Man of High Empire

Man of High Empire

The Life of Pliny the Younger

ROY K. GIBSON

OXFORD
UNIVERSITY PRESS

OXFORD
UNIVERSITY PRESS

Oxford University Press is a department of the University of Oxford. It furthers
the University's objective of excellence in research, scholarship, and education
by publishing worldwide. Oxford is a registered trade mark of Oxford University
Press in the UK and certain other countries.

Published in the United States of America by Oxford University Press
198 Madison Avenue, New York, NY 10016, United States of America.

© Oxford University Press 2020

First issued as an Oxford University Press paperback, 2022

CIP data is on file at the Library of Congress
ISBN 978–0–19–994819–2 (hardback)
ISBN 978–0–19–765483–5 (paperback)

1 3 5 7 9 8 6 4 2

Paperback printed by Marquis, Canada

For
Catherine Delaney

Contents

Contents

List of Maps and Figures

Maps

Figures

References and Abbreviations

References in main text and endnotes in the form '6.16.20' are to Pliny's *Letters* 6.16.20. All other ancient texts and authors are specified in the abbreviated form used by the *Oxford Classical Dictionary* (http://classics.oxfordre.com/page/abbreviation-list/). References in the endnotes in the form 'Chp. 5' are to Chapter 5 in this book. Distances are given in both miles and kilometres. Measurements are given in metres alone. Standard reference works are abbreviated in the endnotes as follows.

AE	*L'Année epigraphique*, Paris, 1888–.
CAH 11²	Bowman, A. K., P. Garnsey, and D. Rathbone (eds.), *The Cambridge Ancient History*, 2nd edition. *Vol. 11: The High Empire, AD 70–192*, Cambridge, 2000.
CIL	*Corpus Inscriptionum Latinarum*, Berlin, 1862–.
IGRR	Cagnat, R., *Inscriptiones Graecae ad Res Romanas Pertinentes*, 4 vols., Paris, 1901–27.
ILS	Dessau, H., *Inscriptiones Latinae Selectae*, Berlin, 1892–1916.
OCD	Cary, M. et al. (eds.), *Oxford Classical Dictionary*, Oxford, 1949 (2nd edition 1970, 3rd ed. 1996, 4th ed. 2012, 5th ed. 2015–).
OLD	Glare, P. G. W. (ed.), *Oxford Latin Dictionary*, Oxford, 1982 (2nd edition 2012).
*PIR*²	Groag, E., A. Stein, L. Petersen, K. Wachtel, M. Heil, W. Eck, and J. Heinrichs (eds.), *Prosopographia Imperii Romani*: A–B (Berlin, 1933); C (1936); D–E–F (1943); G (1952); H (1958); I–J (1966); L (1970); M (1982); N–O (1987); P (1998); Q–R (1999); S (2006); T (2009); U/V–Z (2015).
RP 1–7	Syme, R., *Roman Papers* vols. 1–2, ed. E. Badian (Oxford, 1979); vol. 3, ed. A. R. Birley (1984); vols. 4–5, ed. A. R. Birley (1988); vols. 6–7, ed. A. R. Birley (1991).
TLL	*Thesaurus Linguae Latinae*, Leipzig-Stuttgart, 1900–.

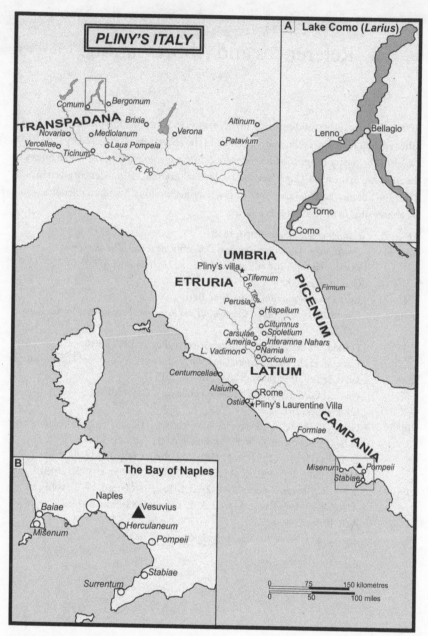

Map 1. Pliny's Italy. *By Catherine Delaney.*

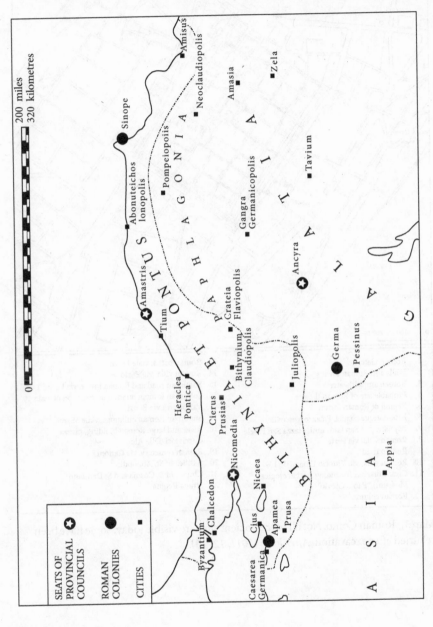

Map 2. Pontus-Bithynia. *After Williams (1990, xii).*

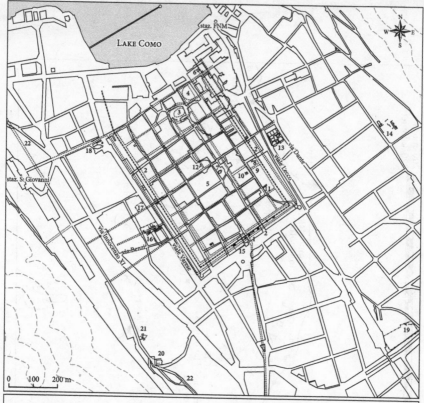

LAKE COMO

1. Roman Gate
2. Walls and Roman towers
3. Roman amphitheatre
4. Probable site of Roman theatre
5. Region of Roman forum
6. Late-antique chapel, Palazzo Vescovile
7. Baptistery of San Giovanni, piazza San Fidele
8. Roman villa, via Perti
9. Roman road
10. Roman villa, via Vittorio Emanuele 107
11. Civic Museum (including Archaeological Museum) "Paolo Giovio"
12. Roman column
13. Roman baths, viale Lecco
14. Roman villa, via Zezio
15. Suburban road and Roman tower, via Parini 1
16. Suburban Roman quarter, intersection of viale Varese and via Benzi
17. Suburban Roman buildings, viale Varese
18. Road and large Roman building, piazza Cacciatori delle Alpe
19. Roman cemetery, via Carloni
20. Basilica of St. Abbondio
21. Church of St Cosma and St Damiano
22. Strada Regina

Map 3. Roman Como. Not all of the ancient sites are visible today: some have been reburied after excavation. *After Jorio (2011, 12–13).*

Introduction

The *Letters* of Pliny the Younger are a literary classic, and have left an unusually detailed record of a Roman senator's life. The Younger Pliny was born to a family from the north of Italy in the early 60s C.E. during the reign of Nero. The emperor's suicide in 68 C.E. brought to an end the imperial dynasty founded by Augustus and a prolonged civil war eventually ushered to power a new dynasty of 'Flavians': Vespasian and his sons Titus and Domitian. By chance the Elder Pliny, the Younger's uncle, had come into friendly contact with Titus during a period of joint military service around a decade before. The Elder ended a long career of duty to empire as commander of the western imperial fleet on the bay of Naples under a Titus newly installed as emperor. The Elder's death in post during the eruption of Vesuvius in 79 C.E.—witnessed and described by the Younger—left Pliny in his eighteenth year without a living senior male relative to guide him on the senatorial career for which personal wealth and literary talents evidently prepared him. The Younger's own father had died before Pliny was fourteen years old.

Connections with the Flavian house likely smoothed access to the ladder of junior posts that led to the senate. Pliny finally entered the senate around 89 C.E. in his late twenties under Domitian. A talent for speaking well was a recognized route to promotion as a senator, along the ladder of offices known as the *cursus honorum*, and Pliny's growing reputation as a star courtroom orator marked him out. Success under an increasingly tyrannical Domitian brought problems. Like many of his generation, including his friend the historian Cornelius Tacitus, Pliny grew defensive about his record after the assassination of Domitian and accession of Nerva in 96 C.E. He nevertheless reached the apex of the consulship in 100 C.E. before he was 40, under a new emperor, Trajan. He published a speech of thanks to the emperor, known today as the *Panegyricus*, to mark the occasion.

By this point Pliny had been married two or perhaps three times. An unnamed wife with connections in the central Italian regions of Umbria and Etruria had passed away early in the reign of Nerva. He was soon remarried to a young woman named Calpurnia from his small north Italian hometown. In Rome, a career as respected former consul in the senate beckoned. Pliny, however, grew increasingly pessimistic under the 'best' of emperors, until appointment as governor of the Asian province of Pontus-Bithynia around 110 C.E. Here he would encounter the 'future' of the Roman empire in two forms: a Greek cultural renaissance now spreading throughout the eastern half of empire; and a puzzling religious group who were the unlikely representatives of a future that would materialize after that renaissance had run its course. These were the Christians of Pontus. Pliny would die before Trajan himself did in 117 C.E.

These are the basic facts of Pliny's career. There is much more to this man than a brief outline can suggest, as this book will try to make clear. The biography has three interlocking aims. The primary purpose is to recreate the life of Pliny in its social, historical, and cultural contexts. A secondary aim is to offer a contribution to biography itself. How can we best write the lives of ancient figures who moved in societies with ideas of self and personhood often quite different from our own? How can we talk about them without unthinkingly imposing modern biographical categories and distorting our subjects out of recognition? A final purpose is to provide the background against which the *Letters* and *Panegyricus* can be best understood. These works place high demands on readers: prior knowledge of people, events, places, and institutions is assumed. In this sense the present volume is a companion to an earlier work with a more obviously literary focus: *Reading the Letters of Pliny the Younger: An Introduction* (2012), co-authored with my friend and former colleague Ruth Morello. The biography, nevertheless, can be enjoyed as a stand-alone work.

The present volume preserves a clear thread of linear narration throughout, but is organized by geographical locale according to the most significant places in the Younger's life. The reasons for this organization, and its significance, are explained in Chapter 2 ('Writing a Modern Biography of an Ancient Roman'). Readers who want to get on with the 'life' are invited to omit Chapter 2 and return to it later. Chapter 3 ('Comum') concentrates on Pliny's childhood milieu, followed by a focus in Chapter 4 ('Campania') on a highly significant event in his eighteenth year. Chapter 5 ('Rome') follows Pliny's political career in Rome under successive emperors from his nineteenth year to the period just before his departure for Pontus-Bithynia. Chapter 8 ('Pontus-Bithynia') takes up the story of Pliny's governorship in that province. Together the Rome and Pontus-Bithynia chapters offer an evaluative narration of intense senatorial and imperial activity across Pliny's adult life. In between come Chapters 6 ('Umbria and the Laurentine Shore') and 7 ('Return to Comum'), which focus less on appraising public and national action, and concentrate more on domestic and local matters, asking questions about Pliny's temperament, personality, and characteristic preferences. They also offer us the opportunity to learn what little is known about Pliny's first and second wives: the unnamed daughter of Pompeia Celerina and Calpurnia of Comum.[1] Together this pair of chapters on Umbria and Comum covers the whole of Pliny's adult life in Italy outside Rome. Appendix 1 provides information on the dating of the *Letters*, as well as an orienting 'timeline' for the great political episodes of Pliny's lifetime, and for events involving Pliny or his broad circle of friends and acquaintances. Appendix 2 offers further information on the sights and modern archaeology of the locales associated with Pliny.

Throughout the book I use the phrase 'the Transpadana' to refer to *transpadana Italia* (Pliny, *HN* 16.66), that is all the Roman lands between the river Po (*Padus*) and the Alps, and not to the more delimited Augustan *regio XI* 'Transpadana', which constituted only the western half of the lands beyond the Po.[2]

Pliny's *Letters* and *Panegyricus* are cited in English, with corresponding Latin in the endnotes. I have made no attempt to downplay the presence of these works within the narrative: they are usually our only source for key events in Pliny's life. (I return to this issue in Chapter 1.) No translation can do justice to the elegance and economy of Pliny's Latin: the *Letters* represent a peak of stylistic achievement in Latin prose. I use or adapt Lewis' 1879 literal translation, with frequent recourse to the excellent translations of Betty Radice (1969) and Walsh (2006), plus Williams (1990) for Book 10, and Radice for Pliny's *Panegyricus*. Lewis' translation renders the meaning of Pliny's words precisely and avoids smoothing out his text into mandarin prose. The translation of connective terms of which Latin is so fond, like modern Italian, makes Pliny sound more fussy in English than he does in the original. The Latin text is that of Mynors (1963). Translations of the *Odyssey* are from Fitzgerald (1961), of Catullus from Lee (1990), of Epictetus from Hard (2014), while those from Augustine also make use of Burton (2001) alongside the *Loeb Classical Library* translation. Translations of all other classical texts are taken or adapted from relevant volumes in the Loeb series. Use of all these volumes is gratefully acknowledged.

I have accumulated many debts in the writing of this book. Chris Whitton and Tony Woodman read drafts of all the chapters, offered invaluable suggestions, and removed errors great and small. Ellen O'Gorman commented on Chapter 2, Kathy Coleman read Chapter 6, and Greg Woolf took on Chapter 8. To each of these readers I am sincerely grateful. Audiences in the UK, Germany, USA, and Australia heard versions of Chapters 1 and 2 and offered stimulating feedback. I owe a debt also to the anonymous OUP readers, particularly the reader who commented on a full draft and offered food for thought. Stefan Vranka at OUP likewise provided (truly) unfailing support and inspired changes of direction and emphasis at crucial moments. Lynda Crawford brought her great expertise to bear on copyediting the manuscript. I am particularly grateful to Professors Pierre Du Prey and Paolo Braconi for their permission and help in the matter of the reproduction of images. Professor Braconi supplied his reconstruction of the site of the Umbrian ('Tuscan') villa (Fig. 6.2.), and Professor Du Prey supplied copies of the perspectives of the Laurentine (Fig. 6.3.) and Umbria villas (Fig. 6.4.) by K. F. Schinkel (1841). Ilaria Marchesi kindly gave permission to use her photo of the view from Misenum to Vesuvius.

Composition of a first draft of the book was made possible by a year's leave provided by the University of Manchester and a Loeb Classical Library Foundation Fellowship. The book was completed during a term's leave provided by Durham University. I express my sincere thanks to all three institutions for their generosity. I am profoundly grateful to former colleagues in Manchester for the supportive research environment they created over a quarter of a century, particularly Ruth Morello, Andrew Morrison, and Alison Sharrock. I wish to thank new colleagues in Durham for the warmth of their welcome, and very much look forward to working with them in the years that lie ahead.

This book is dedicated to Catherine Delaney. We travelled Italy together, from Como to the bay of Naples, and visited the sites of ancient Bithynia. She taught me to take Pliny's eye for landscape seriously; brought with her a (much-needed) geographer-geologist's ability to read a map; took many of the photographs in this volume; and drew the map of Pliny's Italy. Our children, David and Michael, were occasionally recruited as companions. Their entirely justified refusal to leave the car in sweltering summer heat in the Tiber valley to look at a pond in a field is a cherished memory.

Notes

1. Or second and third wives: see Chp. 5 on the controversy over the number of Pliny's wives and for fleeting mentions by Pliny of the daughter of Pompeia and of Calpurnia in Rome.
2. The use of 'Transpadana' to refer to the Augustan *regio* gradually becomes standard in the early empire, but remained intelligible as a reference to all the lands north of the Po; see Roncaglia (2018, xix–xxi) for definitions and geographical place names of northern Italy.

1

Pliny the Younger

Life and *Letters*

Como or Verona?

Within a century of his death, the Younger Pliny was already being confused with his uncle and adoptive father, the Elder Pliny. The mistake was not hard to make. Both were authors. The reputation of the Younger rested on his published sets of *Letters*, that of the Elder on his massive encyclopedia, the *Natural History*.[1] The pair also shared the names C. Plinius Secundus, although the Younger Pliny possessed the additional name Caecilius, inherited from his natural father, to distinguish him from his famous relative.[2] An eyewitness report among the Younger's *Letters* on the death of his uncle during the eruption of Vesuvius in 79 C.E. ought to have made it clear that the Elder and Younger were separate people.[3] Neither this letter nor any other was enough to save the Younger from the planetary pull of the *Natural History* and eventual identification with its author.

Eleven centuries later, in the early 1300s, the canon of the cathedral in Verona authored what has been hailed as the first work of critical literary history in the Renaissance.[4] Giovanni de Matociis gave his essay the title 'A Short Notice on the Two Plinii of Verona', and tried to establish some basic biographical and bibliographical facts about the pair.[5] The library of the Veronese cathedral possessed an important manuscript of the *Letters*, now lost, and on its basis de Matociis was able to attribute them correctly to Pliny the Younger while distinguishing the Elder as the author of the encyclopedia. If de Matociis brought illumination, he also spread error. De Matociis had come across the Elder Pliny's reference to the poet Catullus as 'my fellow countryman' (*Catullum conterraneum meum*) in the opening sentences of the *Natural History*. The only manuscript of Catullus in existence had been brought to the library of de Matociis' cathedral not long before: the document allowed the inference that the poet was a native of Verona.[6] De Matociis concluded that the Elder Pliny too must be Veronese, and as evidence for the identical origin of the Younger Pliny could cite a letter that referred to 'our Veronese' (*Veronensibus nostris*).[7]

The conclusion that the Younger was Veronese involved turning a blind eye to plentiful evidence that the Younger was in fact from another north Italian town: Comum, modern Como, over 90 miles/150 kilometres to the west of

Man of High Empire. Roy K. Gibson, Oxford University Press (2020). © Oxford University Press.
DOI: 10.1093/actrade/9780199948192.001.0001

Verona.[8] The possibility that both Plinii were fellow townsmen of de Matociis, however, was too useful to be subjected to searching scrutiny, at least in Verona, and received a boost from Petrarch, who in the later fourteenth century spread the word to several humanist authorities, including the eminent scholar Lorenzo Valla. Important counter-evidence was available.[9] The biographer Suetonius, a protégé of the Younger Pliny, had written a 'life' of the Elder Pliny that was later positioned at the head of numerous manuscripts and early printed editions of the *Natural History*.[10] This life, heavily abbreviated since antiquity, had as its opening words 'Plinius Secundus of Novum Comum' (*Plinius Secundus Nouecomensis*).[11]

A tussle of notably high artistic standards ensued. Civic leaders in Como and Verona, keen to assert the antiquity of their towns and independence from dominant nearby communities in Milan and Venice, put out commissions for statues and scholarly treatises. Larger-than-life representations of the Elder and Younger Plinii were ready for the cathedral in Como by the early 1480s (Fig. 1.1.). Flanking the main door, the two statues display all the iconography of patron saints of the town. 'Honouring Romans without any Christian connections whatsoever on

Figure 1.1. Statues of the Plinii on Como Cathedral (Santa Maria Maggiore). Installed in the 1480s, these larger-than-life figures were designed to bolster the case that the Plinii were from Como rather than Verona. The Elder is on the left, the Younger on the right. *Photo by C. Delaney.*

a cathedral façade is unprecedented', notes one commentator; 'the city authorities' decision to commission large, isolated sculptures in the most prominent position possible is even more radical'.[12] Opinion was now running in Como's favour, and received a further boost from the affirmation of such luminaries as Angelo Poliziano, among others, that the Elder Pliny belonged to Como. Verona responded in 1492–3 by placing a statue of the Elder Pliny on its handsome new Loggia del Consiglio in the prominent public space of the Piazza dei Signori and commissioning a local historian to compose a treatise on famous ancient citizens of Verona. A relief of the Younger Pliny was added to the façade of the Loggia. The leaders of Como replied in 1498 by adding new inscriptions underneath the statues of the two Plinii, whose ultimate purpose was to make it clear that *conterraneus* ('fellow countryman') found in the preface to the *Natural History* did not signify *conciuis* ('fellow citizen').[13] Verona might share Transpadane Italy as a region with the two Plinii, but could not claim their citizenship.[14]

The civic leaders of Como soon had a reason to regret the erection of a statue to the Younger on the façade of their handsome cathedral. The majority of Pliny's correspondence had been available in print since 1471, but it was only between 1502 and 1508 that the tenth and final book of his letters gradually emerged from its long obscurity.[15] Thrillingly, this installment recorded the personal correspondence of Como's native son with the archetypal 'good' emperor Trajan. Included was a record of Pliny's encounter as Roman governor with a community of Christians on the Black Sea coast of modern Turkey, where it could now be seen that he had described the infant religion, on whose church walls his image currently stood, as a 'vicious and extravagant superstition' (10.96.8). In 1587, at the height of the Counter-Reformation, a visiting bishop of nearby Vercelli demanded the removal of the statues. The local authorities declined to implement his decree.[16]

Biographies of the Younger Pliny

Few biographies can match the short work of de Matociis for engagement of such intellectuals as Petrarch and Poliziano or inspiration of civic leaders to embellishment of cities. But the desire of de Matociis to re-establish some basic biographical facts was a good pointer to the future direction of studies of Pliny the Younger in the wider world outside Como and Verona in the age of print. Alongside the writing of commentaries on the *Letters*, the composition of biographies of Pliny soon became a staple.[17] In 1506 Giovanni Maria Cattaneo published a large and still useful commentary that contained in its preface a first 'life' of Pliny, derived largely from the correspondence itself, but accurate enough within the limits Cattaneo set for himself. Updates to Cattaneo's life followed in the editions of

Cellarius (1693) and Hearne (1703) and in a separate monograph by the Anglo-French scholar Jean Masson (1709),[18] which was to serve as the definitive 'life' until the intervention of the greatest Roman historian of the nineteenth century, Theodor Mommsen. Published in 1869 and twice revised, Mommsen's biographical study brought his outstanding knowledge and unparalleled expertise to bear on the reconstruction of Pliny's career and chronology of the letters.[19] The tradition was sustained by Sir Ronald Syme, the Mommsen of the twentieth century, who produced an extensive series of studies on Pliny and his circle of correspondents.[20] For all this scholar's evident distaste for Pliny, whom he regarded as a tiresome self-promoter, and his personal identification instead with the more reticent Tacitus, Syme advanced and broadened Mommsen's work.[21]

Why such industry on the biography of an individual who was not in Trajan's innermost circle? Thanks to the *Letters, Panegyricus*, and the gradual recovery of some important inscriptions, we know a very great deal about Pliny's life. In fact we perhaps know more about him than any Roman figure, other than members of the imperial household, between Cicero in the first century B.C.E. and Augustine at the end of the fourth century C.E. As is simply not the case with Vergil, Ovid, Livy, or Tacitus, the arc of Pliny's life can be traced in detail—from early life at the foot of the Alps in Comum, through education at Rome under the great Quintilian, to the oppression of the senatorial class by Domitian, and its apparent resurgence under Trajan, and Pliny's suppression in turn of an early Christian community. Through his *Letters* we also catch rare glimpses of the 'domestic' life of the Roman elite, including attendance at literary recitations and dinner parties, tours of country estates, visits to friends, and relationships with wives, freedmen, and enslaved persons, not to mention the wide range of people whom Pliny knew or to whom he wrote, whether names still familiar today (Martial, Tacitus, Suetonius) or significant figures now long forgotten.[22]

Pliny is of intrinsic interest. Quite apart from Pliny's detailed account of the eruption of Vesuvius or first independent witness to Christian communities in the Roman empire, the *Letters* offer a portrait of a consul, leading courtroom orator, patron of literature, innovating landowner, energetic civic benefactor,[23] and man with a surprisingly sharp eye for the natural wonders of the Italian landscape.[24] The capacious variety of the correspondence provides 'the solution to the problem', a modern scholar remarks, 'of self-presentation in face of the anxious question "What do I amount to?" '[25]What Pliny appears to amount to is the first man in his family to enter the senate, a writer of great style, a traditionalist in senatorial politics and a modernist in literature, rather immune to philosophy and its fashions, but a lover of oratory and language, and if inclined to self-praise, also an enthusiastic promoter of the interests of Comum and his wide circle of friends, including a remarkably extensive network of women of his own rank and status.[26] In particular, Pliny offers precious insight into the political life of Rome's 'high empire', from the viewpoint of a rising senator rather than the customary perspective of the emperor and his court. In the first volume of *The History of the Decline and Fall of the Roman Empire*, Gibbon famously opined, 'If a man were called upon to fix the period in the history of the world during which the condition of the human race was most happy and prosperous, he would, without hesitation, name that which elapsed from the death of Domitian to the accession of Commodus'.[27] Pliny's life straddles the opening of Gibbon's 'happy and prosperous' age. Pliny had direct experience both of the last tyrannical years of Domitian and of the allegedly 'good' emperor Trajan. Alongside Tacitus, Pliny successfully sought senatorial promotion from Domitian in the decade before the emperor's assassination. How well Pliny's reputation emerges from these years is a moot question—and one of keen interest in modern times to readers familiar with evasive or self-justifying narratives produced by survivors of oppressive regimes. In producing his own record Pliny will be seen to play with words, as befits a star of Rome's courtrooms.[28] Tacitus preferred silence or avoidance of complete disclosure. Ambitious senators such as these who endured the poor fortune of seeking office and power under 'bad' emperors throng the pages of early imperial history. But we rarely gain more than a glimpse of their lives. The *Letters* of Pliny give the fuller picture.

Shaping Pliny's story

This biography of Pliny tells its story primarily through locale and aims to exemplify and evoke rather than to offer exhaustive narration. One chapter is devoted to each of the most important places in Pliny's life; Comum takes up a pair of chapters. Pliny's life is reconstructed within each region, one by one. Freed from strict chronology, the biography nevertheless maintains an overall movement forward in time. Advance is made, as hinted in the Introduction, from Pliny's earliest years in Comum, through a significant episode in his young adulthood during the eruption of Vesuvius in Campania, on to maturity spent both as lawyer and politician in Rome, to finish with Pliny's stint as governor of Pontus-Bithynia. Between Rome and Pontus-Bithynia come two chapters that briefly pause the forward movement of Pliny's story and focus on issues raised by the villas Pliny owned by the Laurentine shore and in Umbria, and on Pliny's adult life in Comum. The first includes an account of the economic realities of Pliny's farming activities, but focuses also on the issue of Pliny's *persona* and the version of the self that he fostered and particularly cherished in these country locales. The second examines the difference between the Comum of Pliny's childhood and the town he returned to as an adult and successful senator. He may have hardly visited the place during the first fifteen years of his public career in Rome.

The reasons for the privileging of locale alongside chronology and of detailed evocations over cradle-to-grave narration are explained in the second chapter. That chapter examines the somewhat uncomfortable fit between modern biographical norms and an individual such as Pliny. Like many ancient figures, Pliny does not respond quite readily to our expectations. Demands for the reconstruction of a unique personality, for understanding the effect of the child on the man, or for insight into the subject's rich inner life—all of these are not quite suited to most Greco-Roman individuals and the evidence of their lives left us from antiquity. The reasons are complex, and take us to the heart of the difference between ancient and modern conceptions of the individual. A concentration on geographical locale, the second chapter argues, brings the distinctiveness of ancient figures into sharper focus than modern biographical preoccupations might.

Sources: the *Letters*

The *Letters* are our main source for Pliny's life, alongside the speech of thanks to the emperor Trajan for his consulship of 100 C.E., some worryingly poor poetry,[29] and a number of important inscriptions.[30] The *Letters* consist of nine books of 'private' correspondence containing 247 relatively short personal communications with over 100 different addressees across the years 96–109 C.E., and a tenth book of 124 even shorter letters exchanged with the emperor Trajan, mostly during Pliny's stint as governor of Pontus-Bithynia (c. 110–12 C.E.).[31]We are particularly well informed about Pliny's life during the period in which he achieved the highest offices in the state under Trajan, although references back in time within the letters also tell us something about his life in the period before the assassination of Domitian in 96 C.E. A number of inscriptions aside, the only surviving contemporary witness to Pliny's life other than the *Letters* is his protégé the poet Martial.[32]

Ancient biographers value letters as source material, but generally do not make more than modest use of them and appear not to regard letters as an especially privileged category of information.[33] Letters form the backbone to the modern genre, and failure to gain access to a subject's correspondence is regarded as a serious flaw in a 'life'.[34] Biographers often speak of the 'transgression' involved in reading letters meant for the eyes of others—itself one part of a larger set of moral reservations that hover around the genre: 'dislike of gossip, distrust of "low" sources of information, squeamishness about reading private correspondence, suspecting witnesses of having a private agenda'.[35] Gossipers about Pliny have been dead for nearly two millennia. It is modern scholars who harbour private agendas or act as conduits for low speculation. There can be no squeamishness, however, about reading his correspondence. Pliny published his own letters in his own lifetime, and clearly wrote them with one eye on publication all along, editing and revising before publication.[36]

Elite Romans in a slave-owning society lacked the sense that the domestic arena was private: actions at home might have value only in the context of their public reception.[37] Pliny positively welcomed the idea of others writing his biography, even while still alive.[38] What he and his contemporaries feared was not invasion of privacy, but the prospect of negative judgement on their actions.[39] As part of an exercise in seeking approval for private actions, the *Letters* are not likely to contain anything truly damaging to the letter-writer, and rather more likely to offer a controlled and positive version of the self.[40] One symptom of that control is the scarcity of occasions usually prized in published correspondence: those instances where we comprehend more than the letter-writer and know how the story ends. Yet as successive biographers of Pliny have understood, from Cataneus to the current century,[41] none of this makes the *Letters* useless for writing a life. Pliny cannot smooth over every ruffle, nor is he so tightly disciplined as to avoid internal contradiction, forestall the raising of awkward questions, or dampen suspicion of evasiveness or playing with words. If Pliny's letters work for him, they can also be used against him. This is as true for Pliny's defensiveness about his record as a senator under Domitian as it is for the locales of Pliny's life.[42] Comum may be heavily promoted as Pliny's favoured region, but at over two weeks away by road from Rome, and with Pliny's time already restricted by senatorial duties, it is not likely that he went there very often as an adult. At only five days' journey from Rome, Pliny's estates in Umbria were rather more convenient. In his correspondence Pliny paints a more vivid portrait of his life there than in his hometown of Comum, and regards Comum as a venue for *pietas* ('duty') and the burdensome activities of a public benefactor. Umbria was the locale for the literary activities that were vital to him.

If the *Letters* reveal quite as much as they conceal, there still remains the question of the level of factual scepticism that is appropriate to handling a text that has clear literary ambitions. The artistic structure of individual books and the collection as a whole, allied to the frequent literary allusions of the individual letters, make it clear that Pliny meant his collected correspondence to form a counterpart in prose to the verse collections of such contemporaries as Martial or Statius or Augustan predecessors like Horace.[43] Pliny tells us he wrote some elegies in his youth while detained by adverse winds on the island of Icaria during return from military service (7.4.2–3). Is this a useable piece of biographical information, or a literary joke? Writing an elegy while delayed against one's will on a Greek island is precisely the scenario of the most memorable of Tibullus' elegies. And the reference to the sea into which the over-daring young Icarus plunged could be a self-mocking comment on the quality of the elegies written by the youthful Pliny.[44] Others will take a different view. In this instance, I understand the Icarian tale as *both* biographical datum *and* sophisticated insider play. The level of scepticism I judge appropriate is based on observation of the remarkable lengths to which Pliny elsewhere goes *not* to be caught telling actual untruths about his record.[45] Clearly, Pliny plays with words, without taking care to avoid misleading the unwary, and creatively amalgamates literature and life. Charges of fabrication and outright invention, however, rarely stick.

From high empire to Augustine

Cicero and Tacitus are obvious figures to compare with Pliny and provide context for his achievements.[46] Cicero, like Pliny, was a 'new man' (*nouus homo*) from provincial Italy: the first man in his family to enter the senate and attain the consulship. Pliny longed to equal Cicero's successes in the law courts of Rome 150 years before, and yearned for his own published courtroom speeches and letters to achieve some kind of comparison with his great predecessor. Tacitus, only a few years older than Pliny, offered competition both in senatorial career and literary achievement. Pliny confesses as much to Tacitus, with elegant quotation from Vergil's epic boat race: 'I yearned to follow after you—both to be accounted and to be "second to you, though great the space between"' (7.20.4).[47] Senators, nevertheless, ought not be allowed to fill the stage in the manner they would no doubt believe their right. A philosopher, the exact contemporary of Pliny and Tacitus, will make occasional appearances in these pages: Epictetus, Stoic teacher, born enslaved. His thoughts on the emptiness of a life of public ambition will provide a counterpoint to the senatorial world view.[48]

A fourth, perhaps more unexpected, figure will appear alongside Cicero, Tacitus, and Epictetus for comparison with Pliny: St Augustine of Hippo (354–430 C.E.). In his *Confessions*, Augustine provides evidence for features of ancient daily life that can be found nowhere else or better nowhere else. Augustine also wrote the plot for modern life-writing.[49] If almost two thousand years separate us from Pliny, only three centuries separate Pliny from Augustine. The *Confessions* can productively be used to inform questions about Pliny's life, society, set of mind, and notions of individuality, to a degree that the norms of modern biography perhaps cannot. Augustine reveals through contrast what is distinctive to Pliny and his society. One feature of late antique society that seems familiar to a modern readership is the scenario of 'personal growth' apparently exemplified in the *Confessions*. How should we understand this process? On one reading, Augustine is dramatizing his openness to revision of his most fundamental beliefs by portraying successive moves through a range of belief systems, including Manichaeism, a form of Neoplatonism, and varieties of Christianity.[50] These dramatic shifts offer a fresh angle from which to view Pliny. Such change would be anathema to Pliny and his class: it could only be evidence of profound and shocking lack of personal *constantia*. Consistency is Pliny's cardinal virtue.[51] Augustine can usefully make unfamiliar a man who might be misunderstood as often like ourselves.

If Cicero offers a version of a traditional past to which Pliny was attracted, and Tacitus and Epictetus represent two competing versions of Pliny's present, Augustine tells us that changes in society and personal behaviour would eventually come to Rome. Such developments would not be confined to the self and society: the stable political and material conditions of Pliny's era would not last forever. Much that Pliny, man of high empire, could take for granted, had disappeared in the unstable and increasingly impoverished empire of Augustine's time. As will become clear over the course of this biography, the flourishing provincial town is the unspoken hero of high empire. Pliny, like many elite contemporaries, was intimately concerned with its civic health—in Comum, Umbria, and Pontus-Bithynia. Augustine shows no interest even as the infrastructure of many towns reached a state of inertia or decay in parts of the empire.[52] His focus was on the church and above all those who attended it. This biography of Pliny is, in part, also a portrait of an era of high empire. Augustine forecasts the passing of Pliny's world.

Notes

1. On the two Plinii in later antiquity, see Cameron (2016); on the broader history of the reception of the *Letters* and the *Natural History*, see Kempf (2012) and McHam (2013), respectively.
2. See Chps. 3 and 4.
3. 6.16: see Chp. 4.
4. The account of events in Verona and Como offered here and later draws primarily on McHam (2005, 476–86), with some additions and expansions; cf. McHam (2013, 156–8, 168).
5. De Matociis: McHam (2005, 478 with n. 62). His essay *Breuis adnotatio de duobus Pliniis Veronensibus* is reprinted by Merrill (1910, 186–8), and evaluated by Reynolds-Wilson (2013, 128).
6. Catull. 35.3, 68a.28; cf. 31 on Sirmio.
7. 6.34.1.
8. 1.3.1, 1.8.2, 2.8.1, 3.6.4, 4.13.3, 4.13.5, 4.30.1–2, 5.7.1, 5.14.1.
9. The whole course of the debate begun by de Matociis is surveyed with authority by Benedetto Giovio, historian of Como, in the second book of his *Historiae Patriae Libri Duo* (completed c. 1534, first printed 1629), as reprinted in Giovio (1982, 237–43). On B. Giovio and his brother P. Giovio, see Appendix 2.
10. See Reeve (2011, 207).

11. *Nouecomensis* is garbled in some manuscripts: Reeve (2011, 214–5).

12. McHam (2005, 480–1), who outlines the development of the interchanges between Como and Verona; cf. Della Torre (1984, 170–7) on the history, iconography, and attribution of both the Veronese and Comascan statues; also Lucati (1984) more broadly on the Elder in the historiography of Como.

13. The inscription underneath the Younger Pliny states pointedly, 'The senate of Como set up [these] memorials to its greatly missed *fellow citizen*' (*ordo Comensis conciui suo desiderabili* | . . . *monumenta posuit*). The inscription under the statue of the Elder likewise commemorates the work of Pliny's 'fellow citizens' (*conciues . . . meos*). Both inscriptions are the work of Giovio (McHam (2005, 481 with n. 68)), who in his history of Como (see earlier) devotes his considerable skills of close reading to the meanings of *conterraneus* and *conciuis* (Giovio (1982, 237, 240).

14. The debate about the origin of the two Plinii would rumble on well into the nineteenth century (McHam (2005, 485 with n. 76)); Mommsen (1869, 61–2) reasserts the meaning of *conterraneus*.

15. See Reynolds (1983, 317–20).

16. See McHam (2005, 481). Giovio gives Pliny's treatment of Christians full coverage: Giovio (1982, 243–5).

17. For an overview of scholarship on the *Letters* from 1470 to the present, see Whitton and Gibson (2016); cf. Häger (2015) on recent trends. For a history of editions and commentaries on the *Letters*, see Ciapponi (2011).

18. Masson supplied the 'life' for Hearne's 1703 edition, before significantly expanding and publishing it as a separate monograph in 1709.

19. See Whitton and Gibson (2016, 12) on Mommsen (1869), (1873), (1906).

20. Syme's numerous Plinian contributions are included in his *Roman Papers* (1979–91); the seventh and final volume (1991) consists of previously unpublished material originally designed to form a separate book on 'Pliny and Italia Transpadana' (*RP* 6.v).

21. On Syme's identification with Tacitus in contradistinction to A. N. Sherwin-White, an Oxford contemporary who completed a magisterial edition of Pliny's *Letters*, see Griffin (1999, 145–6) = (2016, 362–3); cf. Whitton and Gibson (2016, 38–9). For a brief modern biography of Syme, see Edmond (2017).

22. Literary recitations: 1.13, 2.3, 2.19, 4.27, 5.12, 5.17, 6.15, 6.17, 6.21, 8.21, 9.27, 9.34. Dinner parties: 1.15, 2.6, 3.12, 9.17, 9.23. Tours of estates and visits to friends and relations: 1.4, 1.9, 2.17, 4.1, 5.6, 5.14, 6.10, 6.14, 6.28, 6.30, 8.1, 8.20. Wives: 4.1, 4.19, 6.4, 6.7, 6.24, 7.5, 8.5, 8.10, 8.11. Slaves and freedmen: 1.21, 3.14, 5.19, 8.16, 8.19, 9.21, 9.24. Martial: 3.21. Tacitus: 1.6, 1.20, 4.13, 6.9, 6.16, 6.20, 7.20, 7.33, 8.7, 9.10, 9.14. Suetonius: 1.18, 1.24, 3.8, 5.10, 9.34, 10.94–5.

23. Pliny as consul, orator, patron: Chp. 5; as landowner: Chp. 6; and as energetic civic benefactor: Chp. 7.

24. Rightly emphasized by Radice (1962, 168).

25. Fitzgerald (2016, 7).

26. Pliny as first of his family to enter senate: Chps. 3, 5; his literary style: Chp. 6; conservative senator: Chp. 5; modernist in literature: Chp. 6, *Letters* 6.21, with Gibson

(f'coming) ad loc.; Pliny and philosophy: Chps. 5, 6; inclined to self-praise: Gibson (2003); promoter of Comum: Chp. 7; networks of women: Chps. 5, 7 (note comprehensive treatments by Carlon (2009), Shelton (2013)).

27. Gibbon (1776–88 = 1994, 1.103).

28. See Chp. 5.

29. On Pliny's poetry, see Courtney (1993, 367–70), Hershkowitz (1995), Roller (1998) = (2016), Janka (2015); cf. Chp. 6.

30. The inscriptions are listed at Vidman *PIR*² P 490, with the most important reprinted in the editions of (e.g.) Schuster (1958), Radice (1969), Zehnacker (2009); cf. Sherwin-White (1966, 732–3), Gibson and Morello (2012, 270–3). See also Chp. 6 and Appendix 2 on the brick stamps recovered at the site of the Umbrian estate.

31. On the dates of Pliny's correspondence, see Appendix 1.

32. Martial 10.20 (partially quoted by Pliny in 3.21).

33. See Trapp (2007, 337) on Plutarch's sources for his *Life of Cicero*.

34. See (e.g.) Parker (2010, 10–46) on the central role of letters in biographies of Michelangelo between 1568 and the present day.

35. Lee (2005, 65); cf. Beard (2002, 12).

36. For a succinct overview of the 'authenticity' debate on Pliny's *Letters*, see Whitton (2013, 2–5); cf. Hoffer (1999, 17–18, 26–7, 87). On the publication of the letters, see Appendix 1.

37. On 'public' and 'private' in Pliny's world view, see Riggsby (1998, 80, 83) = (2016, 230–1, 233); cf. Riggsby (1997).

38. 9.8. 9.31; cf. 5.10, where Pliny encourages the publication by Suetonius of his *de Viris Illustribus* (Power (2010), which would contain a biographical sketch of the Elder Pliny (Reeve (2011)).

39. Cf. Dionysius of Halicarnassus, *Letter to Pompeius* 6 on the reputation of the histories of Theopompus of Chios (fourth century B.C.E.).

40. Not solely an ancient problem: see Lee (2005, 66–7) on the correspondence of Jane Austen.

41. Twenty-first-century biographical work on Pliny: Birley (2000a, 1–17) = (2016), Winsbury (2014).

42. Pliny's evasiveness: Chp. 5; Umbria vs. Comum: Chps. 6, 7.

43. See (e.g.) Marchesi (2008), Gibson and Morello (2012, 36–72), Whitton (2013, 11–27); Gibson (2015), Whitton (2015a), (2019).

44. See Tzounakas (2012) on 7.4 and Tibullus 1.3.

45. See Whitton (2015b) and Chp. 5 on Pliny in Domitianic Rome. Nevertheless, there are certain parallels between the present project (which extracts biography from a literary work) and ancient biographies of poets, which are often essentially a form of literary criticism of the writers' work; for the latter, see above all Graziosi (2002) on lives of Homer, and (more recently) Peirano Garrison (2017) on lives of Vergil.

46. See esp. Chp. 5.

47. 7.20.4 *te sequi, tibi 'longo sed proximus interuallo' et esse et haberi concupiscebam*; cf. Marchesi (2008, 135–43) on this letter and the quotation from Verg. *Aen.* 5.320.

48. On the life and works of Epictetus, see Envoi n. 14.

49. See Chp. 2; cf. Fredriksen (2012) and Becker (2014) for short introductions to the *Confessions*.
50. See Brown (2000, 151–9). On another reading, Augustine displays traditional *constantia* by eventually returning to the childhood Christian beliefs inculcated by his mother Monnica. Augustinian change, at any rate, was not conceived as adaptation, but as a shedding of the superfluous and a firmer grasp on the essential (Brown (2000, 354)). On the related question of classical beliefs in the 'fixity' of character, see Riggsby (2004) with reference to older discussions.
51. See esp. Chps. 4, 6. But on 'conversions' from rhetoric to philosophy, particularly in later antiquity, see Lane Fox (2015, 262–7), with reference to older discussions.
52. See Chps. 7, 8.

2

Writing a Modern Biography of an Ancient Roman

The key challenge in most biographical treatments of Pliny until recent decades has been to interpret the sometimes elusive data of the *Letters* correctly and to put the facts and career milestones in the correct order within the right year or even month. If Pliny's life and progress along the ladder of offices on the traditional Roman *cursus honorum* could be established with precision, then his biography might usefully serve as a key reference point for framing the careers of other senators of high empire. A modern life of Pliny faces rather different challenges. We are certainly now less interested in the precise interval between the offices of praetor and consul or the exact length and legal status of Pliny's governorship of Pontus-Bithynia, and rather more likely to want to know something personal and intimate about him. Who was Pliny *really*? What was he like? What forces shaped and drove him on?

Before answering these questions, we must confront the gap between what the modern biographer expects to discover and what Greek and Roman texts like to tell us about individuals. It can be easy to ignore this divergence, since it is emperors and the great generals of classical antiquity who tend to attract most biographies of ancient characters written in modern times.[1] To write biographies of such men is also to write 'history'. The need to ask what modern norms *do* to ancient figures may somehow seem less pressing if a biographer's focus on political and military deeds orients the narrative towards conventional history. The effects of modern biographical treatment on Greco-Roman individuals may then go largely unexamined, despite the fact that there are well-known differences between ancient and modern conceptions or valuations of the self, the individual and society, and the 'inner life'.[2]

In a biography of a 'private' individual, questions of the effect of modern biographic norms pose themselves urgently, since the life is *not* a history of something else in the way that a biography of an emperor is a history of the state. Even biographies of Cicero and Augustine risk leaving these distorting effects unquestioned: significant portions of their lives are transformed with relative ease into ciphers for a history of the last generation of the Roman republic or the development of Christian theology in the late antique west. The life of Pliny the Younger is less clearly the story of a significant historical or ideological development. If

Man of High Empire. Roy K. Gibson, Oxford University Press (2020). © Oxford University Press.
DOI: 10.1093/actrade/9780199948192.001.0001

anything, his life is associated with a senate experiencing revival after the death of Domitian: a body allegedly now ready to command its long plateau across high empire in steady state and optimal condition.[3] Earlier biographers were not wrong to see in him an exemplary senatorial career. This circumstance makes it more urgent we examine some of the norms of modern biography and the problems they create for ancient figures. A partial solution will be proposed at the conclusion of the chapter.

Biography and the 'unique individual'

Modern biographers are expected to construct their subjects as unique individuals. The identification of personal complexity, quirkiness, and contradictory traits is routinely hailed as the authentic mark of successful completion of a biography. The poet Paul Muldoon praised the second volume of Roy Foster's landmark biography of W. B. Yeats for allowing the subject to emerge as 'haughty and humble, polemicist and priest, prig and profligate'.[4] Richard Ellmann's classic life of James Joyce offers a separate index for Joyce's 'personal characteristics', including such promising items as 'birthday, important to', 'bizarre actions', 'litigiousness', and 'superstitions'.[5] A recent prizewinning biography of Van Gogh offers a portrait of a man who 'never could command consistency from himself (not even within the same letter, much less between correspondents)'.[6] In the words of one penetrating critic of the genre, 'if we do not . . . encounter a distinct person whose voices, gestures and moods grow familiar to us, then we judge the biography a failure'.[7]

It would be far from impossible to produce a distinctive portrait of Pliny as a unique individual in this mould. We could focus on a penchant for taking notebooks along while out hunting 'so that if I came back empty-handed, my tablets at any rate would be full' (1.6.1), or on a professed love of reading and composing obscene poetry (4.14, 5.3). To bring this Pliny into being demands we ignore the broad texture of ancient life-writing and Pliny's own practice. In general Greco-Roman texts tend to present us with characters who are somewhat too 'integrated' for modern tastes. The great biographer Plutarch is more thorough than most, but he is representative of an ancient tendency to portray personalities that exemplify, in a recent formulation, 'a "syndrome" of traits which are independent but which one naturally finds in combination'.[8] Plutarch's Mark Antony does not couple personal simplicity with unexpected interest in the arcana of Stoic cosmology, nor is his soldierliness leavened by devotion to love poetry. Antony incorporates a series of qualities—simplicity, soldierliness, leadership, nobility, and a capacity to be inflamed by Roman values—where one tends to lead to another, and which together help to explain how Antony could achieve and squander personal greatness. To paraphrase one critic, it appears more natural to talk of 'a sort of person like Mark Antony' after reading Plutarch's narrative than to talk of 'a sort of person like James Joyce' after reading Ellmann's biography.[9]

Pliny joins Plutarch at the end of the spectrum that prefers thoroughgoing integration of character. He integrates his own allegedly risqué poetry into unexceptionable practice by producing a list of seventeen senators, four emperors, and several others, including Ennius and Vergil, to show that high status and good personal morals are compatible with obscene verse (5.3.5–6). Pliny also writes to a very wide range of people in his *Letters* and mentions numerous others in passing.[10] Surprisingly few of them are especially memorable or distinctive. What do we glean from Pliny about Tacitus, the correspondent to whom he writes more letters than any other?[11] We learn very little that is individualized or authentically personal—except perhaps that Tacitus was less irritated by Pliny than his modern avatar Sir Ronald Syme. The apparent blandness of his friends is often taken as evidence of Pliny's egocentrism or limitations as an artist. There is a better explanation. Pliny is producing integrated portraits, where each person has a mix of traits that already complement one another and few have discordant qualities that cry out for comment.

When Pliny does produce quirky or contradictory characters it is usually a sign that something has gone wrong with that person. (Perhaps they have failed to stem the leakage of some inner life.) Around 106–7 C.E., Pliny reports he has just heard about a public poetry recitation given by his Umbrian friend Passennus Paulus who writes elegiac poetry in the style of his ancestor Sextus Propertius. In the audience was Iavolenus Priscus, an eminent consular jurist and mutual friend of both Paulus and Pliny, who received the honour of a dedicatory address in the opening words of the recitation: 'You command me, Priscus . . .' (*Prisce, iubes*, 6.15.2). Priscus immediately shattered the artistic convention and intended compliment by retorting loudly to Paulus *ego vero non iubeo* ('Indeed I do not command you'). This is very witty, albeit heartless. Pliny is having none of it. To him it is all evidence of Priscus' 'dubious sanity' (*dubiae sanitatis*)—strong words for Pliny to apply to a living person. He is strongly exercised by a discrepancy between the witticism and Priscus' very public position as one regularly consulted on points of civil law. What for us might be evidence of authentic eccentricity is an indication to Pliny of fundamental *instability*. Similar considerations apply to Pliny's grumpy grandfather-in-law, Calpurnius Fabatus, and rather more emphatically to the courtroom orator Aquillius Regulus—the one private individual whom Pliny is willing to go on record as actually loathing.[12] As part of a negative portrayal of Regulus, he mentions a series of personal quirks, including the fact that Regulus used to put make-up around one of his eyes: the right when speaking for the plaintiff and left when acting for the defendant (6.2.2). Even where a portrait of a character is not hostile, the appearance of remarkable personal habits may be a sign that something is not quite right. An obvious case is the Elder Pliny, some of whose characteristics will emerge in the Campania chapter. If the Younger mentions that his uncle refused to walk anywhere because it cut down on the amount of time available for study (3.5.16), this is less endearing quirk and more a hint that the Younger does not consider the monomaniac Elder a model in every aspect of his adult life.[13]

How readily can we reconstruct an idiosyncratic Pliny? We *could* emphasize further oddities and bring together traits and habits that are potentially in conflict. The biographer will then have done the job of portraying a unique individual. It is clear, however, that Pliny and many others in his society did not aspire to be remembered in this sense. Rather, Pliny was evidently aiming in the short term for rigorous personal integration—and for lasting fame through his writings in the long term.[14] Whether or not he succeeded in the former, it is clear that too great an insistence on recreating a distinctive or quirky personality risks distorting things that are important about Pliny.[15] Social norms may impinge not only on the presentation, but also on the formation and even the *experience* of the self.

Biography and the psychology of the child

Richard Ellmann devotes over one hundred and fifty pages of his biography to the first twenty-two years of James Joyce's life.[16] An interest in childhood is not always shared by readers of biography (I normally skip over the earliest years), but there is no getting away from its fundamental importance to the genre. Characters are formed, and important early relationships leave their mark on the subject, as is clear enough in Pliny's own young adulthood at least.[17] Wealth and fame gained later in life provide invigorating contrast with more humble beginnings. A concern with childhood is not always so evident in ancient biography: the available evidence can rarely have been plentiful.[18] Writers often concentrate instead on the actions of the adult, particularly in lives of political figures. Even when childhood does feature, the focus is usually on the public matter of education rather than on early developments of later traits. Nor is social mobility necessarily interesting to ancient biographers.[19] The ancient lives of the legendary Aesop in fact omit parentage and childhood altogether despite his traditional birth into slavery.[20]

Pliny himself has relatively little to say about his own childhood. An exception is the account he offers of his experience of the eruption of Vesuvius in his eighteenth year (6.16, 6.20). The rarity of such detailed insight into a Roman individual's life before maturity has been reached, not to mention the intrinsic interest of the eruption, justify the devotion of an entire chapter of this biography to the event (Chapter 4). Nevertheless, one clear trait in adulthood appears to encourage a return to his earliest years in search of a psychological explanation: Pliny never once talks about his natural father in any published writing. In modern biography, persons are regularly understood to be shaped by being too distant from (or too close to) mothers, fathers, and siblings. Is the same true of Pliny? His father appears only rather indirectly in such asides as 'the generosity of my parents / ancestors' (1.8.5 *munificentia parentum nostrorum*) or 'my estates . . . excepting what had come to me from my mother and father' (7.11.5 *praediis meis . . . exceptis maternis paternisque*). Pliny does go out of his way to criticize fellow senators for having forgotten the father of a young protégé: 'though there are many to whom [the father] was known, yet they honour none but the living' (6.6.4). But even the name by which the Younger is known to us comes not from his father but from the Elder. The Younger was adopted after the death of the Elder and only then became C. Plinius Caecilius Secundus. Before that he had been known only as C. Caecilius Secundus. His father evidently died before Pliny reached his middle teens. Inscriptions from Como may identify this man as the wealthy L. Caecilius Secundus.[21]

It is true that in all the adult inscriptions that have been found in Como and in one of his private estates, the Younger Pliny is identified with his full four names.[22] However the public record of Rome's consuls show that at the pinnacle of his career Pliny registered himself as C. Plinius Secundus, despite the fact that it would have been more normal for a man to display his distinctively paternal nomenclature (Caecilius Secundus).[23] In the headings to his letters Pliny identifies himself even more simply as C. Plinius and it is clear from the contents of the letters that he was routinely referred to by others as 'Plinius'.[24]

The man evidently known in Comum as a Caecilius through his father drops that name on the national stage and in his published writings.[25] One story we could build on the foundation of Pliny's silence about his natural father is an attempt to distance himself from the memory and name of the elder Caecilius Secundus. If we reflect on the prominence allotted in the correspondence to the Elder and to Pliny's guardian Verginius Rufus,[26] and remember also that his mother, the Elder's sister, is given a leading role in the account of the eruption of Vesuvius,[27] or that Pliny highlights connections inherited from his mother and uncle and never those from his natural father,[28] and that even Pliny's childhood nurse gets an entire letter to herself[29]—*then* we might begin to suspect that the father has been deliberately written out of the record of his son's life.

Pliny would not be the first Roman son with an aversion to a *paterfamilias*. Terence's *Adelphoe* (160 B.C.E.) offers a classic fictional portrait of an overly strict father and an embittered son. At the other end of antiquity in the autobiographical *Confessions*, Augustine barely mentions his father, always with notable coolness, and is negative about fathers in general.[30] It is his mother Monnica who is granted an important role in the story of his life.[31] One possible reason for Augustine's reticence is the marital infidelity and anger against his mother revealed as characteristic of his father at a very late stage in the narrative.[32]

A completely different narrative can be built around Pliny's silence about his father and the prominence given to adoptive father and guardian: one with little to say about the psychological effects of childhood on the actions of the adult. It is likely that Pliny's *Letters* began to be published some years after Trajan succeeded the elderly Nerva in early 98.[33] Pliny had ample opportunity to contemplate the circumstances of the transfer of power between emperors and the establishment of stable imperial rule. These had no real parallel in the often bloody history of the principate: the dynasty begun by Augustus had promoted successors from within its own family group, while after the civil wars of 68–9 C.E. Vespasian was eventually succeeded by his sons, with particularly unpopular results in Domitian, at least for the senatorial class. It was Nerva who achieved a first for Rome in adopting as son and successor a man quite unrelated to him, and in seeing him safely installed at the helm of empire. 'In Pliny's work, surrogacy serves as a governing paradigm both for the author's personal experience and for ideal imperial governance', one perceptive scholar has argued; where 'the theme of paternal surrogacy permits him to account for the successes both of his own career and of the new imperial regime'.[34] In the *Panegyricus*, Pliny does not completely omit mention of Trajan's natural father,[35] but of Nerva he declares 'his highest claim to be the father of his country [*publicus parens*] was his being father to you' (*Paneg.* 10.6). So when Pliny reports that his guardian once declared to him that 'even if I had a son, I would choose you in preference to him as my representative' (2.1.9),[36] we can begin to guess Pliny's omission of his father might be less a sign of any childhood trauma or adolescent resentment, and more an indicator of a desire to align the achievements of his life with the success of Trajan's rule. Similarly Pliny's conspicuous support of young men, including fatherless young men,[37] throughout his career might speak less of Pliny's personal psychological history or his own continuing childlessness,[38] and rather more of a canny sense of political capital to be made in recapitulating the surrogate parenthood of the emperor. (Simple personal generosity cannot be ruled out, of course.)

Attempts to read Pliny psychologically encounter serious challenges. Does this make him less interesting or more? It certainly makes him bracingly different and his biography, in part, a mission to comprehend that difference. We need to come to grips with a society quite different from our own in which adoption and guardianship were deeply embedded in social practice.

Biography and the interior life

The reconstruction of a subject's inner life is a standard feature of modern biography, and, so far from being unavoidable, it is hailed by a recent guide to the craft of 'life writing' as something to be embraced:

> In . . . speaking about the inner life of others . . . speculation is not contingent, and not the life writer's fault. It marks the limit of our knowledge of other people's minds . . . But speculation here isn't failing, because you can only fail where you can also succeed. Rather, it marks our respect for the dignity and inviolability of other people, who are . . . sovereign beings. So far from a sign of failure, it is a mark of honour, and should be used without shame.[39]

There are some worrying leaps in the logic of this argument. It is clear, all the same, that the reconstruction of the inner life is felt to be fundamental and not necessarily beyond the biographer's reach. Other critics have emphasized its difficulty or impossibility.[40]

Ancient biographers were less exercised by the conceptual difficulties: they just weren't that interested in the interior life. They attribute motives, doubt, and conflict to their subjects, but rarely maintain a consistent focus on the inner life or evoke it in the rich and extended detail found in many modern biographies. Plutarch adhered to an explicit theory of psychological structure and was clearly capable of making deductions about a subject's interiority.[41] He does so with a frequency and depth of insight, however, that prove 'disappointing'. Often we are left to infer inner thoughts where a modern biographer would speculatively reconstruct them. 'Understanding people was just one among several things [Plutarch] was trying to do', in the judgement of one modern authority; 'it was not always the priority'.[42] Even when a detailed reconstruction of a state of mind is given, as with the portrait of Julius Caesar's hesitation before crossing the Rubicon to begin civil war in Italy, its purpose can wrong-foot us. Caesar's prolonged inner conflict is designed to dramatize and mark a momentous action, not to give an insight into the inner life.[43] Elsewhere Plutarch's Caesar is not generally afflicted by hesitation in action and shows almost no concern for one of the things said to give him pause at the Rubicon: the ills that his actions will unleash upon the world.[44]

If we set ancient biography to one side, the key question in Pliny's case is this: what *material* do we have to work with in the reconstruction of his inner life? Pliny is greatly interested in proper and productive use of time.[45] The question of how to fit into an overstretched life everything he needs and wants to do is of no less concern to him than most modern readers. The subject is potentially emotive and personally revealing. Reflection on how we use time often demands interrogation of the self and clarification of what is core and what is peripheral. And so it would prove in the hands of Augustine in the ancient world. Pliny is characteristically different:

> For a long time I have taken neither book nor pen in hand. For a long time I have not known what rest is or repose, or, in short, that state, so idle yet so agreeable, of doing nothing and being nothing. To such a degree do the multitude of my friends' affairs debar me from seclusion and study. For no studies are of such importance that the duty of friendship should be abandoned on their account—indeed, that this duty should be most scrupulously guarded is a matter which is taught by these very studies.[46]

> Pliny, *Letters* 8.9

There is little regret or anxiety here and no insight into the process of self-examination that appears to lie far beneath the surface of the letter. Instead, a clear assertion of a result. It is right that the current demands of friends trump the alternative of attention to personal preoccupations such as reading, writing, or the pleasure of simply doing nothing. It is the alternative, the study of books, which has *taught* Pliny that duties towards others are paramount: a bare hint that his ethical training has given him 'reason' or the ability to discriminate properly between the claims of competing duties. A single word, *religiosissime* ('most scrupulously'), suggests the effort required to internalize the practice of constraint.

In the *Confessions* Augustine promotes process over results and reimagines an intense bout of self-examination undertaken by his younger self. He remembers himself as a thirty-year-old performing a review of how his life had been spent since the age of nineteen. Recreating the chronological order of the influences on his thinking and pressures on his time, the younger Augustine depicts an internal to-and-fro that eventually adds up to a complex and powerful interior dialogue:

> . . . I reviewed with agitation how much time had elapsed since, in my nineteenth year, I had begun my fervent quest for wisdom. . . . And all the time I said, 'Tomorrow I will find it: look, then it will be clear, and I will master it'.—'Look, Faustus [the Manichee] will come and explain everything'—'What heroes the Academics are! Is it true that "nothing pertaining to the blessed life can be apprehended as a certainty?" '—'No; rather, let us seek more diligently and not despair' . . .—'I shall set my feet . . . until transparent truth is found'.— 'But where will it be sought? When will it be sought? Ambrose [the bishop of Milan] has no time to spare, and I have no time to read. And the books themselves—where shall I seek them? Where and when shall I buy them? From whom shall I get them?'—'Let time be set aside, and certain hours alloted to my soul's welfare'. . . .—'My mornings are taken up with students; what do I do for

the rest of the day? Why am I not getting on with this?'—'But when will I pay my greeting to my powerful friends, whose backing I need? When am I to prepare the teaching which my pupils pay for? When am I to refresh myself, giving my mind a rest from its pressing weight of anxieties?'[47]

Augustine, *Confessions* 6.11.18

Pliny and Augustine, whether abandoning books for friends or yearning to abandon pupils and patrons for books, are both focused on the question of the proper use of time. Pliny offers a moment of outward success and personal integrity maintained. Augustine gives an extended narrative of anguished internal reflection, ethical failure, and personal fragmentation.[48] The gulf between the two can be sensed in the difference between Pliny's simple alternation of present and past time and Augustine's profligate use of present, future, perfect and imperfect verbs, alongside expressions of intense self-exhortation. Pliny deals with essential, ideal, almost timeless qualities. Augustine is fascinated by the interaction between past, present, and future selves.[49]

If Augustine feels 'modern' with his puzzled sense of a lack of interior wholeness and his absence of confidence in the power of reason to impose order on a life,[50] that is because he largely invented the plot for contemporary biography and autobiography: the inner journey from fragmentation to integration.[51] Pliny is not anguished, far from a mystery to himself and clearly intent on offering a model of rational decision-making. The difference between them, however, is not to be accounted for by some story about the ascent towards the modern self that begins with the arrival in late antiquity of a new Christian life of inner scrutiny. Quite apart from the fact that Augustine did not value interiority or the individual human personality per se,[52] almost everything in Augustine can be found already in a poet who wrote four hundred and fifty years before the *Confessions* and a century and a half before Pliny. In his eighth poem, Catullus, writing of a failed love affair, displays an Augustinian will towards integration out of fragmentation ('Wretched Catullus, you should stop fooling | and what you know you've lost admit losing . . .'), realizes that simply initiating a right choice does not bring desired wholeness, and reviews his own behaviour in an anguished internal dialogue of self-accusation and exhortation[53] —the whole accompanied by a parallel profligacy in the evocation of past, present, and future time.[54] Pliny certainly knew the poetry of his *conterraneus* well, and used him in defence of his practice of writing obscene verse,[55] but he is not remotely interested in Catullus' model of interiority. Augustine never mentions Catullus and may not have read him, yet his internal struggles essentially replicate those of the pagan poet half a millennium before.[56]

The question remains: what *material* do we have to work with in the reconstruction of Pliny's inner life? If Pliny experienced inner fragmentation or conducted anguished self-examination to match Catullus, he certainly never tells us about it. Public self-blame would hardly sit easily with the dignity of a senator. A number of his elders and contemporaries *were* beginning to practise a more deliberate, philosophical self-examination. Some have seen in the writings of Seneca, active at the time of Pliny's birth, evidence for the beginning of a new 'turn inwards' where the individual, inspired by Stoic or Epicurean philosophy, might practise intense self-scrutiny with the aim of correcting and improving oneself, without thought of the community or its greater good.[57] The goal of this transformative self-examination was greater personal compliance with 'natural' or universal moral standards: the process is unlikely to have been very revealing of the unique individual.[58] Certainly the philosophical letters of Seneca offer relatively little of the strongly personalized interiority of Catullus or Augustine.[59] Pliny was largely out of sympathy even with this sort of turn inwards, and adhered to more traditional collective standards. For Pliny correctness of thought and behaviour is determined less by interior self-examination and rather more by the opinion of his society.[60] He operates, as one scholar argues, 'in a world in which the most legitimate measure of his worth is whether he fills an appropriate place in the order of the community'. Pliny, in truth, 'seems to devote less energy to controlling himself and more to controlling what others think about him', and 'does not cultivate his character so much as his standing'.[61]

Pliny in a landscape

The broad reasons or motivations for Pliny's actions and behaviour may not be beyond our speculative recovery. Yet any attempt to reconstruct some unique and richly detailed inner life is hampered not only by lack of evidence, but also by the fact that such reconstruction appears false to the set of values by which Pliny directed his life. A glance through his published works, however, reveals that Pliny does not lack for individuality or particularity as a human being. How to frame and grasp these qualities?

A highlight of the *Odyssey* is the moment when the hero finally reveals his name to his hosts on Phaeacia and describes his island home with its conspicuous mountain and other islands nearby:

> I am Laërtês' son, Odysseus...
> My home is on the peaked sea-mark of Ithaka
> under Mount Neion's wind-blown robe of leaves,
> in sight of other islands—Doulíkhion,
> Samë, wooded Zakynthos—Ithaka
> being most lofty in that coastal sea,

and northwest, while the rest lie east and south.
A rocky isle, but good for a boy's training,
I shall not see a place on earth more dear.

Homer, Odyssey 9.19, 21–8

'Odysseus is presenting his *sphragis*, his seal-stone', in a recent summation; 'like his name, the pattern of his landscape affirms the impress of his individuality'.[62] Odysseus binds his identity firmly up with Ithaca, a small, geographically isolated, and rather unimportant place. Such a remote locale is a good match in some respects for Comum. Pliny's small hometown lies as far from Rome as you can travel without actually leaving Italy: nothing important had ever happened there and beyond it lay only the inhospitable Alps. Pliny was conspicuously proud of Comum and wastes no opportunity to give it prominence, to the later delight of the civic leaders of the Renaissance town. 'What news of Comum, your darling and mine?', he writes to a friend in the third letter of his collection.[63] Like Odysseus, Pliny is asserting his particularity in a distinctive way—one that appears not to have occurred to the Elder Pliny, who passes over Comum in the *Natural History* without a flicker of recognition.[64]

Pliny was not the first Roman writer to suggest individuality through locale. Catullus, as de Matociis knew, was linked with Verona, even if the ancient poet occasionally affected a preference for Rome over the 'province'.[65] Vergil spoke of Mantua and the bay of Naples, Horace idealized his Sabine farm, while Propertius pointed to his origins in Umbria and Ovid anticipated a time when his hometown of Sulmo would be famous.[66] The lives and work of each of these poets were set against the regions they highlight in a very readable book published in the 1950s: Gilbert Highet's *Poets in a Landscape*. It inadvertently demonstrates how modest is the role these places play in the corpus of each poet. Not so with Pliny. He gives sustained prominence to a chosen range of landscapes and locations alongside Comum. As civic patron of an Umbrian town, local landowner, and son-in-law to the broader region's aristocracy, Pliny was closely involved with the provinces of central Italy. His luxurious residences on the Umbrian border with Etruria and on the Laurentine shore near Ostia commanded much of his time outside Rome. Pliny also has a distinctive gift for evoking the beautiful and the spectacular in the Italian landscape, whether the source of the river Clitumnus, the disastrous flooding of the Tiber, a miraculous spring on the shores of Lake Como, or Lake Vadimon's floating islands. Most memorable is Pliny's clarity in evoking Vesuvius and the ruin of the bay of Naples.[67]

No Roman writer, perhaps not even Vergil, ties his identity to the regions of Italy more successfully than the Younger. His focus on Italy is in fact remarkable: by the standards of his class, Pliny had very little experience of travel outside the Roman heartlands.[68] What interiority is to a life of Augustine, landscape and locality can be to an account of Pliny. (In the course of a much-travelled life, Augustine himself showed almost no interest in his physical surroundings.[69]) By recreating Pliny's life within each of his treasured regions, we can grasp his particularity without having to impose modern biographical norms focused on his psychology or inner life. We may begin to understand his individuality in a way that is a better reflection of the ancient man than any attempt to reconstruct him as a modern unique individual. What is Pliny's attachment or relationship to a region? What is his persona, what does he *do* there? What does he see, or not see, in a landscape or its inhabitants?[70] Biographies of other Greco-Roman figures might benefit from a similar approach based on region.[71]

From cradle to grave?

Telling Pliny's story through overlapping narratives region by region brings an advantage beyond insight into his individuality. It helps avoid 'cradle to grave' biography.[72] The evidence on which such a life could be written simply does not exist—even for so well documented a Roman. Mary Beard, a consistent critic of contemporary biographies of ancient figures, rightly attacks the 'usual biographical *horror vacui* which drives modern writers to tell a full life story, even where there is no surviving ancient evidence at all'.[73] The biographer's resort to 'would have' is one common sign that the narrative is based largely on inference, speculation, or import from other sources.[74] *This* biography can hardly do without inference or import. Yet by focusing on Pliny's significant places and the evidence we have for his life in each (there is plenty of it), we can concentrate on the material we *do* have and avoid the narrative problems set by linear biography, which would demand coverage of whole swathes of Pliny's life for which we have no real information.

The choice of locale as an organizing principle has precedents in ancient and modern life-writing.[75] Rosamund Bartlett's *Chekhov: Scenes from a Life* offers a biography of the locations in which Chekhov lived. She uses these places to illuminate facets of his character, in recognition of the fact that relationship with landscape was the 'one area of his life where he was unusually expansive'.[76] Bartlett's biography is deliberately episodic rather than comprehensive. The same approach suits Pliny: his life, after all, was fundamentally episodic. Pliny participated in significant events, but his life lacks an overall plot or great pivotal event.[77] The plot of Cicero's life is his failed attempt to save the republic, and the guiding narrative of Augustine's intellectual autobiography is the ascent of the mind.[78] There is no need to exaggerate Pliny's situation, however. His life hardly matches J. R. R. Tolkien's for uneventfulness. A biographer of the latter declares just over one-third of the way through a four-hundred-page life: 'And after this, you might say, nothing else really happened. Tolkien came back to Oxford . . .'[79] Tolkien did not witness a famous natural disaster, hold high office in the state, and go on to persecute a fledgling world religion in one of the provinces of the British empire. Pliny's life lacks a shape all the same: hence a compartmentalized approach in this biography. Of course, the parts of a life cannot be completely segregated from one another. And there is, in any case, a convergence between locality and the phases of Pliny's life. This biography takes advantage of that fact to create forward momentum from early years in Comum through to final years in Pontus-Bithynia.

What did Pliny look like?

Before a start is made, one standard question posed in a biography *cannot* be avoided. What did Pliny look like? No ancient portraits survive. Perhaps the museums of northern Italy or Umbria preserve his likeness in their collections among the many statue heads of 'Roman dignitary (unknown)' long severed from marble bodies. In his biographies of the Caesars and men of letters, Suetonius was greatly interested in personal appearance.[80] Like most ancient letter-writers, Pliny tells us next to nothing. He says only that he was 'slender'— unlike his corpulent uncle.[81]

Notes

1. E.g. the *Roman Imperial Biographies* series published by Routledge.
2. On competing historical conceptions of the self, see Chp. 6; on the inner life, see later in this chapter and Chp. 6.
3. Pliny himself would come to doubt this cheering story of a revived senate under a 'good emperor'; see Chp. 5.
4. Paul Muldoon, *The Times* (London), 20 September 2003, reviewing Foster (2003).
5. Ellmann (1982, 849–50).
6. Naifeh and White Smith (2011, 632).
7. Clifford (1978, 44), on biography and the production of irreducible individuals; cf. Cline and Angier (2013, 152) and Lee (2009, 16, 28–9, 31, 44–6, 54). See also Sturrock (1993, 285–92) on the inevitable connection between modern (auto-)biography and the rise of philosophies of individualism.
8. Pelling (1990a, 236); cf. Pelling (1990a, 235–44) on integrated characters more broadly, and Pelling (1990b, 246–7, 253–5) on the essentially normative characters of Greek tragedy. (For a different view of Plutarch, see Nikolaidis (2014).) There are obvious exceptions to the rule of integration: egregious idiosyncrasies are on display in Horace (e.g. *Ep.* 1.20.20–5) and the *Satyricon* of Petronius, and they attract the

attention of Suetonius (e.g. *Vesp.* 20–2). Suetonius' practice of writing lives according to a series of topic headings (on which see Hurley (2014)) tends to produce characters that are potentially rather complex (Pelling (1990a, 237)); but it is left to the reader of Suetonius to put the parts of the person together to produce a whole.

9. Pelling (1990a, 239).

10. All correspondents and people mentioned by Pliny are catalogued and where possible identified by Birley (2000a).

11. Pliny's letters to Tacitus: see Chp. 1.

12. Calpurnius Fabatus: see Chp. 7 with n. 62. Regulus: see Chp. 5, nn. 140–1.

13. See Keeline (2018) for the argument that the Elder is in fact an anti-model.

14. Pliny and fame: 5.8, 6.16, 6.20, 7.20, 7.33, 9.2, 9.3, 9.14, 9.23, 9.25; cf. 3.18, 4.5, 4.16, 4.19, 4.27, 7.4, 8.13, 9.8.

15. I do not mean to insist that, as a rule, we cannot ask modern questions about ancient characters. We should, however, concede the provisional nature of the results.

16. See Ellmann (1982, 23–179).

17. See Chp. 4 on the Elder Pliny.

18. On childhood in ancient biography, and some exceptions to this rule, see Pelling (1990a, 213–24); cf. Hägg (2012, 6, 75, 125–6, 254, 329–30, 385). On psychology and modern literary (auto-)biography, see Storr (1995), Marcus (2015).

19. On social mobility as an issue of interest to Suetonius (in the *Lives of Grammarians and Rhetoricians*), but not to Pliny, see Gibson (2014).

20. See Hägg (2012, 102).

21. See Chps. 3 and 4 on adoption and Pliny's natural father.

22. Plinian inscriptions from Comum and environs: *CIL* 5, 5262 (Milan), 5263–4 (both Como), 5667 (Fecchio, nr. Como), and *AE* 1972, 212 (Como); brick stamps and roof tiles from his estate in the upper Tiber valley: Chp. 6, Appendix 2. Inscriptions relating to Pliny are discussed in Chapters 3, 5, 6, 7.

23. On Pliny's nomenclature in the *Fasti Ostienses*, see Vidman (1980, 45), Syme *RP* 7.551, Salomies (1992, 59–60).

24. See Gibson and Morello (2012, 109–10).

25. Pliny did not have to drop 'Caecilius' because it lacked distinctiveness: others routinely retain more commonplace names (Salomies (1992, 60)).

26. Elder Pliny: 1.19.1, 3.5, 5.8, 6.16, 6.20, and Chp. 4; Verginius Rufus: 2.1, 6.10, 5.3.5, 9.19; cf. Corellius Rufus (1.12, 4.17); Vestricius Spurinna (3.1, 3.10). See Chps. 4 n. 121, 7 n. 34 on Pliny's admired elders.

27. 6.16, 6.20, and Chp. 4.

28. 1.19.1, 4.19.7, 7.11.4; cf. Shelton (2013, 189–90) on the contrast with the amount of information on the paternal relatives of Pliny's wife Calpurnia, also orphaned in childhood.

29. 6.3, with Gibson (f'coming).

30. E.g. *Conf.* 2.3.6, 3.4.7; see O'Donnell (1992, II.70–1).

31. Lane Fox (2015) 41–50, Clark (2015).

32. *Conf.* 9.9.19, 22; cf. Chp. 3. for marital calamity as an alternative reason for the Younger's silence over his father. Other literary-biographical conundra: Catullus

mentions his deceased brother (68a.15–26, 101), but never his father (who appears to have been alive in the poet's adulthood: Suet. *Jul.* 73); Horace frequently mentions his father (e.g. *Sat.* 1.6.58, 81–4), but never his mother, and so on.

33. See Appendix 1.

34. Bernstein (2009, 250, 256): the analysis in this paragraph is indebted to Bernstein (2009, 249–56); cf. Bernstein (2008) on the theme of surrogate parenthood in Pliny more generally.

35. *Paneg.* 9.2, 14.1, 16.1, 89.2–3.

36. Cf. also 2.1.8, 8.14.6 on his guardian Verginius Rufus as surrogate parent.

37. Supportive interest in the younger generation: 2.9, 5.17, 6.23, 8.23, 9.12 (cf. 1.8, 4.13); particular interest in young men without fathers: 2.8 the children of Arulenus Rusticus, 3.3 the son of Corellia Hispulla, 6.6, 6.10 Iulius Naso (cf. 5.21). Cf. claims of surrogate parenthood at 6.11, 6.26, 6.32, 8.13.

38. Cf. 8.10–11, 10.2.

39. Cline and Angier (2013, 18).

40. Cf. Virginia Woolf's satirical 1928 'biography' *Orlando*, mocking those who 'can see, often when we say nothing about it, exactly what [Orlando] looked like; know without a word to guide them precisely what he thought—and it is for readers such as these that we write' (Woolf (2004, 43). On *Orlando* and the problem of the reconstruction of the inner life, see Lee (2009, 80–82). Woolf also published a biography of Roger Fry (1940) and authored such influential critical essays as 'The new biography' (1927) and 'The art of biography' (1939).

41. See Gill (2006, esp. 412–21) on the Platonic-Aristotelian ideas that inform much of Plutarch's ethical writing and biographies.

42. Pelling (1990a, 234); cf. Momigliano (1985, 88–9), Lee (2009, 21).

43. Plut. *Caes.* 32.4–9, with Pelling (2002, 327–9), (2011, 313–4).

44. To have a theory of the unified self (like Plutarch) is not necessarily the same as having an interest in the internal workings of the self; see Taylor (1989, 115–26). In his classic *Geschichte der Autobiographie* of 1907, Georg Misch went so far as to conclude that no pagan individual prior to Augustine possessed sufficient inner life to write an account of that life; cf. Pelling (1990b) on Wilamowitz-Möllendorff's influential 1907 review of Misch's work, also Güthenke (2016). Yet Plutarch would hardly have been so widely read throughout the centuries 'if his perception of the individual had not satisfied men educated to the Christian inner life' (Momigliano (1985, 90)).

45. See Gibson and Morello (2012, 104, 117–23). In Suetonius, a subject's use of time suggests individuality rather than inwardness (e.g. *Vesp.* 21); in the letters of Seneca the same subject foregrounds inwardness, but without individuality (e.g. 1.1).

46. 8.9 *Olim non librum in manus, non stilum sumpsi, olim nescio quid sit otium quid quies, quid denique illud iners quidem, iucundum tamen nihil agere nihil esse: adeo multa me negotia amicorum nec secedere nec studere patiuntur. nulla enim studia tanti sunt ut amicitiae officium deseratur, quod religiosissime custodiendum studia ipsa praecipiunt.* On *studia* ('study') as intellectual activity, esp. of a literary kind, see Whitton (2013, 88).

47. *Conf.* 6.11.18 *satagens et recolens quam longum tempus esset ab undeuicensimo anno aetatis meae, quo feruere coeperam studio sapientiae . . . dum dico, 'cras inueniam. ecce manifestum apparebit, et tenebo. ecce Faustus ueniet et exponet omnia. o magni uiri academici! nihil ad agendam uitam certi comprehendi potest? immo quaeramus diligentius et non desperemus . . . figam pedes . . . donec inueniatur perspicua ueritas. sed ubi quaeretur? quando quaeretur? non uacat Ambrosio, non uacat legere. ubi ipsos codices quaerimus? unde aut quando comparamus? a quibus sumimus? deputentur tempora, distribuantur horae pro salute animae. . . . antemeridianis horis discipuli occupant: ceteris quid facimus? cur non id agimus? sed quando salutamus amicos maiores, quorum suffragiis opus habemus? quando praeparamus quod emant scholastici? quando reparamus nos ipsos relaxando animo ab intentione curarum?'* On this passage, see O'Donnell (1992, III.179, 371); cf. Baltussen (2010) on ethical self-address in Marcus Aurelius.

48. Pre-Christian ethical self-examination largely lacks the anguish of Augustine, and is more often a matter of 'quality control' (Miller (1998, 184)); cf. Ker (2009) on Senecan self-examination.

49. See Brown (2000, 167–8); contrast Mira Seo (2013, 8–16) on exemplarity and traditional Roman conceptions of character.

50. See Clark (2004, 52); cf. *Conf.* 10.32.48, 10.37.62, and Clark (2004, xiv, 65) on Augustine as a mystery to himself, but without the modern interest in the subconscious.

51. See O'Donnell (2005, 83–4); variants include the triumph of fragmentation or a surface integration that masks deeper fragmentation. For theoretical reflections on how to write the biography of Augustine, see O'Donnell (1999).

52. See O'Donnell (2005, 65–6). On the kind of interiority which Augustine *did* value, namely the appeal 'to our first-person experience of thinking', see Taylor (1989, 127–42). For a variety of further views on the Augustinian inner self and its sources, see Cary (2000), Mortley (2013, 14–27), Stock (2017), also Conybeare (2016, 144–7) on differences from the modern self.

53. Catull. 8.1–15, 19 *Miser Catulle, desinas ineptire, | et quod uides perisse perditum ducas. | fulsere quondam candidi tibi soles, | cum uentitabas quo puella ducebat, | amata nobis quantum amabitur nulla. | ibi illa multa tum iocosa fiebant, | quae tu uolebas nec puella nolebat. | fulsere uere candidi tibi soles. | nunc iam illa non uult: tu quoque, impotens, noli, | nec quae fugit sectare, nec miser uiue, | sed obstinata mente perfer, obdura. | uale, puella, iam Catullus obdurat, | nec te requiret nec rogabit inuitam. | at tu dolebis, cum rogaberis nulla. | scelesta, uae te! quae tibi manet uita? | . . . | at tu, Catulle, desinatus obdura* ('Wretched Catullus, you should stop fooling | And what you know you've lost admit losing. | The sun shone brilliantly for you, time was, | When you kept following where a girl led you, | Loved by us as we shall love no one. | There when those many amusing things happened | Which you wanted nor did the girl not want | The sun shone brilliantly for you, truly. | Now she's stopped wanting, you must stop, weakling. | Don't chase what runs away nor live wretched | But with a mind made up be firm, stand fast. | Goodbye girl. Catullus now stands fast, | Won't ask for or look for

you who're not willing. | But you'll be sorry when you're not asked for. | Alas, what life awaits you now, devil? | . . . | But you Catullus, mind made up, stand fast.')

54. On temporal complexity in Catullus, see Ker (2009, 172), who develops the ideas of Miller (1998, 189–93). The potentially disturbing effect on contemporaries of Catullus' dialogue with himself is brilliantly evoked in section XXVI-B of T. Wilder's 1948 novel *The Ides of March*.

55. Cf. 4.14.15; see Roller (1998) = (2016).

56. Augustine's knowledge of Catullus: Pucci (2009); cf. Conybeare (2017, 510–13).

57. See Foucault (1986) on the turn inwards and the consequent 'care of the self', and Edwards (1997) = (2008) on the letters of Seneca; cf. Bartsch and Wray (2009) for sustained criticism of Foucault's formulations.

58. Cf. Gill (1996) on the distinction between modern subjective-individualist ideas of selfhood, as opposed to the objective and normative concepts of selfhood more dominant in pagan antiquity: see also Zeitlin (2012, 122–6) on the interiority of the Greek novel.

59. See Taylor (1989, 130–1) on the difference between Augustine's 'radical reflexivity' and the Foucauldian care of the self, which is more about the activity of *caring* than the entity of the *self*. On the lack of personal detail in Seneca's letters, see Edwards (2008, 85).

60. Riggsby (1998) = (2016); cf. Whitton and Gibson (2016, 33–5) on the context for Riggsby's argument, and see Chp. 6 for a privileged Plinian sense of self and his limited cultivation of that self. For the limited sort of interiority that is recoverable from Pliny, see Méthy (2007, 175–88).

61. Riggsby (1998, 89, 87, 92) = (2016, 238–9, 236–7, 242). For Pliny's dependence on community for correct behaviour, see Riggsby (1998, 77–83) = (2016, 227–33).

62. Jenkyns (2013, 67).

63. 1.3.1 *Quid agit Comum, tuae meaeque deliciae?* For Comum in the *Letters*, see Chps 3, 7.

64. *Natural History* 2.232, 3.124, 132; 34.144, 36.15. In his great survey of Italy in Book 3 of the *Natural History*, the Elder produces a rather 'flat' picture of Italy, concentrating on the peninsula's *urbes, oppida,* and *populi* (Bispham (2007b)); the Younger's vision of Italy is quite different.

65. For Catullus' preference for Rome and ambivalent attitude to the 'province' (i.e. Gallia Cisalpina before the extension of Roman citizenship), see poems 43, 68a.25–36; but for Catullus' self-conscious identity as a Transpadane Italian in Rome, see Wiseman (1986), Tatum (1997).

66. For Roman poets and writers on their birthplaces and significant locales, see Highet (1957), Watts (1971).

67. Pliny on: the Clitumnus (8.8), the Tiber (8.17), the spring by Lake Como (4.30), Lake Vadimon (8.20), and the bay of Naples (6.16, 6.20).

68. Pliny's record of foreign travel registers only an early stint in Syria and a late stint in Pontus-Bithynia: see Chp. 8. He did not (e.g.) go abroad to command a legion or govern a province as praetor; see Chp. 4 for a contrast with the much-travelled Elder Pliny.

69. See Clark (1995, 122), Brown (2000, 23), O'Donnell (2005, 120, 147–8); on the (positive) reasons for the lack of interest in the topography of Carthage, Rome, and Milan in the *Confessions*, see Fuhrer (2018).

70. Cf. Fitzgerald and Spentzou (2018) and their emphasis on the participant-observer's experience of space in the Roman world.

71. Cicero and Seneca were interested in locale, and fresh biographies might equally be structured by region; cf. Wilson (2014) and Tempest (2014) for recent biographies. However, while placing Pliny or others within a landscape may avoid the imposition of modern biographical norms, it remains true that landscape and region are not the sort of overarching frames that ancient subjects might have expected us to understand them within.

72. A straightforward linear narration of a life remains the default expectation for biography, despite a long history of trial with other forms: 'the battle for "experimental" biography has to be fought anew in each generation' (Cline and Angier (2013, 58; cf. 60), who note the exception of 'memoir', an anti-teleological strand of life-writing, from this rule (2013, 90); cf. Zwerdling (2017) on the rise of the memoir). Lee (2009, 8) suggests that 'this rule [of chronological narration] has been so often broken as not to count'; but it remains a powerful default expectation; see Sturrock (1977, 53–4). For a brief history of experiment with biographical form, see Nadel (1984, 183–205); cf. Lee (2009, 122) on her own thematic rather than chronological biography (1997) of Virginia Woolf, also Lee (2013) on Woolf's *Diary* as inspiration. For criticism of the linear mode in autobiography, see Lejeune (1989, 73), Sturrock (1977), also Sturrock (1993, 75–8, 186–7, 191, 192–3, 204–5, 232, 256–84). For an attack on the idea that all humans experience their lives as a form of narrative, see Strawson (2004) (with Lee (2009, 103–4) for a brief response), and Strawson (2015).

73. Beard (2013, 138); cf. Beard (2013, 124, 172–3), also Shapiro (2015) on the problems created for Shakespeare and his lacunose life by biographers wedded to a *bildungsroman* format.

74. Cf. Lee (2009, 75–85) on the biographer's 'must have'.

75. See Burridge (2004, 192–3, 195–6) on Galilee and Jerusalem in the Christian Gospels (perhaps the most widely read biographies in history); cf. Hägg (2012, 137–9, 333) for other ancient examples, also Woodman and Kraus (2014, 3–4) for praise of a subject's *patria* as a standard part of encomium.

76. Bartlett (2004, xvi); cf. Hurley (2014) on the use of a 'topic' based approach in some modern biographies of Roman emperors (derived in part from the Suetonian model of imperial biography).

77. On an alleged need for plot in biography, see Cline and Angier (2013, 43).

78. See O'Donnell (1992, I.xxxii–xli) on Augustine.

79. Carpenter (1977, 150). For the hostility of an influential nineteenth century theorist of biography to 'static' lives, see Marcus (1994, 25–6) quoting Stanfield (1813, 68, 100, 336).

80. See Hurley (2014) on Suetonius' biographical rubrics.

81. 2.11.15 (quoted in Chp. 5) refers to Pliny's 'slenderness' (*gracilitas*), with a side-ways glance at Cicero's self-description in his youth (Cic. *Brut.* 313): see Whitton (2013, 175), who notes also Trajan's reference to *corpusculi tui* ('your slender frame', 10.18.1), and that 'His uncle, by contrast, was ample (6.16.3), as perhaps was his mother (6.20.12 *corpore grauem*)'.

3

Comum

At the foot of the Alps

As its ancient name Mediolanum supposedly indicates, Milan lies in the middle of a great plain, north of the river Po. Beyond the plain the land begins to rise as the border with Switzerland nears. The road into Como makes its way over a saddle between two high ridges, where a glimpse can be caught of the town settled below at the bottom of Lake Como's westerly branch (Map 1, inset A). Como is surrounded by a horseshoe of heights. The Spina Verde overlooks the town to the west, while to the immediate east a large ridge rises steeply to a height of 500 metres. The snow-covered Alps are visible from the modern *commune* of Brunate on its summit. Down on the lakefront of the town, another high ridge on the left bank of the lake forms the northern horizon. The deep and broad glacial lake bends slowly out of sight to the north-east, hemmed in on both sides by tall hills rising sharply from the water's edge for almost the whole of its nearly 30 miles/50 kilometres extent.

The land beyond the Po, the 'Transpadana', had begun to be Romanized only in the early second century B.C.E. and was not even formally part of the Roman state till 42 B.C.E.[1]—around a century before Pliny's birth. Catullus brought some Celtic terms current in the Po valley to Rome. One, *ploxenum* ('carriage-body'), was sniffily classified under the heading *barbarismus* by Quintilian in his treatise on education.[2] The writings of his pupil Pliny show not a trace of such long-vanished influences. And if Pliny once possessed a local accent, much as Augustine later felt conscious of an African nuance to his pronunciation, we never hear of it.[3] The Comum Pliny knew had been deliberately planned from the start as a Roman foundation. The older Celtic people of the area, the Comenses, had lived in a settlement on the slopes of the far side of the Spina Verde.[4] Roman colonists joined them early in the first century B.C.E. A substantial new influx from the south followed in 59 at the instigation of Julius Caesar. Forebears of the Elder and Younger perhaps took part in the Julian migration: Plinii of rank are attested in the far south of Italy well before the Plinii of Comum rise to prominence.[5] The flat marshy ground between the Spina Verde and the Brunate ridge was now drained through diversion of a river. Comum was refounded here as 'New Comum' (*Novum Comum*).[6]

Man of High Empire. Roy K. Gibson, Oxford University Press (2020). © Oxford University Press.
DOI: 10.1093/actrade/9780199948192.001.0001

New Comum lies at the convergence point of roads from Novaria (modern Novara) to the south-west, Mediolanum to the south, and Bergomum (Bergamo) to the east (Map 1). It became the entry point for navigation by boat to the northern tip of the lake at Summus Lacus (Samolaco), where a road continued over the Alps into the heart of the province of Raetia in modern Switzerland.[7] Caesar had already made sure to equip his colony with walls. Catullus, writing from the town that would dispute ownership of the Plinii with Comum centuries hence, soon mentioned the fortifications in a poem requesting 'my comrade | Caecilius, the tender poet, | to come to Verona, leaving New | Comum's walls and the Larian shore'.[8] (The civic leaders of the Renaissance Como were confident this must be Caecilius Statius, and commissioned a small statue for their cathedral.[9]) Traces of Caesar's walls are preserved near or beneath the remnants of the medieval fortifications which surround Como's old town today.[10] With a rectangular circuit of roughly 1.25 miles/2 kilometres, the walls enclosed a space potentially big enough to house a substantial population of somewhere between eighteen and twenty-two thousand by Pliny's day.[11]

Como clearly preserves the original Roman layout with its chessboard street plan. The medieval town was built directly over the antique: visible remnants of Roman Comum are few (Map 3). There is no sign of the ancient forum, and very little remains of the town's harbour. Subterranean foundations have been discovered of what appears to be a theatre or amphitheatre of perhaps the late first or early second century C.E.[12] Inscriptions and marble fragments recovered in abundance suggest a flourishing early imperial community with a rich agricultural hinterland.[13] These, together with the *Letters*, allow a few gaps to be filled. Long before Pliny's birth the colony had become a *municipium*: a self-governing town featuring four locally elected magistrates known as the *quattuoruiri* and a town senate (*ordo decurionum*).[14] There was a senate house for these decurions (1.8.16–17). In addition, a temple to Jupiter which would later house a statue gifted by Pliny on the occasion of his consulship (3.6). As the principal shrine in a *municipium*, this temple presumably dominated the forum.[15] Epigraphical evidence points to numerous other temples in the town and the existence of public baths.[16] Other complexes, such as the library and bath complex built by Pliny or the colonnade with ornamented gates erected by his grandfather-in-law, belong to the Comum of Pliny's maturity.[17]

One inscription recording the dedication of a major building will soon bring us to Pliny's natural father. A more pressing question first: what effect did a childhood in Comum have on the young Pliny?

Childhood in the lakes

Had Pliny been born in the era of William Wordsworth, he might have written a letter about his boyhood there in romantic terms:

> One summer evening I found a little boat tied to a tree; stepping in I pushed from the shore. I fixed my view on the summit of a craggy ridge and dipped my oars into the lake, when from behind the steep a huge peak upreared its head. I struck and struck again, but growing still the grim shape towered up between me and the stars. With trembling oars I turned and stole my way back to the covert of the tree. After I had seen that spectacle, for many days my brain worked with a dim sense; over my thoughts there hung a darkness. No familiar shapes remained, no pleasant images of trees, of sea or sky.

This 'letter' is an extract from *The Prelude*. (Portions of Wordsworth's original have been omitted, but nothing has been added or re-ordered.) The Wordsworthian scene is traditionally identified as Ullswater in England's Lake District, where steep heights rise almost directly from the water's edge, as in Lake Como. The passage is usually interpreted as suggesting that it was Nature herself who led the young Wordsworth to a sense of morality and proper goodness. A particular environment has left an indelible mark on an *individual*. The prestige of this Romantic conception of the moulding influence of locale has made it a feature of modern biography. A boyhood on the heaths of the southern Netherlands shaped Van Gogh's characteristic outlook.[18] The Russian steppe just beyond Chekhov's boyhood home on the Black Sea affected him personally for life. According to one biographer, ' . . . these boundless plains of waving grasses, streams and gullies were an endless source of fascination for Chekhov, and might partly account for his lifelong restlessness'.[19] The effect of environment is a preoccupation also of ancient thinking. Characteristically, locale moulds *peoples*— and individuals only as members of a people. Half a millennium before Pliny, the school of Hippocrates had established an authoritative link between climate, soil, habitat, and the physical and mental constitution of a nation. Tacitus took it as fundamental in his *Germania*.[20] It was unthinkable that a mountain would impose a sense of morality on a single individual without also affecting others. When Pliny's contemporary the poet Statius declared to his wife that the bay of Naples 'created me for you, bound me to be your partner for many a long year', this was less a claim to a unique upbringing and more a provoking assertion that his birthplace, despite its decadent reputation, was the nurturer of long marriages.[21]

Pliny does write a letter to his boyhood friend Voconius Romanus about Lake Como (9.7). Characteristically, it concentrates on his lakeside villas there.[22] The closest that Pliny comes to a statement about the effect of a childhood in the Italian lakes reflects the Hippocratic tradition. Writing to recommend for the daughter of a valued friend a prospective bridegroom from a town halfway between Comum and Verona, Pliny insists 'His home is in Brixia, in that part of our country which still retains and preserves much of the ancient modesty, thriftiness and even rustic simplicity'.[23] This is an assertion of better *communal* preservation of traditional standards in an Italian region remote from Rome. Pliny was not alone in this unsophisticated belief in the pristine morality of the lands north of the Po. His fellow 'provincial' Tacitus, so often cynical about character and motivation, appears to share it.[24] Pliny was not so naïve as to think that everyone raised in the Transpadana was an exemplar of antique virtue. A wicked consular descendant of the poet Catullus was proof enough of that.[25] But it was useful that others should believe it of Pliny. The prominence of Comum in Pliny's *Letters* is not owed to love of native land alone. As with the farm of Horace in the old hill country of the hardy Sabines, Comum lent Pliny an aura.

Did a boyhood in the Italian lakes leave no discernible mark on Pliny as an individual? Perhaps it did after all.[26] Water is a constant preoccupation: flowing, ebbing, running, and navigable. Pliny makes incidental mention of 'sailing on our lake Comum' in adulthood.[27] Boats remain the most convenient mode of transport around this steep-sided lake. Did Pliny sail there as a boy? He certainly exhibits a fascination with water hard to parallel fully amongst contemporaries. It is explicit enough in lengthy disquisitions on the miraculous spring by lake Como (4.30), the source of the river Clitumnus (8.8), the overflowing of the Tiber (8.17), and the floating islands of lake Vadimon (8.20). His gaze is firmly fixed on lake or sea next to villas owned by himself or others on lake Como (1.3.1, 9.7), the Laurentine coast (1.9.6, 2.17)[28] and Centumcellae north of Rome (6.31.15–17).[29] Even the inland 'Tuscan' villa, close to the upper reaches of the Tiber (5.6.12), highlights running streams and fountains in its most intimate venues (5.6.36–40). The narrative of the Elder's final journey across the bay of Naples is unforgettable in its clarity (6.16.8–12).[30] The most remarkable set piece of description in the *Panegyricus* takes the failure of the annual Nile flood as its subject (*Paneg.* 30–32).[31] And report is made to Trajan on the details of Pliny's journey by boat to Pontus-Bithynia (10.15, 17a). Once arrived Pliny devotes considerable effort to the project of a canal from lake to sea at Nicomedia (10.41–2, 61–2) and to the water supplies of Sinope and Amastris (10.90, 98)—as befits a former curator of the beds and banks of the Tiber and friend of Rome's foremost authority on aqueducts.[32] Catullus, another child of the Italian lakes, writes vividly of his own journey home by yacht from the very province that Pliny would govern a century and a half later.[33] The yacht sails 'right up to this clear lake' (*adusque limpidum lacum*, 4.24) to rest there in retirement. An apparent sequel joyfully greets Sirmio and Lake Garda after the poet's long absence abroad (31).

His greatest mythological poetry gives prominence to episodes of sailing (63.1, 14–16; 64.1–18). A childhood in the Italian lakes perhaps installed in Pliny and Catullus a shared love of water.

L. Caecilius Cilo vs. L. Caecilius Secundus

Not yet formally adopted into the Plinii, the Younger grew up in Comum as Caecilius Secundus. The family name Caecilius invites speculation on a connection with the fashionable young poet who had been the friend of Catullus at the very foundation of New Comum. In reality 'common to excess',[34] Caecilius creates some difficulties of identification even for Pliny's father. Here we turn our gaze away from the lakeshore of ancient Comum and enter the doors of the Museo Archeologico in modern Como's old town. A *tutor* or legal guardian was appointed only for those under fourteen years of age, as evidently for Pliny (2.1.8).[35] His father must then have died before 75–6 C.E. Inscriptions on display in the museum reveal two men who are candidates for Pliny's father: L. Caecilius Cilo and L. Caecilius Secundus. They themselves bear the family name Caecilius, have sons named Caecilius Secundus, and possess epitaphs not inconsistent with premature death. Their texts illustrate the delicate foundations on which much Roman social history rests and the perils of optimistic interpretation.

Cilo's fine testamentary inscription provided a local church with a marble altar table until the sixteenth century. As custom demanded of a former town magistrate, Cilo left a significant benefaction: olive oil for use by his fellow citizens on festal days 'on the *campus* and in all the bathing establishments and baths which are in Comum'.[36] Two sons are also mentioned: L. Caecilius Valens and P. Caecilius Secundus. Cilo's wife is not named. But he evidently had a *contubernalis*, a concubine, whose distinctive style of name appears to identify her as a non-citizen of Celtic descent: 'Lutulla, daughter of Pictus' (*Lutullae Picti f.*). Cilo was the preferred candidate of Theodor Mommsen, Pliny's venerated nineteenth century biographer[37] Cilo is a gift to a biography. If he was Pliny's father, then Cilo must have divorced Pliny's mother at some point and installed Lutulla in her stead as official sexual partner without status as wife. 'Life had knocked [Pliny's mother] about enough as it was—humiliated by her wastrel husband and his ghastly mistress, then left widowed with a boy to bring up'. Such is the excellent use Robert Harris makes of this inscription in his novel *Pompeii*.[38] Perhaps Pliny was silent about his father in the *Letters* because of marital infidelity that the young Augustine would also witness in his own home in north Africa?[39] Unfortunately, Cilo has been generally demoted since Mommsen's day from father to mere collateral relation to Pliny. 'Celtic names and apparent lack of citizen status', in the estimate of one authority, 'suggest that the inscription belongs to a period too early for Pliny and his father'.[40]

We have no reliable evidence for a diminishing supply of Celtic concubines in Comum in the second half of the first century. Just a hunch. And Cilo's rival creates fewer problems of this sort—if we can trust the craft of epigraphers. The inscription which commemorates L. Caecilius Secundus was found in the late nineteenth century alongside over forty others in the garden of a school, the Liceo Classico 'A. Volta', just inside the main gate to the old town of Como. The façade of this former ecclesiastical building carries modern busts of both the Elder and Younger Plinii and is supported by fine Roman marble columns of unidentified provenance.[41] The inscription records the final dedication of a temple of the imperial cult by a Caecilius Secundus, after his father L. Caecilius Secundus had begun it in the name of a presumably deceased daughter named Caecilia:[42]

> [Caeci]liae f(iliae) suae nomin[e] L(ucius) Ca[eciliu]s C(ai) f(ilius) Ouf(entina tribu) Secundus praef(ectus) [fabr(um)] a co(n)s(ule) (quattuor)uir i(ure) d(icundo) pontif(ex) tem[plum] Aeternitati Romae et Augu[stor(um) c]um porticibus et ornamentis incohauit
> [—Caeci]lius Secundus f(ilius) dedic[auit]

> In the name of his daughter Caecilia, Lucius Caecilius Secundus, son of Gaius, of the tribe Oufentina, chief of engineers on the nomination of the consul, magistrate for the administration of justice, priest, began a temple to the Eternity of Rome and the Augusti [i.e. emperors] with porticoes and decorations.
> ... Caecilius Secundus, his son, dedicated it.

> *CIL* 5, Add. 745 = *AE* (1983) 443

Today this limestone inscription is rather faded. But the naked eye can still see what is obscured in transcription by the epigrapher's panoply of square brackets, denoting suggested restorations, and angled brackets, denoting the suggested resolution of abbreviations. The name 'Caecilius' is nowhere preserved in full. The damaged original offers only three different parts of what is evidently the same name: -*liae*, *Ca* . . .*s*, and -*lius*. An optimistic attitude to incomplete inscriptions has played havoc with the biography of the Plinii before. The island of Aradus off the coast of Syria produced an inscription in honour of ']inius Secund['. Who else could this be but Pl]inius Secund[us the Elder in his travels during a long career in military and imperial service? Mommsen was certain. But the current consensus restores a more common name: Can]inius, Com]inius or Gab]inius Secund[us.[43]

Suppose we accept the restoration of the various forms of the name 'Caecilius': why believe L. Caecilius Secundus is the father of our Caecilius Secundus? The answer is technical and demands faith in a discipline based on knowledge of the repetitive formulae of Roman inscriptions and an eye for the number of letters that can be incised on the available space. The key term is 'Augu['. One experienced scholar has persuaded many that a fragmentary parallel inscription suggests, and the surface of the stone allows for, four missing letters, not three. The text originally read 'Augu[stor(um)]' and not 'Augu[sti]': a plural form rather than a singular.[44] If he is right, then the temple was dedicated to 'The Eternity of Rome' and a plurality of emperors not to a single 'Augustus'. A cult of this particular sort, the argument goes, is consistent with a Flavian date—which would suit the Younger well. It was during the final years of Vespasian that Pliny became formally old enough to dedicate a temple as Caecilius Secundus, in the window of time between the early death of his father and adoption by his uncle as a Plinius.[45]

Perhaps neither Cilo nor Secundus is Pliny's father. Delicacies of interpretation aside, the assumption of a connection between surviving texts and available artefacts is as common as it is often unwarranted. At the very least, L. Caecilius Secundus tells us something about the *sort* of wealthy local man Pliny's father clearly was. The army posting 'chief of engineers' (*praefectus fabrum*) indicates equestrian status.[46] He held the more prestigious of his town's four local annual magistracies ('*quattuoruir* for the administration of justice') and, consequently, served in Comum's senate of around eighty to one hundred men drawn from the local elite.[47] This body possessed oversight of the affairs of the town and required significant financial contributions from its members.[48] The landed wealth of the Younger, inherited from both parents,[49] shows his father could well afford these subventions. L. Caecilius Secundus went further in dedicating an expensive temple of the imperial cult in Comum, just as the Younger in later life would donate a library (and baths) to Comum explicitly in a family tradition (1.8.5), and dedicate his own temple of the imperial cult in the Umbrian town of which he was patron (10.8).[50]

So far, so unrevealing, perhaps. If the Comum text of dedication really is to Rome and a plurality of emperors, more can be said. The worship of Rome and the imperial household is an innovation on the older cult of Rome and Augustus. Firm evidence begins to appear at the end of the first century C.E., but the cult likely has roots in the Flavian era.[51] Vespasian and his sons stood in need of legitimizing their new dynasty after the death of the last emperor related to Augustus: Vespasian dropped 'Flavius' from his name and added 'Augustus'.[52] A temple to more than one Augustus usefully mingled cult of the new dynasty with worship of imperial predecessors. Perhaps L. Caecilius Secundus was well attuned to the aspirations of the new regime and an early adopter.[53] It was in the provincial towns of Italy that Vespasian could rely on keen support: he had been born outside Rome to a father who had not been a senator.[54] If a man like L. Caecilius Secundus was the Younger's father, the roots of loyalty to the dynasty went very deep. On the other side of the family, the Elder Pliny appears to have become friendly with Titus even before the Younger was born, a full decade before the unlikely ascent of the Flavians to power. He went on to write a history of their dynasty, and left it for the Younger to publish after his death.[55] Unlike the great intermarried families of Rome who could trace principled criticism of 'bad' emperors back to the days of Claudius, Pliny had no domestic traditions of imperial opposition. His loyal service in later life to the last of the Flavians would eventually imperil his good reputation in senatorial society.[56]

Growing up fatherless in Comum

A father's early death, in one recent estimate, 'stood in the mid-range of life's tragedies in the ancient world. It was not devastatingly rare, as a child's death is today'.[57] Epitaphs fill out the void behind this judgement. The memorial for Caecilius Cilo records family grief in rather small letters beneath the more formal main inscription: 'Time has hurried on. It had to be done. Don't cry mother'.[58] Given generally severe mortality rates and the tendency of men outside the senatorial elite to marry at about thirty, around one-third of children could expect to lose their fathers by their early teens, rising to somewhere between 50 and 60 per cent by age 25.[59] It is true that Pliny all but erases his father from the *Letters* to emphasize the success of surrogate parentship, and proves himself attuned to the regime of Trajan quite as early as L. Caecilius Secundus to the Flavians.[60] But perhaps, also, he did not remember his father very clearly. The same might be true of a sister for Pliny named Caecilia in the temple inscription—another family absentee from the written record of Pliny's life.[61] If Pliny's wife Calpurnia had carried to term the pregnancy whose miscarriage is reported around 107 C.E., his own child would likely not have retained any memories by the time of the Younger's death five or more years later.[62]

The memorial for L. Caecilius Secundus suggests a man lacking in personal ambition beyond eminence in Comum. Unlike the Elder Pliny, he interpreted the requirement of military service laid on his privileged class in a minimalist way: 'chief of engineers' was often an honorary post, with no well-defined duties beyond personal attachment to a consul or proconsul.[63] But he evidently gave some thought, as must most men in his position, to the appointment of a surrogate parent for his child. Whether made by L. Caecilius Secundus or someone like him, the choice indicates no lack of aspiration for the Younger. The early death of a father could represent opportunity as much as tragedy.[64]

The Greek rhetorician Libanius, older contemporary of Augustine, saw his father die at eleven. He later wrote, 'I would gladly have seen my father in his old age, but of one thing I am certain—that if my father had come to a ripe old age, I would now be engaged upon a very different life'.[65] Through his choice of guardian, Pliny's father placed few such limits on the ambitions of his son.[66] The Elder was passed over: he was probably abroad for much of Pliny's youth.[67] Verginius Rufus of Milan was chosen in his stead. Connections with Verginius were local: 'we came from the same part of the country' (2.1.8).[68] More importantly, Verginius was a figure on the imperial stage.[69] By the time Pliny was seven or eight years old, Verginius had been twice consul, a governor of the key military province of upper Germany, and acclaimed as emperor by his troops in the course of action during the insurrection against Nero in 68 C.E. He made the great refusal, and seems to have spent the remainder of his long life in well-advised retirement on the coast at Alsium, 22 miles/35 kilometres north of Rome.[70]

The exact nature of the relationship between Verginius Rufus and the young Pliny can only be guessed at. The bonds of guardianship were regarded as more sacred even than *amicitia*, friendship, but at his faraway seaside retreat Verginius was ill-placed to perform the guardian's onerous main role of property management.[71] He still retained his ward's affection throughout life: 'left by will as my guardian . . . [Verginius] always exhibited towards me the affection of a parent'.[72] Did he guide Pliny towards one of his advantageous marriages? Certainly the wealthy Pompeia Celerina, the mother of the wife immediately prior to Calpurnia, is found in possession of Verginius' house at Alsium ten years after the death of the latter (6.10).[73] Pliny also shared literary interests in verse composition with Verginius (5.3.5), and the elegiac lines that make up the epitaph for Verginius display real elegance (6.10.5).[74]

Not everyone was a fan. Tacitus appears unenthusiastic in his appraisal of Verginius and his behaviour during the events of 68-9 C.E.[75] Pliny loyally defends the record of his guardian (2.1.2, 6.10.4, 9.19). Verginius, after all, was a man ideally placed to foster and shape the senatorial ambitions of his ward, the son of a wealthy but undistinguished father. His knowledge of the inner workings of senate, army, provinces, and emperor can have had few equals amongst contemporaries in the Transpadana. And Verginius would eventually be honoured with an extremely rare third consulship in 97 C.E., in his eighties, under Nerva.[76] Yet, for all that, two decades earlier, it is in the Elder Pliny's company that the Younger can be discovered at the moment of the eruption of Vesuvius. The Elder's connections to the Flavian house were paramount for an ambitious young man in his eighteenth year.[77] If the entrée to senatorial life offered by Verginius was invaluable, the personal relationship with Pliny ultimately seems a distant one.[78]

A Roman childhood: filling in the gaps?

Pliny displays no systematic interest in the events of his childhood. Unlike the Augustine of the *Confessions*,[79] he is not trying to trace the ascent of his mind from ignorance to illumination over the course of a life. Nor, like Marcus Aurelius in the *Meditations*, is he trying to think hard about the formation of his character from earliest years.[80] Reflection on or systematic interrogation of the self is not part of Pliny's plan. The guiding assumption is that his correspondents will want to hear of recent or significant events that Pliny has either witnessed or taken part in.

The *Letters* do offer *some* explicit details about childhood, or at least information from which clear inferences can be made. In a letter lamenting the death of the daughter of a friend in her early teens, Pliny exclaims 'How she cherished her nurses [*nutrices*], her attendants [*paedagogos*] and her tutors [*praeceptores*]' (5.16.3).[81] From this panoply of attendants on a privileged childhood, only a nurse would resurface in Pliny's own adult life. He remained attached enough, even in his mid-forties, to intervene and halt the falling returns from the farm he had gifted her.[82] Like nearly all *nutrices* in non-fictional Roman literature, she goes unnamed, and nothing is said of her nurturing role in childhood. That honour goes instead to Calpurnia Hispulla of Comum, aunt of Pliny's future wife: 'For as you revered my mother in the place of a parent, so from my very boyhood you were in the habit of forming me, of praising me, of predicting that I should be such as I now appear to my wife to be' (4.19.7).[83] Moralists, philosophers, and medical writers were united and emphatic in their opposition to the use of *nutrices*.[84] Elite society ignored them. It could only be to Pliny's advantage, nevertheless, to credit as nurturer a well-born woman of wealthy family from his hometown.

For his schooling, Pliny attended a public classroom in Comum at either the elementary stage of education, under the *ludi magister* ('school master'), or under more advanced instruction in language and poetry from the *grammaticus* ('scholar').[85] This emerges from a letter to a childhood friend, Romatius Firmus, whose status Pliny sought to raise in adulthood from decurion to Roman knight: 'You are my townsman [*municeps*] and my schoolfellow [*condiscipulus*] and have been my associate [*contubernalis*] from the outset of my life. Your father was on terms of intimacy with my mother and uncle . . .' (1.19.1).[86] Unlike other members of local elites,[87] Pliny was not educated at home, and mixed with those somewhat beneath his own wealth and status. He was evidently also a star pupil in this environment, to judge from the information that he attempted to write a Greek tragedy at age fourteen.[88] Quintilian's *Education of the Orator*, produced during Pliny's adulthood, offered retrospective approval for the future public speaker's attendance of a town school. Aware of the fears of anxious parents about the morals of *grammatici* and the neglect that their sons might suffer in a large class, Quintilian argued against home schooling and in favour of the public classroom: 'let the future orator, who has to live in the crowd and in the full glare of public life, become accustomed from childhood not to be frightened of people or acquire the pallor that comes from that solitary life that is lived in the shade' (*Inst.* 1.2.18).[89] Who taught Pliny there? An inscribed statue base of the late first or early second century records the gratitude of the local senate in Comum to a *grammaticus* named P. Atilius Septicianus, albeit not for his teaching but for leaving his estate to the town.[90] The date is too late for any association with someone who taught Pliny,[91] but does suggest the public recognition and prominence which such figures might win. Pliny does not single out for praise or name any *grammaticus* from Comum.[92] But he hardly matches Augustine, of whom one modern critic has said 'He never wrote with admiration or gratitude about any of his teachers.'[93]

Augustine, writing in his forties, complains with evident bitterness of the beatings he received from teachers in the early stages of education.[94] Such thrashings are consistently portrayed as an unavoidable part of ancient schooling. If Pliny was beaten in his first years at school, this is not what worries *him* as an adult about teachers of the young. Pliny shares with Quintilian a concern that seems not to impinge on Augustine: a suspicion of sexual interference with pupils.[95] This lies behind Pliny's assertion that Comum is the best place for 'virtuous supervision . . . under the eyes of . . . parents' (4.13.4),[96] and his determination to find for the son of a friend a teacher 'of the discipline [*scholae seueritas*] and respectability [*pudor*] of whose schoolroom, above all, of whose morality [*castitas*], we are assured. For our young friend . . . possesses remarkable physical beauty [*eximia corporis pulchritudo*], in view of which, at his critical age, not a teacher merely, but a guardian and governor is required' (3.3.3–4).[97] Pliny here is speaking of the dangers of more advanced education under the *rhetor*. Quintilian indicates a continuity with the potential risks of the *grammaticus*: 'If not enough care has been taken about the character of the supervisors or teachers, I blush to mention the shameful purposes for which evil men abuse their right to flog . . . I will not dwell on this subject: what I am hinting at is already too much' (*Inst.* 1.3.17).[98] Augustine, of course, writes with apparent candour on a tangential topic: the experience of adolescent desire and growing sexual maturity.[99] Pliny is a model of reticence. Such things were for the Augustan love poets, not senators. Pliny's 'love letters' in adulthood to his wife Calpurnia would draw on the poets' more decorous pages.[100] Unlike the Augustan elegists, he would not praise his beloved's looks. He comments only on the beauty of young males.[101]

Pliny could not stay in Comum for the final stage of his education in public speaking. The town had no *rhetor* in residence, and students had to go to Milan or elsewhere to finish their education. Pliny later tried to remedy this deficiency with an offer to part-fund the salary of a *rhetor*—whom he undertook to recruit personally from the circle of young men around Tacitus, leading orator of the day.[102] He even made an impromptu speech to the parents of Comum, emphasizing the attractions of local education:

> Let those who are born here be educated here, and from their very infancy let them grow accustomed to love and to throng their native soil. And I hope that you introduce teachers of such repute that this will be a source to which neighbouring towns will resort for learning, and that, just as now your children flock to other places, so strangers may soon flock to this place.[103]
>
> *Letters* 4.13.9

Sound words and encouragement of civic rivalry with Milan, all backed up by Pliny's own cash. But he himself had gone to Rome for *his* training in rhetoric. A later chapter will take up that story.[104]

Pliny, Augustine, and the biography of childhood

This handful of facts represents almost the complete sum of direct evidence that can be gleaned about early years in Comum. Such paucity of information is a problem faced by most modern lives of ancient figures. To solve it, many silently substitute context for biography: generic information on ancient childhood drawn from a variety of sources across space and time does duty for a specific account of a subject's youth.[105] It is better to be explicit. Anyone in search of a larger narrative framework into which the fragments of Pliny's youth can be inserted should read Augustine's *Confessions*.[106] Pliny's nurse comes to life in Augustine's reconstruction of how his mother and nurses fed him milk, how his nurses watched him laugh and cry and later played and joked with him while encouraging him to speak his native Latin.[107] Augustine's reconstruction of his earliest years needs to be treated with caution, since much of the *Confessions* is deeply imbued with the author's reading of Cicero, Vergil, and the Christian scriptures.[108] The first three books of the work, nevertheless, include a largely chronological retelling of the first eighteen years of the Augustine's relatively privileged provincial Roman boyhood, from infant years and schooling at Thagaste in north Africa to education in a school of rhetoric in the provincial capital of Carthage.[109] Differences in assumptions and outlook between Pliny and Augustine are profound, but elsewhere the gap narrows. Education, local civic and social structures, technology, materials—most of these had changed little enough in the three centuries that intervene between the pair. Augustine's father was hardly as wealthy or well-connected as Pliny's. Both were members of the local 'decurion' class, all the same, and lived in towns remote from the centres of power, died early, and had sons who showed obvious rhetorical and literary talent.[110]

Inasmuch as they provide the template for modern biography,[111] the *Confessions* are useful in another way. They provoke the suspicion that the *Letters* would be unlikely to satisfy modern and Augustinian demands for a satisfactory narrative of youth, even if more material were available to us from Pliny's hand. Here we return to reflect on the awkward fit between ancient lives and modern biographical expectations. A note of alienation runs through the Augustine's narration of his early life. He disliked his elementary lessons at school and preferred games with his fellow pupils. He recoils still at the memory of being beaten, and failed to warm to Greek. He regrets the waste of time and energy spent in successfully retelling an episode from Vergil in a class exercise, and criticizes his own pride in success. He could not, then or now, identify with his father's ambitions for his son or the interest he took in his offspring's sexual maturity.[112] Augustine scorns an education system aimed at teaching pupils how to deceive more effectively in the courtroom. 'Was it not all smoke and wind? And was there no other way of training my mind and tongue' (*Conf.* 1.17.27) he asks of the Vergilian exercise. The art of rhetoric is dismissed as 'a damnable end urged on us by the delight men take in vanity' (*Conf.* 3.4.7).[113] Augustine's discomfort has a distinctively Christian origin. But the identification of alienation from prevailing conventional culture is a distinctive feature of modern biography, whether largely personal and aesthetic (Joyce), political (Yeats), or psychological (Van Gogh). If estrangement is a contemporary hallmark of personal authenticity, Augustine appears modern in his willingness to reflect critically on contemporary values and practices, and reject them.

Such sustained alienation is hard to find in the culture of Pliny's high empire. A sense of youthful estrangement from parental ambition and society's ethical expectations can be found in Roman love elegy of the Augustan era. Elegy's alienation is vulnerable to being contained within an older narrative of permitted early indiscretion. It is encapsulated in the shame expressed by the elegist Propertius for making his girlfriend Cynthia famous and his new dedication to *Mens Bona* ('Good Sense') after five years of servitude to his mistress.[114] Parents and teachers appear largely confident that restless adolescent behaviour will burn itself out: alienation is an interlude between longer episodes of integration.[115] For Augustine, youthful estrangement continues into maturity. His sense of alienation finds gradual relief in the series of personal transformations that articulates the *Confessions*. Such changes in the self are viewed positively in the modern world. But ancient pre-Christian society tended to believe, in the estimate of a modern authority, that 'you owed it to yourself and others to know the right thing in the first place'.[116] As emphasized in the immediately following chapter on the young Pliny at Vesuvius: consistency, not evolution, was the supreme value.[117] In this context, if Pliny felt alienated in his youth from the education system or his father's ambitions for him or the prevailing sexual norms, this alienation could not be transformed into a positive story of an evolving critical stance towards society and its values. Such stories could be told to public approval only after the passing of high empire.

Notes

1. See Ando (2016), Roncaglia (2018, 19–60).
2. Catull. 97.6, criticized at Quint. *Inst.* 1.5.8 ('Catullus found it in the Po Valley'); cf. Cic. *Brut.* 171, Adams (2003, 184–5, 442–3). *Basium* ('kiss') has also been suspected: see Fordyce (1961, 106–7) on Catull. 5.7; cf. O'Hara (2017, 53) on Catull. 11.9 *Alpes*. For Vergil's experience as a Transpadane, see Jenkyns (1998, 73–127).
3. Augustin. *de Ord.* 2.17.45, Brown (2000, 79). Syme (1958, 619) uses *Letters* 9.23.2 to suggest that Tacitus possessed non-Italic nuances to his pronunciation. For a general lack of prejudice against western senators from outside the bounds of the old Italy, see Syme (1999, 39–44).
4. On pre-Roman Comum, see *Como fra Etruschi e Celti* (1986), Luraschi (2013b, 10–20); cf. Häussler (2007) on the pre-Roman history of the surrounding area.
5. Bacchiega (1993) cites *AE* 1952, 55 (from Capua, c. 108 B.C.E.) and *AE* 1895, 23 (from Sicily, c. 36 B.C.E.): the first records a Plinius who was a *magister* of a *collegium* of Iuppiter Optimus Maximus, and the second a Plinius who was *legatus propraetore*. The Younger aside, those bearing the name Plinius do not leave an extensive inscriptional record; see Chp. 7 for the Plinii of Comum and their freedmen in the context of the total epigraphic attestations of the name.
6. Cf. Strabo 5.1.6, Appian *BC* 2.26, Suet. *Iul.* 28.3, Luraschi (1999b), De Agostini (2006, 2–4), Luraschi (2013b, 20–28); see also Pelling (2011, 294–6) on the status of the town's inhabitants in the late Republic.
7. On the dangers of crossing the Alps beyond Comum, cf. Strabo 4.6.6.
8. Catull. 35.1–4 *poetae tenero, meo sodali, | uelim Caecilio, papyre, dicas | Veronam ueniat, Novi relinquens | Comi moenia Lariumque litus.*
9. See McHam (2005, 478 with n. 65). The identity of this Caecilius is unknown to modern scholarship (Hollis (2007, 421)), but as Caecilius Statius he is the first *praestans uir* of Como in Giovio's history of the town (Giovio (1982, 234–6): see Chp. 1 on this history).
10. See Luraschi (1999c), (1999d, 469), De Agostini (2006, 30–2).
11. On the population of ancient Comum and the layout of the town in *insulae* of c. 70 x 70m, see Duncan-Jones (1982, 267, 272–3), Luraschi (1999d, 469), Roncaglia (2018, 172 n. 32); cf. modern censuses for the urban centre: 37,537 in 1921 and 56,937 in 1951. See De Ligt (2012, 289–303) for a survey of sizes of cities and towns in the early imperial Transpadana.

12. On Roman Comum, see Roncaglia (2018, 75–88), also S. Maggi (1993), (2013), Sacchi (2013). For a possible amphitheatre or theatre, see Mirabella Roberti (1993), Luraschi (1999e), De Agostini (2006, 111–13). For a survey of written sources on Roman Comum up to late antiquity, see P. Maggi (1993); for an historical survey of archaeological finds in Comum, see De Agostini (2013).

13. On Comum's epigraphic culture, see Sartori (1993), (1994), (2013); on its extensive marble survivals, see Rossignani and Sacchi (1993).

14. On Comum as *municipium*, including economy and territorial boundaries, see Luraschi (1999d), (2013b, 10, 34–42); cf. Pliny on his lands in the area, e.g. 2.1.8, 2.15, 4.6, 5.14.8, 7.11, 7.14.

15. Cf. 3.6.4, with Sherwin-White (1966, 226), Henderson (2002a, 169).

16. Baths: see later on *CIL* 5.5279; for other temples in Comum, see Luraschi (1999d, 470–1).

17. Library, baths, and colonnade: see Chp. 7.

18. See Naifeh and White Smith (2011, 38–9).

19. Bartlett (2004, 44). The endpoint of this Romantic tradition is the commercialization of locales for tourists; see Foster (1997, 23) on 'Yeats country' near the poet's childhood home in Sligo. (For the present biography's partial implication in this trope, see Appendix 2.)

20. See Wear (2008), Rives (1999, 16–17); cf. Thomas (1982) for the influence of the tradition on Horace, Vergil, and Tacitus.

21. Statius *Silvae* 3.5.105–9, Newlands (2012, 157).

22. See Chp. 7.

23. 1.14.4 (Minicius Acilianus) *patria est ei Brixia, ex illa nostra Italia quae multum adhuc uerecundiae frugalitatis, atque etiam rusticitatis antiquae, retinet ac seruat*; cf. Chp. 7 on the virtues of Calpurnia of Comum.

24. Cf. *Agr.* 4.2, *Ann.* 3.55.3, 16.5.1, Woodman and Martin (1996, 405–6), Griffin (1999, 156) = (2016, 375), Birley (2000b, 233–4), Syme (1999, 45–52).

25. On Catullus Messalinus, collateral descendant of the poet, consul and informer under Domitian, cf. 4.22.5–6, Sherwin-White (1966, 300–1). Vibius Crispus, a three-time consul and 'denouncer' from Vercellae, who may conceivably have aided the careers of both Plinii, was another local to live down; see Syme, *RP* 7.506, 524–33.

26. I owe the observation of the biographical importance of water in Pliny to Ellen O'Gorman; cf. Radice (1962).

27. 6.24.2 *nauigabam per Larium nostrum;* cf. Chp. 7 on Pliny's views of the lake.

28. See Chp. 6.

29. See Saylor (1972).

30. See Chp. 4.

31. On the historical realities of the (relative) failure of the Nile flood in 99 C.E. and on Pliny's treatment of it in the *Panegyricus,* see Bonneau (1971, 171–4, 238–40), Manolaraki (2013, 234–46), Gibson (2019); on the importance of water and seascapes in the *Panegyricus* more generally, see Manolaraki (2008).

32. See Chp. 5; cf. 4.8, 5.1, 9.19 on Pliny's friendship with Iulius Frontinus, author of *de Aquaeductu Urbis Romae.*

33. Catullus in Bithynia: see Chp. 8; cf. poem 101 on a visit by sea—imagined or real?—to the tomb of his brother in Asia Minor (68b.91–100).

34. Syme (1985c, 195) = *RP* 5.644.

35. See Sherwin-White (1966, 144); cf. later on Verginius Rufus and the duties of a *tutor*.

36. *CIL* 5.5279; Cilo's premature death is suggested by *aetas properauit* ('time has hurried on'). On bathing benefactions, see Patterson (2006, 157).

37. See Chp. 1. On Cilo, his concubine, and his 'divorce', see Mommsen (1869, 59–61), who points out that Pliny's mother is still alive when Pliny is in his late teens in 79 C.E. (6.16, 20). The bottom of the inscription contains, in much smaller letters, an address to a mother (*noli plangere mater*, 'don't cry mother'): Mommsen interpreted this as the speech of the *manes* ('ghost') of Cilo to his own mother, and not as a reference to Cilo's erstwhile wife. Note that Caecilius Valens and Caecilius Secundus, however, might equally be understood as the dead man's brothers.

38. Harris (2003, 172–3); cf. Hales and Paul (2011b) for an interview with Harris on his novel.

39. See Chp. 2.

40. Sherwin-White (1966, 70); cf. Ando (2016, 285–6) on the persistence of Celtic elements in the Transpadana up to early imperial times.

41. See Sacchi (2013, 162) on the possible origin of the columns from a site tentatively identified in Chp. 7 as that of Pliny's library.

42. *CIL* 5, Add. 745 = *AE* (1983) 443 = Alföldy (1983) = (1999b); cf. Krieckhaus (2006, 215). The second half of the inscription reappears in even more lacunose form as *CIL* 5, Add. 746 (discovered in the same location as 745); cf. Krieckhaus (2006, 215). The form of the inscription likely implies that Caecilia predeceased her father; see Sherwin-White (1966, 70). On her absence from the *Letters*, see later.

43. See Syme (1969, 205) = *RP* 2.745–6; *RP* 7.497.

44. Alföldy (1983) = (1999b) argues for the restoration of *CIL* 5, Add. 745 from a fragment assumed to belong to the same building: *CIL* 5, Add. 746 'Au]gustor[um' (itself restored from rather doubtful lettering). On the Flavian date, see later.

45. See Chp. 4 on adoption after the death of the Elder.

46. See Syme (1985c, 195) = *RP* 5.644.

47. See Luraschi (1999d, 472–7). The *quattuoruir* post held by Caecilius Secundus dealt with the public finances, presided over public cults, and administered justice within certain limits.

48. See Sherwin-White (1966, 129–30, 721–2) on 1.19.2, 10.112.

49. Cf. 7.11.5; see Chp. 6 on Pliny's total wealth.

50. See Chps. 7 and 6 respectively.

51. See Alföldy (1983, 367–71) = (1999b, 216–18), who cites also later evidence from 10.35–6, 83, 100–1; *Paneg.* 67.3. The addition of 'Eternity' to the cult's name shifted attention away from individual emperors to the institution of the principate as a whole.

52. On Vespasian's imperial ideology in general, including links particularly with Augustus and Claudius and his change in nomenclature, see Griffin (2000a, 11–25), Cooley (2016b, 121–3).

53. A contemporary narrative, with which Pliny and Tacitus were in sympathy, saw Vespasian break with the decadence of the Julio-Claudians; see Sherwin-White (1966, 431–2), Woodman and Martin (1996, 401).

54. On Vespasian's background, generosity, and appeal to the provincial cities of Italy, cf. 1.14.5, Tac. *Ann.* 3.55.3–5, Suet. *Vesp.* 9.2, Griffin (2000a, 2–3, 31), Levick (1999, 130–4).

55. See Chp. 4.

56. See Chp. 5. Tacitus, by contrast, may have had some family connections with one of the dynasties of the 'Stoic' opposition; see Birley (2000b, 231–3).

57. Golden (2009, 59).

58. *aetas properavit faciendum fuit noli plangere mater* (*CIL* 5.5279); see earlier on this inscription.

59. See Scheidel (2009, 32) and Parkin (2011) validating the conclusions of Saller (1994, 9–69). On the age of first marriage for men, see Saller (1994, 25–41).

60. See Chp. 2.

61. In the *Confessions* Augustine commits the more obvious crime of failing to mention a living sister, Perpetua, who went on to be an abbess; a hitherto unmentioned brother Navigius turns up at his mother's deathbed (*Conf.* 9.11.27); cf. Clarke (2004, 5).

62. Cf. 8.10–11, Bernstein (2009, 251–2 with n. 41).

63. See Healy (1999, 4–5), Buraselis (2000, 67–70); cf. Chp. 4 on the extensive military career of the Elder.

64. See Golden (2009), Hallett (2009), Müller (2009), Cribiore (2009).

65. Libanius *Or.* 1.6—where it is implied that his father would have preferred a career in local politics or law.

66. For the expectation that a father chose as *tutor* at least one man of greater power and wealth than himself, see Saller (1994, 201–2); cf. Bernstein (2009, 243–6) on criticism of those who failed to appoint a *tutor*.

67. See Chp. 1.

68. 2.1.8 *utrique eadem regio.* Verginius from Milan: *ILS* 982.

69. Verginius had no son (2.1.9); Syme, *RP* 7.508 speculates that he was also (attractively) childless.

70. On Verginius, see Chp. 4 n. 121; on his ambiguous role in the revolt against Nero, cf. 2.1.2–3, 9.19.5, Tac. *Hist.* 1.8.2, 1.52.4, Shotter (2001); on Verginius at Alsium, see later, also Appendix 2.

71. See Saller (1994, 181–203).

72. 2.1.8 *ille mihi tutor relictus adfectum parentis exhibuit.*

73. Cf. Chp. 6 n. 38, and see Gibson (f'coming) on 6.10.

74. 6.10.5 *Hic situs est Rufus, pulso qui Vindice quondam | imperium adseruit non sibi sed patriae,* 'Here lies Rufus who after Vindex had been defeated once | liberated supreme power not for himself but for his country'.

75. See Shotter (1967, 379–80), Syme, *RP* 7.517.

76. Cf. 2.1 with Whitton (2013, 65–83); see also Chp. 5.

77. See Chp. 4.

78. In his most pessimistic phase, Pliny hints darkly at the limitations of all his elders, including Verginius; see Chp. 5, Gibson (2015, 208–19).

79. See Chp. 2.

80. On Marcus Aurelius in *Meditations* Book 1, see Pelling (1990a, 224), Dickson (2009), Gill (2013, lxxv–lxxxiv).

81. On Minicia Marcella, deceased daughter of Minicius Fundanus, see Shelton (2013, 275–82), Bodel (1995), Caldwell (2015, 23–7). Quintilian devotes separate attention to the attendants he assumes will surround his elite male charges in early childhood: nurses must pronounce their words properly, and enslaved persons or freedmen attendants must either be well educated or know they are uneducated (*Inst.* 1.1.4–6, 1.1.8–1); on these figures, see further Bradley (1991, 143–5), Cribiore (2009, 260–1), Laes (2011, 113–22).

82. Cf. 6.3. On nurses, see Shelton (2013, 178–84) with specific reference to 6.3; more generally see Bradley (1991, 13–36), Laes (2011, 69–77).

83. 4.19.7 *nam cum matrem meam parentis loco uererere, me a pueritia statim formare laudare, talemque qualis nunc uxori meae uideor, ominari solebas.* On Hispulla, see Chp. 7; for intergenerational relationships between opposite sexes in Pliny, see Centlivres Challet (2011).

84. Cf. Tac. *Germ.* 20, *Dial.* 29, Plut. *Mor.* 3c–e, *Cato* 20, Gell. 1.1.1–24, Galen *de San. Tuen.* 1.7, Soran. *Gyn.* 2.7.17–18.

85. On the various (and flexible) stages of Roman education under *ludi magister* and *grammaticus* from roughly 7–15 years-old, see Rawson (2003, 146–209), Horster (2011), Laes (2011, 122–37).

86. On 1.19 to Romatius Firmus, see Henderson (2002c).

87. Cf. 3.3.3 on the son of Corellia Hispulla, evidently taught at home by a *grammaticus.*

88. Cf. 7.14.2; see Gibson and Steel (2010) on Pliny's literary career.

89. Quint. *Inst.* 1.2.18 *futurus orator, cui in maxima celebritate et in media rei publicae luce uiuendum est, adsuescat iam a tenero non reformidare homines neque illa solitaria et uelut umbratili uita pallescere*; cf. *Inst.* 1.2.17–31 for Quintilian's broad opposition to home schooling. On competing ideas of childhood education in contemporary authors, see Uden (2018).

90. *CIL* 5.5278; similar awards of the *ornamenta decurionalia* to *grammatici* are known at Verona (*CIL* 5.3433) and Beneventum (*CIL* 9.1654). On municipal *grammatici*, see further Sherwin-White (1966, 288).

91. The date does allow a possible association with the teacher whom Pliny proposed in adulthood to fund for Comum (4.13: see later); cf. Roncaglia (2018, 82, 172 n. 39).

92. The rise to social prominence by *grammatici* is the underpinning narrative of the chapters awarded to these figures by Suetonius in his work *De Viris Illustribus*: previous authors of lives of illustrious literary men appear to have excluded coverage of *grammatici* and *rhetores* altogether; cf. esp. Suet. *Gramm.* 25.3, Kaster (1995, xxix–xxx, xliv). Pliny is quite uninterested in the idea of social mobility for paid educators; see Gibson (2014, 217–21).

93. Chadwick (2001, 8).

94. *Conf.* 1.9.14, O'Donnell (1992, II.61); see Laes (2011, 137–47) for a survey of the broader evidence.

95. See Lane Fox (2015, 59–60).

96. 4.13.4 *pudicius continerentur . . . sub oculis parentum.*

97. Cf. 3.3.5 *licentia temporum,* 'the looseness of our age'.

98. Quint. *Inst.* 1.3.17 *iam si minor in eligendis custodum et praeceptorum moribus fuit cura, pudet dicere in quae probra nefandi homines isto caedendi iure abutantur . . . non morabor in parte hac: nimium est quod intellegitur.* On recurrent worries about sexual interference with pupils, cf. Hor. *Sat.* 1.6.76–84, Quint. *Inst.* 2.2.1–3, 14–15, Kaster (1995, 235) on Suet. *DGR* 23.2. On the societal context for such worries, see Laes (2011, 222–77).

99. The growth of sexual desire dominates the second book of Augustine's *Confessions*; cf. the Augustan love poet Propertius 3.15.3–10. See Laes and Strubbe (2014, 221–7) for continuity and change in attitudes to adolescent sexuality across antiquity.

100. Cf. 6.4, 6.7, 7.5, Chp. 7 n. 72.

101. Klodt (2012, 58–61) points out that while Pliny comments on the beauty of young men (e.g. 1.14.8, 3.3.4, 3.16.3, 7.24.3), not even in the letter on the death of the young daughter of Minicius Fundanus (5.16: see earlier) does he comment on female beauty, despite encouragement from the literary traditions behind the letter.

102. Cf. 4.13, with Manuwald (2003); see also Sherwin-White (1966, 287) for imperial encouragement of municipal schooling. Note that Pliny is proposing to hire a teacher, on a private rather than municipal basis, not to build a school (Sherwin-White (1966, 200)).

103. 4.13.9 *educentur hic qui hic nascuntur, statimque ab infantia natale solum amare frequentare consuescant. atque utinam tam claros praeceptores inducatis, ut in finitimis oppidis studia hinc petantur, utque nunc liberi uestri aliena in loca ita mox alieni in hunc locum confluant!*

104. See Chp. 5.

105. See Beard (2013, 124–5). For a broad overview of the evidence and issues pertaining to the first seven years of a Roman child's life, see Laes (2011, 50–106).

106. Augustine's 'narrative of childhood is not especially Christian', at least in Book 1: O'Donnell (1992, II.8); cf. O'Donnell (2005, 53).

107. Cf. *Conf.* 1.6.7–8, 1.14.23. Just visible in Augustine also are the enslaved children of wet nurses who provided companions for the free children of the house: *Conf.* 1.7.11, with Bradley (1991, 149–55); see also Shaw (1987) on Augustine and his experience of the Roman family. Vignettes of stereotypical daily life, including lives of children, can be recovered from texts designed to teach Latin to Greek speakers; see Dickey (2016) and, in more detail, Dickey (2012–15).

108. See (e.g.) Shanzer (1992), Bennett (1988); cf., more broadly, Wills (2010), O'Donnell (2015), Shanzer (2012).

109. For a narrative overview of Augustine's life as he presents it in the *Confessions*, see O'Donnell (2005, 37–41). On Augustine in Thagaste and Carthage, see Sears (2017).

110. On the financial and municipal status of Augustine's father, see O'Donnell (1992, II.117–18); on Augustine's early education, see Lane Fox (2015) 51–61.

111. See Chp. 2.

112. Augustine's alienation in the *Confessions*: dislike of lessons (1.12.19, 1.13.20) and preference for games (1.19.15); resentment at beatings (1.9.14); 'failure' at Greek (1.13.20, 1.14.23); success with Vergilian exercise and later self-recrimination (1.17.27); and scorn for father's ambition and pride (2.3.6, 8).

113. *Conf.* 1.17.27 *nonne ecce illa omnia fumus et uentus? itane aliud non erat ubi exerceretur ingenium et lingua mea?*; 3.4.7 *fine damnabili . . . per gaudia uanitatis humanae.*

114. Cf. Propertius 3.24.4, 18–20; 3.25.1–4; Fear (2005).

115. See Laes and Strubbe (2014, 42–8, 136–63, 228–32).

116. Fulkerson (2013, 196).

117. See Chp. 4 with reference to Fulkerson (2013).

4

Campania

Cape Misenum

At the northern tip of the great crescent that describes the bay of Naples (Map 1 inset B), the via Lido Miliscola runs along a narrow spit of land between the beach and the Mare Morto: a great lagoon of 'dead' or landlocked water.[1] Derived allegedly from the Latin *militum schola* ('soldiers' school'), the name of the road hints at the existence of an old Roman naval base in the area. Further along the peninsula, the road leads to the via Plinio il Vecchio ('Pliny the Elder Rd.'), and directly ahead can be seen the strange mass of rock that rises suddenly from sea level to a height of 100 metres before beginning a gentle descent along a wide plateau. This is Cape Misenum, an imposing oblong headland, and all that remains of a volcanic crater long sunk beneath the waves. In ancient times its resemblance to a huge burial mound gave rise to the story that it was the last resting place of Aeneas' trumpeter Misenus. The story of his death is told in Vergil's *Aeneid*—the opening of whose sixth book is dominated by the distinctive landscape of the bay of Naples.

From the top of Cape Misenum, there are impressive views in all directions.[2] It was from here that the Elder Pliny, uncle of the Younger Pliny, had his first view of the eruption of Vesuvius to the east (Fig. 4.1). The Younger's own accounts of events that day are filled with striking instances of the 'long view' across the bay of Naples.[3] To the north-west can now be seen in its entirety the lagoon—site of the imperial naval base which lay under the command of the Elder Pliny at the time of the eruption in 79 C.E. (Fig. 4.2). The Elder mustered a flotilla of ships from this base to lead a rescue mission across the bay. Immediately behind the lagoon, to its west, rise the heights of Monte di Procida and, to its north, are found the hills which conceal from sight on their far side the ancient seaside resort of Baiae. It was in the direction of the former that the Younger, then in his eighteenth year, fled with his mother from Misenum, after the approach of a 'black and terrible cloud' (6.20.9) emanating from across the bay.[4] Barely visible in the far distance beyond the Baian hills is a stretch of open coast, home to ancient Cumae and to Vergil's prophetess, the Sibyl, who directed Aeneas to enter the underworld at nearby lake Avernus. This lake, adjacent to Baiae, cannot be glimpsed from the heights of the cape. But to the north-east can now be clearly seen a town that had been largely hidden from view at ground level: Pozzuoli,

Man of High Empire. Roy K. Gibson, Oxford University Press (2020). © Oxford University Press.

DOI: 10.1093/actrade/9780199948192.001.0001

Figure 4.1. View of Vesuvius from the raised plateau of Cape Misenum, eastward across the bay of Naples. *Photo by I. Marchesi.*

Figure 4.2. View of Mare Morto (lago Miseno) north-westwards from the raised plateau of Cape Misenum. The lagoon provided the inner harbour that was home to the Misene fleet commanded by the Elder Pliny at the time of the eruption of Vesuvius in 79 C.E. The Younger Pliny and his mother perhaps fled Misenum along the route traced by Miseno beach, towards Monte di Procida. *Photo by C. Delaney.*

ancient Puteoli, the port which received the grain convoys from Egypt so vital to Rome's economy. Appointed to his post by the new emperor Titus, son of the recently deceased Vespasian, the Elder's task was to police the waters which these grain ships traversed.[5]

Rather further to the east, across the brilliant blue of the bay, the naked eye can make out the urban sprawl that continues beyond the south-eastern fringes of modern Naples. It will struggle to make out Herculaneum, modern Ercolano. The ancient town nestles near the sea at the foot of the towering mass of Vesuvius, just to the south of two distinctive patches of greenery formed by local parks amid the urban growth at Portici. Just beyond the southern slope of Vesuvius a small flat plain can be made out which is home to Pompeii—itself naturally invisible from this distance. The via Plinio, formerly known as the Strada Reale, runs to the south of the excavations of the ancient town. In truth neither of the Plinii has any direct connection with Pompeii. The town goes unmentioned in Pliny's account of the eruption, and the closest the Elder may have come in his mission was a spot a little further north back up the coastline towards Vesuvius, home to a friend named Rectina. To the south again, beyond Pompeii, the impressive heights of the Monti Lattari become visible as the bay begins its turn back out to sea in completion of its crescent shape along the Sorrentine peninsula. At the point where the bay turns decisively south-west sits Castellammare di Stabia, site of the ancient settlement of Stabiae (Map 1 inset B), and home today to a school named after the Elder: Liceo Classico 'Plinio Seniore'.[6] It was here, on a cliff above the modern town, that the Elder took shelter from the eruption, having diverted course from the attempted rescue of Rectina towards another friend, Pomponianus. The Elder later died on the beach below. From Cape Misenum, the eye can make out only the broad outline of the peninsula. (In the reverse direction, the distinctive raised plateau at Misenum can be seen on a good day from the resort of Sorrento.) Clearly visible out to sea, not far beyond the end of the Sorrentine peninsula, lies the isle of Capri, home to the last years of the emperor Tiberius, who had died while the Elder was in his youth. The visible blanketing of this island first made the Younger aware of the approach of the ominous cloud across the bay.

Pliny in Campania

Campania, the region that is home to the bay of Naples, does not rank high in the affections of the Younger Pliny as an adult. Few of his friends come from the region.[7] Pliny first mentions Campania around 103 C.E., some six or seven years after the earliest recorded communication in the Letters. The context is notably jaundiced: a lukewarm obituary for Silius Italicus, poet, consul, and alleged delator ('denouncer') under Nero.[8] He had passed away in his luxurious villa near

Naples (3.7.1). Pliny's grandfather-in-law, Calpurnius Fabatus of Comum, also owned a villa in the region, and the Younger presumably spent some time there. Pliny's wife Calpurnia certainly did (6.4, 6.30). Gone from Rome to convalesce in Campania, she receives a letter from him asking 'whether . . . you passed through the retreats, pleasures and the richness of the region without receiving any hurt [*inoffensa*]' (6.4.2).[9] Implicit here is one likely explanation for Pliny's attitude to Campania: his relative silence is less a marker of youthful trauma, more evidence of a desire to be seen to adhere to high personal standards. Traditionalists from Cicero to Seneca remained suspicious of venues like Baiae.[10] Even the Augustan elegist Propertius had denounced the town as 'corrupt' and criticized its beaches as 'harmful to virtuous girls'.[11] And Pliny's friend and protégé, the poet Martial, suggested a woman might arrive at Baiae a 'Penelope' and leave a 'Helen' (*Ep.* 1.68). Comum, 400 miles/650 kilometres north at the foot of the hardy Alps, gave Pliny moral substance, small and unimportant as the place was. But such views of the bay of Naples were beginning to recede into the past. The poet Statius, Pliny's older contemporary and a native of Campania, praises the flourishing population, towns, beaches, climate, fertility, Greek culture, and peaceful atmosphere of the bay of Naples.[12] This is his attempt to counter traditional stereotypes and promote the reputation and regeneration of a region devastated by the eruption witnessed decades before by Pliny.[13]

The son of northern Italy may be reticent or even cool towards Campania, but the twenty-four hours surrounding the eruption of Vesuvius also form the single day in Pliny's life about which we are best informed. Pliny's own later narrative of events brings us close to key figures in his life, his mother and above all his uncle. Neither is ever portrayed by Pliny in their shared native town of Comum. Pliny's pair of letters on the eruption also raise a host of questions about early formation, career, connections, and character: all at a moment just a year or perhaps even months before he made his first appearance as an advocate in Rome's courts, and stepped onto the first rung of the ladder of offices that led to the senate.[14] No less important is the fact that Pliny's eyewitness account of the events of 79 underpins almost all modern narratives of the eruption and provides many of their most telling details. The story is rarely told from Pliny's point of view, however. Nor is there always proper scrutiny of the meaning or reliability of some of the details of an account written a quarter of a century after the events described. The opening scenes of Paul W. S. Anderson's visually spectacular, if historically alarming, movie *Pompeii* powerfully deploy quotations from Pliny's Vesuvius letters intercut with moving images of prone bodies that resemble the macabre plaster casts made of the victims of Pompeii.[15] Pliny's words, as will become clear, in fact describe the reactions of the crowds at faraway Misenum, and are almost certainly meant as criticism rather than expression of empathy for the despair of those caught up in the eruption.

A cloud of unusual size and shape

The Elder Pliny was not the first family member to notice something very unusual on the far side of the bay. That distinction belonged to the mother of the
Younger, sister of the Elder:

> [My uncle] was at Misenum, in personal command of the fleet. The ninth day
> before the Kalends of September [i.e. 24 August], at about the seventh hour
> [i.e. noon], my mother indicated to him the appearance of a cloud of unu-
> sual size and appearance. After sunning himself, he had next gone to his cold
> bath and taken a light meal (while reposing) and began to study. He called for
> his sandals and climbed to a spot from which this wonder could best be seen.
> A cloud was rising—from what mountain was a matter of uncertainty to the
> distant spectators: afterwards it was known to have been Vesuvius—whose like-
> ness and shape would be better represented by a pine than any other tree.[16]
>
> *Letters* 6.16.4–5

The admiral's residence was evidently on the low ground of the peninsula at Misenum, perhaps on the punta Sarparealla near the *collegium* of the
'Augustales'—a site for the cult of the imperial family that has been excavated
in the vicinity.[17] It was a small but very densely populated area: perhaps three
to four thousand people lived there.[18] From the top of the cape, the Elder could
take in the panoramic view. His post at Misenum was manifestly not a full-time
occupation. More to the point, he hated interruptions to his studies, and normally allowed little to get in the way of research for the many works he produced
during his lifetime.[19] The Younger reveals elsewhere the full extremity of the
Elder's devotion, in retreat at one of his own county villas: 'only his bathing-time
was exempted from study. When I say bathing, I am speaking of when he was actually in the water, for while he was being rubbed and dried he was read to or he
dictated' (3.5.14).[20] An exception could be made for a remarkable sight by a man
whose recently completed encyclopedia, the *Natural History*, demonstrated so
marked an interest in *mirabilia* ('wonders').[21]

It became clear only later that the unusual cloud was emanating from
Vesuvius. The scrupulousness of the detail is deliberate: at the end of his first
letter on the eruption, the Younger implies a parallel between himself and the
Greek historian Thucydides for credibility as a reporter.[22] At least some Romans
intuited that Vesuvius had been a volcano in the past, and pondered the parallels
with Mount Etna.[23] The Elder did not include it in his survey of volcanoes in
the *Natural History* (2.236–8). The Augustan geographer Strabo says that in his
time the eminence 'save for its summit, has dwellings all round, on farm lands
that are absolutely beautiful' (5.4.8). A famous wall painting from the House of

the Centenary in Pompeii shows the volcano's slopes abounding in vegetation as they rise to a near-perfect cone—blown off by the 79 eruption.[24] For someone looking across the bay on a hazy day, with no reason to suspect Vesuvius in particular, there might be equal cause to think of the heights behind Stabiae or the Appenines further inland to the rear of Vesuvius. Whether the Elder looked across the bay on the 24th of August is a matter of debate: archaeologists have begun to suggest that evidence from Pompeii points to a time later in the autumn, and one part of the medieval manuscript tradition of the *Letters* might possibly allow for a later date.[25]

That the eruption was now visible from Misenum meant that residents to the south and east of the volcano had only a short time before pumice stones would begin to fall from the cloud now above their heads. None of this could have been guessed by those at Misenum: the main explosion had not even been audible.[26] The author of the *Natural History* immediately conceived a desire for a closer look. This was a way of continuing by other means the study which had been so forcibly interrupted by the appearance of the strange cloud:

> To a man of my uncle's erudition, it seemed important, something to be observed from a nearer point of view. He ordered his fast-sailing cutter [*liburnica*] to be got ready, and he offered me the chance of going with him if I wanted to. I replied that I preferred to go on with my studies, and it so happened that he had given me something to write.[27]
>
> *Letters* 6.16.7

The Younger found his own way to continue with his studies in this scholarly family.[28] It later appears that the task set by his uncle was to make extracts from a historian (6.20.5). This was a practice at which the Elder himself excelled: 'he read nothing without making extracts', famously insisting that 'there was no book so bad as not to contain *something* of value' (3.5.10)[29]. Making extracts from Livy may have saved the Younger's life, but it has naturally given rise to incredulity. An incredulity with particular resonance among those tasked in their own youth with construing this verbose Roman historian. Here is the young man who preferred Latin homework to the chance of witnessing the greatest natural disaster of the era. From the Younger's point of view, the incident reveals two things: a willingness as an adult to expose his youthful self as unheroic, and the extent to which he modelled himself at that time on the Elder and the latter's excessive devotion to study. Roman culture did allow for admission of flaws in a youth, but hardly in the behaviour of adults, as we shall see later. Pliny himself would correct his youthful excess by making clear his preference in maturity for a life systematically varied by work, study, and leisure. We also learn that the Elder was, at this stage in life, personally in charge of the Younger's education.

This reflects the authority and confidence of the author of 'The Student, in three volumes [studiosi tres] . . . in which the orator is trained from his very cradle and perfected' (3.5.5).[30] This work by the Elder had perhaps been written around the time of the Younger's birth in 61 or 62 C.E., and would only be eclipsed three decades later by a rival work written by the man whom the Younger identifies as responsible for his education in Rome, the great Quintilian.

In the act of leaving the house

The sudden arrival of a message from across the bay decisively changed the Elder's reaction to events from that of studious scholar to military man with a sense of mission. The launch of a naval flotilla was now called for:

> [My uncle] was leaving the house when a note was handed him from Rectina the wife of Tascus. She was frightened by the imminence of her danger (her villa lay under the mountain, and there was no escape except by ship), and begged him to rescue her from overwhelming peril. He changed his plan, and having started on the task as a scholar [studioso animo] carried it out in the spirit of a hero [animo . . . maximo]. He launched his four-ranked galleys [quadriremes] and embarked in person, to carry assistance, not only to Rectina, but to many others, for the charms of the coast made it thickly populated. He hastened in the direction from which everyone else was flying, holding a direct course . . .[31]
>
> Letters 6.16.8–10

A scene of perhaps some hours is compressed into a short paragraph. The nearby naval station, seen from atop Cape Misenum, can be imagined as awash with activity in the wake of the admiral's orders (Fig. 4.2). It is not clear how many quadriremes the Elder launched. The Younger does not allow them much of a role in his account of subsequent events, preferring to concentrate instead on the actions of his uncle. Apart from some moles and the impressive underground reservoir which supplied the station with drinking water, almost nothing remains today of the base for these ships. Home to many thousands of sailors, the lagoon of the Mare Morto was presumably ringed by a series of large boat sheds.[32]

Rectina sent the decisive message. Epigraphic evidence suggests a Spanish origin for this owner of a villa on the far side of the bay: a testimony to the attractions of the Neapolitan coast even for far-flung members of the wealthy Roman elite. She makes a trio with two other Roman Spaniards who make prominent appearances in the Younger's narrative: Pomponianus, owner of the villa overlooking the beach at Stabiae, where the Elder would die the next morning, and an unnamed Spanish guest at the admiral's residence in Misenum, who would urge the Younger and his mother to flee the effects of the eruption during the night to come.[33] But this network of Spaniards centered on the Elder is not the real oddity here. After all, the Elder had spent part of his earlier career as imperial functionary in one of the Hispanic provinces.[34] Rather, Rectina's villa lay under Vesuvius, 12–18 miles/20–30 kilometres from Misenum as the crow flies and considerably further by land. How did her message arrive so soon after the eruption cloud became visible?

There is evidence of volcanic activity at Vesuvius prior to the noonday eruption, in the form of a fine layer of ash that fell on areas to the east of the volcano. This may have begun to fall five to ten hours before the eruption could no longer be missed at Misenum. Explosions which produce this kind of ash-layer are relatively small, and were presumably invisible in 79 C.E. from Misenum. Yet, in the opinion of one modern expert, they were likely 'alarming in certain areas, especially close to and east of Vesuvius'.[35] It is possible that Rectina sent her message to the Elder either around or across the bay during the earliest phases of the event, in time for her plea to arrive at Misenum not long after the start of the main eruption around midday. Pliny comments on the message sent by Rectina: 'there was no escape except by ship'. During later phases of the eruption escape by boat become impossible, owing to strong onshore winds (6.16.12). But whether the note arrived by horseback or boat, why could Rectina herself not escape by these routes? Perhaps she wanted to take her belongings with her—like Pomponianus later at Stabiae (6.16.12), or Rectina's near neighbours at the Villa of the Papyri next to Herculaneum, who appear to have been in the process of moving the library when the site was suddenly abandoned.[36]

The arrival of Rectina's message is not the only puzzling feature of the Younger's account. The source for the details of the Elder's final moments (6.16.19) is both unclear and contradicted by a rival version in a contemporary biography of the Elder. Other perplexities will emerge. Together they underline a tension at the heart of Pliny's narrative. Volcanologists have found the 'scientific' details of Pliny's narrative remarkably reliable as a report of the mechanics of the very specific type of eruption his account indicates.[37] No other ancient account of *any* eruption is comparable. The phase of an eruption in which hot gas and stone fragments are ejected from a volcano to form a distinctive mushroom cloud is commonly described in geological circles as 'Plinian' in honour of the Younger, who memorably compares the emanation to a Mediterranean pine (6.16.5–6).[38] It is also clear that Pliny's narrative of the involvement of the Elder does not achieve, or even aim for, the levels of veracity attributed to the contextual details. Umberto Eco has persuasively argued that a rather different story about the Elder can be extracted from Pliny's account. A story, as we shall see, which encourages the suspicion that the Elder was completely unable to cope with the emergency. The Younger conceals nothing in his account. Yet, through eminent skill as narrator, he is able to channel us towards a view of the Elder as entirely heroic.[39]

Caught between an impulse to trust the Younger's report of the eruption and wariness about the overall objectivity of the letter, we stand to learn a great deal about the author of the account. Pliny emerges as a man with a good eye and ear for the natural world around him, able to evoke atmosphere and event without exaggeration or fantasy. His passion for accuracy extends to a decidedly unheroic self-portrait. But it does not disturb his loyalty to an uncle famous for his literary achievements. In fact the Younger's decision to portray himself in a somewhat unflattering light may well be part of a plan to boost the impression of the Elder's own heroism.[40] We also learn, more indirectly, of the interest taken by both Elder and Younger in a network of personal elite contacts around the bay. The mass of humanity caught up in the eruption of Vesuvius hardly registers with Pliny.

A divided narrative

While the Elder was making preparations to leave, pumice stones had already begun to fall from the eruption cloud onto areas south and east of Vesuvius. Herculaneum, just to the west of the volcano, would remain largely untouched until the first collapse of the eruption column in the early hours of the next morning.[41] It would take the Elder some time to reach the other side of the bay. With the exit of the Elder, the Younger's own narrative divides into two parts. In his first Vesuvius letter (6.16), the Younger stays focused on the Elder from the moment of the departure of the flotilla until his death the next morning on the beach at Stabiae. The second Vesuvius letter (6.20) narrates events from the Younger's own viewpoint at Misenum. He and his mother's household evacuate their residence during the night and abandon Misenum itself after dawn in the face of increasingly violent tremors and the approach of the ominous cloud.

This division in the story provides an opportunity to say something about these letters, both classics of world narrative literature. Pliny's split-screen account is related to the formal promptings for each letter. Both are addressed to Tacitus. In the first letter Pliny responds to a specific request about the Elder: 'You ask me to write you an account of my uncle's death, so you can transmit a more truthful account to posterity' (6.16.1).[42] In the second letter, Pliny answers an additional query from Tacitus about his own experience, left behind at Misenum. In 106–7 C.E., around the time these letters were written or published, Tacitus was engaged on his *Histories*, a work of twelve or fourteen books covering events from the year of the four emperors in 69 C.E. to the assassination of Domitian in 96 C.E. The *Histories* could hardly avoid a narrative of the devastation of Vesuvius. The terms in which Tacitus appears to have written to Pliny for the first letter suggest a distinctive emphasis to his now lost version. Accounts of the 'deaths of famous men' (*exitus inlustrium uirorum*) were a fashionable genre of the day.[43] Thucydides described the great plague at Athens only to pass over in silence the death of Pericles, its most famous victim. Perhaps Tacitus concentrated on the death of Pliny the Elder, the best-known victim of Vesuvius, and passed over others in silence.[44] The particular nature of Tacitus' request is, at least, partially responsible for the Younger's omission in his first letter of any focus on the wider effects of the eruption.

More importantly, Pliny insists that the second Vesuvius letter is a mere pendant to the first: his own experience at Misenum, unlike that of the Elder under Vesuvius, must be counted as 'irrelevant to an historical account' (6.16.21).[45] This is the cue for an elaborate stylistic ploy on Pliny's part. The second letter is written up to the standards expected by ancient audiences of 'history': it is replete with allusions to other historians, in particular Livy, whom Pliny was reading at the time of the eruption, and keeps up an extended dialogue with epic poets, especially Vergil.[46] Having declared that the first letter is suitable for incorporation into history (6.16.22), while the second is ultimately fit for discarding (6.20.20), Pliny seems determined to wrongfoot both Tacitus and later readers by lavishing the historian's art only on the letter detailing his experiences at Misenum. Of course, what made the second letter recognizable to ancients as history is often what generates modern questions about reliability.

A direct course and rudder set straight . . .

The Elder set off 'holding a direct course and his rudder set straight for the danger' from which everyone else was fleeing, but with the residual instincts of a scholar: 'he dictated and noted down all the movements and outlines of the disaster as he caught sight of them' (6.16.10).[47] His flotilla encountered falls of ash and pumice the closer it came to the Vesuvian coast. His destination was clearly well to the south of Herculaneum, which experienced no significant inundations during this phase of eruption. Perhaps he was aiming for the region of 'Oplontis'—where visitors today can visit an outstanding luxury villa buried by the eruption.[48] At a distance from Misenum of 17 miles/28 kilometres, Oplontis takes around four hours to reach by boat, even at a sustained maximum speed of eight knots assumed for a heavy quadrireme.[49] Most of the day was already gone.

The Elder could not land near Rectina's villa: 'There had been a sudden retreat of the sea, and debris from the mountain made the shore unapproachable' (6.16.11).[50] Did the Younger have access to the last notes made by the Elder on his journey across the bay?[51] Even so, it is not clear what blocked the path of the Elder. Perhaps a seabed raised by volcanic activity or a floating 'carpet' of pumice sometimes encountered in eruptions of this type near water.[52] A quick change of plan ensued. Rejecting calls from his helmsman to return to Misenum, the Elder diverted course to Stabiae at the far south-east of the bay. Rectina and her subsequent fate go unmentioned. The quadriremes likewise disappear from view at this point, although there may have been a small naval station at Stabiae.[53] Whatever outpost there may have been, the Elder's concern is rather to reach a second friend with Spanish connections: *Pomponianum pete*, 'Make for Pomponianus!' (6.16.11). The 5 miles/8 kilometres journey down the coast of the bay took the Elder's ship past a Pompeii that was already largely deserted.[54]

On arrival it became apparent that Pomponianus was well aware of the danger spouting from Vesuvius immediately to the north. He was on the beach, his belongings stowed on boat ready for departure. The strong north-westerly wind created by the eruption that brought the Elder to shore, however, also ensured that Pomponianus could not escape by sea against its force.[55] Today the community of Castellammare di Stabia effectively sits beneath ancient Stabiae on a shore greatly extended into the bay by the 79 eruption. When the Elder landed there, the distance from the water to the bottom of the cliffs on which Stabiae sat may have been as little as 200 metres.[56] Forty metres above, Stabiae itself was made up of a series of luxury villas strung out along the extensive cliffs, with panoramic views of the bay.[57] Ruins of up to six of these villas have been found in the area, known today as Varano hill. No ancient owners have been positively identified. At least one villa, San Marco, was an imperial possession, while the villa Arianna yielded up the famous set of miniature paintings of Flora, Medea, Diana, and Leda.[58] It was in one of these wealthy residences that the Elder took shelter from the rain of ash and pumice:

> [My uncle] embraced his trembling friend [Pomponianus], consoling and encouraging him, and in order to calm his fears by his own nonchalance, gave instructions for being conducted to his bath. After washing, he took his place at the table, and dined cheerfully, or (which was equally heroic) with an air of cheerfulness.... Then he gave himself over to rest.[59]
>
> *Letters* 6.16.12, 13

The Younger glosses the behaviour of the Elder as heroic in the Stoic mould: the protagonist experiences *securitas* himself and offers *consolatio* to others.[60] The Elder, however, has no plan for action, now or later, even to the extent of dissuading Pomponianus from thinking about escape. Is this bravery in the face of almost certain death, or evidence of a leader who is completely out of his depth? The Younger would prefer us to believe the former. The latter appears more likely.

Meanwhile at Misenum, the Younger had been following essentially the same routine: 'After the departure of my uncle, I devoted what time was left to study (that was the reason I remained behind); a bath soon after, then dinner and a short and troubled sleep' (6.20.2).[61] Both were evidently strongly wedded to routine, endeavouring to retain a semblance of ordered behaviour even in the most threatening of circumstances.[62] This is less a family quirk than a strongly developed sense of adherence, as we shall see, to the ancient ideal of constancy (*constantia*). Events during the night would force each far outside their routines.

During the night

The Elder slept soundly through the continuing eruption. His snoring could be heard from outside the bedroom. He could not be left to sleep the whole night: 'the courtyard from which [his] suite of rooms was approached was already so full of ashes mixed with pumice stones that its level was rising, and a longer stay in the bedroom would have cut off any exit' (6.16.14).[63] Excavations at the villa Arianna show that Stabiae, fully 9 miles/14 kilometres south of Vesuvius (Fig. 4.3), experienced an inundation up to 2 metres in depth.[64] It was around this time or a little later that a fitfully sleeping Younger Pliny was roused from *his* bed in Misenum (6.20.4). Before either could rise from their rest, devastation had already reached Herculaneum. The town experienced a deadly 'pyroclastic' surge some five or six hours before Pompeii endured the same fate.

Until a few decades ago, it was thought that the inhabitants of Herculaneum were overwhelmed by massive flows of mud, those of Pompeii overcome by a devastating fall of pumice and ash even deeper than the one experienced at Stabiae. As long ago as 1902, reports had reached Europe and North America of the fate of the island of Martinique, where nearly all twenty-five thousand inhabitants of the town of St Pierre had been killed within minutes. (Pompeii and particularly Herculaneum were rather smaller towns, with estimates of the percentage of casualties somewhat lower.[65]) In the report of a later volcanologist, they had been overtaken 'by a cloud of hot volcanic gas and particles that had travelled down the slopes of the volcano at hurricane speed. These deadly clouds were described as glowing avalanches . . .'[66] E. T. Merrill, American classicist and distinguished student of Pliny the Younger, had been the first to connect reports of the Martinique disaster with the Vesuvius letters.[67] His views were largely ignored in geological circles. It was not until the 1980s that research led by the Icelandic volcanologist Haraldur Sigurdsson began to win general acceptance for the deadly role in the 79 eruption of pyroclastic flows and surges.[68]

Pyroclastic events are created when the column of material forced upwards by an eruption suddenly undergoes a dramatic collapse in pressure. Superheated,

Figure 4.3. View of modern Castellammare di Stabia from near the summit of Vesuvius. The town sits 9 miles/14 kilometres from the volcano, at the point where the bay begins to curve south-west towards Sorrento. Ancient Stabiae sat on Varano hill, visible as a dark line just above Castellammare di Stabia. It was in one of the villas on Varano hill that the Elder Pliny sheltered from the eruption. He died on the ancient beach at the foot of Varano hill. *Photo by C. Delaney.*

ground-hugging plumes now spread laterally. The plumes carry a higher concentration of material at their base ('flows'), while the upper layers, more extensive in their spread, are comparatively diluted ('surges'). The Vesuvian column would undergo collapse six times in the early hours of the morning. It was not until the fourth collapse, around 6.30 a.m., that the remaining inhabitants of Pompeii would be directly affected. The citizens of Herculaneum were not so lucky. Undoubtedly the earthquakes and the sight of the eruption column towering above them 9–19 miles/15–30 kilometres into the sky were alarming. The city, nevertheless, had not become impassable from falls of pumice and ash: high altitude winds had carried the debris of the erupting column away from the town. When the column collapsed, superheated plumes spread down the sides of the mountain. The initial surge reached the town between two and five minutes after the first collapse.[69] It instantly killed every living thing. With air temperatures of up to 500°C, in the estimate of recent research, the 'heat was enough for sudden and complete vaporization of soft tissues of the victims'.[70] Only an 85-metre strip of seafront at Herculaneum has been excavated, but 139 victims were discovered there in the 1980s.[71] The base of the plume, the pyroclastic flow, followed soon after and deposited a layer of volcanic debris up to 1.5

metres thick. Repetition of the process a further five times in the next few hours completely buried the city to a depth of 23 metres.[72] The sheer rock faces that form the modern perimeter of the excavated ancient site are silent testimony to the vehemence of the event.

No details of how the victims died could have reached Pliny. In any event, strong earth tremors were now affecting both the Elder and the Younger.[73] At Stabiae, violently rocking buildings forced a debate over whether to remain inside or to risk the hail of pumice outside (6.16.15).[74] At Misenum, the same tremors forced the evacuation of both the Younger and his mother into the fore-court of their residence, away from the immediate risk of collapsing buildings (6.20.3–4). This seemed a good moment to the young Pliny to emulate his uncle's work ethic. The latter's devotion to study routinely extended to rising between midnight and 2 a.m. to begin work for the day (3.5.8). The Younger would now attempt to complete the homework assigned before the Elder's departure:

> We sat down in the forecourt of the house, between the buildings and the sea close by. I do not know whether to call it steadfastness [*constantiam*] or impru-dence [*imprudentiam*], seeing that I was only in my eighteenth year; but I called for a volume of Livy, and read it as though quite at my ease, and even made extracts from it, as I had begun to do.[75]
>
> *Letters* 6.20.4–5

To the frustration of historians and biographers, specific indications of date are vanishingly rare in almost all ancient letter collections.[76] The precious piece of information that Pliny was at the time of the eruption in his 'eighteenth year' allows it to be inferred that he was born in 61 or 62 C.E. We can be sure that Pliny has supplied the information with a quite different purpose in mind. He is providing ethical context. In the ancient world, 'youth is . . . a time for learning and progress', in the words of one critic: 'With maturity . . . comes the responsi-bility to have got it right first time'.[77] If Pliny acts in a way that requires reflection or revision in hindsight, then he needs to let us know such behaviour belonged to a time before full maturity. In adulthood there was little room for admitting to amendments or improvements in behaviour. Consistency rather than evolu-tion was applauded. In perhaps the year immediately after Vesuvius, on his first appearance in court as an advocate, Pliny would by his own account show great inner strength in refusing to give in to his own fear of facing 'friends of Caesar' on the opposing bench (1.18.3–5). The transition to the ethical plateau of matu-rity has taken place. Pliny is careful, all the same, to limit the damage for injudi-cious acts in earlier youth by setting a question: was he displaying *constantia* or *imprudentia*? Even when behaving a little foolishly, the Younger was aiming for the adult virtue of consistency.

Dawn arrives: the death of the Elder

The sudden intervention of a 'friend of my uncle's, who had lately come to him from Spain' (6.20.5) made no dent on Pliny's youthful version of constancy. A well-known eighteenth-century painting by Angelica Kauffmann, now hanging in the Princeton University Museum, illustrates the moment (Fig. 4.4).[78] The friend's horror at the 'apathy' of Pliny's mother and the 'insensibility to danger' of her son elicits little reaction, either in the painting or in Pliny's own account. The Spaniard later abandons the Plinii in the face of their simple refusal to consider their own predicament while still unsure of the safety of the Elder (6.20.10–11). Pliny's denial of a name to this character, unlike Iberian compatriots Rectina and Pomponianus, conveys strong disapproval, even twenty-five years after the event. The refusal of the Plinii to leave indicates

Figure 4.4. *Pliny the Younger and his Mother at Misenum, 79 AD*, by Angelica Kauffmann. Painted in 1785, the image depicts the moment when the Younger Pliny and his mother are accosted by their Spanish guest at Misenum, during the absence of the Elder, and are urged to flee the effects of the eruption at Vesuvius. The Younger displays youthful *constantia* by making extracts from the historian Livy. *Reproduced by courtesy of Princeton University Art Museum. Museum purchase, gift of Franklin H. Kissner. Photo by Bruce White. © Photo SCALA, Florence.*

more than apathy. There is no sign of a wife for the Elder Pliny.[79] The Younger's own natural father, husband to his mother, had died before Pliny reached the age of fourteen.[80] Perhaps the Elder and his sister were particularly close as siblings. Also revealing is the refusal of Pliny's mother to direct or overrule her son, either now or during subsequent events in the night. She emerges as a signally passive character, even later willing to be abandoned for the sake of her son's safety when the decision is taken to flee Misenum. Nor do we gain much insight into the nature of the relationship between mother and son.[81] Both Pliny and his parent appear focused on the Elder, even in his absence.

A fitful dawn light had now arrived in Misenum (6.20.6). Across the bay, under the eruption cloud at Stabiae, 'it was night, the blackest and thickest of all nights' (6.16.17), and the Elder and his friends were making their way down to the shore, pillows tied over their heads for protection against the falling pumice. Destruction was edging nearer. It was around dawn that the fourth successive collapse of the eruption column produced the pyroclastic flow that killed the remaining inhabitants of Pompeii.[82] Between the first pyroclastic event and dawn, there had been two fresh collapses of the column, each more powerful than its predecessor. The third surge reached the walls of Pompeii. An associated flow completely buried Herculaneum. The inhabitants of Pompeii had been given every warning to leave long before. By the previous evening or late afternoon, the accumulated pumice fall had caused roofs in the town to collapse.[83] A majority of the c. 1,100 'bodies' recovered from Pompeii were found by modern excavators on top of rather than within the layers created by the pumice deposits.[84] These Pompeians were killed here, within seconds, by the intense heat of the fourth pyroclastic event[85]—followed within minutes by an even more deadly fifth. The cavities left by their decayed corpses amidst the pyroclastic debris allowed excavators to produce the town's grim plaster casts. The majority who had already fled Pompeii were hardly guaranteed survival. A late nineteenth-century excavation at Fondo Bottaro, just south of ancient Pompeii, revealed corpses scattered along the main road between Pompeii and Stabiae.[86]

The Elder's party had descended to the beach at Stabiae in the vain hope of escape by sea. The sixth and largest pyroclastic event now passed over Pompeii, all but burying the town, and appears eventually to have reached Stabiae:[87]

... an outbreak of flame and smell of sulphur, warning of further flames, put some to flight and roused [the Elder]. With the help of two slave boys he rose from the ground, and immediately fell back, owing (as I gather) to the dense vapour obstructing his breath and blocking his windpipe, which was weak and narrow and often inflamed. When day returned ... his body was found whole and uninjured, in the clothes he wore; its appearance was of one resting rather than dead.[88]

Letters 6.16.18–20

Evidence of a surge layer has been found at Stabiae.[89] Situated on the edge of the area affected by the pyroclastic events, it is possible the Elder was not exposed to the acute temperatures that killed the remaining inhabitants of Pompeii. Yet the surge was enough to end his life. Did it also kill the slave boys, or did they live to be the source for the Elder's final moments? Perhaps it only killed the Elder, an apparent asthmatic.[90] A further challenge is offered by an alternative story in circulation about the passing of the Elder. This story is mentioned by none other than the Younger's own later protégé, Suetonius,[91] who reports in a brief biography of the Elder that he 'succumbed to the quantity of dust and ash, or *as some believe* was dispatched by one of his slaves whom he had begged when the heat overwhelmed him to expedite his death'.[92] The Younger's own account appears to go out of its way to scotch this version, with its insistence the Elder's body was 'found whole and uninjured' (*inuentum integrum inlaesum*, 6.16.20). Evidently the Elder must resist to the end. The true version is beyond recovery. Note will be taken of Pliny's broader insistence on the heroic behaviour of the Elder in the face of evidence of a man out of his depth.

Meanwhile at Misenum . . .

What the death of the Elder meant for the Younger is a subject to ponder later. More immediately, the effects of the same pyroclastic surge which killed the Elder would soon reach even Misenum. At some point after dawn, Pliny and his mother had finally decided to leave the town altogether, since even the small open area outside their house in which they were sitting was at risk from falling buildings (6.20.6). So began a general exodus from Misenum that must mirror the evacuations taking place all around the bay of Naples during the previous eighteen hours:

> Then at last we decided to leave the town. The mass of the inhabitants followed us thunder-struck, and preferring the guidance of others to their own—an effect of panic causing it to resemble prudence [*prudentia*]—they pressed on us as we were making off, and impelled us forwards by their crowded ranks. When we had got beyond the buildings we stopped.[93]

Letters 6.20.7

This second Vesuvius letter began with a quotation by Pliny from Vergil's *Aeneid*. Pliny responded to Tacitus's request for an account of events at Misenum, using Aeneas' reply to Dido's plea for the story of the fall of Troy: 'Though I shudder to think of the memory . . . I will begin' (*quamquam animus meminisse horret . . .*

incipiam, Verg. *Aen.* 2.12–13). Pliny continues the Vergilian theme now with a hint in his words at how Aeneas stumbled into leadership of the defeated Trojans exiting their doomed city. Ancient historians liked to add epic allusions to their narratives: Pliny's reference to Vergil brings the flavour of historiography to his letter. But the implication of his allusion is misleading. Pliny is *refusing* the leadership that the inhabitants of Misenum appear to be thrusting on the young nephew of the commander of the Misene fleet. The inhabitants of the densely populated settlement await the Younger's initiative as the one closest to authority. Pliny is untroubled by concern. The behaviour of the masses resembled *prudentia*, but was in fact an expression of terror. Pliny's own earlier *imprudentia*, we are assured, could at least be thought of as a kind of youthful *constantia*. Evidently Pliny shares with Tacitus a lack of concern for the effect of the eruption on the people of the bay of Naples. There was no code held in common among the Roman elite to tell Pliny that he *should* care about people unconnected to him by the bonds of personal patronage. This youthful moment of leadership refused prefigures the adult Pliny in another way. He appears to be uncomfortable with standing out too starkly against the background of his fellow senators.[94]

Further terrors followed. The carriages accompanying the Younger and his mother would not stand still on level ground, even when braked with stones (6.20.8). The sea suddenly receded from the shore (6.20.9), as if in anticipation of a tsunami.[95] An ominous cloud could be seen:

> On the other side of us a black and terrible cloud, broken by forked and quivering bursts of flame, parted to reveal great tongues of fire: these were like lightning, but on a larger scale ... Not long after, the cloud descended on the earth and covered the sea. Already it had enveloped and hidden from view Capri, and blotted out the promontory of Misenum.[96]
>
> *Letters* 6.20.9, 11

Pliny and his mother are now well beyond the town, since Capri and the promontory of Misenum are only fully visible from the hills above Baiae or the heights of Monte di Procida.[97] The apocalyptic aspect of the cloud is given special emphasis by Pliny: its portents are visible at the very hour that the Elder dies on the far side of bay, unknown as this was at the time to the Younger.[98] His mother now begs the physically able Younger to think of his own rescue, since 'retarded by her years and her body, she would die happily as long as she had not been the cause of my death' (6.20.12).[99] He refuses to be saved, except in her company, and grasps his mother by the hand to aid her progress. The moment contains irresistible echoes of the famous scene in which Vergil's hero insists on rescuing his elderly and disabled parent, Anchises, from the ruin of Troy.[100] It is in relation to a family member, not the frightened masses of Misenum, that Pliny becomes Aeneas. There is no mention of the panoply of enslaved persons that will have accompanied the Younger's every step, just visible in earlier details of braked carriages and the request for a copy of Livy.

The cloud descends

The vivid details that Pliny supplies next seemed the stuff of fantasy to earlier generations more familiar with stately lava flows than the glowing avalanches produced by pyroclastic events:

> And now came a shower of ashes, but only a scattered one. I looked back: a dense fog was closing in behind us, following us like a torrent as it streamed along the ground. 'Let's get off the road,' I said, 'while we can still see, or we shall be knocked down and trampled underfoot in the dark by the crowd behind'. We had scarcely sat down when night came on, not the dark when there is no moon, or when there are clouds, but the night of a closed place with the lights put out.[101]
>
> *Letters* 6.20.13–14

Surge clouds can travel long distances over water. In the catastrophic 1883 eruption of Krakatau in Indonesia, settlements and islands on the southern coast of Sumatra were swamped by surge clouds from the volcano.[102] Pliny's cloud evidently cooled on its journey across the waters of the bay, since the symptoms of heat underlined in the context of the Elder's death at Stabiae go unmentioned at Misenum. Somewhat disturbingly for the scientific authentication of Pliny's account, no trace has been found of a surge layer at Misenum, despite the Younger's apparent insistence on deep deposits of ash (6.20.16, 18).

Even less susceptible to verification is Pliny's gripping narrative on the sounds that could now be heard in the enveloping darkness:

> You could hear the shrieks of the women, the cries for help of the children, the shouts of the men: some were calling for their parents, others for their young ones, others for their spouses, and recognising them by their voices. Some were lamenting their own misfortune, others that of those dear to them. There were those who, through fear of death, prayed for death. Many raised their hands to the gods, but still more concluded that there were no gods anywhere, and that that night was the eternal and last night for the world.[103]
>
> *Letters* 6.20.14–15

This is the passage raised to modern prominence in the opening voice-over scene of Anderson's movie *Pompeii*. The Latin original derives its colour and power from a wealth of allusions to cataclysmic passages in Vergil, Lucretius, and Livy. The cries of people in great distress, their prayers for death through dread of death, fears of the divine and the final apocalypse—all find clear parallels in earlier poetic, philosophical, and historical accounts of the sack of cities, murder and public disorder in the streets, the onset of plague, and even mere existential distress.[104] Whatever the frightened reactions of others, Pliny is concerned to emphasize that he did not share them: 'I could boast that not a groan or cry of fear escaped me in these perils' (6.20.17).[105] The terror of those around him is depicted for implicit criticism, not empathetic evocation. This underlining of his younger self's level-headed approach is meant to suggest a link with the spirit of scientific enquiry and Stoic resilience displayed by his uncle, and to establish continuity with the firmly rational and restrained character of the narrative of the eruption supplied by the adult Pliny. As the great Plinian commentator Sherwin-White notes, Pliny's 'account contains none of the nonsense about giant spectres imported into the story by Dio', the Greek historian.[106] Pliny's *constantia*, we are meant to infer, can now confidently be traced back to his youth. Even so, Pliny immediately qualifies his boast with a disarming echo of the philosopher Seneca: '[I could boast] . . . were it not for the fact that I believed myself to be perishing in company with all things, and all things with me, a miserable and yet a mighty consolation in death' (6.20.17).[107]

Aftermath

There were false reports of the destruction of Misenum, fire loomed in the darkness, and heavy falls of ash continued. At last, the sun reappeared and revealed a changed world: 'the sun . . . shone out, but luridly, as during an eclipse. Our still trembling eyes saw everything changed and covered in deep ashes like snowdrifts' (6.20.18).[108] Eventually the Younger and his mother returned to Misenum to spend a fearful night amidst further earth tremors. The sole purpose was to wait for news of their brother and uncle (6.20.19–20). The Younger does not narrate the denouement. When the news of the Elder's death arrived, it marked the moment when the Younger was adopted as son, in the Roman fashion, by his dead relative, and could look forward to inheriting the Elder's name, estates, and role as patron of an Umbrian town.[109] It would also fall to the Younger's lot to publish the Elder's history of the deeds of the Flavian house of Titus, his father Vespasian, and brother Domitian: a work deliberately held back from wider circulation by the Elder until after his own death.[110] Such publication

would benefit the Younger as he stood on the threshold of his own public career, without the presence of a father or now uncle to guide him. In the year after
Vesuvius, Pliny would begin his distinguished civil career in the Roman courts,
and receive from the emperor Titus the *latus clauus*, the 'broad stripe' on the toga
given to those aiming for the senate. His career as a holder of public office would
begin not long afterwards.[111] It would eventually prove necessary to live down
the Elder's work of history, just under two decades later, after the assassination of
the final member of the Flavian dynasty.[112]

The influence of the Elder

The next chapter will take Pliny's story forwards from the beginning of his public
career in Rome. Now is the time, as this chapter draws to a close, to reflect briefly
on the broader influence of the Elder on the Younger. How much time did the
Younger actually get to spend with his uncle? In his life of the Elder, Suetonius
mentions a 'succession of eminent administrative posts' (*procurationes . . .
splendidissimas atque continuas*). It was open to a man of the Elder's wealth and
status to pursue a career first in the army, then in imperial civil administration
across the provinces of the empire. The duties of such a 'procurator' might include fiscal responsibility in a province or even a governorship of one of the
smaller provinces.[113] Some would gain entry to the senate by this route. Only
one of the Elder's several procuratorships can be positively identified: Spain
(3.5.17), source of the personal connections visible in the Vesuvius letters. The
date of this service is unknown, although various factors point to a time in the
70s C.E.[114] It has been vigorously argued that nearly all of the Elder's postings
belong to the early Flavian era, between 70 and 76 C.E. In truth, this is far from
certain, and one widely conjectured procuratorship in Africa may well belong
to the 60s, during Nero's reign.[115] What is clear is that, by the Younger's account,
the Elder was a very busy man even when back in Rome: 'Before daybreak he
used to make his way to the Emperor Vespasian (who also worked by night),
and after that to his official duties. On his return home, he gave the rest of his
time to study' (3.5.9).[116] This 'study' produced 102 volumes over the lifetime
of the Elder. (Only the thirty-seven volumes of the *Natural History* survive in
full.) They are proudly catalogued in chronological order by the Younger for a
friend from Comum, culminating with the books of the *Natural History* (3.5.3–
6). The Younger adds, 'you will be still more astonished when you learn that for
a considerable time he practised in the law courts, that he died in his fifty-sixth
year, and that between these two periods he was much distracted and hindered,
partly by the discharge of important offices, and partly by his friendship with
the emperors' (3.5.7).[117]

Born in the early 60s C.E., the Younger may well have had little opportunity for extended time with his uncle. When his natural father died, the highly distinguished Verginius Rufus was appointed to the role of guardian for the Younger,[118] perhaps in part because of the Elder's absences abroad. Even so, the Younger can provide an account of the Elder's typical working day in Rome (3.5.8–13), in the country (3.5.14), and when travelling (3.5.15–16). That day, as suggested at the chapter's outset, left little room for ordinary human intercourse amidst the obsessive reading and note-taking. Some close acquaintance is implied by incidental remarks: 'sleep came over him very easily' (3.5.8); 'I remember that one of his friends . . .' (3.5.12); 'I remember being reproved by him for taking a walk . . .' (3.5.16); 'He himself used to relate that when he was procurator in Spain . . .' (3.5.17).[119] How long does one have to spend in the company of a workaholic uncle to acquire an impression of his habits, especially if stories current amongst other family members might fill in the gaps? We cannot know. It is significant that, as noted earlier, the Elder is never once depicted in Pliny's correspondence at home in Comum. The portrait of the Elder, nevertheless, is decidedly more intimate, though not necessarily more affectionate,[120] than that of men such as Verginius Rufus, Vestricius Spurinna and Corellius Rufus, who between them guided Pliny's career in its next stages.[121] Well into his adult life, the Younger both measured himself against and attempted to transcend the example set by the Elder.[122]

Equally important for the Younger were the connections that the Elder could supply. Talk of a career in the imperial civil service or senate can create the misleading impression of standard entry-points and ladders. In reality, as one modern historian emphasizes, 'Personal factors dominate all through—choice or luck or patronage'.[123] A lack of his own powerful patrons may explain why the Elder, born into wealthy obscurity in distant northern Italy, pursued a career in the imperial civil service rather than seeking entry to the senate.[124] Or it may well be that procuratorial employment, with its opportunities to travel and collect information, appealed to the future author of the *Natural History*.[125] As eventual commander of the Misene fleet, the Elder could give his nephew direct access to the imperial house and the accompanying possibility of a senatorial career, not to mention a host of other contacts gained during service abroad.[126] That he was able to provide imperial entrée is evidence enough of the influence of luck on a Roman career. The *Natural History* is dedicated to Titus. In its prefatory letter the Elder uses the rare term *conterraneus* ('fellow countryman') that would cause so much trouble between Como and Verona thirteen-hundred years later in their battle over the ownership of the two Plinii. For Titus' more immediate benefit, the Elder adds 'you recognize even this army term', warming to his theme with the assertion 'what a good comrade you were to us in the companionship of the camp [*in castrensi contubernio*]!' (*HN* pref. 1, 3).[127] The phrase *castrense contubernium*, as a modern authority observes, 'implies something more than merely belonging to the same army'.[128] The exact nature of the association is beyond recovery. The pair may well have undertaken some form of joint military service in lower Germany around 57–8 C.E., when Titus was in his late teens and the Elder was in his middle thirties.[129] The Elder, then, was personally acquainted with a member of the Flavian house, perhaps a full decade before it came to power, unforeseeably, in the aftermath of the revolt against Nero in 68–9 C.E.

The value of this chance connection can hardly be overstated. It explains why the Elder enjoyed access to the imperial inner circle, to the *amicitia principum* ('friendship of the emperors') that kept him so busy when in Rome.[130] It provides the context for the Elder's promotion to his admiralship, and explains the Elder's deeply partisan devotion in turn to Titus. The prefatory letter to the *Natural History* praises Titus's record of public service, singling out his command of the praetorian guard under Vespasian for particular mention (*HN* pref. 3). In his life of Titus, Suetonius would later underline the cruelty of Titus' conduct in the same role, declaring that the future emperor 'incurred such odium at the time that hardly anyone ever came to the throne with so evil a reputation or so much against the desires of all' (*Tit.* 6.2).[131] Titus was widely expected to become *alium Neronem*, 'a second Nero' (*Tit.* 7.1).[132] Personal loyalties trump ugly political records: an early lesson for the Younger. It was not for nothing that the Stoic philosopher Epictetus reserved special scorn for the friends of Caesar.[133] In the case of Titus, at least, there would be nothing for the Younger to live down later. On succeeding Vespasian, soon after the publication of the *Natural History*, Titus became the 'love and darling of human kind' (*Tit.* 1.1).[134] Suetonius praises him for his responses to three natural disasters he faced in his short reign: a three-day conflagration at Rome, a major outbreak of plague in Italy, and, of course, the disaster of Vesuvius (*Tit.* 8.3–4).[135]

There may also have been disappointment for the Elder in his relationship with the Flavians. In his sixth decade the Elder had succeeded neither to the senate nor to the governorship of a major province achieved by other procurators under the same dynasty.[136] The western imperial fleet did not rank as high in esteem as command of the forces at Ravenna, and imperial freedmen had been appointed to the Misene role in recent times. 'A modest question therefore intrudes', suggests Sir Ronald Syme, 'touching the nature and efficacy of Pliny's friendship with Vespasian. In any age and society, converse with an old soldier or a polymath can become tedious'.[137] Or perhaps he just lacked the requisite skills for a provincial post. The Younger, at any rate, would succeed in the senate where the Elder had not. Key to this success was encouragement offered by another signal feature of the Elder's career. Literary endeavour might raise a man to notice: a lesson that could be acted upon rather than, like the luck of meeting a future emperor, merely envied. At a very early stage in his career, the Elder had written a biography of the general and litterateur Pomponius Secundus (3.5.3), perhaps after serving under his governorship in the key military province of Upper Germany in the 50s C.E. The Younger describes Pomponius as 'a man who had cherished a singular regard' for his uncle (3.5.3).[138] If we ask what Pomponius saw in the Elder, one answer springs to mind: a shared love of *studia*, literary work. Commenting on the triumphal honours which Pomponius received for his actions against the Chatti in Germany, Tacitus, expressed the flattering opinion that such *ornamenta* were 'only a modest part of his fame with posterity, among whom he excels for the glory of his poems' (*Ann.* 12.28.2).[139] In the words, again, of Syme, 'The Ceasars set a high premium on polite letters and the social graces. The commander of an army may turn out to be an orator or a writer'.[140] If literary interests had visibly aided the promotion of the Elder, the lesson was hardly lost on the Younger. It was to the development of his skills as a public speaker and writer that the Younger was already giving the utmost attention, even during the eruption of Vesuvius.

From Vesuvius to Rome

Around a decade after Vesuvius, Pliny would enter the senate. There were perhaps few members of that body in 89 C.E. who had experienced the momentous incidents that Pliny had seen in person on the bay of Naples in 79. The later request from Tacitus to supply information not only on the death of his famous uncle, but also on Pliny's own experience (6.20.1 *casus*) of the catastrophe, is perhaps testimony to the celebrity that attended Pliny for his eyewitness role. The long-term effects on Pliny of the disaster can only be imagined. The vividness of his recall of the events of 79, his determination to offer a calm and rational account, and the not entirely flattering self-portrait—all tell their own story. Equally, we can only guess at the personal effect on Pliny of the unexpected loss of his uncle at a key moment of transition from higher education to public career. Pliny's long journey to the senate would begin with a public appearance in Rome within a year of the eruption of the Vesuvius.

Notes

1. In this chapter I provisionally accept as authoritative the account of the course and timings of the eruption provided by Sigurdsson and Carey (2002). The latter synthesizes much previous research, e.g. Sigurdsson, Cashdollar, and Sparks (1982), Sigurdsson, Carey, Cornell et al. (1985). Among the three Sigurdsson et al.

contributions: (1985) provides the hard scientific data and detailed discussion, and updates some of the views put forward in the (1982) piece; while (2002) provides further updates along with a more concerted attempt to reconcile the scientific data to the account provided by Pliny. Other views on the precise timing and phases of the eruption have been offered, and new research will almost certainly revise current thinking, perhaps radically, not least because conjectured timing depends on estimates of the total amount of ejected material and of rates of deposition, and so on. Given such foundations, all statements made about the actual eruption and its relation to the Younger's narrative must be regarded as possessing provisional validity at best. A useful chronology of events, much of it set against *Letters* 6.16 and 20, is provided at Sigurdsson and Carey (2002, 58–62); it can be supplemented from Sigurdsson et al. (1982), who also provide a map of the Elder Pliny's conjectured journey across the bay of Naples; cf. the addendum to Sigurdsson et al. (1982), and Sigurdsson et al. (1985, 336, 376). For another account of the eruption that largely follows Sigurdsson's reconstructions, but with slightly differing provisional times, see Scarth (2009, 53–83); contrast the radically different chronology of (e.g.) Marturano and Varone (2005, esp. 243–6, 257–8). My own account has benefited from the clarification of problems and details offered by the online commentary of Pedar Foss at the quemdixerchaos.com website. These commentaries will be superseded by Foss (f'coming): a monograph that will provide a definitive account of the Pliniii and the Vesuvian eruption.

2. Frequent reference is made by ancient authorities to luxury villas on the peninsula (D'Arms (1970, 9–10, 21–31) = (2003, 22–3, 36–42)), although few traces of any ancient buildings have been found on top of the cape (Keppie (2009, 60)). Today it is largely covered with scrubby vegetation; cf. Appendix 2.

3. Cf. 6.16.4, 5, 12, 13; 6.20.11, 18; also Cic. *Fam.* 7.1.1, Stat. *Silu.* 2.2.1–2.

4. 6.20.9 *nubes atra et horrenda*. On the likely route taken by the Younger, see later in this chapter.

5. See Healy (1999, 22–3) on the Elder's largely administrative rather than military role; cf. D'Arms (1970, 80–2) = (2003, 85–7) on the role of the Misene fleet.

6. Cf. Appendix 2 on ancient Stabiae.

7. Pliny's Campanian friends: 5.14, 6.28 (Pontius Allifanus), 7.3 (wife of Bruttius Praesens); cf. Gibson and Morello (2012, 49, 66) for the suggestion that Campania's unique prominence in Book 6 of the *Letters* is intended to create a sympathetic context for the book's two Vesuvius letters (6.16, 20).

8. Cf. 3.7; see Henderson (2002a, 102–24) for the career of Silius Italicus and Pliny's attitude to him. For Campania in Silius' own epic, see Augoustakis (2015).

9. 6.4.2 *ecquid . . . secessus uoluptates regionisque abundantiam inoffensa transmitteres*; see Gibson (f'coming) for the implication of moral 'hurt'.

10. Cf. Cic. *Cael.* 27, 35, 38, 47, 49; Sen. *Epist.* 51.

11. Cf. Propertius 1.11.27 *corruptas . . . Baias*, 29 *castis inimica puellis*. For Baiae in Propertius, see Leonard (2015).

12. Statius *Silv.* 2.2, 3.5.72–107, Newlands (2012, 136, 138–9, 149–57); cf. Newlands (2010) on Vesuvius in Pliny and the poetry of Statius.

13. On the repopulation of areas affected by the eruption in the period after 79 C.E., see Camardo (2013). On Campania's significance as a centre of literary activity and 'imaginative fulcrum', see the essays collected by Fielding and Newlands (2015). On Roman Naples, see Lomas (2016).

14. See Chp. 5.

15. Anderson (2014); cf. Stähli (2012) on Pompeii in the cinema. On the Pompeian plaster casts and their reception, see Sigurdsson and Carey (2002, 50 with fig. 44, 61), Beard (2008, 1–9), Hales (2011), Seydl (2012, 26–9), Gardner Coates (2012, 47–9), Coates, Lapatin, and Seydl (2012, 154, 158–63, 217–20, 232–5).

16. 6.16.4–5 *erat Miseni classemque imperio praesens regebat. nonum kal. Septembres hora fere septima mater mea indicat ei adparere nubem inusitata et magnitudine et specie. usus ille sole, mox frigida, gustauerat iacens studebatque; poscit soleas, ascendit locum ex quo maxime miraculum illud conspici poterat. nubes—incertum procul intuentibus ex quo monte (Vesuuium fuisse postea cognitum est)—oriebatur, cuius similitudinem et formam non alia magis arbor quam pinus expresserit.* For explication of the Latin formulation of date and time in this passage, see Gibson (f'coming).

17. On the location of the admiral's residence (mentioned also at 6.20.4), see Gigante (1989, 39–40), Starr (1983, 14–16), Pitassi (2009, 205). The *collegium* was discovered by chance in 1968; its inscriptions reveal something of life in imperial Misenum; see D'Arms (2000) = (2003, 439–73)

18. See D'Arms (2000, 134) = (2003, 454–5).

19. Cf. 3.5.3–6, 12, 15–16, Healy (1999, 33–5).

20. 3.5.14 *solum balinei tempus studiis eximebatur (cum dico balinei, de interioribus loquor; nam dum destringitur tergiturque, audiebat aliquid aut dictabat).*

21. The *Natural History* is conventionally dated to 77 C.E. (Beagon (2005, 1–2)); it has strong ties to the genres which recorded *mirabilia*: see Beagon (2011), Naas (2011).

22. 6.16.22 makes reference to Thuc. 1.22.2: see Gibson (f'coming) ad loc.

23. See Connors (2015).

24. The wall painting is widely reproduced and discussed: e.g. Sider (2005, 12), Rowland (2014, 16–17).

25. Doubts about the August date of the eruption go back at least to the biography by Masson (1709, 27–30) and resurface in the nineteenth century (see Merrill (1903, 336)). These doubts are currently attaining critical mass, based on the discovery in Pompeii and environs of autumnal fruits, heavy clothing, and a post-September 79 coin, not dropped by looters; see Beard (2008, 17–18, 319), and, in more detail, Pappalardo (1990), Borgongino and Stefani (2001–2), Stefani and Borgongino (2007). Rolandi, Paone, Di Lascio et al. (2008) add the argument that the distribution of the 79 C.E. deposits is more consistent with autumnal wind patterns than with those normal in August. (A charcoal graffito, newly discovered in Regio V and bearing an October date, awaits publication and contextualisation.) Some scholars bolster their arguments with references to an alternative later date in the manuscript tradition—although the evidence is suggestive rather than definitive. Standard texts of 6.16.4 offer *nonum kal. Septembres*. Mynors' authoritative edition (1963) comments: '*Septembres* Ma, *om.* γ', i.e. the reading 'September' is found in one of the

most important manuscripts (the M[ediceus]) and independently in the landmark Aldine edition of 1508 (a[ldinus]), but it is omitted by an entire branch of the manuscript tradition (represented by γ). The latter tradition displays only *nonum kal.*; i.e. the name of the month is omitted. Five early printed editions, appearing between 1474 and 1506, offer variants of *November Calend.*, as may also two late manuscripts; see Stout (1962, ix–10, 179), Borgongino and Stefani (2001–2, 186–7). Is *November* an attempt by Renaissance editors to supply the name of the missing month from *nonum* ('ninth'), or is it a witness to an independent lost tradition? The supposed further variant of *nonum Kal. Decembris* makes its debut as an editorial emendation in an edition of 1797. For a defence of the traditional date, see Sigurdsson and Carey (2002, 58), also Carey and Sigurdsson (1987, 307–8), Sigurdsson et al. (1985, 340, 376)). Foss (f'coming) will provide an authoritative account of the whole issue.

26. Contrast Dio Cassius 66.22, who emphasizes the tremendous noise both immediately before and during the first eruption; cf. Sherwin-White (1966, 372).

27. 6.16.7 *magnum propiusque noscendum ut eruditissimo uiro uisum. iubet liburnicam aptari; mihi si uenire una uellem facit copiam; respondi studere me malle, et forte ipse quod scriberem dederat.*

28. This theme runs though Pliny's Vesuvius letters; see Gibson and Morello (2012, 110–15).

29. 3.5.10 *nihil enim legit quod non excerperet; dicere etiam solebat nullum esse librum tam malum ut non aliqua parte prodesset.*

30. 3.5.5 *'studiosi tres', in sex uolumina propter amplitudinem diuisi, quibus oratorem ab incunabulis instituit et perficit.* The work is mentioned by Quintilian at e.g. *Inst.* 3.1.21, 11.3.43.

31. 6.16.8–10 *egrediebatur domo; accipit codicillos Rectinae Tasci imminenti periculo exterritae (nam uilla eius subiacebat, nec ulla nisi nauibus fuga): ut se tanto discrimini eriperet orabat. uertit ille consilium et quod studioso animo incohauerat obit maximo. deducit quadriremes, ascendit ipse non Rectinae modo sed multis (erat enim frequens amoenitas orae) laturus auxilium. properat illuc unde alii fugiunt, rectumque cursum . . . tenet.*

32. On the base at Misenum, see McKay (1967, 8), Casson (1995, 365), D'Arms (1970, 80–82, 136–7) = (2003, 85–7, 135); cf. Appendix 2. On ancient ship sheds, see Blackman and Rankov (2014).

33. See Gibson (f'coming) on 6.16.8, 11; 6.20.5, 10.

34. See later in this chapter.

35. Sigurdsson and Carey (2002, 46), with fuller analysis at (2002, 44–7).

36. Scattered find-spots of papyri at the villa may suggest attempts to move the library; see Sider (2005, 62).

37. E.g. Sigurdsson and Carey (2002, 41); cf. Sigurdsson et al. (1985), Carey and Sigurdsson (1987, 313), Marturano and Varone (2005, 243).

38. See Sigurdsson and Carey (2002, 42–3), Carey and Sigurdsson (1987, 303).

39. See Eco (1990) = (2016).

40. See Jones (2001).

41. See earlier n. 1 in this chapter for estimates of timing and deposition.

42. 6.16.1 *Petis ut tibi auunculi mei exitum scribam, quo uerius tradere posteris possis.*

43. Cf. e.g. 5.5 (on Gaius Fannius), 8.12 (on Titinius Capito), Sherwin-White (1966, 239), Ash (2003, 222–4); cf. Tac. *Hist.* 1.2.1, *Ann.* 16.16.3, Pomeroy (1991, 192–225).

44. See Gigante (1989, 36). Tacitus' lost account of the death of the Elder was perhaps eventually published c. three years after Pliny's Vesuvius letters; only around one third of Tacitus' *Histories* survives, up to the year 70 C.E.

45. 6.16.21 *nihil ad historiam.*

46. See Marchesi (2008, 171–89).

47. 6.16.10 *rectumque cursum recta gubernacula in periculum tenet . . . omnes illius mali motus omnes figuras ut deprenderat oculis dictaret enotaretque.*

48. On Herculaneum's relative freedom from inundation and Oplontis as a possible destination for the Elder, see Sigurdsson et al. (1982, 48), with figures for ash and pumice fall further revised down in Sigurdsson et al (1985) (cf. Sigurdsson and Carey (2002, 53)). On the villa at Oplontis, see Clarke and Muntasser (2014), Clarke (2018), Zarmakoupi (2018). It is not known whether the area was known in antiquity as 'Oplontis', nor to whom the villa belonged (despite popular associations with Poppaea, wife of Nero).

49. See Sigurdsson et al. (1982, 44–5).

50. 6.16.11 *iam uadum subitum ruinaque montis litora obstantia.*

51. The Younger emphasizes at 6.16.22 that he gathered information immediately after the event (in an allusion to Thucydides); see earlier.

52. See Sigurdsson et al. (1982, 44 n. 19, 48), Lefèvre (1996, 198 n.19); for another view, see Marturano and Varone (2005, 244).

53. See Scarth (2009, 61). On the naval outpost at Stabiae, see Ferraro (2004, 39–40).

54. See later in this chapter.

55. On the force and direction of the winds (on the evidence of pumice falls), see Sigurdsson and Carey (2002, 58).

56. See Zarmakoupi (2014, 68).

57. See Zarmakoupi (2014, 54, 56), with archaeological map of the area and a detailed overview of three of the six Stabiae villas and their gardens (Arianna A, Arianna B, and San Marco) at Zarmakoupi (2014, 54–74, 254–63); also Howe (2018) on the social status of the owners of the villas, with map at (2018, 98); cf. Appendix 2. Ancient ramps lead down from villas Arianna A and San Marco to the Roman sea level; see Zarmakoupi (2014, 63–5, 68), with figures and illustration.

58. See Zarmakoupi (2014, 27–8), also *In Stabiano* (2004, 114–18).

59. 6.16.12, 13 *complectitur trepidantem consolatur hortatur, utque timorem eius sua securitate leniret, deferri in balineum iubet; lotus accubat cenat, aut hilaris aut (quod aeque magnum) similis hilari . . . tum se quieti dedit.* Unlike even the grandest villas at Pompeii and Herculaneum, the villas at Stabiae do possess private baths; see Howe (2018, 109).

60. See Gibson (f'coming) on 6.16.12–13.

61. 6.20.2 *profecto auunculo ipse reliquum tempus studiis (ideo enim remanseram) impendi; mox balineum cena somnus inquietus et breuis.*

62. See Gibson and Morello (2012, 110–15).

63. 6.16.14 *area ex qua diaeta adibatur ita iam cinere mixtisque pumicibus oppleta surrexerat, ut si longior in cubiculo mora, exitus negaretur.*

64. See Sigurdsson and Carey (2002, 39 fig. 33, 50, 61); but see Sigurdsson et al. (1982, 41–2) for a slightly higher estimate for Stabiae. Pompeii endured a fall of 2.4–2.7 metres; see Sigurdsson and Carey (2002, 48).

65. See later in this chapter.

66. Sigurdsson and Carey (2002, 37–8).

67. Merrill (1918), (1920).

68. On the contributions of Sigurdsson et al. from the 1980s on, see earlier in this chapter.

69. See Sigurdsson and Carey (2002, 54, 59–60).

70. Mastrolorenzo, Petrone, Pappalardo, and Guarino (2010); older accounts assume gradual asphyxiation (Sigurdsson and Carey (2002, 57)).

71. On the excavations on the shore at Herculaneum and the number of victims found there, many in the seafront arches, see Sigurdsson and Carey (2002, 55–8), Bisel and Bisel (2002). For illustrations of the seafront arches and a map of where the skeletons were found, see Wallace-Hadrill (2011, 25–35), who offers a higher estimate of 'more than 300 victims'. For estimates of casualties in Pompeii, see later in this chapter.

72. See Sigurdsson and Carey (2002, 53–5).

73. See Sigurdsson et al. (1982, 46).

74. Most of the pumice fragments falling in nearby Pompeii during the opening hours of the main eruption appear to have been relatively small (at most a few centimeters in diameter), but with a lethal 10 per cent admixture of fist-sized lithic fragments; see Sigurdsson and Carey (2002, 48, 58–9).

75. 6.20.4–5 *resedimus in area domus, quae mare a tectis modico spatio diuidebat. dubito, constantiam uocare an imprudentiam debeam (agebam enim duodeuicensimum annum): posco librum Titi Liui, et quasi per otium lego atque etiam ut coeperam excerpo.*

76. See Riggsby (2003, 180 n. 25), Gibson (2012, 61 n. 24), Appendix 2.

77. Fulkerson (2013, 187); on the broader topic of ancient consistency vs. modern evolution, see Fulkerson (2013, 186–200); cf. Chp. 2.

78. On Kauffmann and the painting entitled *Pliny the Younger and his mother at Misenum*, see Gardner Coates (2011), Gardner Coates, Lapatin, and Seydl (2012, 128–9). Close inspection of the painting reveals that the Younger is depicted with two left feet (a defect attributed to Kauffmann's less talented husband): a hilarious, if unintended, comment on the behaviour of the Younger. For more eighteenth to nineteenth-century paintings of the eruption, including P. H. de Valenciennes' 1813 representation of the death of the Elder on the beach at Stabiae, see Gardner Coates et al. (2012, 126–53). On further receptions of the Plinii at Vesuvius, see Rowland (2014, 111–12, 133–4, 140, 144–5, 252–3).

79. For surmise of a (deceased) wife for the Elder from the families of Verginius Rufus or Vestricius Spurinna, see Syme (1985a, 350) = *RP* 5.468; 7.510–11.

80. See Chps. 2, 3.

81. See Shelton (2013, 188–99). It is temptingly easy for modern readers to draw a straight line between Augustine and the 'unnerving certainty' of his mother Monnica

(Brown (2000, 277)). Pliny asks us instead to evaluate the relationship between himself and the Elder.

82. See Sigurdsson and Carey (2002, 48–50, 61), Sigurdsson et al. (1985, 350–53).

83. See Sigurdsson and Carey (2002, 48, 58–9).

84.. Around 400 bodies have been discovered in the pumice levels (most killed by collapsing buildings) and 700 in the pyroclastic levels immediately above; see Beard (2008, 4), Mastrolorenzo et al. (2010, 5–6), and the more detailed estimates of Luongo, Perrotta, Scarpatia, De Carolis, Patricelli, and Ciarallo (2003). The number of corpses found in Pompeii is relatively low by comparison with the conjectured total population, and may be evidence of the emptying of the town before the arrival of the pyroclastic flows; see Beard (2008, 9–11). On G. Fiorelli, the nineteenth-century inventor of the technique of making body casts, see Rowland (2014, 168–73). For estimates of casualties in Herculaneum, see earlier in this chapter.

85. See Mastrolorenzo et al. (2010, 11).

86. See Sigurdsson and Carey (2002, 59); cf. Beard (2008, 1–3).

87. See Sigurdsson and Carey (2002, 50).

88. 6.16.18–20 . . . *flammae flammarumque praenuntius odor sulpuris alios in fugam uertunt, excitant illum. innitens seruolis duobus adsurrexit et statim concidit, ut ego colligo, crassiore caligine spiritu obstructo, clausoque stomacho qui illi natura inualidus et angustus et frequenter aestuans erat. ubi dies redditus . . . corpus inuentum integrum inlaesum opertumque ut fuerat indutus: habitus corporis quiescenti quam defuncto similior.*

89. See Sigurdsson and Carey (2002, 50, 61); cf. Sigurdsson et al. (1985, 352, 380–1).

90. On the Elder as perhaps asthmatic, see Sherwin-White (1966, 374) on 6.16.19, noting the heavy snoring of 6.16.13. The exact cause of the Elder's death, on the Younger's account, has been much discussed: see most recently Schönberger (1990, 529), Lefèvre (1996, 204–5), Scarth (2009, 75–6).

91. On the Younger and Suetonius, see Gibson (2014).

92. *ui pulueris ac fauillae oppressus est, uel* ut quidam existimant *a seruo suo occisus quem deficiens aestu ut necem sibi maturaret orauerat*: Suetonius takes no responsibility for the truth of the report. On the Suetonian life of the Elder, see Reeve (2011).

93. 6.20.7 *tum demum excedere oppido uisum; sequitur uulgus attonitum, quodque in pauore simile prudentiae, alienum consilium suo praefert, ingentique agmine abeuntes premit et impellit. egressi tecta consistimus.* For references in this passage to Verg. *Aen.* 2.450 *agmine denso,* 796–8 *atque hic ingentem comitum adfluxisse nouorum | inuenio admirans numerum, matresque uirosque, | collectam exsilio pubem, miserabile uulgus,* see Marchesi (2008, 178).

94. See Woolf (2015, 137–8) on 3.11 (discussed in Chp. 5); cf. Chp. 5 for Pliny's lack of a leading role in the 'opposition' to Domitian.

95. See Sigurdsson et al. (1982, 48–9), Foss (2017).

96. 6.20.9, 11 *ab altero latere nubes atra et horrenda, ignei spiritus tortis uibratisque discursibus rupta, in longas flammarum figuras dehiscebat; fulguribus illae et similes et maiores erant. . . . nec multo post illa nubes descendere in terras, operire maria; cinxerat Capreas et absconderat, Miseni quod procurrit abstulerat.*

97. On the possible routes taken by the Younger and his mother, see Sherwin-White (1966, 379), Foss (2017). The latter presents convincing arguments for a route along the modern via Lido Miliscola (mentioned at the outset of this chapter) towards Monte di Procida.

98. On the narrative confluence of portents and the death of the Elder, see Gigante (1989, 41, 61); on the geological confluence, see Sigurdsson et al. (1985, 381). The last intervention from the Spanish friend of the Elder at this point ('If [the Elder] has perished, it *was* his wish that you should survive him': 6.20.10) carries particular narrative significance as a marker of the moment that the Elder dies.

99. 6.20.12 *tum mater orare hortari iubere, quoquo modo fugerem; posse enim iuuenem, se et annis et corpore grauem bene morituram, si mihi causa mortis non fuisset.*

100. The parallels with Aeneas and Anchises at 6.20.12 (Verg. *Aen.* 2.638–40, 647–8, also 2.287, 619) were first noted by Lillge (1918, 289–90); cf. Görler (1979, 427), Cova (2001, 56). Pliny's mother may have been only in her 40s in 79 C.E.: this makes the parallel with Anchises the more artificial and deliberate (Shelton (2013, 193)).

101. 6.20.13–14 *iam cinis, adhuc tamen rarus. respicio: densa caligo tergis imminebat, quae nos torrentis modo infusa terrae sequebatur. 'deflectamus' inquam 'dum uidemus, ne in uia strati comitantium turba in tenebris obteramur.' uix consideramus, et nox non qualis inlunis aut nubila, sed qualis in locis clausis lumine exstincto.* The cloud like a flood is a Vergilian touch; cf. Verg. *Aen.* 2.304–8.

102. On the surge cloud produced by Krakatau in 1883, see Sigurdsson and Carey (2002, 62). On the nature of the surge described by Pliny, and its ability to travel large distances over water, see Sigurdsson and Carey (2002, 58,) Sigurdsson et al. (1982, 44, 50), Sigurdsson et al. (1985, 381), Scandone, Giacomelli, and Gasparini (1993, 8).

103. 6.20.14–15 *audires ululatus feminarum, infantum quiritatus, clamores uirorum; alii parentes alii liberos alii coniuges uocibus requirebant, uocibus noscitabant; hi suum casum, illi suorum miserabantur; erant qui metu mortis mortem precarentur; multi ad deos manus tollere, plures nusquam iam deos ullos aeternamque illam et nouissimam noctem mundo interpretabantur.*

104. Literary echoes in this passage: (i) 6.20.14 (the cries of the populace): cf. Verg. *Aen.* 2.313, 2.486–90, 4.667–8; Liv. 2.23.8, 33.28.3; (ii) 6.20.15 (fear of death): cf. Lucr. 3.79–82, 87–90, 6.1256–8, 1276–7; (iii) 6.20.16 (the gods / the end of the world): cf. Lucr. 6.565–7; Verg. *Georg.* 1.468, *Aen.* 2.324–5, 351–2. See further Gibson (f'coming).

105. 6.20.17 *possem gloriari non gemitum mihi, non uocem parum fortem in tantis periculis excidisse.*

106. See Sherwin-White (1966, 373) on Dio 66.21–4; cf. Sherwin-White (1966, 372, 380). It appears to be part of Dio's purpose to set the scene for the death of Titus and accession of Domitian; see Connors (2015, 132–4). Note that the author of an anti-Roman prophecy in the Sibylline oracles would soon link the eruption with the sack of Jerusalem by Titus almost nine years before to the day; cf. *Sibyll. Orac.* 4.115–35, with Shanks (2010). None of Pliny's Misenes appears to have connected their plight with divine vengeance for personal or imperial wrongdoing.

107. 6.20.17 *nisi me cum omnibus, omnia mecum perire misero, magno tamen mortalitatis solacio credidissem.* For the reference in this passage to Seneca *Nat.Q.* 6.2.6, 9, see Gibson (f'coming).

108. 6.20.18 *sol . . . effulsit, luridus tamen qualis esse cum deficit solet. occursabant trepidantibus adhuc oculis mutata omnia altoque cinere tamquam niue obducta.*

109. For the standard view that the Younger's adoption was testamentary, see Sherwin-White (1966, 70), Syme (1985c, 195) = *RP* 5.644, Birley (2000a, 1); cf. Gibson and Morello (2012, 115–16). On inheritances from the Elder, see Chps. 1, 2 (name), and Chp. 6 (Umbrian estates).

110. Cf. *HN* praef. 20 'I have given a full account of all your family—your father, yourself, and your brother, in a history of our own times, beginning where Aufidius Bassus concludes. You will ask, where is it? It has been long completed and its accuracy confirmed; but I have determined to commit the charge of it to my heirs, lest I should have been suspected, during my lifetime, of having been unduly influenced by ambition' (*uos quidem omnes, patrem, te fratremque, diximus opere iusto, temporum nostrorum historiam orsi a fine Aufidii. ubi sit ea, quaeres. iam pridem peracta sancitur et alioqui statutum erat heredi mandare, ne quid ambitioni dedisse uita iudicaretur*).

111. See Chp. 5.

112. Among the Elder's listed works at 3.5.3–6, this history is the only one to receive no explanatory comment from the Younger and is demoted from the leading position in his oeuvre that Elder himself had awarded it; see Gibson and Steel (2010, 127–8), Gibson (2011, 196–201).

113. On careers for wealthy men like the Elder of the equestrian class outside the senate, see Syme (1969, 207–8) = *RP* 2.747–8, Healy (1999, 2).

114. See Syme (1969, 216–17) = *RP* 2.755–6; *RP* 7.503–4 (doubted by Sherwin-White (1966, 213).

115. The Elder's career received extensive investigation from Syme, who built on the work of Friedrich Münzer (1868–1942); see Syme (1958, 60–3, 127, 291–3), (1969) = *RP* 2.742–73; *RP* 7.496–511. Syme's version has the Elder undertaking three separate periods of military service in Germany from c. 47 to c. 58 C.E., plus four procuratorships between 70 and 76 C.E. in (with varying degrees of certainty) Narbonensis, Africa, Tarraconensis, and Belgica. The main sources for this reconstruction are the Younger's long letter on the working practices and bibliography of the Elder (3.5) and the *Natural History*, where descriptions of phenomena in the provinces of the empire imply (or can be interpreted so as to imply) personal autopsy. Sherwin-White (1966, 219–21) rightly criticized the incautious approach to the evidence of the *Natural History*, and restricted known procuratorships to Tarraconensis and (perhaps) Africa. Syme later retracted his argument about the date of the African posting; see Syme (1969, 215 n. 5) = *RP* 2.754 n. 5; *RP* 7.503. The best recent survey of the Elder's career reaffirms Sherwin-White's more sceptical position; see Healy (1999, 1–23); cf. Beagon (2005, 1–5).

116. 3.5.9 *ante lucem ibat ad Vespasianum imperatorem (nam ille quoque noctibus utebatur), inde ad delegatum sibi officium. reuersus domum quod reliquum temporis studiis reddebat.*

117. 3.5.7 *magis miraberis si scieris illum aliquamdiu causas actitasse, decessisse anno sexto et quinquagensimo, medium tempus distentum impeditumque qua officiis maximis qua amicitia principum egisse.*

118. See Chp. 3.

119. 3.5.8 *erat sane somni paratissimi*; 3.5.12 *memini quendam ex amicis*; 3.5.16 *repeto me correptum ab eo, cur ambularem*; 3.5.17 *referebat ipse potuisse se, cum procuraret in Hispania.*

120. Shelton (2013, 190) suggests that the affectionate element of the Younger's relationship with Verginius (2.1.8, 6.10) is not necessarily present in relations with Elder.

121. On Verginius Rufus, Vestricius Spurinna, Corellius Rufus, see Syme, *RP* 7.512–20 (on Verginius), 7.541–50 (on Spurinna), also Chp. 7 n. 34 (on Corellius), and Gibson and Morello (2012, 105–8, 115–23, 126–35) (on all three); cf. Chp. 2 n. 26.

122. See Cova (2001), Lefèvre (1996) = (2009, 123–41); Henderson (2002a, 69–102), (2002b); Gibson (2011), Gibson and Morello (2012, 108–23).

123. Syme (1969, 208) = *RP* 2.748.

124. The personal wealth of the Elder is suggested not only by equestrian status (apparently confirmed by the discovery of a horse-bridle at Xanten on the Rhine bearing the words *Plinio praef. eq.*: *CIL* 13.10026, with Healy (1999, 5)), but also by his ownership of the Umbrian estate inherited by the Younger; see Chp. 6.

125. On the appeal of procuratorships, cf. Sen. *Ep.* 79.1ff., Syme (1969, 203–5) = *RP* 2.743–5, Healy (1999, 2).

126. Syme attempted to identify such contacts through the *Letters* of the nephew, adducing, with various levels of conviction, such luminaries as Arrius Antoninus, Iulius Frontinus, Iulius Ursus, Iulius Servianus, and the father of Cornelius Tacitus; see Syme (1969, 227–36) = *RP* 2.766–73; *RP* 7.506–11

127. *HN* praef. 1, 3 *agnoscis et hoc castrense uerbum . . . nobis quidem qualis in castrensi contubernio.*

128. Syme, *RP* 7.500.

129. See Syme (1969, 205–7) = *RP* 2.746–7, making use of Pliny, *HN* 33.143, 34.47, Suet. *Tit.* 4.1, Tac. *Ann.* 13.54ff.; cf. Syme *RP* 7.499–501 (with added qualifications), Healy (1999, 5–6). The argument is doubted by Sherwin-White (1966, 220), who argues (1966, 221, 221–2) instead for 'a period of service c. 56 when he may have been with the young Titus in Upper Germany'.

130. On the nature of the Elder's access to Vespasian's inner circle, see Sherwin-White (1966, 222).

131. Suet. *Tit.* 6.2 *ita ad praesens plurimum contraxit inuidiae, ut non temere quis tam aduerso rumore magisque inuitis omnibus transierit ad principatum.*

132. On Titus, his reputation and rule, see Griffin (2000a, 46–54).

133. For Epictetus on friendship with Caesars, cf. Arr. *Epict. diss.* 2.14.18, 4.1.6–13, 45–8, 60, 95; Millar (1965, 144–5) = (2004d, 111–12).

134. Suet. *Tit.* 1.1 *amor ac deliciae generis humani.*

135. On the reaction of the emperor to Vesuvius: '[Titus] chose commissioners by lot from among the ex-consuls for the relief of Campania; and the property of

those who lost their lives by Vesuvius and had no heirs left alive he applied to the rebuilding of the buried cities' (Suet. *Tit.* 8.4).

136. Even equestrians from the provinces of empire achieved entry into the senate; see Madsen (2009, 64–79).

137. Syme, *RP* 7.505–6. For Syme's unsympathetic attitude to the Plinii, see Chp. 8 n. 84.

138. 3.5.3 *a quo singulariter amatus.* On Pomponius Secundus, see Malloch (2013, 212–3) on Tac. *Ann.* 11.13.1, Champlin (2012, 377–8). Pomponius is mentioned by the Elder at *HN* 7.80, 13.83, 14.56, and again by Tacitus (*Ann.* 5.8.2, 6.18.1), and receives some attention from Quintilian (*Inst.* 10.1.98); see also Salomies (1992, 114).

139. Tac. *Ann.* 12.28.2 *modica pars famae eius apud posteros in quis carminum gloria praecellit*; cf. *Letters* 7.17.11 on the tragedies of Pomponius.

140. Syme (1969, 203) = *RP* 2.743. On personal wealth and the acquisition of literary culture as two of the main drivers of social mobility amongst the Roman elite, see Tacoma (2015).

5

Rome

Early life in Rome: an education in rhetoric

The youthful Pliny encountered living in his uncle's shadow 'in his eighteenth year' near Vesuvius (6.20.5) is found a year later in the heart of Rome: 'I began to speak in the Forum in my nineteenth year' (5.8.8). This was hardly his first time in Rome. Comum had no *rhetor* (4.13), but Pliny did not accompany classmates to Milan to finish his education.[1] This option might be sufficient for wealthier sons of Comum's local elite, but not for Pliny. Three centuries later, Augustine's family considered education in a small town near their home in north Africa insufficient, and waited until they could secure funds to finish his education in public speaking at the provincial capital of Carthage (*Conf.* 2.3.5). Pliny possessed the wealth and the connections to take him to Rome: Verginius Rufus had been twice consul even before Pliny reached 10 years old.[2] The various stages of Roman education show considerable flexibility, so it cannot be known exactly when Pliny began his course of instruction at Rome. It is clear that he spent much of this period with a fellow pupil who would become a lifelong friend (2.13.4–5, 10.4.1): Voconius Romanus of Tarraconensis, another Spanish connection no doubt supplied by the Elder Pliny.[3]

Pliny's teacher in Rome was Quintilian, another native of Tarraconensis, appointed Rome's first public professor of rhetoric by Vespasian.[4] Pliny mentions his teacher only twice in passing (2.4.9, 6.6.3), but the *Letters* bear witness to the profound influence of Quintilian's great treatise *Education of the Orator* (*Institutio Oratoria*) on his speech and thought. No other ancient author engages so extensively with the work:[5] the language and thinking of Quintilian are woven into the text of the *Letters* quite as deeply as those of Cicero or Tacitus.[6] Quintilian had done much to re-establish Ciceronian style as the gold standard for prose in Rome, after the perceived baroque excesses of the Neronian age. *Education of the Orator* was composed towards the end of Quintilian's life, in the 90s C.E., but likely gives some idea of the education in public speaking undergone by Pliny two decades earlier. The work proceeds systematically from elementary rhetorical exercises, through broader questions of arrangement of topics and appropriate level of style, to the attainment of proper facility in public speaking and on to issues of delivery. The final book of the treatise insists on a traditional Roman ideal of the orator as a consummate moral figure: 'a good

Man of High Empire. Roy K. Gibson, Oxford University Press (2020). © Oxford University Press.
DOI: 10.1093/actrade/9780199948192.001.0001

man skilled in speaking' (*uir bonus dicendi peritus, Inst.* 12.1.1). Pliny did not feel bound to follow his teacher in every regard. Quintilian concentrates on oratory as a practical art for the courtroom. The adult Pliny is at least as interested in the achievement of fame through the *publication* of his forensic speeches as a form of literature. He parades preferences for length (1.20) and audacity (9.26) of speech that Quintilian would find excessive.[7] There can be little doubt, however, that Pliny is included in the high praise of contemporary courtroom oratory that Quintilian offers towards the end of his great work (*Inst.* 10.1.122).[8]

An invitation to visit the schools of rhetoric as an adult, in search of a suitable teacher for the children of one of Domitian's senatorial victims, elicits Pliny's nostalgia for his school days in Rome: 'I resume that delightful age. I sit among young people, as I did in my youth' (2.18.1).[9] He adds a detail which hints at a boisterous atmosphere in the schools (2.18.2). This is tame by comparison with Augustine's experience. Now a teacher, Augustine relates that the violent rowdiness of his charges in Carthage caused him to leave after he had 'heard that the young students at Rome were quieter and better disciplined' (*Conf.* 5.8.14). The students in Italy, certainly less destructive, could cause other problems: they routinely avoided paying their fees by transferring en masse to other teachers (*Conf.* 5.12.22). Pliny's more orderly world has space neither for pupils' rowdiness nor sharp financial practices. And as a student of the optimistic Quintilian and the ideal of the *uir bonus dicendi peritus*, Pliny harbours none of Augustine's dark thoughts about learning rhetoric in the schools: 'the better I could deceive, the more I would be praised' (*Conf.* 3.3.6). Augustine's doubts multiplied as a teacher: 'in all honesty I taught them trickery—not so that they could employ these tricks to have an innocent man condemned, but so that, when the occasion required, they could act on behalf of a guilty man' (*Conf.* 4.2.2).[10] Pliny's superb talent for trickery on behalf of a guilty man will emerge in the final chapter on Pontus-Bithynia. It is not a matter for reflection on Pliny's part: elite codes of behaviour scarcely allowed for public interrogation of the self on such matters.

From schoolroom to courtroom

The central purpose of Quintilian's education was to fit a pupil for appearance in a court of law. In Rome, successful courtroom speaking was a traditional route to *gloria*.[11] An outstanding rhetorical performance might matter in a Roman law court rather more than evidence or witnesses. The *dignitas* (social standing) and *auctoritas* (reputation) of the speaker were equally important, and both were best communicated through an impressive style of speech—whether inside the courtroom or in daily social interaction.[12] The law court was not the only route to renown. Others might achieve *gloria* through military service or, more rarely, mastery of the law. Someone evidently spotted Pliny's rhetorical talent and encouraged him to continue developing it—whether Verginius Rufus or other senatorial patrons such as Vestricius Spurinna or Corellius Rufus.[13]

Pliny began his bid for *gloria* in the twelve months after the eruption of Vesuvius, around the time of the third great natural disaster of Titus' brief reign: a plague, 'the like of which had hardly ever been known before' (Suet. *Tit.* 8.3).[14] The great trials of the late Republic devoted to public disorder or interference with operations of the state had long since been removed from the public sphere: these were largely the preserve of either the emperor or the senate in closed session. The tradition of making an early name in the courts lived on. Unless one wished to undertake prosecutions on behalf of the imperial house against troublesome members of the elite,[15] the highest the rising orator could aim was Rome's Centumviral or 'Hundred Men' courtroom. This was the most distinguished of the civil courts, devoted to trying the cases of inheritance that so thoroughly dominated Roman law.[16] Defence was safer than attack: better to make one's name through aiding the vulnerable rather than assailing fellow members of the elite classes, no matter how obviously guilty.

It may well be that the case undertaken by Pliny in his nineteenth year is one mentioned elsewhere as conducted in the Centumviral courts 'while yet a very young man' (*adulescentulus adhuc*, 1.18.3).[17] Appropriately, the trial appears to have involved the defence of a fellow northern Italian, Iunius Pastor.[18] Recalling the episode over a decade and a half later, Pliny remembers that 'in my sleep, my mother-in-law appeared to me, in a suppliant posture at my feet, begging me not to plead' (1.18.3). The cause of anxiety was not simply that of youthful inexperience: Pliny was appearing 'against men of the highest influence in the state, and, what is more, friends of the Emperor' (1.18.3). Pliny persevered and won both his case and his name: 'it was that very speech which opened for me the ears of men and the gates of fame' (1.18.4).[19] Despite the lack of a father and recent death of his well-connected uncle, Pliny apparently now displays the adult *constantia* that had been imperfectly grasped the previous year.[20] Pliny presumably acted as a junior member of the legal team, much as he would insist a quarter of a century hence on bringing *his* young protégé on board to 'exhibit him to the Forum, introduce him to fame (6.23.2).[21]

Towards the senate and marriage

The gates of fame could hardly be opened without entry also into the senate.[22] The right to stand for offices leading to the senate was symbolized by the grant of a broad stripe (*latus clauus*) on the tunic. It was given automatically to the offspring of senators. Sons of *equites*, like Pliny, were obliged to acquire it directly from the emperor.[23] In later life Pliny makes reference to occasions on which he acquired the *latus clauus* from the emperor on behalf of his own protégés.[24] In his own case, he had direct access to the imperial house through the services and later the memory of the Elder Pliny: Titus's loyalty to the *amici* of his father Vespasian was well known (Suet. *Tit.* 7.2).[25] Between assumption of the stripe and entry to the senate via the office of quaestor (c. 89–90 C.E.), around a decade would elapse. A further decade would take Pliny to the consulship in 100 C.E.

The twenty years of Pliny's life in Rome after Vesuvius would be entirely concentrated on ascending this summit of a senator's career. His success in doing so as a new man, one without senatorial pedigree, commands interest. A parallel narrative, however, will dominate this chapter, namely Pliny's record in Rome as a rising senator in favour with Domitian—and the questions raised by Pliny's own incomplete account of that rise. Two legal actions in the senate conducted by Pliny against fellow senators punctuate the story: the successful prosecution of the corrupt provincial governor Baebius Massa c. 93–4 C.E., and the attempted indictment of the alleged 'collaborator' Publicius Certus in 97, the year after the death of Domitian. The final part of the chapter will include an account of one of the civil trials conducted by Pliny before a public court c. 106–7, and round out the portrait of the courtroom orator that is central to Pliny's identity in Rome. But ultimately the focus here will be on the little understood pessimism felt by Pliny under Trajan. Pliny's growing despair after the emperor's return from Dacia in 107 reveals complexity in a man often belittled for his apparent optimism, and throws doubts on the conventional narrative about the 'best' (*Optimus*) of emperors.

Before entry to the senate, Pliny held two minor offices at Rome.[26] Each gave notice of future prospects: both holders and onlookers keenly evaluated their worth. The first required Pliny to preside at the Centumviral courts. Duties were not onerous. The second post as *seuir equitum Romanorum* ('Commissioner for the Roman knights') was purely ceremonial. It marked a distinct rise in his prospects: *seuiri* were selected personally by the emperor. In between came a period of service as military tribune in the wealthy and cultured province of Syria, with Domitian now installed as emperor after the early death of Titus in September 81 (8.14.7). The post was not obligatory, but had come to be expected from those of non-senatorial backgrounds.[27] The traces which this period of service left on Pliny's life are distinctive, as will become clear in the final chapter on Pliny's dealings with the Greek half of the empire.

Pliny may have already married for the first time. If the Iunius Pastor case does represent Pliny's debut in the Forum, then he had a mother-in-law in his nineteenth year. Early marriage was not uncommon for aspiring senators, who might marry well before the standard age of thirty.[28] The reasons for such youthful unions were firmly linked with career: marriage, if accompanied by children, offered material advantages in the race for senatorial promotion. The *ius liberorum* ('privilege of children') allowed a reduction in the minimum age at which one could stand for a post: one year per child for the first three children.[29] A contemporary, Calestrius Tiro, would produce enough children to beat Pliny to a senatorial post (7.16.2).[30] Whether or not Pliny did marry young, this first marriage did not produce offspring. His desire for children is underlined in a letter to Trajan written almost two decades after the first appearance in the Forum: 'All the greater is my longing for children, whom I wished to have even in the dismal period that is past, as you may judge from my two marriages. But the gods have decreed better . . . I preferred that I should become a father rather at this time' (10.2.2–3).[31] Pliny's last wife, Calpurnia, would become pregnant some years after this letter, only to miscarry (8.10–11). None of Pliny's marriages would produce children.

The identity of Pliny's first wife is uncertain: it is unclear whether the two marriages Pliny mentions were prior to, or include, the marriage to Calpurnia of Comum.[32] If Pliny was married three times, we know nothing whatever of the first wife's identity. If he married twice, then the first wife is the daughter of Pompeia Celerina. Pliny refers affectionately to this woman as mother-in-law even when married again after her daughter's death. He does not name the daughter. Pompeia Celerina owned numerous properties in Umbria and Etruria (1.4.1, 6.10.1) and was evidently wealthy (3.19.8). Marriage to her daughter cemented the ties that Pliny already had in Umbria thanks to inheritance of an estate from the Elder.[33] Celerina's daughter is not evoked by Pliny as a living figure in Rome. More will be said on her family in the chapter devoted to Umbria and the Laurentine shore.

Who kept Pliny company in the years before entry to the senate? Curiously, Pliny reveals actual details of early attachment only for those who failed to enter the senate or whose senatorial careers would eventually stall. Alongside days spent with schoolmate Voconius Romanus, Pliny reveals of another 'We served in the army together, and we were Caesar's quaestors together. He preceded me in the tribunate, in virtue of his having children, but I overtook him in the praetorship . . .' (7.16.1–2).[34] This is Calestrius Tiro, whose career would halt permanently at praetor.[35] Youthful acquaintance with Tacitus appears to have been admiring but distant: 'When I was still a very young man,' Pliny writes many years later, 'while you were already flourishing in glory and renown . . . I yearned to follow after you' (7.20.4).[36] Tacitus was four or five years older than Pliny and would make it to the consulship three years before him. He receives more letters from Pliny than any other correspondent.[37]

Pliny's first letter to Tacitus occurs in Book 1 of the *Letters*, usually dated to the years immediately after the assassination of Domitian, c. 96–8 C.E. Here Tacitus keeps company with a glittering cast of figures whose consulships surround

Pliny's own of 100 C.E., including Domitius Apollinaris (consul 97 C.E.), Sosius Senecio (99), Fabius Iustus (102), Minicius Fundanus (107), Pompeius Falco (108), and Catilius Severus (110).[38] Two of them, Apollinaris and Fundanus, are from the Transpadana.[39] Perhaps they give a flavour of Pliny's youthful milieu. Fundanus developed an interest in philosophy, although Pliny would later warn a friend *not* to urge the usual harsh philosophical commonplaces on Fundanus after the loss of a much-loved daughter just before her marriage (5.16.8–11). Like Fundanus, Sosius Senecio would become a close associate of Plutarch, who came to Rome on several occasions during the Flavian era.[40] Pliny's silence on Plutarch suggests *he* did not develop the interest in the Platonic philosophy that Fundanus and Senecio appear to have shared with Plutarch.[41]

Pliny adhered to his beloved rhetoric. His philosophically inclined friends were taught logic, physics, and ethics. Ethical teaching concentrated on the practical restraint of the emotions esteemed as a badge of honour by elites across the Greco-Roman world. 'Envy and benevolence, ambition and thirst for glory, love and hate, masculinity and shamelessness, excitability and unaffectedness, pretense': these were the common topics of discussion.[42] The saturation of his published works in the thought and language of Quintilian suggests that rather different issues may have filled Pliny's head. Rhetoric did not obviously encourage habits of critical or innovative thinking. Instead, the orator was trained 'to make educated guesses about the psychological make-up of his audience and their grasp of the material' at issue.[43] Was encomiastic, deliberative, or forensic oratory called for (Quint. *Inst.* 3.3.15)? In composing the speech, there were then five issues to consider: the 'discovery' (*inuentio*) of the appropriate material, then ordering, style, memorization, and delivery (Quint. *Inst.* 3.3.1). Finally, it was expected that the speech would consist of five essential parts: exordium, narration, division and partition, confirmation and refutation, and peroration. All of these elements were a matter of vigorous discussion and dispute amongst practitioners of the art.

Ideally, the ability to speak well went hand in hand with the ability to express oneself elegantly on the page. Pliny was already active here. He associates his return journey from military service in Syria with the composition on an Aegean island of some elegies (7.4.2–3). The 80s C.E. under Domitian were in fact a fertile time for literature: Martial, Statius, and the epic poets Valerius Flaccus and Silius Italicus were all active, most towards the end of the decade. Later, Quintilian would be asked to tutor the nephews of the emperor and receive the insignia of a consul.[44] Domitian himself had given up literary composition on his accession. The example of Nero did not encourage it. He emerged as a personal promoter of literary talent. Contests were initiated, including the annual Alban games at the imperial villa and the Capitoline games in Rome celebrated three times between 86 and 94 C.E., not to mention a lavish celebration of the century since Augustus'

Secular Games in 88.[45] A growing literary reputation, achieved in courtroom or in the public recitation of literary works, could only benefit Pliny's career. Such costly patronage of the arts worsened Domitian's financial position. Nerva and Trajan, financially more prudent, put no particular premium on the arts. A literary renaissance would be proclaimed, all the same, after Domitian's death.[46]

Quaestor: entry to the senate

Pressure was building on Domitian. Already in 85 C.E., there is a suggestion that Domitian was beginning to resort to prosecutions in Rome and exactions in the provinces to make up for financial shortfalls.[47] There was war on the empire's frontiers. The emperor insisted on conducting campaigns in person: military prowess was the supreme imperial virtue. Domitian led his troops in Germany and on the Danube four times between 83 and 92 C.E.[48] Decades later, contemporaries offered conflicting accounts of the decisive change in Domitian's rule. Suetonius highlights a moment before 89, when Domitian became 'rapacious through need, cruel through fear' (*Dom.* 3.2), and emphasizes the rebellion in that year of the legionary commander Antonius Saturninus in Germany as the occasion on which Domitian became 'even more cruel' (*Dom.* 10.5).[49] Senatorial writers like Tacitus and Pliny pointed to 93–4, the year when Domitian turned decisively against their class.[50] But the enforced suicide and execution of leading men became increasingly common as the 80s wore on. Was political life reverting to the last years of Nero's reign?[51]

It was in this atmosphere that Pliny finally entered the senate with election to the office of quaestor in the late 80s C.E. Precisely when does matter. Like his contemporaries, Pliny was obsessed with acquiring posts at the minimum legal age: the earlier the achievement, the greater the prestige and promise. Pliny lets drop the information that he reached both consulship and a prestigious priesthood several years before his fellow new man Cicero (4.8.5). The normal minimum age for the quaestorship was a man's twenty-fifth year. Pliny does not let it be known he became quaestor *suo anno* ('in his [exact] year'): he may have been a late starter, entering the senate in 89 or 90 C.E., three years after the minimum age. Perhaps his lack of senatorial family had counted against him. Or he had been ill—touched in some way by the plague or its aftermath.[52] What is clear is that the type of quaestorship acquired by Pliny points to an emphatic rise in his stock. Elections were delegated to the senate, and Pliny evokes on several occasions the tension around canvassing and election day itself (2.9, 3.20, 4.15, 6.6, 6.19).[53] He exaggerates. Care had been taken to match the number of pre-senatorial posts in any one year to the twenty quaestorships available annually. Pliny himself was assured of election: not only was he a candidate supported by the emperor, but he joined Calestrius Tiro in being one of only two quaestors picked out for formal attachment to the person of the emperor (7.16.1).[54] It would be their task to read out the emperor's speeches or letters to the senate:[55] an 'uncomfortable apprenticeship in the arts and hypocrisies of public life', in Syme's estimate.[56] This 'distinction seldom awaited a man of equestrian parentage, being the preserve of patricians or sons of consuls', Syme adds elsewhere; 'For companions the Caesars liked men endowed with literary or social accomplishments'.[57] The devotion to *studia*, evident already at Vesuvius, had paid off.

After this prestigious entry into the senate, Pliny soon acquired the post of tribune of the plebs.[58] (The Stoic Epictetus scornfully imagines a scene of domestic rejoicing on just such an occasion: 'his slaves kiss his hands. He arrives home to find lamps being lit'.[59]) He was then granted by Domitian a reduction of the standard interval that others had to endure before seeking election as praetor (7.16.2). Pliny reached the praetorship in the turbulent years of 93 or 94 C.E.[60] His troubles begin here.

Pliny the 'collaborator': modern biographical imperatives

The period of Pliny's praetorship coincides with the moment when Domitian turned on the senatorial class with a series of treason trials and executions. Around the time of these events, Pliny appears to have accepted from the emperor a post at Rome's military treasury: an employment known only from inscriptions, not once mentioned in the *Letters*. Pliny does claim proximity to the executed, insists his own life was in danger after the executions (3.11.3), and that as praetor he still undertook a risky visit to one of the philosophers who had been banished from Rome at the time (3.11.2).[61] Elsewhere he insists that, while his career advanced under Domitian, at least until the emperor 'confessed his hatred of good men', thereafter he 'halted', preferring the 'longer route' (*Paneg.* 95.2–4).[62] After the assassination of the emperor in 96 C.E., Pliny adds, documents laying information against Pliny were found on the emperor's desk (7.27.14). Their source, Pliny assures us, was the very man who had initiated the executions.[63]

Pliny's *record* of continuing imperial favour is somewhat at odds with his *commentary*, which asserts a stalled career and personal peril, and implies covert opposition to Domitian. Pliny himself would no doubt choose the consulship achieved under the 'good' emperor Trajan as the main focus of his biography: the broad narrative of the *Letters* begins just a few years prior to the surmounting of this pinnacle. He might be disappointed to learn that modern critics have been far more interested in his record during the last years of Domitian. Each generation creates the biographies that it needs. As biographer Hermione Lee remarks, Virginia Woolf has successively taken on the guise of 'a difficult modernist preoccupied with questions of form, or comedian of manners, or neurotic high-brow aesthete, or inventive fantasist, or pernicious snob, or Marxist feminist, or historian of women's lives, or victim of abuse, or lesbian heroine, or cultural analyst.[64] Pliny is hardly so protean. Modern study of Pliny, nevertheless, finds the question of his 'collaboration' with a corrupt and tyrannical regime of over-whelming significance. A recent biography of Pliny arraigns him on this very question: 'If Pliny were on trial, what would our verdict be?'[65] There is not much interest in the topic in lives of Pliny from earlier centuries. Cattaneo (1506) glides over Pliny's Domitianic record in a single sentence and gives the bulk of his at-tention to Pliny's friends, family and literary achievements. This pattern is es-sentially replicated in Cellarius (1693), who takes additional detailed interest in the question whether Pliny converted to Christianity on his return from Pontus-Bithynia. Masson (1709) is greatly concerned with the exact year of Pliny's prae-torship (93 C.E.), skips straight to 96 C.E., and accepts without question Pliny's narrative of a halt in his career.[66] Mommsen largely follows suit, remarking only that Pliny's prefecture of the military treasury demonstrates the timeless ability of lesser players in great events to 'move forward unhindered'.[67]

Serious doubts about Pliny's honesty and political integrity surfaced with urgency for the first time just after the First World War, in Germany. In 1919 Walter Otto re-examined Pliny's career in 94–6 C.E. and declared his claims to have opposed the monstrous Domitian as 'humanly highly unpleasant'.[68] This view gained momentum after the Second World War, driven along by Sir Ronald Syme, and continues to the present day.[69] The reasons for the resonance of an individual's record under tyranny scarcely need spelling out. The de-Nazification of Germany in the mid-twentieth century, the fate of citizens in post-Soviet states, and the truth and reconciliation committees that proliferate after civil op-pression or war—all have served to keep the issue topical in a way that Mommsen could scarcely have anticipated. In the estimate of one recent German historian, Pliny was a 'fellow traveller', a man 'who would have made a career under any to-talitarian and despotic regime'.[70] What, then, is the relationship between Pliny's apparent record and his commentary on it? The problems faced in answering this question are highly technical.[71] The answers are involved, messy, and revealing.

The trial of Baebius Massa

Domitian was absent from Rome for much of 92 C.E., conducting campaigns against the Sarmatae and Suebi on the Danube.[72] Iunius Arulenus Rusticus, brother of Pliny's friend Iunius Mauricus, and member of a family linked to others in a dynasty of opposition to imperial houses, accepted a consulship in that year from Domitian. Rusticus' career had suffered a long interval since his praetorship of 69 C.E.: perhaps an association with Thrasea Paetus had retarded him. Paetus had been a principled critic of the imperial regime under Nero. Rusticus had tried to aid him as tribune in the year of Paetus' execution by the emperor in 66 C.E., and would later write Paetus' biography (Tac. *Agr.* 2.1). In this biography Rusticus appears also to have praised Helvidius Priscus the Elder (Suet. *Dom.* 10.3), a son-in-law of Paetus who would be executed by Vespasian c. 74 C.E. for persistent abuse and lack of respect (Suet. *Vesp.* 15). That Domitian was willing to offer a consulship, and Rusticus willing to accept it, might seem to indicate a willingness on both sides to move on. A personal anecdote told by Plutarch, which may belong to this period, conjures a more ominous atmosphere. During a lecture given by Plutarch in Rome, a soldier entered the auditorium to present Rusticus with a letter from Domitian. Plutarch paused to give Rusticus a chance to read the letter, but 'he refused and did not break the seal until I had finished my lecture and the audience had dispersed. . . . everyone admired the dignity of the man' (Plut. *Mor.* 522e).[73] By the end of the year after his consulship, or not long after, Rusticus would be executed.

The chain of events which led to this execution has some missing links. The beginning is clear, and it involves the first of two significant legal actions by Pliny in the senate mentioned earlier. Baebius Massa, senatorial governor of Baetica in Spain, was accused of the serious crime of 'aggravated extortion' during his term in office (7.33).[74] A lengthy investigation into the charges began perhaps in late 92 C.E., and Massa's formal trial took place in the last months of 93 C.E. or even slightly later.[75] Pliny himself was handed the prestigious task of prosecution: the first such role assigned to him and an indication of the esteem in which his courtroom talents were already held. Trials of corrupt governors were *not* show trials. The senate often proved reluctant to convict one of its own.[76] The *dignitas* of the defendant, as hinted earlier, might count for more than mere evidence. Such trials, if admitted by the presiding consuls to the senate, were nevertheless taken very seriously.

Pliny's co-prosecutor was the Baetican senator Herennius Senecio.[77] The latter had declined promotion beyond the office of quaestor: a dangerous echo of Helvidius Priscus, who had refused from Nero advancement beyond tribune of the plebs. In a long letter sent around fifteen years later to Tacitus, Pliny tells the story of the trial for inclusion in his friend's *Histories*, concentrating particularly on the aftermath (7.33). The likely sequence of the actual court action can be reconstructed from other accounts.[78] Trials took place before the senate in full session. The venue was usually the Curia Iulia in the Forum Romanum, where in theory up to six hundred senators might be present.[79] After a reading of the charges and comment from the president of the court or the emperor, the prosecution offered its complete case first, followed by the case for the defence. Occasionally, the speeches of the two co-prosecutors might alternate with speeches for the defence.[80] Either arrangement maximized the impact of persuasive eloquence. Only then was written or oral evidence called for, with witnesses open to cross-examination. It was the convention that in trials of accused governors, only the prosecution had the right to summon witnesses from the province.[81] The whole process lasted several days, not including adjournments. At the conclusion of the trial, verdicts were requested from the assembled senators.

Each prosecutor was normally allotted three hours for his speech, although in complicated cases four to five hours or even more might be allotted.[82] The physical demands were considerable. In a later case of provincial corruption heard before the senate, Pliny tells how 'the emperor . . . frequently advised my freedman, who stood behind me, that I should spare my voice and my strength, whenever he thought I was exerting myself with greater vehemence than my delicate frame might be able to bear' (2.11.15).[83] All the training provided by Quintilian on arrangement, delivery, and memory of the points to be developed came into play here. A vigorous and fulsome style would count for much. Some of Pliny's more forceful letters may contain an echo of his favoured courtroom mode.[84]

The prosecution of Massa was successful. Whatever the aftermath of the case, the demonstration of effective public oratory before the senate, by one who had only just reached the status of praetor or praetor designate, can only have impressed Pliny's peers and provided a significant boost to his career and status. The gratitude of the citizens of Baetica towards their new patron was also guaranteed (3.4.2–4).[85]

For the guilty defendant, 'relegation' from Rome and repayment of funds to the Baeticans was the likely punishment. Senecio, evidently worried that Massa might engineer a reduction in his financial worth, approached the consuls. He was now open to counter-attack.[86] Massa accused Senecio of exceeding his duty to Baetica: a serious charge, *impietas*, perhaps equivalent to *maiestas* or treason (7.33.7).[87] In Pliny's view, his own omission from Massa's new charge implied the arraignment of Pliny on *praevaricatio* or 'collusion'. His quick-witted declaration of this fact earned a written congratulation from the future emperor Nerva, then perhaps serving in Domitian's inner circle. Massa's manoeuvre, it appears, failed.[88]

Treason trials

What happened next is mysterious and is narrated in detail by no author. Not long after the Massa action, Senecio is found on trial for his life. The charge was a biography of the same Helvidius whom Rusticus had praised (Tac. *Agr.* 2.1).

Included in the indictment was Senecio's willful refusal to pursue the honours of the *cursus honorum*.[89] Had the attempted action against Massa raised the quaestor to unhelpful prominence? Now, somehow, the net widened far beyond Senecio. Arulenus Rusticus was arraigned for his writings on Thrasea Paetus and Helvidius Priscus (Tac. *Agr.* 2.1, Suet. *Dom.* 10.3). Perhaps a little later, Helvidius the Younger, son of the subject of Rusticus's writings and consul as recently as 87 C.E., was brought to trial for *his* writings: 'in a farce composed for the stage [Helvidius] had under the characters of Paris and Oenone censured Domitian's divorce from his wife' (Suet. *Dom.* 10.4).[90] The literary efforts of Helvidius, and perhaps of all three, may not have been very recent. The prosecutors were raking up what they could.[91] Peripherally involved in the onslaught was one Publicius Certus: a name that will recur in Pliny's story after the assassination of Domitian.

The results were disastrous: a spate of executions and the public burning of the offending works in the Forum itself (Tac. *Agr.* 2.1). The sentences were passed by the senate. Tacitus admits the guilt of his class:

> Our hands it was that dragged Helvidius to his dungeon; it was we who were [put to shame] by the look which Mauricus and Rusticus gave, we who were soaked by the innocent blood of Senecio. Nero after all withdrew his eyes, nor contemplated the crimes he authorized. Under Domitian it was no small part of our sufferings that we saw him and were seen by him.[92]
>
> Tacitus, *Agricola* 45.1–2

What Tacitus does not say is that he himself was likely absent from Rome at the time: an admission of senatorial complicity is made, but where it is understood that its author is *de facto* excluded.[93] A senator could hardly make a confession of guilt under any other terms. The three authors were executed without choice as to the manner of their deaths. Mauricus was exiled, along with several female members of the dynasties of imperial opposition. For good measure, an edict ejected philosophers first from Rome, then more generally from Italy (Tac. *Agr* 2.2, Suet. *Dom.* 10.3). The implication was that noxious philosophy had inspired the executed senators.[94] Rhetoric was a worthier pursuit, as the Flavian public funding of Quintilian had confirmed.[95] In fact, it is more likely that the trials resulted from feuds between competing factions in the senate.[96] The award of a consulship to Rusticus had raised to apparent immunity a grouping of senators known for their disaffection from the imperial house. Their rivals were perhaps provoked into open enmity. No one, not even a recent consul, was untouchable.

Such incidents, repeated throughout Rome's history under the emperors, were shocking and painful for the senators and families involved. It is worth adding, briefly, that they also tend to obscure the bigger picture. So far from being *victims* of the imperial system, senators were its prime beneficiaries. The senate took for itself a range of legislative, electoral, and judicial powers that, under the republic, had once belonged to the people. Senators continued to enjoy a monopoly of the highest offices of state and used these to increase their already considerable wealth at the expense of less fortunate others.[97]

The treason trials and Pliny's record

Pliny makes it clear that he was praetor at a moment after the treason trials (3.11). It is known the prosecutions postdated the death of Tacitus' father-in-law Agricola in August 93 C.E. (Tac. *Agr.* 44.1, 45.1–2). By how much is not clear. Late 93 or 94 C.E. seem the obvious dates for the trials. Pliny then likely held his praetorship either in 93 or 94: precisely during or immediately after the months when his friends were on trial for their lives. The coincidence in time has partly motivated modern attempts to move his praetorship back a few years, as if Pliny's integrity were under threat.[98] Praetors were officially designated in mid-January, however, a full year before they entered office on the first of January of the next year.[99] Pliny was designated in either January 92 or January 93 C.E.: well before the treason trials had started. Nor could the prosecutions have been easily antic-ipated: Rusticus will not have expected to be on trial for his life so soon after a consulship. Even had Pliny been gifted with preternatural foresight, it was dan-gerous to refuse promotion. Those who had refused honours, such as Priscus or Senecio, came from a lineage whose family business was dissidence, shared between interrelated dynasties and sustained within the senate over genera-tions.[100] Pliny had only Flavian loyalists in a family tree that, among equestrians from distant Comum, displayed one faithful servant who had not even achieved entry into the senate.[101] Resignation *during* a praetorship was hardly an option. Nor is Pliny concealing his involvement, as has sometimes been thought, as praetor either in the executions of the condemned or the burning of their works. Senatorial trials were not part of the jurisdiction of praetors, and sentences were instructed by and contracted to others.[102] He shared with his six hundred fellow senators the guilt of complicity described by Tacitus and acknowledged in the *Letters* (8.14.9).[103]

A reign of terror began—at least in the memory of senators. Tacitus asserts it was Agricola's good fortune not 'to see the Senate-house besieged, the Senate surrounded by armed men, and in the same carnage so many consulars butch-ered, the flight and exile of so many honourable women' (*Agr.* 45.1).[104] This is the gloomy context for the most significant act of 'resistance' that Pliny can dig up for later readers in the happier age of Trajan: a visit to a philosopher friend from Syrian days in Rome's suburbs. Philosophers had evidently been banned from the city itself, but the date for their exile from Italy had not yet passed:[105]

... after the banishment of philosophers from Rome, I went to see Artemidorus at his house in the suburbs, and what made the thing more subject to remark (in other words more dangerous), was the fact that I was praetor at the time. I also advanced to him without interest (though I had to borrow it myself) a considerable sum of money, which he required for the purpose of paying debts contracted under the most honourable circumstances—while some of his great and wealthy friends were humming and hawing over it. And I did this when seven of my friends had either been put to death or banished—Senecio, Rusticus and Helvidius had been put to death; Mauricus, Gratilla, Arria and Fannia had been banished—and when scorched by so many thunderbolts falling around me, I prophesied from certain sure signs that the same destruction was awaiting me.[106]

Letters 3.11.2–3

The uncompromising philosopher Epictetus would suffer ejection in the same event, as perhaps also would Plutarch.[107] Pliny's journey to an unwelcome subversive will hardly have gone unnoticed. He does not need to tell a Roman correspondent what it meant to travel as praetor on public or private business: an entourage of six lictors, each holding the *fasces*.[108] The Roman equivalent of a motorcade. 'A brave deed (duly paraded)', in the judgement of Christopher Whitton; 'but—of course—a scrupulously legal one'.[109] Spirited behaviour and loyalty to old friends within statutory limits: an advance on the youthful reserve of 79 C.E. Heroism was for aristocrats, the descendants of consuls.

Pliny clearly knew some of the condemned and exiled well, not least his coprosecutor Senecio.[110] Regional fellow feeling perhaps provided an entrée. The executed Rusticus and his brother the exiled Mauricus appear to have been from northern Italy, as Thrasea Paetus had been.[111] It was on behalf of Mauricus that Pliny returned to school, after the return of the exiles under Nerva, to find a teacher for the children of Rusticus.[112] An origin in the Transpadana was no guarantee of disaffection from the regime. Pliny attributes to Mauricus a revealing anecdote about the notorious Domitianic 'denouncer' and fellow northerner Catullus Messalinus.[113] While dining with the new emperor Nerva, Mauricus was asked 'What do we think would have happened to [Catullus Messalinus] if he were still living?' Mauricus replied immediately: *nobiscum cenaret*, 'he would be dining with us' (4.22.6). The anecdote encapsulates the politics of the era.

Pliny also takes care to drop sustained hints at long friendships with Arria, wife of Paetus, and her daughter Fannia, wife of Helvidius the Elder.[114] They were part of a wider network of dissident upper-class women of whom he claimed knowledge or connection. Strikingly, Pliny asserts that the behaviour of these women is worthy of emulation by both sexes at Rome (7.19.7).[115] A friendship with the executed Helvidius the Younger may have been less secure.[116] Pliny can say only that 'there was an *amicitia* between myself and Helvidius, as far as *amicitia* was possible with one who, through dread of the times, hid in seclusion his great name' (9.13.3).[117] Pliny retrospectively overplays this relationship, in pursuit of a good image in front of fellow senators. Many no doubt understood, and sympathized.[118]

Prefect of the military treasury

It is Pliny's next posting at the military treasury, not his praetorship, that is a threat to his honesty. Pliny's account of it allows evaluation of a character under pressure: a pressure more intense in the modern world that in the ancient. Pliny does not conceal the post, since it is recorded on two inscriptions found in northern Italy, one of which Pliny likely authored himself.[119] It does not appear in his published works. Perhaps, like other postings in his career, it was not worth mentioning.[120] This three-year praetorian office was in the gift of the emperor, but decidedly unglamorous, overseeing inheritance and sales taxes and the maintenance of army veterans.[121] It did not guarantee a consulship. That promise belonged to the prefecture of the treasury of Saturn: a post Pliny would gain under Nerva. Pliny's own record in the *Panegyricus* points to a discomfort with the military prefecture. In the peroration to this speech of thanks to Trajan, Pliny lists all the recent honours of his career: prefect of the treasury of Saturn (*Paneg.* 90.6–91.1, 92.1), then tribune, praetor, services as senatorial advocate, and consul (*Paneg.* 95.1–2). The single omission from this overview of his career since entry into the senate is the military treasury post. The resonant silence points to a lingering sensitivity, and offers some confirmation, among other considerations, of the dating of the post. The context in the *Panegyricus* is precisely a celebration of the confidence placed in Pliny by Nerva and Trajan, as evidenced in his career and recent promotion from Saturnian treasury to consulship. Had Nerva also appointed Pliny to the military treasury, the closing paragraphs of the *Panegyricus* would hardly have omitted this fact.[122]

Pliny's good name, some think, might be saved if it was Nerva who appointed him to the military treasury after Domitian's reign of terror.[123] He is not a villain for accepting the post from Domitian. Who was he to refuse promotion from the emperor?[124] His frequent claims to have been hated by Domitian or to have lived in fear of him, and the revelation that he was denounced before the emperor (7.27.12–14), are as unprovable as they are irrefutable.[125] They are not incompatible with holding office under a tyrannical regime. The real problem, appropriately for a leading courtroom performer, lies in Pliny's words. At the end of the *Panegyricus* he declares:

si, cursu quodam prouectus ab illo insidiosissimo principe, antequam profiteretur odium bonorum, postquam professus est substiti <et>, cum uiderem, quae ad honores compendia paterent, longius iter malui.

If, having been advanced at something of a pace by that most treacherous emperor, before he confessed his hatred of good men, I halted once he had confessed it and I preferred, when I saw what shortcuts to magistracies lay open, the longer route.[126]

Paneg. 95.3–4

Pliny's implicit claim to have 'halted' in his career after the praetorship is technically correct. There was a distinction between magistracies on the *cursus honorum*, such as praetor and consul, and lesser administrative offices like the military treasury post. It would be another six or seven years until Pliny's consulship. The additional assertion that Pliny preferred 'the longer route' begs questions. Pliny could be taken to imply that he preferred a mundane treasury posting with other similar offices in prospect: a 'longer route'. The alternative 'short cut' was an accelerated run to the consulship—presumably through acting as one of Domitian's agents in the final years of his reign. The likelihood of the latter is impossible to prove. As it was, he would reach the consulship in a time well under the decade between praetor and consul that was normal for all except patricians.[127] Above all, in the analysis of Christopher Whitton, Pliny is guilty of failing to spell the matter out. The prefecture of the military treasury 'goes forgotten, and the inference is all too easy that he held no post at all. Yet if Pliny had really been able in the *Panegyricus* to brandish several years without office, would he have settled for so understated a claim as *longius iter malui*?' He adds, incisively: 'Admire or condemn Pliny's careful footwork as you please: tendentious, yes; dishonest, not quite. . . . Take Pliny's word at your peril. But he will not be caught lying'.[128]

Under pressure, Pliny plays with words. Today, to be convicted of toying with meaning or massaging a record under a despotic regime means destruction of personal reputation. Domitian's government was not Soviet Russia or Nazi Germany: no high empire regime had the means to be totalitarian. Domitian's court resembles rather the brilliant but turbulent Florentine rule of Lorenzo de Medici (1449–1492) or the cultured and increasingly tyrannical reign of England's Henry VIII. Mere survival might matter more than rectitude. Augustine was hostile to rhetoric's propensity to deceive. By the standards of his own times, did Pliny betray Quintilian's ideal of *uir bonus dicendi peritus*? The answer may be a qualified 'yes'. Pliny, however, could hardly admit wrong or regret and promise to do better next time: his was the responsibility to 'get it right first time', or at least claim that he had done so.[129] Tacitus is a case in point. His *Histories* begin with the declaration: 'That my standing was begun by Vespasian, developed by Titus, and advanced some way by Domitian, I should not deny' (*Hist.* 1.1.3).[130] Tacitus is sparing with details, and avoids full disclosure. He had not been just praetor under Domitian. The year of his consulship (97 C.E.) would coincide with Nerva's only full year as emperor. Tacitus had accepted designation from Domitian as consul in the previous year, some months before the tyrant was assassinated.[131] It was better not to spell the matter out.

Pliny's accelerated promotion to the consulship suggests his fellow senators had fewer problems with Pliny's version of his record. And no wonder. Both Nerva and Trajan himself had well-founded reputations as Domitianic loyalists: Trajan would not have been trusted with the legions of Germania and Pannonia in the last years of Domitian under any other circumstances.[132] It is only when Trajan's reign had been well established that Pliny would look back and reflect pessimistically on the Domitianic senate and his complicity in it:

> We also had a view of the senate, but a cowering and speechless senate, at a time when it was dangerous to speak according to one's wishes and vile to speak against them. What could be learnt from such a period? And what could be the advantage of learning? When the senate was summoned either to fall into a profound sleep or to sanction some vile crime, and, detained for a joke or its own humiliation, pronounced decisions which were never serious, though oftentimes sad. These same evils we witnessed and endured for many years after we had ourselves become senators and sharers in them, by which our intellects were permanently dulled, broken and bruised.[133]
>
> *Letters* 8.14.8–9

The permanent damage to the senate might not make encouraging reading for Trajan.

A new era

The new era began with the violent death in September 96 C.E. of the emperor in a palace conspiracy fronted by freedmen of the imperial house and with the likely support of powerful figures among Domitian's friends.[134] The reaction was mixed.[135] The army, whose pay Domitian had raised to his own ruin, was angered and demanded revenge. The people remained indifferent. Senators celebrated: they 'raced to fill the House, where they did not refrain from assailing the dead emperor with the most insulting and stinging kind of outcries. They even had ladders brought and shields and images torn down before their eyes and dashed upon the ground; finally, they passed a decree that his inscriptions should everywhere be erased, and all record of him obliterated' (Suet. *Dom.*

23.1).[136] This last measure was convenient to all who had been promoted under Domitian: Pliny need not now inscribe in stone the name of the Caesar to whom he had been *quaestor*.[137] How Pliny felt at the time of the assassination, he does not tell us. He focuses instead on the reaction of an alleged agent of Domitian, M. Aquillius Regulus:

> Since the death of Domitian, have you ever seen anyone more cowed and abject than Marcus Regulus—under whom he perpetrated infamies as great as under Nero, though with more concealment? He began to fear that I was angry with him; and he was not mistaken, for I *was* angry. He had fostered the dangers which threatened Arulenus Rusticus, and so rejoiced in his death that he recited and published a book in which he insulted Rusticus...[138]
>
> *Letters* 1.5.1–2

Regulus approached one of Pliny's mentors, the distinguished elderly consular Vestricius Spurinna, to act as intermediary for reconciliation. Spurinna and Pliny met in the Portico of Livia on the Esquiline hill, midway between their houses. Pliny insisted that he could do nothing: 'I am waiting for Mauricus' (1.5.10)—to return from exile.[139]

If Pliny ever seriously thought of prosecuting Regulus, nothing came of it. The whole is overdone. Regulus was a trivial delinquent, one who may have been a willing prosecutor of imperial victims under Nero, but whose actual crimes under Domitian not even Pliny can name, beyond the writing of a defamatory pamphlet. Pliny's enmity can only have been sharpened by Regulus' position as leading light of the Centumviral court under Domitian.[140] Ten years hence Pliny would write a vengefully magnanimous tribute to his rival: Regulus is missed in the lawcourts 'because he held our profession in honour' (6.2.2); but 'he did well to die, and would have done better if he had died sooner' (6.2.4).[141] Pliny soon had a better idea: 'during the first few days of restored liberty, every one of his own account had been at once impeaching and crushing his own private enemies (at least the smaller ones) with a confused and turbulent clamour. I deemed it a more temperate and more courageous course to attack a monstrous criminal' (9.13.4).[142] He was determined to avenge the death of Helvidius the Younger, despite the lack of a well-developed relationship with him in Domitianic days. Pliny approached his widow and asked her to inform Helvidius' stepmother, Fannia, and Fannia's mother Arria. They did not dissent (9.13.4). The target was Publicius Certus, a praetorian senator who had gained the Saturnian prefecture and was destined for the consulship (9.13.11). The role of Certus in the death of Helvidius is quite unclear:[143] the senate was not a public court, Certus cannot have acted as prosecutor. Did he propose the sentence? It is hard to believe that a praetorian played more than a minor role in the factional infighting that likely caused Helvidius' death. As often in the aftermath of assassination of tyrants or revolutions, the main offenders suffer few consequences, their agents bear the brunt of the attack, and the compromised do the attacking. Consuls and military men were beyond Pliny's reach.

Pliny's second significant legal action in the senate is now at hand. He could not instigate a formal trial of Certus single-handedly.[144] Pliny's best hope was to persuade fellow senators to petition the emperor for legal action. First, Pliny had to gain permission to speak 'out of order' (*extra ordinem*), prior to the main business of the session of the senate. He takes up the story, over a decade after the event, for the benefit of a young aristocratic protégé who has been reading the speech which Pliny later wrote up as a record of his intervention in the senate.[145] The event was already receding into history, and the young protégé needed to understand the context in which the speech was given. The scene in the Curia Iulia is vividly recreated:

> When I began to touch on the charge, and to hint at a person to be accused (without naming him), there were shouts from all sides. One said 'Tell us who is the object of this irregular attack'. Another, 'Who can be charged before notice is served?'. A third, 'Spare us who survive!'[146]
>
> *Letters* 9.13.7–8

A paranoid senate, if this is accurate reporting by Pliny; one conscious that 'our hands it was that dragged Helvidius to his dungeon'. What better way for Pliny to establish distance from his shared compliance in the execution than by attacking a man more directly implicated? Permission to speak *extra ordinem* was refused: Pliny was told he must wait until the conclusion of the main business before re-opening the affair (9.13.9). He had, quite uncharacteristically, failed to consult his then still-living patron Corellius Rufus in advance. The old man was too habitually cautious (9.13.6).[147] Worse was to follow. Pliny was approached by one consular who made dark allusions to the danger of making oneself known in this manner to future emperors (9.13.10). The current emperor Nerva was already an elderly man, and childless. Another insisted that Certus had powerful backers, including someone at the head of a powerful army in the east, about whom rumours were circulating in the uncertainty of Nerva's tenure (9.13.11).[148]

Pliny's proposal for a petition to the emperor was taken up by other senators as their turn came to speak on the main business of the session, in order of seniority.[149] Finally, it was the turn of the praetorian senators to speak, and Pliny had his chance to reply to the points made by the previous supportive or oppositional speakers (9.13.18). After further uproar, the consul called for a division. Pliny presents the result to his young correspondent as a triumph both for himself and for a senate now freed from its previous reputation for harshness towards others and leniency towards its own (9.13.21). His phrasing requires, once more, careful scrutiny: 'Caesar, it is true, did not send back to the senate any communication on Certus; nevertheless, I obtained what I had aimed at. For the colleague of Certus got the consulship, and Certus himself was superseded' (9.13.22–3).[150] The motion for a petition was passed by the senate. Then Nerva quietly let the matter drop. No further action was taken against Certus. Such characteristic behaviour was one of Nerva's attractions to those who had recently installed him as emperor: moderate and consensualist by nature, Nerva was not likely to instigate a witch-hunt against those members of the senate who, like himself, had served Domitian with apparent loyalty.[151] Pliny insists he got what he wanted: Certus did not rise to the consulship which his tenure as the prefecture of Saturn had marked him out for.[152] Not long after, Certus, who had anyway been ill and absent from the senate, passed away (9.13.24–5). A qualified triumph for Pliny. It may be wondered how much satisfaction the stalled career of a minor player gave to the families of the executed.

One of Pliny's motives for attacking Certus was the 'opportunity... for bringing oneself to notice' (9.13.2).[153] He states it openly, expectant not of modern condemnation of self-interest, but of acceptance within a long-standing elite tradition of making a name through high-profile prosecution. Pliny was now in his mid-thirties, his eyes fixed on the consulship. Cicero had made *his* name with a spectacular success over Verres, corrupt governor of Sicily, at around the same age. Pliny has no need to explain to his addressee the success of the aim to bring himself to notice: it was a matter of public knowledge. Certus was 'superseded' at the Saturnian treasury—by Pliny himself: Pliny was now a safe bet for the consulship.[154] The Saturnian posting would bring a considerably heavier workload than its military treasury predecessor, and elicit some not entirely disingenuous complaints from the rising Pliny (1.10.9–11).[155] He would spend his time here interpreting complex rules on inheritance tax and overseeing funds for the administration of Italy and the provinces assigned to senators.[156]

A new emperor, deaths, remarriage: 97–99 C.E.

Pliny was appointed to the Saturnian treasury by Nerva and Trajan conjointly (10.3a.1, 10.8.3): events had compelled that Trajan be adopted as co-regent in autumn 97 C.E, just a year after Nerva's installation as emperor. In October 97 the Praetorian Guard, perhaps already foiled in an attempt to replace Nerva with their own candidate, rioted in the city. They demanded the execution of Domitian's assassins, and got their way. In the aftermath the elderly and increasingly impotent Nerva was forced to adopt Trajan as his partner and successor.[157] It was a coup in all but name.[158] Trajan's succession was secured largely on the brute fact that he controlled the legions on the Rhine: the greatest concentration of military resources close to Rome. The real threat of civil war was averted.

Later in the autumn Tacitus, now consul, delivered in Rome the funeral oration for Pliny's patron Verginius Rufus (2.1.6). He had died after a fall while rehearsing a speech of thanks for his third consulship (2.1.5). Verginius had been recalled to office three decades after his ambivalent role in the insurrection against Nero and great refusal of imperial power.[159] Perhaps this was a suitable occasion for Tacitus to draw a contrast between the violence which had so tragically torn the Roman world apart in 68–9 C.E., and a repeat of the same crisis now thankfully averted by the adoption of Trajan.[160] In January 98, Nerva died, perhaps fortunately. The new emperor stayed away from Rome and would not enter the capital until the autumn of the next year (99 CE). Trajan had a mission: to tour the frontiers, where the bulk of the military was stationed, and ensure the loyalty of his generals and their men. Like others of his class, Pliny preferred an emperor who was not too close to his generals, one who shared the cultural and literary interests of some in the senate. They would take care to praise Trajan for his *ciuilitas*, his qualities as a citizen (*ciuis*), in hopes of discouraging too great an emphasis on the army.[161]

There were more deaths. Another of Pliny's elderly patrons, Corellius Rufus, passed away c. 97 C.E. (1.12).[162] Pliny himself suffered a life-threatening illness (10.5).[163] We are in fact unusually well informed about Pliny's domestic life in these years: the earliest of the *Letters* date from this period. It was only now that senators could speak and write freely. Or so they said. A somewhat questionable general 'rebirth' of literature was offered as further proof.[164] Thanks to this new freedom of expression, Pliny is able to tell us how he fills his time with the pleasantries of elite life: coming of age ceremonies, betrothals, witnessing of wills, appearances as a witness in court, and consultations on behalf of friends (1.9.2). One other death in the family Pliny might have been expected to say more about is that of his wife, the daughter of Pompeia Celerina. She passed away while Pliny was planning his attack in the senate on Certus. He does not mention the fact until around a decade later (9.13.4).[165] Nor does Pliny acknowledge his remarriage to Calpurnia soon after, probably in 97–8 C.E. Mention of her is delayed until c. 104 C.E. (4.1). Legislation encouraged swift remarriage amongst senators.[166] The union with Calpurnia no doubt also improved Pliny's chances of gaining the 'privilege of three children' (*ius trium liberorum*), acquired around this time from Trajan (10.2). This privilege, granted as a mark of honour to those with less than three children (or none), improved the ability of its holder to inherit. There will be more to say about Calpurnia in Chapter 7, and about the library and alimentary scheme funded in this same period by Pliny in their shared hometown of Comum.

Pliny's consulship

Following his success in prosecuting Baebius Massa under Domitian, further commissions to prosecute corrupt governors followed under Trajan. Pliny was invited to undertake cases against Marius Priscus governor of Africa,[167] and against another governor of Baetica, Caecilius Classicus.[168]

The consulship beckoned. Pliny takes up the story for Trajan's benefit: 'We had not yet completed our second year in an exacting and important office when you offered us the consulate, and this you did, noblest of princes and most valorous of emperors in the field, so that to its supreme honour might be added the further distinction of rapid promotion' (*Paneg.* 91.1).[169] Before Pliny and his colleague Cornutus Tertullus had completed a second year at the treasury of Saturn, they were appointed by Trajan to consulships. The exemption of the pair from the normal interval of a year between offices is valued as a public sign that no cloud hangs over Pliny.[170] He had reached the consulship at the age of 38 or 39, before the average age of 42, and certainly well before the age of the considerably older Cornutus Tertullus (5.14.5).[171] It gave him particular pleasure that he reached the consulship earlier than Cicero (4.8.5). He was the first son of Comum to reach the summit of the *cursus honorum,* and immediately gave instructions for an inscription to be set up in the most important temple of his hometown (3.6).[172] Epictetus reflects on the true cost of what it would take any man to reach this pinnacle: 'If you want to be consul, you must stay up at night, rush this way and that, kiss men's hands, rot away at other men's doors, say and do much that is not suitable for a free man, send presents to many people . . . And what is the result of all this? Twelve bundles of rods . . .' (Arr. *Epict. diss.* 4.10.20–1).[173]

Trajan held his third consulship in the position of honour at the start of the same year, 100 C.E. (*Paneg.* 92.2). Pliny had to wait until September–October for his 'suffect' (successor) consulship.[174] When he rose to give his customary speech of thanks to the emperor for the honour, the senate was half-full, at best. September was a traditional time of senatorial recess and a month filled with public holidays.[175] Trajan was in Italy, at least, although soon to depart Rome once more for war on the frontiers. Pliny was not to be thwarted. The renowned orator gave public readings of a revised version of his speech to enthusiastic audiences (3.13, 3.18), with a view to wider circulation in due course. The publication of this 'speech of thanks' (*gratiarum actio*), known today as the *Panegyricus,* was Pliny's own innovation. He took the opportunity to develop within it his own vision of the standards of behaviour expected by the senate of the emperor.[176] It does not lack the flattery that would disgust Augustine. In his position as professor of rhetoric at Milan, Augustine was required to deliver similar speeches: 'I was preparing to recite a panegyric to the emperor. In that panegyric I would tell many lies, and be applauded for my pains by many who knew that they were lies' (*Conf.* 6.6.9).[177] But, whatever Trajan or fellow senators thought of the speech, Pliny's seriousness of political intent cannot be missed. The impudence of appearing to instruct the emperor is offset by presentation of the material in the form of confirmation that Trajan's behaviour adheres to those expectations. It seemed a model to later generations. The literary reputation of Pliny, of Tacitus, and of all their contemporaries and immediate predecessors went into steep decline in the later second and third centuries. Literary taste took a misguided aesthetic diversion back to the era of Cato the Elder, prior even to Cicero.[178] One of the first works of high empire to recover its standing was Pliny's *Panegyricus*—well before Tacitus began to be read again. His speech was used throughout the later third and fourth centuries as a template for addressing the emperor in prose.[179] When the citizens of Como in the late fifteenth century were choosing scenes from Pliny's life to insert beneath the statue on the façade of their cathedral, they chose to depict Pliny's address to the emperor on that day in September 100 C.E.[180]

Pliny's high hopes for the Trajanic era cannot be missed. He ends the *Panegyricus* with a prayer for Trajan's safety, prefaced with a vow of the emperor's own devising: 'If he rules the state well and in the interests of all . . .' (*Paneg.* 94.5).[181] Trajan was determined to distinguish himself from the despotic Domitian. Pliny reports that on the first day of Trajan's consulship, the emperor had entered the Curia Iulia and 'exhorted' senators 'individually and collectively, to resume our freedom, to take up the responsibilities of the power we might be thought to share, to watch over the interests of the people, and to take action' (*Paneg.* 66.2).[182] This was the ideological atmosphere Trajan wished the senate to breath: free and shared governance of empire in the interests of all its inhabitants.[183] Here was no Evil Empire. Pliny predicted that the title *Optimus* would always remain with Trajan (*Paneg.* 88–9), and later ages embraced this image of the 'best' of emperors. New incumbents would be hailed with the formula 'More fortunate than Augustus, better than Trajan'.[184] Yet there was a troubling inconcinnity in Trajan: contradictions in his disposition and behaviour. 'Something elusive and perhaps discordant, not easily to be estimated in words' lay behind the official façade, in Syme's diagnosis; 'Discipline and modesty concealed a devouring ambition . . . It might all end in anger, conceit, and obstinacy'.[185] Within seven years of his consulship and the delivery of the *Panegyricus*, Pliny would be expressing a gloom and a sense of pessimism that has been overlooked and certainly not properly understood in the man. As will become clear, this pessimism is clearly connected with Trajan and coincides with the emperor's longest period of residence in Rome.

Pliny in Trajan's Rome

There was still much for Pliny to enjoy in the city. Trajan's Rome is best appreciated from the vantage point of late antiquity, in particular from the perspective of Constantius II, third son of Constantine the Great. He had never seen Rome. Constantius' attention had focused largely on his father's city of Constantinople, new capital of the eastern half of the empire. He belatedly paid a ceremonial visit to the old imperial capital in May 357 C.E.[186] The historian Ammianus Marcellinus, a contemporary, records the 'awe and amazement' of Constantius, who 'complained of Fame as either incapable or spiteful, because while always exaggerating everything, in describing what there is in Rome, she becomes valueless' (16.10.17).[187] The list of what Constantius saw includes not a single building from the golden age of Augustus—for all that emperor's pride in finding Rome made of brick and leaving it in marble.[188] Ammianus focuses almost entirely on the glories of the later first and second centuries, from Vespasian and Domitian to Marcus Aurelius. Pride of place in Ammianus' account is reserved for the forum of Trajan. Constantius 'stood fast in amazement, turning his attention to the gigantic complex about him, beggaring description and never again to be imitated by mortal men' (16.10.15).[189] Trajan ranks as one of Rome's greatest architect emperors. His forum, baths, and Pantheon brought new monumentality to an already imposing cityscape.[190] It was towards the middle stretch of his tenure, after his final victories in Dacia c. 106 C.E., that the emperor began to invest in such architecture.[191] Around the start of his reign, Trajan had been praised by Pliny for refraining from the emperor's prerogative of filling the city with his own buildings (*Paneg.* 51.1). Contemporaries did not need to be told that the intended contrast was with Domitian, whose cripplingly expensive additions to Rome were still supremely visible to Ammianus over a quarter of a millennium later.[192] Trajan, rich on the spoils of conquest in Dacia, could not be praised for such caution by the end of the first decade of the second century. He refuses Pliny's request for architects to be sent out to Pontus-Bithynia, on the telling ground that 'I have scarcely enough surveyors for the public works in progress in Rome or in the neighbourhood' (10.18.3).[193]

Many writers of the late republic and early empire, among them Cicero, Vergil, the Elder Pliny, and Tacitus, exhibit a concentric vision of the world, with the city of Rome at its very centre.[194] Pliny the Younger is quite different. Rome must compete for space and attention in his universe with Comum, Umbria, and the Laurentine shore near the capital. Arrestingly, while the environs of Pliny's estates and villas in all three regions outside the city are strongly visualized, Rome itself rarely comes into focus for Pliny.[195] The city is constantly present as backdrop to his roles as senator and leading courtroom orator. The temples of Concord and of Vesta and the latter's next door neighbour, the Regia, residence of the *pontifex maximus*;[196] the great courtroom of the Basilica Iulia;[197] the statue of the divine Julius Caesar and the nearby senate house;[198] the emperor's residence on the Palatine hill and the Circus Maximus;[199] and the Portico of Livia on the Oppian[200]—all feature incidentally or as backdrops for Pliny's daily life in Rome. With the obvious exceptions of Livia's Portico and the Circus, all these sites are in or adjoin the Forum Romanum, the capital's traditional legal centre.[201] Pliny's Rome is clustered around the scene of his adult triumphs as a public speaker.[202] Yet there are few evocations of individual monuments or of characteristic features of Rome's cityscape. Pliny shows little interest in the particularities of the city both at the start of Trajan's reign, when it was fashionable to underscore imperial restoration rather than addition of buildings,[203] and later during the first phase of the emperor's building boom. Remarkably, during 107–9 C.E., the timespan covered by Books 7–9 of the *Letters*, Pliny makes not a single reference to Trajan's *grands projets*[204]—despite the proximity of the stunning new bath complex on the Oppian to Pliny's house on the Esquiline.[205] It is the emperor who alludes to his building works during Pliny's residence in Pontus-Bithynia, not Pliny. A foretaste, here, of Pliny's late political disaffection from the emperor.

Pliny has no taste for the kind of quiddity that features so abundantly in Martial's evocation of the capital, or for his crowded and jostling streets.[206] The poet's description of the itinerary from his own house in the Subura to Pliny's Esquiline residence takes a keen interest even in a wayside pool decorated with statues from a mythological scene: 'the effort of climbing | the uphill path doesn't take long, once through Subura. | There you will immediately see Orpheus | standing slippery at the top of his watery theatre, | and the wondering beasts and the royal bird' (Mart. 10.20.4–8).[207] Pliny quotes from this poem's eulogy of his abilities as an orator, but omits the lines that give the details of Martial's journey (3.21.5).[208] Later, Augustine spent important periods of his life in Rome. Both his classical education in Cicero and Vergil and his Christian upbringing will have made him only too aware of the significance of the imperial capital. Despite arriving only a quarter of a century after his fellow Christian Constantius II, Augustine tells us almost nothing in the *Confessions* about his experience of Rome's magnificent urban environment. Rome is not picked out for special treatment, however. Augustine nowhere shows interest in his physical surroundings.[209]

Indoor scenes: the Centumviral court and literary recitations

Rome's cityscape was evidently of little interest to Pliny.[210] To the Younger, Rome meant a career inside courtroom and senate, not the long history visible in the city's buildings outside. Characteristically, vividness is reserved for *indoor* scenes. Pliny evokes a crowded setting as he prepares to make an appearance in a scandalous inheritance case in Rome's leading public court:

> The 180 jurors (this is the sum of the four panels sitting together) took their seats. There were several advocates on the two sides, and the benches were jammed; in addition a densely packed crowd of bystanders surrounded the very extensive court-room in a thronged circle. The tribunal also was crowded, and in the gallery of the basilica both men and women loomed over us in their eagerness to hear (which was difficult) and to see (which was easy). Fathers, daughters, even stepmothers all awaited with great anticipation.[211]
>
> *Letters* 6.33.3–4

The venue is the Basilica Iulia, home of the Centumviral court, near the Curia Iulia in the Forum Romanum.[212] Rome is shocked by goings-on in high society: Attia Viriola, a woman of high birth and the wife of a praetorian senator, had been disinherited by her octogenarian father within eleven days of his remarriage. Attia, with Pliny as her advocate, is seeking to regain her lost inheritance.[213]

Cases were normally heard in the Centumviral courts by single panels of forty-five jurors, with the speeches of advocates restricted to less than an hour.[214] The celebrity of the Attia Viriola case ensured that Pliny was heard by all four panels sitting at once, and had rather more time at his disposal (6.33.7).[215] With both the ground floor and upper gallery of the Basilica Iulia full, there were perhaps in excess of two thousand people present to hear Pliny's speech for the prosecution.[216] Conditions amongst the throng of bystanders could be boisterous. In a parallel case Pliny mentions that a 'young man of some distinction had his tunic torn . . . but he stayed on, clad only in his toga.'[217]

Pliny's action on behalf of Attia was partially successful (6.33.5–6), but he remained very proud of the speech he delivered, and circulated a revised version to friends. Writing to Voconius Romanus in Tarraconensis, he expressed hope that the written speech retained 'its freshness by its abundant matter, its clear divisions, its several short anecdotes, and its varied eloquence'. Passages in the speech were by turns 'sublime', 'aggressive', and 'delicate': 'for it was often necessary to interrupt the impassioned and noble passages to make calculations and virtually to demand counters and a games-board' (6.33.8–9).[218] Such were the challenges of presenting a speech concerned with domestic finances and inheritance law. Pliny remained optimistic that such cases might still prove of interest to a broader public. Tacitus appears not to have shared this view.[219]

In a further 'indoor' scene, Calpurnia is pictured waiting at the house on the Esquiline hill for news of her husband in court: 'She posts individuals to report to her the assent and the applause that I have received, and the outcome which

I have imposed on the judge' (4.19.3).[220] Pliny does not expect his wife to attend in person. She is never portrayed on the streets of Rome. Calpurnia's only other 'appearance' in Rome is in fact behind a curtain, in decorous but distant attendance at one her husband's many literary events: 'Whenever I am giving a recitation, she sits close by, concealed by a curtain, and listens most avidly to the praises heaped on me' (4.19.3).[221] Whether such concealment was due to the young Calpurnia's shyness or to Pliny's overly traditional expectations of marriage, we are not told.[222]

Recitations in public auditoria or in houses belonging to himself or friends in Rome interested Pliny as an adult greatly, and he offers a good many vivid reports.[223] Audiences drawn from the capital's elite were not invariably attentive or polite, although in Pliny's account poor behaviour and audience heckling or disapprobation largely take place at performances given by others.[224] The judgements of literary immortality that he was wont to make on the basis of these public readings are predictably mixed. He foresaw the longevity of Tacitus (6.16.1–3), but did not anticipate that of Martial (3.21.6).[225] Other pronouncements, such as that on the mediocrity of the epic poetry of Silius Italicus (3.7.5), have proven a challenge to shift. Pliny's own *recitationes* are characterized by useful comments or praise from an assembled audience of friends, although he admits that he is criticized for his reading voice and for the novel practice of performing revised courtroom speeches in public.[226] Martial and the satirist Juvenal give the viewpoint of less cooperative members of the audience, all too prone to become bored or restless.[227] Perhaps they would rather have been at one of Rome's many theatres, or the Colosseum or the Circus. Of the latter Pliny comments: 'I have been passing all this time between my writing tablets and my books in the most delicious calm. "However", you ask, "have you been able to do this in Rome?" The Circus races were on—a species of exhibition which does not attract me even in the faintest degree' (9.6.1).[228] The city's theatres Pliny mentions only incidentally, the gladiatorial spectacles in Rome, not at all.[229] His is the Rome of the elite litterateur.

A priesthood

There were more prestigious posts to come for Pliny in Rome before Trajan's victorious return from Dacia, further high profile trials to undertake in senate and courtroom. In 104–6 C.E., he would become 'curator' of the Tiber (*curator aluei Tiberis et riparum et cloacarum urbis*): a consular post which put the holder in charge of drainage and flood defences along the Tiber and in Rome. Pliny refers to the post indirectly (5.14.2–3), preferring elsewhere to approach it obliquely in a manner that conveys his abiding interest in water.[230] He writes in detail about the flooding of the Tiber and its accompanying devastation above and below Rome (8.17). His term in office was by then over.[231] Just before after the period of his curatorship and towards its end, defence would be undertaken in the senate of two successive governors of Pontus-Bithynia: Iulius Bassus (4.9) and Varenus Rufus. That they were on trial was due to factional infighting among the Bithynian elites. The obvious guilt of the pair cannot have endeared Pliny to some locals when he went out himself as governor just a few years after the termination of the second trial. A return will be made to these trials in the chapter on Pontus-Bithynia.[232]

More than further official posts or trials in the senate, Pliny had long hankered for admission to one of Rome's four priestly colleges. There were only sixty places available for the 150–200 consular senators likely competing for entry at any one time.[233] Verginius Rufus had consistently supported his suit (2.1.8), as had Iulius Frontinus (4.8.3), another rare holder of three consulships and distinguished author of works on military strategy and Rome's aqueducts.[234] Pliny wrote to Trajan himself to press his case for co-option (10.13). In the event, around 103 C.E., Pliny would be nominated for the distinguished college of augurs in Frontinus' place, after he passed away (4.8). The frequent ritual dinners of the colleges provided an important venue for interaction with senior senators, although the priesthoods themselves did not lack for religious meaning or significance.[235] It was the particular duty of augurs to rule on cases of faults in public ceremony that might interfere with the ritual taking of omens, to preside at augural rites, and on occasion perform inaugurations of temples.[236]

Roman senators were perfectly capable of intensely individual apprehensions of the divine.[237] These tended to happen abroad, away from Rome. Tacitus recorded one such experience for the sober Vespasian, before he became emperor, at the temple of Serapis in Alexandria (Tac. *Hist.* 4.82). Religion has no recorded place in Pliny's domestic life in Rome, although a public concern for the prosperity of the empire and safety of the emperor permeates the prayers to gods found at either end of the *Panegyricus* (1, 94). Pliny's personal religious sensibility is reserved for Umbria, for a famous shrine at the source of the Clitumnus river (8.8), and the dedication or repair of temples on or near his Umbrian estates (4.1, 9.39, 10.8).[238] The Christians of Pontus would prove a challenge but not inspire curiosity (10.96.7–8).[239]

Disillusion

After 106 C.E., following Pliny's demission of the Tiber posting and around the time of the termination of the trial of Varenus Rufus, pessimism sets in. The coincidence with Pliny's freedom from office and major trials cannot be missed. His pessimism also overlaps with Trajan's longest stay in his capital. Entering Rome as emperor in September 99 C.E., Trajan was soon off to conduct the first Dacian campaign in modern Romania around March 101, returning only in December 102. Two and half years intervened before the start of the second Dacian war and the departure of Trajan in June 105. Upon returning in the first half of 107, Trajan would be continuously present in Italy until the Parthian war of September 113. Pliny's pessimism and hints of discomfort with Trajan are initially hard to spot. Criticism of emperors in published writing, no matter how muted, could only be expressed indirectly. Pliny has a reputation for optimism.[240] That positive outlook leaks away in Books 7–9 (107–9 C.E.). These books are read rather less frequently than their sunnier predecessors.[241] Book 6, which contains the Vesuvius letters, is a high point of Pliny's enchantment with Trajan.[242] A sequence of epistles traces Trajan's return from Dacia in 107 C.E. and sees him installed back at the heart of Rome's legal system, away from his armies (6.13, 19, 22, 27, 31). Thereafter a gloom gently descends, easily missed if Pliny's outlook is assumed to be unchanging.[243]

References to illnesses and deaths begin to pile up in Book 7 (7.1, 7.19, 7.21, 7.26). Unlike in earlier times (5.21.6), Pliny is unable to achieve the determination to rise above his grief (7.1.1, 7.19.1, 11).[244] Trajan is mentioned briefly at an early stage (7.6, 7.10). Thereafter Pliny's thoughts focus on the spectre of Domitian and the terror and fear which he inflicted on Rome in the 90s C.E. (7.19.4–6, 7.27.12–14, 7.33). The atmosphere darkens further in Book 8. Nearly one-third of the book's letters are concerned with death and serious illness (8.1, 8.5, 8.10, 8.11, 8.16. 8.19, 8.23). Pliny remains tangled up in his emotions, unable to lift his eyes above his current situation (8.19.2, 8.23.8), prone to expressing 'uncharacteristic' sentiments on the futility of life in the face of death (8.23.6–7). Natural disaster supervenes. Book 8 is the home of Pliny's reports on the devastating effects of the inundation of the Tiber after 'continual storms and frequent flooding' (8.17).[245] The channel dug by the emperor to reduce the impact of the flooding has only limited effect (8.17.2). Trajan is mentioned only once elsewhere in the book, in a letter on his military triumph in Dacia (8.4). Trajan's success with controlling and diverting rivers in Dacia is underlined (8.4.2): an obvious contrast with his ultimate failure to control the Tiber at home in Rome. The metaphorical potential of the contrast is obvious.[246]

More explicit personal criticism is impossible. But a broader political pessimism of cannot be missed. Pliny laments the pitiful ignorance of proper behaviour among the senatorial elite in forthright terms: 'The slavish situation of former days casts a kind of forgetfulness and ignorance over senatorial procedures as over other most honourable pursuits . . . the resumption of freedom has found us ill-educated and ignorant, but, fired by the sweetness of that freedom, we are compelled to perform certain duties before we are acquainted with them' (8.14.2–3).[247] Over a decade before, Pliny had celebrated the return of political freedom (1.5.1, 1.10.1, 1.13.1). Now he expresses a sentiment unthinkable in those earlier times: the return of liberty encountered a senate unfit to exercise it.

The debilitating series of illnesses and deaths is gone in Book 9.[248] Pliny looks more confidently to the future and anticipates in letter after letter a bright future for his reception as a writer by posterity.[249] This is literary not political optimism. Trajan himself is entirely absent. No mention is made, now or earlier, of the emperor's *grands projets* in Rome.[250] The only great enterprise Pliny does mention is one *outside* Rome: Trajan's new deepwater harbour at Centum Cellae, modern Civitavecchia, some 43 miles/70 kilometres north of Rome (6.31).[251] Pliny ends the book, and his whole collection of private correspondence, with a marked retreat to his country estates, away from the politics of the capital (9.36, 37, 39, 40). Letters at the heart of the book reveal a new willingness to confront the darkness of the past. Pliny reveals the turmoil in the senate just after the assassination of Domitian (9.13): a turmoil that Pliny had rather glossed over at the time. He admits what he had previously denied implicitly (2.1.12): that the behaviour of his patron Verginius Rufus in 68–9 C.E. was open to adverse interpretation (9.19.5). Pliny also condemns the behaviour of an audience which asked an unnamed historian to stop reading from a work on recent history (9.27). The silenced work appears to have been the *Histories* of Tacitus and its account of senatorial conduct under Domitian.[252]

The coincidence between the personal and political pessimism of Books 7–9 and the sustained sojourn of the emperor in Rome is hardly fortuitous.[253] Pliny's journey from the light of the *Panegyricus* into the darkness of the last books of the private *Letters* anticipates the political journey that Tacitus was himself undertaking, from the Trajanic enthusiasm of the *Agricola* to the pointed silences and increasing imperial disillusionment of the *Annals*.[254] Prolonged contact with Trajan in the capital, where he was publicly subject to the competing demands of a range of interest groups,[255] had perhaps strained relations or created disappointment. The aspiration for a free and independent senate working in partnership alongside the emperor had proven illusory.[256] The vast scale of Trajan's forum and baths gave the lie to any talk of equality with senatorial peers. And despite the boost to personal merit over bloodline that Trajan's adoption by Nerva had apparently provided, the new emperor was showing worrying signs of dynastic ambitions for his family.[257] A repeat of the mistakes of the Flavian era appeared not unlikely. There are also hints that financial disaster was averted for Trajan only by the windfall of treasure from the victory in Dacia.[258]

It is testimony to the shrewdness of Pliny as a political participant, and to his depth and complexity as a human observer, that he grew to perceive a shadow at the heart of Trajan's reign. Once grasped, Pliny's political pessimism cannot be forgotten. The senator was capable of moving on decisively from the enthusiasm of the *Panegyricus* and his conviction that Trajan would remain *Optimus*.

Notes

1. See Chp. 3 for the earlier stages of Pliny's education.
2. See Chp. 4 n. 121 on Pliny's guardian.
3. On Voconius Romanus, see Syme (1960, 364–8) = *RP* 2.480–3 = (2016, 70–3), Gibson and Morello (2012, 149–54), Whitton (2013, 66–7); on his connection with the Plinii, see Syme (1969, 230–1) = *RP* 2.768–9. Voconius receives the high total of eight letters from Pliny (1.5, 2.1, 3.13, 6.15, 6.33, 8.8, 9.7, 9.28), and is mentioned elsewhere in 2.13 and 10.4. In later life Romanus would rise to high position in his native province as president of its council; see Whitton (2013, 196). For Pliny's attempt to gain entry to the senate for Voconius and the possibility that the latter accompanied Pliny to Pontus-Bithynia, see Chp. 8.
4. On Quintilian, see Kaster (1995, 333–6), López (2007); especially as he relates to Pliny, see Whitton (2019, 20–68). On Roman rhetorical education more broadly, see Corbeill (2007), Connolly (2011). For an overview of Pliny's rhetorical training and early career in Rome's courts, see Procchi (2012, 23–36).
5. See Whitton (2019).
6. See Marchesi (2008, 97–206) on the literary relationship between Pliny and Tacitus, and Marchesi (2008, 207–40, 252–7) on Pliny's literary relationship with Cicero. On the strong intertextual relations between the *Letters*, the *Dialogus* of Tacitus and Quintilian, see Whitton (2018). For a broad view of the varying influences of Cicero, Tacitus, and the Neronian Seneca on Pliny, see Whitton (2013, 2–6, 32–4).
7. For significant differences between Pliny and Quintilian, see Whitton (2019, esp. 60–68, 122–32, 136–51); cf. e.g. 1.2, 2.19, 4.9, 5.8, 5.12, 7.12, 7.17, 9.4, 9.15, on the revision, circulation, public reading, and publication of courtroom speeches. For Pliny and Quintilian on length and audacity, see Whitton (2019, 192–261) on 1.20, 9.26, and *Inst.* 12.10.
8. For Quintilian on contemporary oratory, cf. *Inst.* 10.1.118ff.; 12.10–11, and see the overview of Syme, *RP* 7.555–9.
9. 2.18.1 *illam dulcissimam aetatem . . . resumo: sedeo inter iuuenes ut solebam*: Pliny is here seeking a tutor for the children of the deceased Iunius Arulenus Rusticus, at the instigation of the latter's brother Iunius Mauricus; see later for these characters.
10. *Conf.* 5.8.14 *audiebam quietius ibi studere adulescentes et ordinatiore disciplinae cohercitione sedari; Conf.* 3.3.6 *hoc laudabilior, quo fraudulentior; Conf.* 4.2.2 *eos sine dolo docebam dolos, non quibus contra caput innocentis agerent sed aliquando pro capite nocentis.* On Augustine's students in Carthage and Rome, see Lane Fox (2015, 159, 175).
11. See Mayer (2003) for the centrality of *gloria* as an orator to Pliny.
12. On the relative worth of evidence, argument, and prestige in Roman courtrooms, see Meyer (2016).
13. See Chp. 3 for these figures.
14. Suet. *Tit.* 8.3 *pestilentia quanta non temere alias*; see Syme, *RP* 7.552 for scarce literary traces of this plague.

15. According to Tac. *Hist.* 4.42, Regulus had undertaken prosecutions *iuuenis admodum* (i.e. probably before becoming quaestor) in the late Neronian epoch against the Licinii Crassi and Salvidienus Orfitus; cf. Syme, *RP* 7.555.

16. On the Centumviral courts, see later in this chapter. For the overwhelming dominance of inheritance cases in Roman legal thinking and practice, see Winsbury (2014, 50), with reference to Kelly (1976, 71–92).

17. On the identification of the trial undertaken in Pliny's nineteenth year with the Iunius Pastor case, see the cautious views of Sherwin-White (1966, 128). Syme, *RP* 7.555 places the Iunius Pastor trial *after* Pliny's military service in Syria, but without engaging Sherwin-White on the language of 1.18; Birley (2000a, 9) takes a more neutral position.

18. Pliny speaks of the considerations of *patria* and *fides* in the case (1.18.4). A probable descendant of this Iunius Pastor is identified by Syme (1968a, 148) = *RP* 2.718, 7.555, and by Salomies (1992, 145–7); but the latter opts for a domicile in Patavium against the Brixia of Syme.

19. 1.18.3–4 *mihi quiescenti uisa est socrus mea aduoluta genibus ne agerem obsecrare . . . contra potentissimos ciuitatis atque etiam Caesaris amicos . . . adeo illa actio mihi aures hominum, illa ianuam famae patefecit.*

20. See Chp. 4.

21. 6.23.2 *ostendere foro, adsignare famae.* Pliny himself later complains about the premature introduction of young men to the Centumviral court (2.14.2–3); Quintilian remained flexible on the appropriate age (*Inst.* 12.6.1–4).

22. The dates of Pliny's senatorial career from earliest pre-senatorial postings in the early 80s C.E. to prefect of military treasury in the late 90s C.E. are a matter of long-standing controversy: underlying the present account is the persuasive overview of Whitton (2015b), which revises (or supersedes) the older accounts of (e.g.) Mommsen (1869), Otto (1919), Harte (1935), Syme (1958), Sherwin-White (1966), Birley (2000a).

23. See Talbert (1984, 11–13).

24. Cf. e.g. 2.9.2 (Erucius Clarus), 8.23.2 (Iunius Avitus), perhaps also 10.4.2 (Voconius Romanus).

25. See Griffin (2000a, 58–60).

26. Pliny's two pre-senatorial offices (the first was membership of *decemuiri stlitibus iudicandis,* 'Board of Ten for Judging Lawsuits') are recorded on the great Comum inscription (*CIL* 5.5262: reproduced in Chp. 7); see Eck (1974, 177), Talbert (1984, 13–14), Syme, *RP* 7.552, Birley (2000a, 7–8) on the duties and prestige of each.

27. Pliny in Syria (also recorded on *CIL* 5.5262): on dates, see Whitton (2015b, 11); on the place of the post in a senatorial career, see Talbert (1984, 14); cf. Chp. 8 for a fuller account.

28. See Saller (1994, 25–41).

29. See Whitton (2015b, 9–10), with further references. On marrying 'at the right moment for the *cursus*', see Sherwin-White (1966, 420).

30. Cf. the parallel case of Ummidius Quadratus, cited at 7.24.3 and contextualized by Sherwin-White (1966, 420), Birley (2000a, 9).

31. 10.2.2–3 *eoque magis liberos concupisco, quos habere etiam illo tristissimo saeculo uolui, sicut potes duobus matrimoniis meis credere. sed di melius . . . malui hoc potius tempore me patrem fieri, quo futurus essem et securus et felix.* Syme, *RP* 7.554–5 conjures the context for a choice of bride for Pliny, based on the advice of family friends; cf. Chp. 7 on marriage to Calpurnia. Paradoxically, childlessness might increase a new man's chances of personal favour from the emperor; see Hoffer (1999, 229–32).

32. The evidence for Pliny's marriages and relations through marriages—including the key passages at 9.13.4, 13; 10.2—is set out with exemplary clarity by Birley (2000a, 2–4) and Shelton (2013, 96–8, 260). A total of three wives is favoured by (e.g.) Sherwin-White (1966, 71, 128, 264, 559–60), Syme, *RP* 7.510, 554, *PIR*² P 490 (p. 206); and of two wives by (e.g.) Birley (2000a, 3)—all with references to earlier literature.

33. On Pompeia Celerina, see Chp. 6 n. 38.

34. 7.16.1–2 *simul militauimus, simul quaestores Caesaris fuimus. ille me in tribunatu . . . praecessit, ego illum in praetura sum consecutus.* For Pliny and Tiro on military service in Syria, see Chp. 8.

35. On Pliny's relationship with Tiro and Romanus (who receive four and seven letters respectively from Pliny), see Gibson and Morello (2012, 147–54); cf. Syme, *RP* 7.565–6 on the stalled career of the former (marked by his praetorian governorship of Baetica: 9.5, Chp. 8).

36. 7.20.4 *equidem adulescentulus, cum iam tu fama gloriaque floreres, te sequi . . . concupiscebam.*

37. Tacitus receives eleven letters from Pliny (1.6, 1.20, 4.13, 6.9, 6.16, 6.20, 7.20, 7.33, 8.7, 9.10, 9.14); on their relationship, see Chp. 7 n. 47; on their literary interactions, see earlier n. 6.

38. Pliny's coevals: Domitius Apollinaris (Chp. 7 n. 33); Sosius Senecio (Jones (1970, 100–4), (1971, 54–7), Stadter (2015, 36–40)); Minicius Fundanus (Chp. 7 n. 33) and his daughter (Bodel (1995)); Pompeius Falco (Salomies (1992, 121–5)); and Catilius Severus (Syme (1985d, 352–3) = *RP* 5.555–6).

39. On Pliny's contemporaries from the Transpadana, see Chp. 7.

40. On Plutarch, Fundanus, and Senecio, and the ethical works that Plutarch addressed to the latter, see later in this chapter.

41. On Pliny and Plutarch, see later in this chapter.

42. Hahn (2011, 124); see Hahn (2011) for an overview of high empire philosophical education as a form of sociopolitical acclimatization.

43. Connolly (2011, 107)—whose summary of rhetorical training I follow here.

44. Quint. *Inst.* 4 pref. 2, Auson. *Grat Act.* 10.7.204ff.

45. See Griffin (2000a, 60–61, 69–70) on Domitian and the arts.

46. See later in this chapter.

47. See Griffin (2000a, 72); cf. (2000a, 74–6) for a survey of the evidence for later depredations.

48. See Griffin (2000a, 63–5), Jones (1992, 128–31, 138–9, 141–53).

49. Suet. *Dom.* 3.2 *inopia rapax, metu saeuus*; 10.5 *post ciuilis belli uictoriam saeuior.* On the revolt of Saturninus, see Griffin (2000a, 65–6); the future emperor Trajan was

rewarded for his loyalty in helping to put down the rebellion with the position of *consul ordinarius* for 91.

50. On conflicting accounts of the turning point in the reign of Domitian, see Griffin (2000a, 60); see later in this chapter for the events of 93–4 C.E. highlighted by Pliny and Tacitus.

51. For the voicing of such fears, cf. Tac. *Agr.* 45.2 (with Woodman and Kraus (2014, 319)).

52. On Pliny as a late entrant to the senate c. 89–90 C.E., see Whitton (2015b, 9–13); for older contributions to the debate, cf. Sherwin-White (1966, 73–5), *PIR*[2] P 490 (p. 205), Syme, *RP* 7.561–3; Birley (2000a, 9, 14). On possible reasons for the delay in entry, see Sherwin-White (1966, 74), Syme (1958, 653), *RP* 7.562, 564.

53. On canvassing and election, see Sherwin-White (1966, 157–8, 260–2, 362), Talbert (1984, 14–18, 204–7, 343–4).

54. On *quaestores Caesaris*, see Birley (2000a, 8–9); the post also appears in Pliny's inscriptions (*CIL* 5.5262, 5.5667, and probably 11.5272). Both Birley and Sherwin-White (1966, 3, 157) interpret 2.9.1 as referring to the fact that, as *candidatus Caesaris* for the quaestorship (and perhaps some subsequent offices), Pliny did not have to canvass for election.

55. On the duties of a *quaestor Caesaris*, see Sherwin-White (1966, 419); on the duties of the other eighteen quaestors, see Talbert (1984, 17).

56. Syme (1958, 76).

57. Syme, *RP* 7.565–6 (who goes on to puzzle over why the unimpressive Calestrius Tiro should be so favoured). To these years also belong the execution by Domitian of the Vestal Virgin Cornelia, as recounted in 4.11; cf. Traub (1955, 213–19) = (2016, 124–30), Sherwin-White (1966, 84–5).

58. See Whitton (2015b, 12–13); cf. Sherwin-White (1966, 74–5), Syme, *RP* 7.563, Birley (2000a, 9–10), *PIR*[2] P 490 (p. 205). Cf. Pliny on the proper conduct of a tribunate (1.23), and references to his own behaviour as a tribune (6.8.3, *Paneg.* 95.1–2).

59. Arr. *Epict. diss.* 1.19.24.

60. The exact date of Pliny's praetorship is strongly contested, but 93 or 94 C.E. seems most likely; see later in this chapter.

61. Cf. 1.5.5–7, 1.7.2, 1.14, 2.18, 3.11.3, 4.21, 4.24.4–5, 7.19, 7.27.12–14, 7.33, 9.13, and see later in this chapter.

62. For the full passage, see later in this chapter.

63. Mettius Carus: a layer of information against Pliny (7.27.14) and prosecutor of Senecio (7.19.5); cf. 1.5.3. On this notorious figure, mentioned also at Mart. 12.25.5, Juv. 1.35–6, see Woodman and Kraus (2014, 316) with reference to Rutledge (2001, 245–6); he may have been involved also in the condemnation of Cornelia, the Vestal Virgin (see earlier in this chapter).

64. Lee (1997, 769).

65. Winsbury (2014, 2); cf. Winsbury (2014, 11–12, 91–107) for a trial specifically on the issue.

66. See Masson (1709, 59–66) on 93 C.E., (1709, 67–8) on 96 C.E.; he assigns the prefecture of the military treasury to 98 C.E. (1709, 85).

67. Mommsen (1869, 86–9), with quotation from (1869, 89).

68. Otto (1919, 43–50), with comment at (1919, 52): 'Es is daher menschlich höchst unerfreulich, wenn uns Plinius später nach des Kaisers Ermordung als einer der schlimmsten Schreier gegen diesen entgegentritt'.

69. See Syme (1958, 76–8, 656–8), *RP* 7.561–5; cf. above all Strobel (1983), (2003).

70. Fellow traveller ('Mitläufer'): Strobel (2003, 313) 'Plinius war ein Mann, der unter jedem totalitären und despotischen System Karriere gemacht . . . hätte'.

71. For attempts to defend Pliny's integrity, including efforts to redate his career, see Harte (1935), Kuijper (1968), Birley (2000a, 10–16), Strunk (2013), Winsbury (2014). For a broad outline of the historiography of the debate, see Whitton (2015b, 1–4), adding now Strunk (2015), who makes a broader case: 'the fact that one held or did not hold high political office cannot be used as evidence of collaboration or dissent' (2015, 56).

72. See Jones (1992, 152–3).

73. On the possible date of the incident (late 92 C.E.) and Plutarch's connections with Rusticus, see Jones (1971, 23, 51) (doubted by Russell (1972, 7)). On the rarity of such contemporary illustrations in Plutarch's ethical works, see Van Hoof (2010, 192–3). Plutarch evidently came to Rome several times before the death of Domitian (Jones (1971, 20–27)), and acquired an extensive network of senatorial Roman friends dominated by northern Italians and *noui homines* (i.e. men very like Pliny); see Jones (1971, 48–64). The extant works of Pliny and Plutarch reveal up to seven shared friends and acquaintances, of whom the most significant are Minicius Fundanus and Sosius Senecio (both mentioned earlier n. 38). Fundanus is the main speaker in Plutarch's *On the Restraint of Anger* and is mentioned at the start of *On Tranquillity*, alongside being addressed or mentioned in five letters of Pliny (1.9, 4.15, 5.16, 6.6, and 7.12). Sosius Senecio is the dedicatee of the *Parellel Lives, Table Talk*, and *On Progress in Virtue*, and receives two letters from Pliny (1.13, 4.4)—who is acquainted both with Senecio's father-in-law, Iulius Frontinus (4.8.3, 5.1.5, 9.19), and with his son-in-law, Pompeius Falco (1.23, 4.27, 7.22, 9.15). It is possible that in the year after the Rusticus incident (i.e. in 93 C.E.), Pliny personally defended the wife of Plutarch's brother Timon at a time when Plutarch himself was in Rome; see Jones (1971, 23–4) (Carlon (2009, 33–4, 39–40) takes a different view). It is hard to imagine that the pair were unaware of each other—yet neither mentions the other in extant writings; see Gibson (2018) for an overview of their literary relationship.

74. See Woodman and Kraus (2014, 317) on Tac. *Agr.* 45.1, with reference to Rutledge (2001, 202–4), Powell (2010, 240–1); Massa reappears in villainous guise at Tac. *Hist.* 4.50.2 and Juv. 1.35–6.

75. On dates, see Whitton (2015b, 13–15), revising older estimates; cf. 3.4.4, 6.29.8 for Pliny's other references to the trial.

76. See Chp. 8 on prosecutions of corrupt governors of Pontus-Bithynia.

77. On this figure, see Syme, *RP* 7.571, 575, with reference to Dio Xiph. 67.13.2.

78. See Talbert (1984, 482–7).

79. For the size of the senate, its usual meeting place in the Curia Iulia, and layout of the seating, see Talbert (1984, 113–28, 131–62, Figs. 3–7).

80. Cf. the varying accounts given by Pliny of trials of provincial governors in which he was involved: 2.11–12 (Marius Priscus: see n. 167 later), 3.9 (Caecilius Classicus), 4.9 (Iulius Bassus), 5.20, 6.5, 6.13, 7.6 (Varenus Rufus). On the latter pair of defendants, see Chp. 8.

81. For Pliny's own willingness to break this convention when acting for the defence, see Chp. 8.

82. See Sherwin-White (1966, 167), noting 2.11.14 (four to five hours for a case of provincial corruption), 4.9.9 (five hours for the same), and 4.16.2 (an exceptional seven hours for a civil case). The defence normally received a larger allotment of time than the prosecution.

83. 2.11.15 *Caesar . . . libertum meum post me stantem saepius admoneret uoci laterique consulerem, cum me uehementius putaret intendi, quam gracilitas mea perpeti posset.*

84. Cf. e.g. 6.8, with Gibson (f'coming). For Pliny's distinctive emphasis on the performance and delivery of a speech, see Tempest (2017). On the overwhelming importance of memory as a skill for an orator, see Small (2007).

85. For Pliny as civic and provincial patron, see Chps. 6, 7.

86. See Sherwin-White (1966, 445).

87. See Bauman (1974, 33–5), Hennig (1978); cf. *Paneg.* 33.3 and Suet. *Dom.* 10.1.

88. See Sherwin-White (1966, 447, 766).

89. Cf. Dio Xiph. 67.13.2 with Eck (2010, 352), also Tac. *Hist.* 1.2.3.

90. Suet. *Dom.* 10.4 *quasi scaenico exodio sub persona Paridis et Oenones diuortium suum cum uxore taxasset.*

91. See Syme *RP* 7.575, Whitton (2015b, 14 n. 77).

92. Tac. *Agr.* 45.1–2 *mox nostrae duxere Heluidium in carcerem manus; nos Maurici Rusticique uisus <foedauit>; nos innocenti sanguine Senecio perfudit. Nero tamen subtraxit oculos suos iussitque scelera, non spectauit; praecipua sub Domitiano miseriarum pars erat uidere et aspici.* On the contested construal of the second clause of this quotation and the supplement of a missing verb, see Woodman and Kraus (2014, 318).

93. See Woodman and Kraus (2014, 76–7) on Tac. *Agr.* 2.1; cf. Woodman and Kraus (2014, 318).

94. Carlon (2009, 21–2) acknowledges that the families of the victims were not bound by their philosophical adherence to Stoicism, but argues reasonably that the term 'Stoic opposition' is a still useful title for encapsulating their 'political allegiance to resisting imperial authority and restoring senatorial power'. For the influence of Roman Stoicism on political thought and action, see Brunt (2013, esp. 275–330).

95. See Jones (1978, 16).

96. See Syme, *RP* 7.576.

97. See Lavan (f'coming); cf. Roller (2015) on the republican and imperial senate in this context.

98. The date of Pliny's praetorship is much contested. Mommsen (1869, 79–88) argued for 93 C.E., and was followed by Syme (1958, 76–8, 656–8), *RP* 7.561–5, and Sherwin-White (1966, 763–71). Otto (1919, 43–50) argued for 95 C.E., Harte (1935) (followed by Kuijper (1968)) moved the date out of the danger zone of 93

C.E. and argued for 90–1 C.E. His arguments were belatedly endorsed by Birley (2000a, 9–16), who moved the praetorship back further still to 89–90 C.E.; this same position underlies (e.g.) Strunk (2013) and Winsbury (2014, 91–107). The matter has been authoritatively re-investigated by Whitton (2015b), who argues for 93 or 94 C.E.

99. See Talbert (1984, 207).

100. For a family tree and clear portrait of the interconnections between the dissident figures of 93–4 C.E. and their families, see Carlon (2009, 21–36, 221–2); cf. 7.19.4–5 for a glimpse of the dynastic connections in a snapshot from the trial of Senecio.

101. See Chps. 3 and 4.

102. See Whitton (2015b, 15–16 n. 86).

103. The praetorship is not then an issue for Pliny's reputation; see Whitton (2015b, 15).

104. Tac. *Agr.* 45.1 *non uidit Agricola obsessam curiam et clausum armis senatum et eadem strage tot consularium caedes, tot nobilissimarum feminarum exilia et fugas.* 'So many consuls butchered': Woodman and Kraus (2014, 316) note that of the twelve consulars executed by the emperor in the account of Suetonius (*Dom.* 10.2–4, 11.1, 15.1), only three can be assigned to this particular period: in addition to Helvidius and Rusticus, one Flavius Clemens, consul of 95 C.E. (Suet. *Dom.* 15.1).

105. On the number and dates of the bans on philosophers, se Whitton (2015b, 5–9), with revision of older studies.

106. 3.11.2–3 *cum essent philosophi ab urbe summoti, fui apud illum in suburbano, et quo notabilius (hoc est, periculosius) esset fui praetor. pecuniam etiam, qua tunc illi ampliore opus erat, ut aes alienum exsolueret contractum ex pulcherrimis causis, mussantibus magnis quibusdam et locupletibus amicis mutuatus ipse gratuitam dedi. atque haec feci, cum septem amicis meis aut occisis aut relegatis, occisis Senecione Rustico Heluidio, relegatis Maurico Gratilla Arria Fannia, tot circa me iactis fulminibus quasi ambustus mihi quoque impendere idem exitium certis quibusdam notis augurarer.* 'Certain sure signs' and other phrases like it (e.g. 1.7.2, 4.24.2) probably refer to the prosecution of Massa (7.33) and perhaps also to the incident in another trial recorded at 1.5.

107. Epictetus: cf. Gell. 15.11.5; Plutarch: see Jones (1971, 24–5), noting the favourable reference to the exiled Mauricus at Plut. *Galb.* 8.8.

108. See Whitton (2015b, 6 with n. 20).

109. Whitton (2015b, 9).

110. See Carlon (2009, 21–67); cf. Shelton (1987), Baraz (2012).

111. See Birley (2000a, 67), with further references, also Syme, *RP* 7.477; cf. Syme, *RP* 7.568–87 for a study of the larger political grouping.

112. See earlier on 2.18.

113. See Chp. 3 for Messalinus' collateral descent from the poet Catullus' family.

114. For letters to Mauricus, cf. 1.14, 2.18 (the return to school), 6.14. For letters involving Arria and Fannia, cf. 3.11.3 3.16, 7.19, 9.13. Sherwin-White (1966, 243) notoriously labelled the latter 'this tedious pair'; but Shelton (2013, 15–91) offers a sympathetic and detailed study of the duo as part of a larger group of dissident women, including Arria the Elder, Gratilla, and Anteia; cf. Carlon (2009, 18–67).

115. See Langlands (2014) for a nuanced study of these claims; cf. Centlivres Challet (2008).
116. See Carlon (2009, 60).
117. 9.13.3 *fuerat alioqui mihi cum Heluidio amicitia, quanta potuerat esse cum eo, qui metu temporum nomen ingens paresque uirtutes secessu tegebat.*
118. Cf. Madsen (2009, 110–11, 116) on Dio of Prusa maximizing his record of opposition to Domitian.
119. *CIL* 5.5262 (Comum: authored by Pliny: Chp. 7), 5.5667 (Vercellae); cf. Strunk (2013, 100–1) on Pliny's non-suppression of the post here.
120. In the *Letters*, Pliny does not mention his early presidency of the Centumviral court or post as *seuir* (see earlier), and makes only indirect allusions to his Saturnian prefecture in the private letters (1.10.9; but explicitly at 10.3.1) or to his curatorship of the bed and banks of the Tiber (5.14.2).
121. For the little that is known about the prefecture of the military treasury, see Whitton (2015b, 16, 18), with reference to Corbier (1974), Eck (1979), Günther (2008). As prefect of the military treasury, Pliny was *not* involved, as has sometimes been claimed (e.g. by Bartsch (1994, 168–9), Winsbury (2014, 100)), in recovering debts on behalf of the state from the estates of convicted traitors such as Senecio, Rusticus, and Helvidius. That function seems to have belonged, if it can be clearly assigned to anyone, to Saturnian prefects; see Whitton (2015b, 18–19).
122. On the Domitianic dating of the military treasury post, see Whitton (2015b, 16–18), endorsing and revising the earlier views of Mommsen, Syme, and Sherwin-White (documented in connection with the date of Pliny's praetorship: see earlier), and refuting the views of Otto (1919, 43–50) and in particular of those who move the post either forward to a Nervan appointment in 96–7 C.E. (Oertel (1939), Birley (2000a, 9–16); cf. Strunk (2013, 101–3), Winsbury (2014, 91–107)) or back to the safer period of 91–3 C.E. (Harte (1935), Kuijper (1968, 62–6)).
123. See earlier.
124. See Strunk (2013, 102); cf. Whitton (2015b, 17).
125. Cf. 1.5.5–7, 1.7.2; 3.11.3, 4.24.4, *Paneg.* 95.3, 95.4; Whitton (2015b, 18–19).
126. Text and translation from Whitton (2015b, 2), where see (2015b, 2 n. 6) for the conjectured <*et*>.
127. See Syme (1958, 652–6), *RP* 7.561–3.
128. Whitton (2015b, 19, 20).
129. Fulkerson (2013, 218–19), cited in Chp. 4.
130. Tac. *Hist.* 1.1.3 *dignitatem nostram a Vespasiano inchoatam, a Tito auctam, a Domitiano longius prouectam non abnuerim.*
131. See Syme (1958, 70); cf. Whitton (2015a, 19 n. 119).
132. See Bennett (2001, 42–6) for Trajan's Domitianic record; cf. earlier in this chapter for Nerva under Domitian.
133. 8.14.8–9 *iidem prospeximus curiam, sed curiam trepidam et elinguem, cum dicere quod uelles periculosum, quod nolles miserum esset. quid tunc disci potuit, quid didicisse iuuit, cum senatus aut ad otium summum aut ad summum nefas uocaretur, et modo ludibrio modo dolori retentus numquam seria, tristia saepe censeret? eadem*

mala iam senatores, iam participes malorum multos per annos uidimus tulimusque; quibus ingenia nostra in posterum quoque hebetata fracta contusa sunt.

134. Cf. Suet. *Dom.* 17.1–2, Jones (1992, 193–6).

135. For a fuller narrative of the events of 96–8 C.E, see Griffin (2000b, 84–96); cf. Syme (1958, 1–18, 627–36), Grainger (2004, 45–108), Bennett (2001, 42–52), Birley (1997) 35–7, Collins (2009).

136. Suet. *Dom.* 23.1 *repleta certatim curia non temperaret, quin mortuum contumeliosissimo atque acerbissimo adclamationum genere laceraret, scalas etiam inferri clipeosque et imagines eius coram detrahi et ibidem solo affligi iuberet, nouissime eradendos ubique titulos abolendamque omnes memoriam decerneret.*

137. The great Comum inscription, set up during Trajan's reign, records only *quaestor Imperatoris* (*CIL* 5.5262: Chp. 7).

138. 1.5.1–2 *Vidistine quemquam M. Regulo timidiorem humiliorem post Domitiani mortem? sub quo non minora flagitia commiserat quam sub Nerone sed tectiora. coepit uereri ne sibi irascerer, nec fallebatur: irascebar. Rustici Aruleni periculum fouerat, exsultauerat morte; adeo ut librum recitaret publicaretque, in quo Rusticum insectatur.* On this letter, see Hoffer (1999, 55–91) = (2016).

139. 1.5.10 *exspecto Mauricum.* On Vestricius Spurinna, see Chp. 4; cf. Pliny's lengthy eulogy of his mentor in 3.1.

140. On Regulus, see Syme, *RP* 7.577–8, Lefèvre (2009, 50–60), Gibson and Morello (2012, 68–73), Ash (2013), Marchesi (2013), (2018); Whitton (2013, 16–17, 19–20, 268–70). He appears in 1.5, 1.20.14, 2.11.22, 2.20, 4.2, 4.7, 6.2.

141. 6.2.2, 4 *habebat studiis honorem . . . bene fecit Regulus quod est mortuus: melius, si ante.* On Pliny's rivalry with Regulus in the Centumviral court, cf. 1.5.4–7, 4.7.4–5, also Mart. 6.38, Syme (1958, 101–104).

142. 9.13.4 *primis quidem diebus redditae libertatis pro se quisque inimicos suos, dumtaxat minores, incondito turbidoque clamore postulauerat simul et oppresserat. ego et modestius et constantius arbitratus immanissimum reum . . . urgere.*

143. See Sherwin-White (1966, 492), with reference to 9.13.16 *cruentae adulationis.*

144. On procedures for laying charges in the senate, see Sherwin-White (1966, 493–4), Talbert (1984, 480–81).

145. Pliny's speech, probably known as 'On the vindication of Helvidius' (9.13.1 *de Helvidi ultione*), receives frequent mention in the *Letters*: 1.2.6, 4.21.3, 7.30.5; see also Syme, *RP* 7.579, who conjectures its influence on Tac. *Hist.* 4.42 (the denunciation of Regulus by Curtius Montanus in 70 C.E.). On Ummidius Quadratus, and his family (including his grandmother Ummidia Quadratilla: subject of 7.24), see Syme (1968b) = *RP* 2.659–93; (1979) = *RP* 3.1158–78; (1982, 235–6) = *RP* 4.55–6; (1984a, 406–7) = 4.169–70.

146. 9.13.7–8 *ubi coepi crimen attingere, reum destinare, adhuc tamen sine nomine, undique mihi reclamari. alius: 'sciamus, quis sit de quo extra ordinem referas', alius: 'quis est ante relationem reus?', alius: 'salui simus, qui supersumus'.*

147. On Pliny's deliberate delay of his account of the trial—including the observation about Corellius Rufus—till more than a decade after the event, in Book 9, see Gibson and Morello (2012, 27–32, 128–31), also Mratschek (2018, 217–21).

148. Probably M. Cornelius Nigrinus Curiatius Maternus; for his role in the events of 97 C.E., see Eck (2002), Griffin (2000b, 90).

149. See Sherwin-White (1966, 497). Pliny has omitted the contents of his own *sententia* or formal proposal, presumably that the 'conduct of Certus should be subject to an investigation, provided that the *princeps* concurred' (Sherwin-White (1966, 497)).

150. 9.13.22–3 *relationem quidem de eo Caesar ad senatum non remisit; obtinui tamen quod intenderam: nam collega Certi consulatum, successorem Certus accepit.*

151. On the constitutional technicalities of Nerva's (non-)response to the senate's motion, see Sherwin-White (1966, 498); cf. Griffin (2000b, 88 and n. 31), and Murison (2003) on Nerva and the Flavians.

152. The interpretation of Certus' fate in the treasury posting is disputed: some argue that *successorem accepit* ('was superseded') must mean that Certus was removed from the Saturnian position; but Sherwin-White (1966, 498) rightly argues that no such dismissal can be read into the words (as does Syme (1958, 658)). For the view that illness (and death) snatched the consulship from Certus, see Griffin (1999, 154 n. 52) = (2016, 372 n. 52). Certus' colleague at the Treasury of Saturn, Bittius Proculus, did gain the consulship. This Proculus was stepfather to Pliny's wife (Salomies (1992, 120–1)), who had died shortly before these events in the senate (9.13.4), and had spoken in defence of Certus during the senatorial debate (9.13.13). Perhaps he and Pliny were able to rise above their differences; see Chp. 6 for the Umbrian connection.

153. 9.13.2 *materiam . . . se proferendi.* Such a motive does not however appear among those approved by the high-minded Thrasea (Pliny must add it himself); see Gibson (f'coming) on 6.29.

154. The exact sequence of events that brought Pliny to the Saturnian treasury and thence to the consulship is disputed; for a variety of views, see Syme (1958, 658), *RP* 7.564–5; Sherwin-White (1966, 491), Griffin (2000b, 88). The precise dates of Pliny's Saturnian posting are likewise a subject of disagreement; see Syme (1958, 658–9), Sherwin-White (1966, 75–8), *PIR²* P 490 (p. 206). On the high success rate of prefects of the treasury in their later careers, see Syme (1984b, 55–6) = *RP* 4.320–1.

155. On 1.10.9–11 as a reference to the Saturnian prefecture, see Sherwin-White (1966, 110); cf. 10.8 for further references to the burdens of the office.

156. On the duties of the prefects of the treasury of Saturn, see Millar (1964) = (2004c). Pliny's colleague at the Saturnian treasury was Cornutus Tertullus, who would join him in the consulship of 100 C.E.; see later in this chapter.

157. See earlier for the narrative of events in 97–8.

158. See Syme, *RP* 7.519; cf. also Berriman-Todd (2001), Eck (2002), Hoffer (2006, 74–7).

159. See Whitton (2013, 65–83) on 2.1.

160. See Syme, *RP* 7.518–19.

161. On Trajan's trademark *ciuilitas*, see Griffin (2000b, 102–6); on Pliny's attempt to play this up, at the expense of Trajan's military affiliations, see Noreña (2007) on Book 10; cf. Syme (1964) = *RP* 6.142–9 on Pliny's strategy of silence over the Dacian wars. On Pliny's handing of the accession of Trajan and the emperor's return to Rome, see Gibson and Morello (2012, 24 with n. 60).

162. See Hoffer (1999, 141–59) on the death of Corellius.

163. Cf. 10.6–7, 10–11 on the same subject. The date of 97 C.E. appears to be guaranteed by 10.8.3, where the illness is said to take place during the reign of Nerva, but before Pliny's assumption of the post of prefect of the treasury of Saturn in 98.

164. Cf. 1.10, 1.13; cf. 3.20.10–12, Tac. *Agr.* 3.1–3 (with Woodman and Kraus (2014, 87–93), Gibson and Morello (2012, 25–26), Hoffer (1999, 161–63, 170). Despite the riches of non-senatorial literature in the late Flavian era (see earlier), a literary renaissance could be declared at least for senators: alongside Pliny's work on his speeches and *Letters*, Tacitus would author the *Agricola, Germania,* and *Dialogus de Oratoribus* before starting on the *Histories.* For the 'silencing' of Flavian literature by Trajanic authors, see Buckley (2018).

165. See Gibson and Morello (2012, 27–35) on the effect of this delayed revelation, and Chp. 7 on the reason for the delay; see Chp. 6 for Pompeia Celerina and her daughter.

166. See Hoffer (1999, 229–33) on the Augustan marriage laws and the date of Pliny's marriage to Calpurnia (doubted by Shelton (2013, 98)); cf. earlier n. 32 for the controversy over the number of Pliny's marriages.

167. The various stages of the Priscus trial described in 2.11–12 (with Whitton (2013, 154–92)) appear to stretch from initial indictment in the second half of 98 to the final sessions in front of the senate in January 100; see Sherwin-White (1966, 160). Pliny's co-prosecutor was Tacitus; he makes further references to the trial at 3.9.2–4, 6.29.9, 10.3a.1–2, *Paneg.* 76.1–3. Later generations would come to disagree with Pliny's estimate of the importance of the trial: the leniency of Priscus' sentence would become proverbial (Juv. 1.47–8; cf. 8.119–20).

168. 3.4, 3.9, 6.29.8. Classicus was prosecuted despite being dead; see Sherwin-White (1966, 213–5, 230–8).

169. *Paneg.* 91.1 *nondum biennium compleueramus in officio laboriosissimo et maximo, cum tu nobis, optime principum fortissime imperatorum, consulatum obtulisti, ut ad summum honorem gloria celeritatis accederet*; cf. 91.2 on the exemption of a year as a mark of favour.

170. Pliny makes much of the fact that he and Cornutus Tertullus continued in office at the treasury right up till the moment that they became suffect consuls, in September 100 C.E., although this also been used to suggest that Pliny held the treasury post right through his consulship into 101 C.E.; see Sherwin-White (1966, 77–8), Syme (1958, 659).

171. A suppressed competitiveness between Pliny and Cornutus Tertullus is evident in 5.14. Cornutus would continue to lag behind Pliny slightly, succeeding the younger man in Pontus-Bithynia (see Envoi). Cornutus was a guardian to the daughter of Helvidius and one of the speakers in the senate who supported Pliny's motion against Certus (9.13.15–16). Tertullus is a rare example at this period of a consul from the eastern empire; see Chp. 8 n. 50.

172. Comum's second consul may well be Baebius Macer: consul of 103 C.E. and addressee of Pliny's long letter on the books and working habits of his uncle (3.5); cf. Birley (2000a, 41) for further information on Macer.

173. Epictetus on senatorial ambition: cf. Arr. *Epict. diss.* 1.25.26–7, 4.1.55, 173. Millar (1965, 145) = (2004d, 113) contrasts Arr. *Epict. diss.* 4.10.20–1 and Pliny's sanitized picture of canvassing at 6.19.

174. For a reconstruction of the consular *fasti* for 100 C.E., see Sherwin-White (1966, 78), noting the revisions of Syme, *RP* 7.546–7. On the exact length of Pliny's tenure as suffect consul, see Sherwin-White (1966) 78. The September start is guaranteed by the references to superintendence by Pliny and Cornutus of celebrations in that month, such as the triple celebration on 18 September of Trajan's birthday, Domitian's death, and Nerva's accession (*Paneg.* 92.4–5; cf. Chp. 8).

175. Cf. 10.8.3, Suet. *Dom.* 35.3, Geisthardt (2015, 83–146).

176. On the context and content of the *Panegyricus*, see the essays collected in Roche (2011a).

177. Aug. *Conf.* 6.6.9 *cum pararem recitare imperatori laudes, quibus plura mentirer et mentienti faveretur ab scientibus.*

178. See Cameron (2011, 399–420); cf. Chp. 8 for the influence of the Second Sophistic.

179. See Cameron (2011, 403–4); cf. the essays gathered by Gibson and Rees (2013) for the fate of the *Panegyricus* in late antiquity; see also Chp. 8 for early Christian readers of Book 10 and general revival of the *Letters* in the fourth century.

180. See Della Torre (1984, 175–6).

181. *Paneg.* 94.5 *si bene rem publicam, si ex utilitate omnium regit.*

182. *Paneg.* 66.2 *nunc singulos, nunc uniuersos adhortatus es resumere libertatem, capessere quasi communis imperii curas, inuigilare publicis utiltatibus et insurgere.*

183. For Trajanic ideology, insofar as it can be recovered from the *Panegyricus* and the kingship orations of Dio of Prusa, see Bennett (2001, 63–73).

184. Eutropius *Breuiarum* 8.5.3 *felicior Augusto, melior Traiano.*

185. Syme (1958, 41); cf. the analysis of Griffin (2000b, 96–100).

186. See Matthews (1989, 11–12, 231–4).

187. Amm. Marc. 16.10.17 *multis igitur cum stupore uisis horrendo imperator in fama querebatur ut inualida uel maligna, quod augens omnia semper in maius erga haec explicanda quae Romae sunt obsolescit.*

188. See Jenkyns (2013, 263, 337); cf. Suet. *Aug.* 28.3 (brick and marble).

189. Amm. Marc. 16.10.15 *haerebat adtonitus per giganteos contextus circumferens mentem nec relatu effabiles nec rursus mortalibus adpetendos.*

190. See Jenkyns (2013, 326, 345–64) for an overview. The Pantheon is now widely redated from the reign of Hadrian to that of Trajan; see Jenkyns (2013, 351–2), with reference to the work of Hetland (2007).

191. See Roche (2011b, 48–9); but for Pliny's own building activities in Comum in the mid-late 90s C.E. see Chp. 7.

192. For an overview of the Flavian architectural contribution to Rome, including Vespasian's Colosseum and Forum of Peace, and Domitian's Odeum, Stadium, and Temple of Jupiter (all mentioned in Amm. Marc. 16.10.14), see Griffin (2000a, 19–21, 57–8), Jenkyns (2013, 325–6, 343–5). On Domitian's financial troubles, see Griffin (2000a, 69–76).

193. 10.18.3 *mensores uix etiam iis operibus, quae aut Romae aut in proximo fiunt, sufficientes habeo.*

194. See Jenkyns (2013, 122–6). In his review of Rome's greatest building, the Elder Pliny had offered a paean to the city: 'If we imagine the whole agglomeration of our buildings massed together and placed on one great heap, we shall see such grandeur towering above us as to make us think that some other world were being described, all concentrated in a single place' (*HN* 36.101). The marvels of Rome are reviewed at length at *HN* 36.101–25.

195. In the *Panegyricus,* Pliny reviews the buildings of Rome under the sunlight of Trajan's rule and produces a chillingly sinister portrait of Domitian's former residence on the Palatine hill (*Paneg.* 48.2–49.3); see Jenkyns (2013, 298–300); cf. Clark (2007, 17–19), Roche (2011b, esp. 50, 65). There was a strong link between monuments and encomium (Roche (2011b, 47–8)); the *Letters* perhaps give a better idea of Pliny's *personal* interests (or lack thereof).

196. Cf. 5.1.9, 7.19.2, 4.11.6 (with Hoffer (1999, 79) and Clark (2007, 20) on the particular symbolism of Pliny's rare mention of specific public buildings other than the Basilica Iulia).

197. Cf. 2.14.4, 8; 5.9.1, 6.33.4.

198. Cf. 8.6.13–14 (with Clark (2007, 22–3 and n. 73) on the location of the statue).

199. Cf. 1.13.3 and 9.6.1, 9.23.2.

200. Cf. 1.5.9 (see earlier in this chapter for Pliny meeting there).

201. Cf. 1.17.1, 4; 2.1.6, 2.14.2, 5.8.8; cf. mention of a handful of homes and estates in the suburbs of Rome or on the far bank of the Tiber (3.11.2, 4.2.5, 6.19.1). On the Roman forum, see Appendix 2.

202. In *his* letters, Cicero ranges more widely, taking in the Capitol, the Campus Martius, the via Appia, and a good number of houses belonging to friends and associates; cf. e.g. Cic. *Att.* 2.1.7, 4.1, 13.33 (Capitol); *Att.* 1.1, 4.3, *Fam.* 7.30 (Campus Martius); *Q.Fr.* 1.1.17, 3.5.8, *Att.* 16.10 (via Appia); *Att.* 1.12.3, 3.2.1, 4.3 (houses of friends and associates). For a complete list of the capital's sites in Cicero's letters, see Clark (2007, 4–7).

203. Cf. *Paneg.* 51.1, 3–5, with Roche (2011b, 54–9), who points out that the Trajanic project of restoration of the Circus Maximus was almost certainly Domitianic in origin.

204. See Gibson (2015, 212–19), and later in this chapter for hints of political disaffection.

205. On the location of Pliny's house, see Appendix 2.

206. On Martial's Rome, see Sullivan (1991, 147–55), Roman (2010).

207. Mart. 10.20.4–8 *breuis est labor peractae | altum uincere tramitem Suburae. | illic Orphea protinus uidebis | udi uertice lubricum theatri | mirantisque feras auemque regem.* On Pliny's quotation from this poem in 3.21, see Henderson (2002a, 50–5); cf. Förtsch (1993, 17 n. 55).

208. Pliny's Rome is full of movement of other kinds: he writes of doing the rounds in public and private places to canvass on behalf of friends (2.9.5); evokes journeys through a Forum crowded with audiences for the great trials of the day (2.14.6–8, 4.16.1, 5.9.1–2); and pointedly criticizes those who are sluggish in attending literary recitations (1.13.2).

209. Augustine on Rome: see Clark (2004, 16–18), O'Donnell (2005, 120), Lane Fox (2015, 163–7), Gwynn (2017).

210. Contrast Rome in the writings of Pliny's friend and rival: 'The richest sense of the physical presence of Rome in any prose author belongs to Tacitus' (Jenkyns (2013, 134, with elaboration at 135–41).

211. 6.33.3–4 *sedebant centum et octoginta iudices (tot enim quattuor consiliis colliguntur), ingens utrimque aduocatio et numerosa subsellia, praeterea densa circumstantium corona latissimum iudicium multiplici circulo ambibat. ad hoc stipatum tribunal, atque etiam ex superiore basilicae parte qua feminae qua uiri et audiendi (quod difficile) et (quod facile) uisendi studio imminebant.* On the difficulties of interpreting physical layout here, see Bablitz (2007, 68–9).

212. On the operation of Rome's civil courts in general, see Bablitz (2011), (2016); on the operation of the Centumviral courts in particular, see Bablitz (2007, 61–70), Whitton (2013, 201–3), all with further references.

213. To complicate matters, Suburanus, a nephew or cousin of Attia, and himself disinherited, is seeking not the restitution of his own part of the estate, but rather to gain Attia's share; see Carlon (2009, 113, 132–4) for the possible bearing the case has on Pliny's relationship with Trajan via Attia's putative brother; see also Gibson (f'coming) on 6.33.

214. On the length of speeches in the courts, see Bablitz (2007, 172–3, 179–85), Whitton (2013, 173–4), Gibson (f'coming) on 6.2.3. 5.

215. See earlier n. 82 for variations in length of time allowed.

216. See Bablitz (2007, 70).

217. 4.16.2 *quidam ornatus adulescens scissis tunicis . . . sola uelatus toga perstitit.*

218. 6.33.8–9 *et copia rerum et arguta divisione et narratiunculis pluribus et eloquendi uarietate renouatur . . . elata . . . pugnacia . . . subtilia . . . intervenit enim acribus illis et erectis frequens necessitas computandi ac paene calculos tabulamque poscendi.*

219. Note the gloomy sentiments attributed to Maternus in Tacitus' *Dialogus*, where at a dramatic date of c. 75 C.E. he contrasts the prestige of the great criminal trials of the late Republic with the low reputation in that era of inheritance cases tried before the Centumviral courts (*Dial.* 38.2); see further Marchesi (2008, 132–5), Dominik (2007).

220. 4.19.3 *disponit qui nuntient sibi quem adsensum quos clamores excitarim, quem euentum iudicii tulerim.*

221. 4.19.3 *eadem, si quando recito, in proximo discreta uelo sedet, laudesque nostras auidissimis auribus excipit.*

222. Cf. Shelton (2013, 113) and see further Chp. 7 for Calpurnia.

223. See Johnson (2010, 32–62) on the *recitatio*. For public recitations of new literature in Pliny (both his own and that of others), cf. 1.13, 2.3, 2.10, 2.19, 3.18, 4.5, 4.19, 4.27, 5.3, 5.12, 5.17, 6.15, 6.17, 6.21, 7.17, 8.12, 8.21, 9.17, 9.27, 9.34.

224. E.g. 1.13, 6.15, 6.17.

225. On Pliny and Martial, see further Fitzgerald (2018), Mratschek (2018).

226. Cf. 5.3, 5.12 (helpful criticism), 7.17, 9.3 (criticisms of Pliny). On cooperation and competition in the culture of the contemporary *recitatio*, see Roller (2018).

227. Cf. Mart. 6.60, Juvenal *Sat.* 1.1–18.

228. 9.6.1 '*quemadmodum*' inquis '*in urbe potuisti?*' *Circenses erant, quo genere spectaculi ne leuissime quidem teneor.*

229. Cf. 7.24.6, also 7.11.4 (a very brief mention of the *ludi* over which Pliny presided during his praetorship). For gladiatorial games *outside* Rome in the new Trajanic era, see Chp. 7.

230. For Pliny's tenure in this curatorship (104–6 C.E.), see Syme (1958, 659), Sherwin-White (1966, 79). Not long after Pliny's time, this post would become a stepping stone to the governorship of a province; see Syme (1984b, 56–7) = *RP* 4.321–2. For further possible references to the post, other than on inscriptions (*CIL* 5.5262, 5263, 5667), cf. 7.15.1, 7.21.1.

231. Cf. Sherwin-White (1966, 467)) on 8.17: 'Pliny writes with the knowledge of a *curator Tiberis*, but without any official connexion with the matter'.

232. Cf. 5.20, 6.5, 6.13, 6.29, 7.6, 7.10; see Chp.8.

233. For the size and prestige of priestly colleges and competitive entry through co-option, see Sherwin-White (1966, 272), Várhelyi (2010, 56–69).

234. On Frontinus, see Rodgers (2004, 1–20), Malloch (2015); on Frontinus and Pliny, cf. 4.8.3, 5.1.5, 9.19, König (2013).

235. See Várhelyi (2010, 75–7); on the religious significance of priesthoods, see Várhelyi (2010, 58).

236. See *OCD*[4] s.v. *augures*.

237. See Jenkyns (2013, 235–55).

238. See Chp. 6.

239. See Chp. 8.

240. See Jal (1993), Griffin (1999) = (2016), Hoffer (1999, 1), Wolff (2003). But for a recognition of Pliny's tendency to pessimism, see Strunk (2012).

241. See Gibson (2015, 211–12).

242. See Gibson (2015, 203–4). On Trajan's return from Dacia in Book 6, see Gibson (f'coming).

243. Syme understood the descending gloom of the later books: he noted that 'illnesses seem to pile up in the period covered by Books VII and VIII', and suggested as explanation 'a sequence of unhealthy seasons' (cf. 8.1.1) or 'an epidemic supervening in the train of second war against the Dacians' (Syme (1985b, 182) = *RP* 5.486). But the gloom spreads beyond the personal to the political; see later.

244. The argument in this paragraph is set out in greater detail, and with further supporting evidence, in Gibson (2015, 204–19).

245. The use of the flooding of the Tiber to create an ominous political atmosphere has a long history; cf. e.g. Horace *Odes* 1.2.

246. 8.4 also hints at tyrannical behaviour. Pliny here refers to two famous episodes in the Dacian wars: the king of the Dacians diverted the course of a river in order to bury his treasure, only for Trajan to re-divert the river and recover the treasure; Trajan also managed to throw a miraculous stone bridge over the Danube. Ever since Herodotus, the diversion of rivers had been associated with the behaviour of tyrants (3.117, 7.129–30). And the building of a bridge over the Danube had been

one of the most egregious signs of the tyrannical nature of Darius and very nearly the occasion of his death (4.89, 97–8, 133–42); see further Gibson (2015, 214–15).

247. 8.14.2–3 *priorum temporum seruitus ut aliarum optimarum artium, sic etiam iuris senatorii obliuionem quandam et ignorantiam induxit . . . reducta libertas rudes nos et imperitos deprehendit; cuius dulcedine accensi, cogimur quaedam facere ante quam nosse;* cf. Gibson (2015, 215–19) on this letter in the context of Book 8, also Whitton (2010).

248. The argument in this paragraph is set out in greater detail, and with further supporting evidence, in Gibson (2015, 194–203, 219–20).

249. Cf. 9.2, 9.6, 9.8, 9.11, 9.14, 9.18, 9.23, 9.25, 9.31.

250. On Trajan's *grands projets*, see earlier in this chapter.

251. On the archaeology of Centumcellae and the literary texture of Pliny's description and the harbour as metaphor for Trajan as imperial bulwark, see Appendix 2. Note that this positive framing of the emperor appears in Book 6, before the pessimism of Books 7–9.

252. See Whitton (2012, 363–4).

253. See Gibson (2015, 221–2).

254. See Woodman (2009).

255. See Seelentag (2011, 77–81).

256. See Gibson (f'coming) on 6.19; cf. 3.7.14, 3.20.10, 5.13.6–8.

257. See Griffin (2000b, 99–100).

258. See Griffin (2000b, 113–14).

6

Umbria and the Laurentine Shore

The present chapter will cover Pliny's life in Umbria and the Laurentine shore, from his youthful adoption as patron of the Umbrian town of Tifernum Tiberinum, through early marriage into the aristocratic networks of Umbria and Etruria, on to mature ownership of the two great villas near Rome and Tifernum and their characteristic activities of study, writing, and farming. The chapter covers roughly the same period of time as the previous chapter on Rome, from Pliny's youth under the Flavians to prime of life under Trajan. Markers of passing time and milestones achieved, as befits country villas away from the capital, are not so frequent or so clearly discerned as in Rome. The following chapter, on Pliny's adult life in Comum, focuses on an overlapping but slightly later time period, from the final years of Domitian's reign in the 90s C.E. to the moment of Pliny's departure for Pontus-Bithynia. It includes an account of the new marriage to Calpurnia of Comum that Pliny would contract after the death of his previous wife, whose connections had embedded him in Umbria and Etruria. The concerns of this pair of chapters will be local, domestic, and personal. Questions of who Pliny *is* will arise more urgently than in the Rome chapter, where the focus was often on what Pliny *did*. The chronological story of Pliny's political life, covered in the Rome chapter as far as the end of the first decade of the second century, will be taken up again in the final chapter on Pontus-Bithynia, with Pliny's arrival there as governor c. 110 C.E.[1]

Approaching two villas

Pliny writes a great deal about two impressive residences he owned besides those in Rome and Comum. The first lay directly south-west of Rome on the *ager Laurens*, the 'Laurentine domain' by the sea (Map 1). Reaching this beachfront from the centre of modern Rome takes just over an hour. A metro ride to Piramide will allow a glimpse of the striking Augustan-era pyramid of C. Cestius amidst heavy traffic, as the visitor transfers above ground to the Roma-Lido railway line. Railway cars embossed with graffiti transport the visitor at length towards the sea, past the stop for Ostia Antica and the distant sight of planes landing at Fiumicino on the far bank of the Tiber, through humdrum seaside suburbs to the final stop, Cristoforo Colombo. The traveller emerges beside a

Man of High Empire. Roy K. Gibson, Oxford University Press (2020). © Oxford University Press.

DOI: 10.1093/actrade/9780199948192.001.0001

broad and busy road that must be crossed to reach the sea. The seafront is taken up with bars, private beaches, and leisure facilities for the summer crowds. The strand itself is featureless. In antiquity the shoreline lay several hundred metres inland, along a seafront far more articulated and irregular, before the centuries-long advance of the Tiber mouth.[2] The ancient seashore is largely concealed amongst the dense vegetation that grows in the modern pine forests of Castelfusano and Castelporziano (the private estate of the Italian president). Pliny's villa lies somewhere here, still unidentified amongst the remains of villas repeatedly modified in antiquity and despoiled thereafter by plunder and often undocumented excavation.[3]

Pliny describes a rather different journey to his Laurentine villa that allows arrival at nightfall after a busy morning's work in the city:[4]

It is tucked away seventeen miles from Rome, so that after concluding your business, you can go and stay there with the setting sun. There is access to it by more than one road, since the Laurentine and Ostian highways lead in the same direction; only, you must branch off from the Laurentine at the fourteenth milestone and the Ostian at the eleventh. Either way, the next part of the road is for some distance sandy, somewhat taxing and long by carriage, short and easy on horseback. The view is varied all around: the road is now narrowed by woods blocking its way, now it spreads out and extends over broad expanses of meadow: you see numerous flocks of sheep, and herds of horses and cattle, driven down from the mountains by winter, grow sleek with the grass and spring warmth.[5]

Letters 2.17.2–3

Pliny's description elongates as busy highways are left behind.[6] Vistas expand and contract as woods close in or recede. He travels light: horseback is better than carriage. The retinue that accompanies a senator is elided. Flocks down from the Alban hills hint at an ancestral past, remote from the busy city. Their attendants go unmentioned.[7] Spring warmth and untrammeled nature enrich the scene.

The overall sense of remoteness, depopulation, and hints of wildness all draw on the cultural reputation of the Laurentine shore. The area had a name for seclusion and desertion. This was the 'landscape of Aeneas' arrival', the location of the Trojans' first temporary settlement in Italy and the vanished site of the city of king Latinus.[8] In the *Aeneid*, Vergil has his hero spot a 'huge grove' populated only by birds on his arrival by sea near the Tiber mouth (*Aen.* 7.29–32). The heroes Nisus and Euryalus lose their way in the overgrown woods (*Aen.* 9.381–6). It was here that virtue could flourish in adversity, isolated from the site of the future Rome. In reality, as a critic observes, 'no landscape was a desert if it had a Roman ex-consul in it'.[9] Pliny reveals that the supplies for the Laurentine villa come from nearby Ostia, that the next-door village possesses three sets of public baths, and the seafront features a millionaires' row of luxury villas, 'at one place continuous, at another broken, so as to present the appearance of a number of towns, whether you look at them from the sea or the shore itself' (2.17.26–7).[10] He is teasing readers with the gap between cultural reputation and the facts of contemporary real estate.

Pliny consistently refers to a second beloved residence near Tifernum Tiberinum in the upper Tiber valley as 'Tuscan' (*Tuscos meos*, 5.6.1). This appellation does not signify Tuscany in its Anglophone sense. Pliny's estate and nearby Tifernum lay on the east bank of the Tiber in Umbria (Map 1); the region of Etruria lay to the west. The inhabitants of the region were ethnically Tuscan, from Etruria: the origin of Pliny's name for his estate.[11] Pliny's own personal connections with individuals and towns in the region lay mostly to the east of the Tiber, down through the considerable extent of Umbria. He had fewer relationships to the west. Yet this eastern region is quietly played down, with the apparent intention of giving Comum and the Transpadana greater prominence. This chapter refers to the Tuscan residence as 'Umbrian' by way of highlighting what Pliny wished to leave in the shade and of unifying his various interests in the region beyond the villa.

Pliny provides no account of a scenic approach to the Umbrian villa equivalent to the Laurentine. He says his estate lay over 150 Roman miles from the capital (10.8.6), that is 137 miles/222 kilometres. This was a journey of five days if the seventeen-mile journey to Laurentum could be covered in a long afternoon.[12] Not a trip to be taken on a whim in the middle of a senator's busy schedule;[13] Pliny implies the Umbrian villa was mainly a summer residence (9.36).[14] This is the season in which he reports details of travel to the villa. He has arrived there safely, albeit with 'some of my people rendered ill by the scorching heats' (8.1.1).[15] Particular regret is reserved for Encolpius, Pliny's prized *lector*, whose job it was to read his master's literary productions to him (8.1.2): the enslaved man's throat had become 'so irritated by the dust that he spat blood' (8.1.1). The salubrious surroundings of the estate held good prospect for recovery.

For evocation of atmosphere we must turn to Gilbert Highet's *Poets in a Landscape* and his chapter on the Umbrian poet Propertius, composed sixty years ago:

> North of Rome, the land changes. It becomes richer and more fertile, but also bolder and stranger. The rocky Apennine backbone of Italy sends out curving ribs and throws up harsh vertebrae of stone. There are high ridges of hill, with cool glens and forests among them. There are fruitful plains, often commanded by steep spurs of rock which have always made splendid natural fortresses. It is not an easy country to travel through, even now.[16]

Pliny reserves *his* scenic flourish for the site of the Umbrian villa under the Apennines:

> The lie of the area is charming: imagine a kind of amphitheatre of immense size, such as nature alone can construct. A broad and spreading plain is surrounded by mountains; the mountains on their highest summits are crowned with high and venerable forests, and in them there is hunting in plenty and variety. Next to these are woods for cutting . . . Below them, vineyards stretch along the whole side of the mountain, and present a uniform appearance far and wide. . . . They are terminated . . . by plantation vineyards. Then come meadows and cornfields, fields which are broken up only by the largest oxen and the strongest ploughs . . . there is no marsh, because the land, being on an incline, pours into the Tiber all the moisture it receives and does not absorb. That river runs through the middle of the fields . . . You would be greatly charmed if you viewed the topography of the area from the mountains; you would fancy yourself looking not so much at country, but at a kind of landscape painted with the most exquisite beauty. . . . My villa, though situated at the foot of a hill, commands a view as if from a top; so gentle and gradual is the unperceived rise to it that you find you have made an ascent, without knowing that you have been ascending. At its back it has the Apennines, but some way off. From these it enjoys breezes, however calm and unruffled the day. . . It has, for the most part, a southerly aspect . . .[17]
>
> *Letters* 5.6.7–15

There is less taste for wildness here than in Highet's Umbria. Pliny's scene is presented as a spectacle for viewing.[18] The surrounding bowl of hillsides is compared to the banked seating of an amphitheatre; the view from the hillsides is like looking at a painting. There are hints that Pliny is taking in the landscape with the eye of a man financially dependent on the crops the estate produces: vineyards, fields for ploughing, a river to take the produce downstream to Rome. Finance is ultimately subordinated to the aesthetic pleasure of looking at an ideal, ordered landscape and to the enjoyment it gives the owner of the hillside villa as he takes in the wide-angle view of his domain. Such carefully worked descriptions of landscape in prose are thoroughly familiar to modern readers. They are not to be taken for granted in the ancient world. In the century after Pliny, Pausanias wrote the ancient world's most detailed guide to the sites of Greece largely without comment on landscape or vista. It is human geography that interests Pausanias.[19] In Pliny's own day, intense evocation of scenery was associated with poetry.

A bowl of hills and a situation for a villa at the top of a gentle rise underneath the steeper Apennines: such topographical features are not in short supply in the upper Tiber valley beyond Perugia. There were some false starts

Figure 6.1. View from the foot of Colle Plinio near San Giustino in Umbria, towards the Tiber and the west flank of the upper Tiber valley. As Pliny says, 'so gentle and gradual is the unperceived rise to it that you find you have made an ascent, without knowing it' (5.6.14). Pliny's villa lies on Colle Plinio, under the eastern flank of the Tiber valley; cf. Figure 7. *Photo by C. Delaney.*

in the attempt to locate the remains of Pliny's villa.[20] In the mid-fifteenth century Biondo Flavio authored *Italia Illustrata*, a review of the settlements of the peninsula modelled on the survey of the Italian *regiones* produced by the Elder Pliny in the third book of his *Natural History*. He confidently located the villa at Sansepolcro at the very top of the Tiber valley largely on the basis of the theatrical aspect of the surrounding hills.[21] The likely site further down the valley near San Giustino was first identified by a local, Francesco Ignazio Lazzari (1633–1717),[22] and finally investigated in the late twentieth century by a team of archaeologists from nearby Perugia and from Alicante (Figs. 6.1, 6.2).[23] Excavations uncovered the *pars rustica* or agricultural buildings of the estate— the very part ignored by Pliny in his focus on the interaction of the residential buildings with surrounding landscape.[24] Excavation on the occupied residential site was impossible. Brick stamps discovered in the course of work confirmed what had been long suspected: Pliny inherited the estate from the Elder Pliny.[25] Other discoveries suggest older and grander connections with the Augustan proconsul M. Granius Marcellus.[26]

Figure 6.2. Hypothetical reconstruction of Pliny's villa, its location, and the relationship between archaeological remains and the residential villa proper. Digs on the Campo di Santa Fiora at the base of Colle Plinio near San Giustino in Umbria have uncovered the agricultural buildings of the estate and the remains of a shrine. (This was perhaps also the site of the villa of the former owner, M. Granius Marcellus.) The probable site of the residential part of Pliny's estate complex lies on top of Colle Plinio, within the modern private estate of the Marchesi Cappelletti. *Image reproduced by kind permission of P. Braconi: from Braconi and Uroz-Sáez (2008, 109 fig. 5).*

Inside the villas (and the man)

Pliny is eager to show the addressees of his two great villa letters, Gallus (2.17) and fellow northern consular Apollinaris (5.6), around the inside of his pair of spacious residences.[27] The visitor to the Laurentine villa (Fig. 6.3) is conducted around the central section of the house (2.17.4–5), the south-east wing (2.17.6–9) and the north-west wing with their baths and tower (2.17.10–12), followed by a second tower with its views of attached gardens (2.17.13–15), ending with a long covered walkway (2.17.16–19) and Pliny's own private suite set apart from the main residence (2.17.20–4). The Umbrian villa tour (Fig. 6.4) ultimately follows a similar structure as we begin with the rooms, courtyards, bedrooms, dining areas, swimming pool and baths, exercise area, and covered walkways of the main building, to end with Pliny's private apartment set in the spacious ornamental gardens of the residence (5.6.38–40).[28]

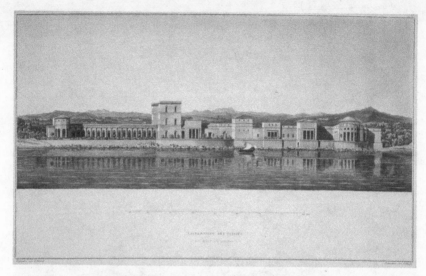

Figure 6.3. Perspective of Pliny's Laurentine villa by K. F. Schinkel (*Architektonisches Album*, Berlin 1841).

Figure 6.4. Perspective of Pliny's Umbrian (Tuscan) villa by K. F. Schinkel (*Architektonisches Album*, Berlin 1841).

There are numerous modern guides to accompany readers through the many rooms and gardens of Pliny's mansions.[29] A biography demands interest in a related sort of interiority: the Plinian self.[30] In the remainder of this chapter, the Umbrian Pliny comes under the spotlight first, before attention switches to the Laurentine. Umbrian friends, connections, and a marriage come to light, and questions are asked about the warm persona that he evinces in the region and his tendency to apprehend the wondrous and the divine there. For the Laurentine Pliny, the focus lingers ultimately on the activities that take the place of farming at the Roman seaside villa: reading, writing, and the improvement of the self (4.6.1–2). There follows a brief reconnoitre of ancient ideas of the 'true self' and the relationship of the Umbrian and Laurentine Pliny to this concept. The chapter ends firmly back on earth—in the Umbrian soil. The extensive leisure that allowed Pliny to read and to think was based on the labour of the families who worked his huge estates. Questions will be asked about Pliny's record and practices as an elite landowner.

The Umbrian Pliny: patron of Tifernum, marriage to 'Venuleia', local networks

For all the prominence Pliny liked to give Comum in his writings, he had been deeply embedded and widely connected on the east bank of the Tiber since at least the time of the eruption of Vesuvius.[31] He became patron of Tifernum Tiberinum, the nearest town to his Umbrian estate, 'while still little more than a boy' (4.1.4): an era compatible with the death of the Elder Pliny when the Younger was in his eighteenth year (6.20.5).[32] Perhaps the Younger inherited patronage of Tifernum and ownership of the estate together on the death of his uncle.[33] Tifernum is modern Città di Castello, around 5 miles/8 kilometres south of the villa site near San Giustino.[34] Pliny would maintain a lifelong connection with the town. He built a temple of the imperial cult there at his own expense around 104 C.E. (3.4.2, 10.8), to an enthusiastic reception (4.1).[35] The locals came to regard him as 'judge or arbitrator' in their affairs (*iudicem aut arbitrum*, 7.30.2). He would be praised by the 'whole region' for his handling of a crisis during the grape harvest (*regione tota*, 8.2.8), and the temple of Ceres on his nearby estate was allegedly thronged each year by a 'large crowd from the whole district' (*magnus e regione tota . . . populus*, 9.39.2).[36]

Pliny would not marry Calpurnia of Comum until the reign of Nerva or Trajan. He had married the daughter of Pompeia Celerina perhaps as much as fifteen years earlier.[37] This woman's name may have been 'Venuleia'. She died not long after the assassination of Domitian. Pliny carefully maintained a relationship with his erstwhile mother-in-law all the same.[38] The latter was an extensive property owner in central Italy, with houses at Narnia (modern Narni) and Carsulae (near San Gemini) in Umbria and at Ocriculum (Otricoli) and Perusia (Perugia) immediately adjacent to the western and southern borders of the region (1.4.1). If, as has often been assumed, Pompeia Celerina's father is L. Pompeius Catellius Celer, then the family had Umbro-Etruscan origins, perhaps ultimately at Volsinii in Etruria.[39] Pompeia's first husband, and the father of Pliny's wife, may well have been Lucius Venuleius Montanus Apronianus: hence the conjecture of the name 'Venuleia' for their daughter.[40] His family came from Pisae, also in Etruria.[41] Pompeia's second husband Bittius Proculus had strong links with families just beyond Ocriculum.[42]

This was distinguished company for a new man like Pliny to keep. Pompeia Celerina was not only a wealthy woman, but a well-connected one. Her putative father, Catellius Celer, had been consul in 77 C.E. and governor of Lusitania in 77–8 under Vespasian. Venuleius Montanus Apronianus was suffect consul in 92 under Domitian. Montanus' own father was likely Lucius Montanus, proconsul of Pontus-Bithynia at the outset of Nero's reign. 'The Venuleii', in Syme's estimate, 'are an eminent and opulent family at Pisae . . . Also, perhaps of some antiquity'.[43] Proculus, the stepfather of 'Venuleia', reached the consulship around 98. He spoke in defence of the Publicius Certus whom Pliny attempted to arraign in the aftermath of the assassination of Domitian (9.13.4).[44]

'Venuleia' was both the daughter and granddaughter of Flavian consuls. Members of the family had been senators since at least the age of Nero, perhaps even as far back as the era of Julius Caesar. The Elder Pliny's substantial estate near Tifernum had given the Plinii a foothold in central Italy: it perhaps ultimately smoothed the Younger's entrée into an aristocratic milieu. Yet this distinguished network acquired by marriage and domiciled in Umbria and Etruria leaves only the faintest of traces in Pliny's record of his life. Writing to Pompeia Celerina around 97 C.E., Pliny expresses thanks for use of her properties in the region: 'What a wealth of appointments at your houses at Ocriculum, Narnia, Carsulae, and Perusia. At Narnia there is even a bathhouse!' (1.4.1).[45] The sites of these houses are located in sequence on the route from Rome to Pliny's villa near Tifernum (Map 1).[46] Pliny neither specifies the final destination of his journey nor offers any hint that Pompeia's daughter had recently passed away. The letter is best understood as a silent tribute to 'Venuleia', whose death is revealed only in a brief and belated aside (9.13.4).[47] It also acts as a pointer towards the Umbro-Etruscan networks in which Pliny was so strongly embedded up to the time of her death. Pliny's repeated evocations of days spent enjoying *otium* or supervising affairs on his Tifernum estate may carry with them a vestige of the earlier marriage.[48] Certainly Calpurnia is never glimpsed on the set of the Umbrian villa, aside from a long-delayed and fleeting appearance at dinner (9.36.4).[49] The young bride from Comum, as will emerge in the next chapter, nevertheless had strong symbolic value for Pliny, of a kind that 'Venuleia' and her Flavian consular networks could not provide.[50] In the post-Domitianic era, there were reasons to focus on Calpurnia and to let 'Venuleia' fade into the background.

A circle of friends in Umbria fills out the picture of Pliny's wide and deep attachments in the region. Despite his claim that 'there are no neighbours to disturb me' (5.6.45) at the Tifernum villa, the habitual presence of nearby friends is recorded (9.36.5). Friends with Umbrian origins or properties can be identified, with varying degrees of certainty in Carsulae, Spoletium (Spoleto), Hispellum (Spello), Asisium (Assisi), Perusia, and Iguvium (Gubbio).[51] Pliny himself evidently had close ties with Hispellum near the source of the Clitumnus river he so memorably describes (8.8). A fragment of a large testamentary inscription, the equivalent of the great Comum inscription, was recovered in the town: evidence of some major act of patronage there in life or posthumously.[52] Pliny makes passing mention of the town in the Clitumnus letter (8.8.6). 'There is a whole fabric of unknown social ties represented here', E. J. Champlin observes, 'one which Pliny did not choose to represent in his letters.'[53]

The persona of the Umbrian Pliny: apprehension of the divine

A distinctive *persona* emerges for Pliny over time at the Umbrian villa. Horace's *persona* at the Sabine villa in *his* letters had been idiosyncratic: he was inclined to become inward-facing there, more prone to testiness, even prickly.[54] Not so Pliny, who evinces a warmer character.[55] The self-praise tapers off: he gets on with his writing at the villa,[56] but entertains flashes of realism about its value and prospects of longevity.[57] Laziness creeps in, allegedly.[58] He devotes time to thinking about his extended *familia* of enslaved and formerly enslaved persons.[59] He goes hunting to exercise the body, although the mind is equally put to work with literary notebooks often brought alongside the nets.[60] Pliny rides around the district on horseback (9.15.3), knows its history well (3.19), shows familiarity with the people there, famed for their long life, and listens to 'old stories and talk of men of the past' (*fabulas ueteres sermonesque maiorum*, 5.6.6). He has literary neighbours, and friends gather to hear bookish entertainments at dinner.[61]

It is in Umbria that Pliny, more unexpectedly, emerges as a keen observer of the temples, rituals, and worshippers to be encountered at the local cult sites of Italy. He had extensive religious responsibilities elsewhere. In addition to the probable dedication of his father's temple of the imperial cult in Comum, Pliny himself held a priesthood of the divine emperor Titus in the Transpadana, and eventually secured co-option to a prestigious college of augurs in Rome.[62] As governor of Pontus-Bithynia, he would encounter problems thrown up by religious procedure and even civic disturbance inspired by cult gatherings.[63] The northern temple, however, receives a very general reference, the priesthood is passed over, the augurship is recorded only as a mark of distinction in Pliny's senatorial career, and the Christians of Pontus would be found to practice mere *superstitio*—unacceptable religion. Something like a religious sympathy or sensibility is on display only in Umbria. The construction (3.4.2), dedication (4.1), and transfer of statues (10.8.1–2) to his public temple of the imperial cult in Tifernum occupy Pliny at various points. The temple of Ceres is built on private ground, at his own estate (9.39).[64] The goddess was presumably the guardian divinity of the *pagus* ('district'). The shrine had become dilapidated, and on the advice of local soothsayers (*haruspices*) Pliny decides to rebuild and enlarge it. A new cult statue is to be sculpted, since the old wooden image is very fragile. Colonnades are to be added to shelter the throng of worshippers: 'many ceremonies are performed' on the Ides of September, 'many vows are undertaken and many are paid, yet there is no refuge near at hand against either the rain or the sun' (9.39.2).[65]

An expertise in religious matters is quietly on show at a shrine near the source of the river Clitumnus further south in Umbria in the vicinity of Hispellum.[66] Pliny tells his childhood friend Voconius Romanus, 'you will also be able to study, and will read a variety of inscriptions by a variety of people, written on every column and every wall in honour of the spring and the god' (8.8.7).[67] He sets himself apart from the naivety of some vows recorded, but is keen to emphasize respect for local piety and tradition (8.8.5, 7). It is at this Umbrian site alone that Pliny evinces a sense of the numinous (Fig. 6.5):

> There rises a hill of moderate size, wooded and shaded by ancient cypresses, at whose base the spring emerges, forced out through many but unequal channels, and after struggling through a troubled pool of its own formation, opens out to view with broad expanse, clear and transparent, so you can count the small coins thrown into it and the glistening pebbles. The water is driven on, not by the slope of the ground, but by its very own abundance . . . Close by is a temple ancient and venerable. Clitumnus stands there in person, clothed and adorned with purple-bordered toga. Oracular responses indicate the presence of divine and prophetic power. Scattered around are a number of chapels and as many gods. . . . Besides that spring, which is (as it were) the parent of the rest, there are smaller ones, separated from the fountainhead, but flowing into the river, which is spanned by a bridge. This marks the boundary between sacred and secular.[68]

Letters 8.8.2–6

Figure 6.5. Le Fonti del Clitunno near Spoleto in Umbria. Pliny describes the numinous source of the Clitumnus river in letter 8.8. The modern site is a nineteenth-century recreation; the flow of the river is much reduced. *Photo by C. Delaney.*

It was perhaps inevitable that water would elicit Pliny's apprehension of the divine. It is while visiting old Fabatus' estate at Ameria in southern Umbria that he is shown another sacred body of water just across the Tiber in a nearby region. This is Lake Vadimon, home to water of striking hue and floating islands made of reed beds (8.20.4–5). Pliny hails it a 'wonder' (*miraculum*, 8.8.2), worthy to be set beside those of Greece, Egypt, or Asia.[69] The Tiber, which ran past his estate, would inspire despair when the river's floods wreaked devastation downstream (8.17).[70] In Pliny's sight, even landlocked regions are filled with water.

The Laurentine Pliny: reading, writing, and the improvement of the self

An eye for water was more readily satisfied at the villa near Rome. In the course of his long description of the Laurentine villa (2.17), Pliny mentions the sea and its views nearly twenty times.[71] He tells us of 'a rather handsome dining room which projects on to the shore', whose base is 'just wetted by the last spray of the breakers' (5). This dining area is fitted with windows 'so that with its sides and its front it faces as it were three different seas', while at the back there is a view 'right to the woods and distant hills' (5). There is even 'a splendid warm swimming bath, from which the swimmers have a view of the sea', and an upper storey containing a dining room that 'looks upon a broad expanse of sea and a long line of coast with idyllic villas' (11, 12).[72] Pliny's consistent emphasis on sea views is perhaps one reason why modern artists have generally preferred the Laurentine villa as a subject over the Umbrian residence.[73]

Lacking the extensive farming lands of the Umbrian villa (4.6.2), the Laurentine residence was free to become, in the memorable formulation of one critic, a 'factory of literature'.[74] Pliny outlines an ideal day at the villa, focused on reading, writing, and listening to literature, interspersed with thinking, walking, and exercise.[75] A winter invasion of court cases for nightly preparation is admitted (9.40.2), and Pliny was hardly likely to escape social calls from fellow millionaires in nearby residences along the Laurentine coast. It was wise of him to play them down: Trajan might be reassured to hear that senators were not regularly in and out of each other's villas.[76] There were no tenants, dealers, or harvests to worry about. Pliny returns to the villa as a place where he can read and write, and repeatedly contrasts busy Rome with the 'productive leisure' of the Laurentine shore (*studiosum otium*).[77]

The seaside villa proves superior in one further respect to estates in Umbria and Comum:

> My Tuscan produce has been damaged by hail. In the country over the Po we are informed of great abundance, but proportionate low prices. My Laurentine property is the only thing that brings me in anything. . . . there I write a good deal, and improve, not the land (which I have not got), but *myself* by means of study [*ipsum me studiis excolo*]; and, while in other places I can show you a full barn, here I can actually show you a full escritoire.[78]
>
> *Letters* 4.6.1–2

A rare example here of Pliny's sympathy with the turn inwards or cultivation of the self-popularized by Seneca and apparently practised by more philosophical contemporaries. He puts it on show, one commentator suggests, 'much as he might display a work of art'.[79] It is not followed up systematically elsewhere.

What does 'improve myself by means of study' actually mean in practice? The answer is revealing. A narrative of personal development through reading remains a central plank of modern intellectual and literary biography. Augustine has a version of it already. In his youth at Thagaste, Augustine wept for the death of Vergil's Dido (*Conf.* 1.13.20–1), but was left unaffected, he says, by Greek literature (*Conf.* 1.13.20). As a young student in Carthage he came upon the *Hortensius* of Cicero and its 'exhortation to philosophy': 'it was this book', says Augustine, 'that changed my way of feeling [*mutauit affectum meum*]' (*Conf.* 3.4.7). He adds:

> I took up that book not as a means to hone my tongue, the skill which I was ostensibly purchasing with my mother's money (I was now eighteen years old, and my father had been dead for two years). It was not in order to hone my tongue that I took it up, nor was it Cicero's manner of speech that swayed me, but what he was saying.[80]

> Augustine, *Conf.* 3.4.7

Augustine is further challenged and shaped in Milan when he is given books of Platonic philosophy to read in Latin translation (*Conf.* 7.9.13). These volumes fire his imagination and provide ideas about how to tackle the Christian gospels that he had otherwise found difficult or unimpressive.[81]

What Pliny reads is a subject of great interest. Cicero aside, he is emphatically a modernist with an overwhelming interest in the literature of his own era.[82] Taking a swipe at Tacitus he declares, 'I do not, like some, disparage the intellects of our own time' (6.21.1).[83] *Why* Pliny reads is a question whose answer proves harder to assimilate to modern biography. He reads in order to develop not his ideas or his person but his literary style: the very opposite of Augustine's purpose in tackling the *Hortensius*. When Pliny reads, he 'perceives from the comparison how badly I write' (7.30.4). A long letter of advice to a young protégé ends with endorsement of the 'saying . . . that a man should be deeply, not widely, read' (7.9.15).[84] The point of such immersion is that an aspiring orator be empowered to improve his speaking style in court and any courtroom speeches he might publish (7.9.5–7). The closest Pliny comes to a biography of intellectual development focuses on his attempts to master the style of a range of poetic genres, from an abortive Greek tragedy at the age of fourteen through the elegies composed during his return from military service in Syria to a current well-received volume of occasional poetry in the hendecasyllabic metre (7.4). The sober senator, of course, wrote such apparently trivial poetry throughout his life for good reason: literary skills and tastes might mark a man out for imperial favour.[85]

Pliny, at any rate, is being consistent rather than shallow. A person wedded to the ethic of *constantia* may admit progress in youth or even failure, but maturity brings the 'responsibility to have got it right first time'. In this moral culture there is little room for books to do anything other than confirm or reinforce a person's apprehension of what is instinctively known to be right.[86] Some might turn to philosophy, where Epictetus hoped for progress among his students towards virtue (Arr. *Epict. diss.* 1.4).[87] Agricola, the father-in-law of Tacitus, learnt an early and valuable lesson from his mother: she 'imposed a check upon his enkindled and growing imagination' when Agricola 'was inclined to drink more deeply of philosophy than is permitted of a Roman and a senator' (*Agr.* 4.3).[88] Pliny and Tacitus might concur. As traditional members of the elite they avoided immersion in systematic philosophy.

The closest Pliny comes to the notion of personal development through literature is in a matter connected to the notion of style. From the beginning of his private epistolary career (1.2) through to its end (9.40.2), he insists on the practice of revising his works before publication. Perfecting the style and presentation of the works is his aim. Given the strong connection in Roman thought between literary style and personal character, to perfect the work was, in a sense, to perfect the writer.[89] If Pliny's style in the *Letters* is characterized by 'brevity, clarity and rhetoricity', there were conclusions for contemporary audiences to draw about the author.[90] Augustine was quite different. Through his reading and writing he aimed to achieve something inconceivable to men of an earlier generation: to transcend his classical education.[91]

The 'true self' in Umbria and the Laurentine shore

Pliny does not care for self-transformation. He does possess a clear sense of a private or domestic self. And this self emerges most clearly in Umbria and by the Laurentine shore. Of the seaside villa Pliny writes:

> No hope, no fear agitates me; no gossip disturbs my mind. I converse only with myself and my books [*mecum ... et cum libellis loquor*]. What a straightforward and genuine life [*o rectam sinceramque uitam*]! What delightful and what honourable leisure, nobler than virtually any active occupation! The sea and shore, my true and private haunt of the Muses [*uerum secretumque mouseion*], how many thoughts do you inspire, and how many do you dictate![92]
>
> *Letters* 1.9.5–6

Of the more remote Umbrian estate he adds:

> I can enjoy a profounder leisure there, more comfort, and fewer cares [*altius ibi otium et pinguius eoque securius*]; I need never wear a formal toga and there are no neighbours to disturb me; everywhere there is peace and quiet [*placida*

omnia et quiescentia], which adds as much to the healthiness of the place as the clear sky and pure air. There I enjoy the best of health, both mental and physical [*ibi animo, ibi corpore maxime ualeo*], for I keep my mind in training with work and my body with hunting. My slaves too are healthier here than anywhere else.[93]

Letters 5.6.45–6

Pliny places marked emphasis on quietness, peace, and personal freedom at the villas, indicates a more intense relationship there with himself and with his books, and suggests a species of authenticity, truth, and soundness in conditions of privacy or secrecy, not to mention evident literary inspiration and increased health in body and mind.[94]

Is Pliny suggesting that his Laurentine and Umbrian villas reveal a true self, or at least a cherished self that he particularly privileges? Modern thinkers have not always liked the idea of a self, much less the notion of a true self. There even appears to be no agreement on what the object of study understood as the self ought to be.[95] Ancient thought had few doubts about the existence of the self, although terms for the phenomenon ranged as widely as opinion about its nature. Various aspects of the individual were privileged as the true self or inviolable self, or self to be cultivated in tranquility, or self to feel particular attachment to—or conversely the self which itself feels detachment. Platonists selected 'reason' or 'intellect' as the essence or 'true self' of an individual. Epictetus characteristically saw the 'will' as his inviolable self: an entity that could be moulded. Other Stoics of the same era put 'mind' at the centre of their conception of self.[96]

None of these disembodied ideas gets us very close to the privileged self that makes its appearance in Pliny. It is not 'mind' that can go without a toga in Umbria. More informal ideas provide illumination. At the opening of a verse epistle to the steward of his Sabine farm, Horace declares: 'Bailiff of my woods and of the little farm *that returns me to myself* (*Vilice silvarum et mihi me reddentis agelli, Ep.* 1.14.1). A generation earlier, Cicero had used the same phrase at the beginning of a speech to the senate after returning from exile in 57 B.C.E.: 'you have given us back to us ourselves' (*nosmet ipsos nobis reddidistis, Red. Sen.* 1.1).[97] The sense of self lost by Cicero in exile encompassed family, personal status, and public activity in senate and forum.[98] Horace's sense of self is restored by an escape from Rome to his farm in the hills. On this private estate, as Horace declares in an earlier epistle, 'I live and I reign, as soon as I have left behind | what you townsmen extol to the skies with shouts of applause' (*Ep.* 1.10.8–9).[99] Free from the duties and interferences of Rome, Horace 'really lives' on the Sabine farm: selected aspects of his person are highlighted as especially deserving to be called the self.

Pliny is closer to Horace than to Cicero. Under the empire, it was risky to declare one's sense of self identical with activities of state. Very much like Horace, Pliny thinks of the countryside away from Rome as a place for reading, writing, and investment in personal interests.[100] Unlike Horace, he will not be studying ethics in the country. Pliny lets it be known in a letter immediately after the appearance of the Laurentine 'haunt of the Muses' that philosophy can be *practised in the city* in a man's role as a magistrate (1.10.10).[101] Epictetus, it may be added, thoroughly disagreed on this very point.[102] Philosophy on the Laurentine shore would have to wait for the early third-century writer Minucius Felix, who sets the prologue to his dialogue *Octavius* on the beach near Pliny's villa.[103] (Augustine went one better in the fourth century with a mystical experience in a now deteriorating Ostia, that was also experiencing blockade brought on by civil war.[104]) Pliny's privileged self, like Horace's, is strongly associated with named locales outside Rome.[105] For Pliny, these places are Umbria and the Laurentine shore, not Comum—for all the affection and promotion of his hometown.[106] It will emerge in the course of the next chapter, however, that Comum was an invaluable resource and emblem for Pliny in his *political* career.

From superstructure to base: economic realities in Umbria

The activities of reading, writing, and thinking, central to Pliny's sense of a privileged self away from Rome, inevitably represent a superstructure founded upon an economic base. The farms in Umbria and the Transpadana provided Pliny with the means to purchase the leisure-time that facilitated the flourishing of the self he particularly cherished. Luckily, he was interested just enough in the economics of farming, above all at his Umbrian estates, to provide glimpses into the process of turning a profit from a large group of tenant farmers.[107] His primary purpose, of course, in writing so extensively about his farms was to set himself up as moral exemplar for landowners.

Pliny was a rich man. He had inherited property from his mother and father, from the Elder Pliny, and, undoubtedly, from one or more of his elderly patrons. His marriages brought dowries; social connections delivered inheritances. He had been very substantially enriched from all these sources during youth and adulthood.[108] As a courtroom orator in the traditional mould, Pliny depended on legacies rather than fees for his services.[109] His wealth, as elite tradition dictated, was invested in his estates: 'nearly all my capital is in land' (*sum . . . prope totus in praediis*, 3.19.8).[110] The sums needed to finance a senatorial career, as he well knew, were considerable.[111] Senators were not paid: liquidity in cash was paramount. Pliny lent some money out at interest.[112] Trade was unthinkable; gross or sustained extortion in a province unwise.[113] His attempts to maintain cash flow from his estates, it will emerge, combined the risk-averse, hands-off approach typical of his class, with some urgent interventions in the affairs of his tenants at moments of apparent crisis. Pliny may have made over one million sesterces a year from his combined agricultural holdings.[114]

What did the Umbrian estate produce? In his description of the environs of the villa, quoted at the chapter's outset, Pliny's eye moves down the mountains towards the plain. It takes in game for hunting, woods for timber, vines first on trellises and then those mounted on trees for support (5.6.9 *arbusta*),[115] and finally meadows and fields for sowing with crops. A mixed economy of cereals and different types of wine production is evidently at work: diversification was a strategy to minimise exposure to the failure of individual crops.[116] Pliny's lens includes no view of the 'centuriation' in evidence all around his villa.[117] The valley in which his residence lay had been divided up into small parcels of land and distributed to 'colonists' for cultivation, most recently under Tiberius. Pliny and the ancestral owners of his villa had no doubt acquired the farms of the colonists piecemeal, so that his estate resembled a patchwork of individual properties rather than a parkland.[118]

Whatever the variety of produce coming from his lands, including timber, Pliny engages with one staple above all others: the grape harvest.[119] There were cultural reasons for this focus, not least the long-standing association of wine with aristocratic society and literature. The export of wine to Rome, nevertheless, was fundamental to his finances. Mass consumption of wine had become normal in Italy only by the close of the first century B.C.E.[120] The broad area around Pliny's villa produced wine of low alcohol content and quality in antiquity. There was a market precisely for such produce among persons of modest means in the capital, where vintages from the upper Tiber valley appear to account for nearly 25 per cent of all wine consumed.[121] The navigability of the Tiber down to Rome during winter and spring (5.6.12) was key to connecting Pliny's otherwise rather isolated Umbrian estates to this market.[122] He may even have benefited commercially from the disruption caused by Vesuvius. The region around the volcano had been one of Rome's main suppliers of wine up to 79 C.E.[123] The remains of Pliny's *pars rustica*, which are presumably part of the central farm on his estate, display significant investment in wine storing and pressing facilities during the phase of his ownership.[124]

Who worked Pliny's farms on the Umbrian estate? In a letter that appears to refer to the vicinity, Pliny declares 'nowhere do I employ chained slaves myself, and no one uses them here' (3.19.7).[125] Whether or not Pliny employed *unchained* enslaved persons extensively on his home farm, it seems certain that much of his land was divided into smallholdings worked by free tenant farmers on a five-year lease.[126] Such farmers were of relatively substantial means. They perhaps had their own smallholdings elsewhere, and were expected to bring with them their own enslaved persons and draft animals to work the fields they rented.[127] Tenant farmers suited the elite, since the purchase and supervision of teams of enslaved people were very costly in both time and money.[128] Wealthy landowners wanted, or said they wanted, minimum involvement in agricultural affairs. Pliny parades the attitude of his class: 'Some time, though not, as *they* think, enough, is given to my tenants, whose rustic grumblings give fresh zest to my literary interests and the more civilized pursuits of the town' (9.36.6).[129] Men of his rank valued a steady income over maximizing revenue through investment in their properties.[130]

Pliny's desire to minimize financial risk to himself is key to understanding his actions as a landowner. Tenants paid owners a cash rent (9.37.3, 10.8.5), and bore themselves the consequences of an unexpectedly low yield or a failed crop.[131] They had some power over the landlord, all the same: desirable tenants could be hard to find, as Pliny himself found (3.19.7, 7.30.3). Landlords might face a choice between enforcing payment of arrears and tolerating tenants in the absence of suitable alternatives.[132]

The story of Pliny's Umbrian farms, in so far as it can be reconstructed during the early years of Trajan's reign,[133] is one of a series of poor harvests, tenants falling repeatedly into arrears, and Pliny's piecemeal attempts to ensure a more regular cash flow. The larger story is undoubtedly one where rents were unrealistically high and large landowners prospered at the expense of tenants. Pliny was thoroughly typical of his class in not seeing things from the viewpoint of those who worked his land. His interventions, however, though marked by a tendency to wait till matters reach crisis point, do represent attempts to respond creatively.

Around 98–9 C.E., the leases for Pliny's Umbrian estates were up for renewal: 'successive bad harvests are forcing me to consider reducing rents' (10.8.5).[134] Whether or not Pliny did bring the payments down, tenants at a neighbouring estate would soon fall into an even more desperate situation. To offset losses from rent owed in arrears, the owner of the nearby domain simply sold off the capital pledged by the tenants, including the enslaved persons they used to work the land. The tenants, unable to farms their holdings efficiently, then fell into debt to the landlord once more (3.19.6–7). Pliny wonders whether to buy the estates at the reduced price they currently commanded—with money borrowed from Pompeia Celerina (3.19.7–9). Some years later, Pliny announces that the leases on his farms are again due for renewal, although 'suitable tenants' (*idoneos conductores*, 7.30.3) are in short supply. Repeated references are made to a poor grape harvest.[135] It is reported that the dealers (*negotiatores*) who purchased the vine crop from Pliny's estates in advance have made a significant loss. He evolves a detailed scheme of compensation so that the *negotiatores* are not ruined by their investment (8.2).[136] The vine crop included produce belonging to Pliny's tenants.[137] Unsurprisingly, Pliny is besieged by their complaints (9.15.1,

9.36.6). They have yet again fallen seriously into arrears, despite his continued reduction of their rents (9.37.2). Matters come to a head: some tenants 'even seize and consume the produce from the land, since they now think it is not in their interest to keep their hands off it' (9.37.2).[138] A solution to the woes of both land-owner and tenants is proposed: instead of a cash rent, Pliny is prepared to receive rent in kind (9.37.3–4).[139]

Long-term problems of farms repeatedly in arrears are to be 'solved' not by eviction but through turning tenants into sharecroppers. Everyone, it seems, can go away happy. A sharecropping scheme, however, would ultimately provide less incentive to farm efficiently, since the greater the produce the larger the benefit to the owner. Yet there is no doubting the optimism of Pliny's belief that he is acting fairly and humanely by the standards of his day.

In the next chapter we move north and return to Comum. Here Pliny has relatively little to say about his villas or his farms, or about his 'privileged' self and the reading, writing, and even apprehension of the divine that went with it. The focus is on the public man, on large donations to his hometown, and marriage to Calpurnia of Comum, successor to 'Venuleia'.

Notes

1. A conceptual debt in this chapter to Champlin (2001) = (2016) on 'Pliny's other country' (Umbria) is gratefully acknowledged.

2. For the historical and physical evolution of the Laurentine shore from antiquity to today and survey of excavations there since the eighteenth century, see Claridge (1997–8), (f'coming); cf. the still useful Lanciani (1909, 306–31). For a cultural history of the *ager Laurens*, see Purcell (1998a) = (1998b).

3. For a survey of archaeological discoveries in the area, see Lauro and Claridge (1998), with fold-out map at p. 40. For a history of attempts to locate Pliny's villa on the shoreline, see Du Prey (1994, 82–106, 148–9), Miziotek (2016, 72–4). On the possible locations of Pliny's villas, see Appendix 2.

4. For the half-day journey after normal conclusion of business at noon, see Whitton (2013, 225).

5. 2.17.2–3 *decem septem milibus passuum ab urbe secessit, ut peractis quae agenda fuerint saluo iam et composito die possis ibi manere. aditur non una uia; nam et Laurentina et Ostiensis eodem ferunt, sed Laurentina a quarto decimo lapide, Ostiensis ab undecimo relinquenda est. utrimque excipit iter aliqua ex parte harenosum, iunctis paulo grauius et longius, equo breue et molle. uaria hinc atque inde facies; nam modo occurrentibus siluis uia coartatur, modo latissimis pratis diffunditur et patescit; multi greges ouium, multa ibi equorum boum armenta, quae montibus hieme depulsa herbis et tepore uerno nitescunt.*

6. For ancient roads in the district, see Appendix 2.

7. See, respectively, Spencer (2010, 115–16 with n. 173); Whitton (2013, 226) with reference to 8.1.1, Sen. *Ep.* 87.2; Whitton (2013, 227); and Purcell (1998a, 18) = (1998b, 8).

8. Purcell (1998a, 18) = (1998b, 8); cf. Purcell (1998a, 27) = (1998b, 17) for venerated relics of Aeneas in the area. For the cultural reputation of the area and the influence of Vergil on it, see Purcell (1998a, 18–21) = (1998b, 8–11); cf. the richly detailed study of Verg. *Aen.* 7.1–135 by Boas (1938).

9. Purcell (1998a, 23) = (1998b, 13).

10. 2.17.26–7 *litus ornant uarietate gratissima nunc continua nunc intermissa tecta uillarum, quae praestant multarum urbium faciem, siue mari siue ipso litore utare.*

11. 'Tuscan': the matter is complex. The Augustan division of Italy into administrative regions led to the inclusion within Umbria of areas and towns that were ethnically Etruscan; see Sisani (2008), developing the ideas of Kolendo (1969). Such boundary changes had little impact on local identities; hence Pliny's reference to his estate and nearby Tifernum as Tuscan. (The Augustan regions leave their only substantial historical mark in the work of the Elder Pliny; see Bispham (2007b).) The ethnic boundary between Etruria and Umbria may have lain much further to the east (Sisani (2008, 60–1). I use the Augustan region of Umbria to unite Pliny's connections on the east bank of the Tiber without making claims for the relevance of that region to all of its inhabitants. For Pliny's connections on the east bank of the Tiber, see later in this chapter.

12. The assumption of a five-day journey coheres with the route traced in 1.4.1; cf. Sherwin-White (1966, 574–5), using also 2.17.2, 6.10. For sceptical reflection on speeds of travel within Italy reported in Cicero and Tacitus, see Woodman (2017, 109).

13. Senators' freedom to travel from Rome might be effectively confined to periods of recess from the senate, although there may have been a relatively high rate of absence precisely for the purpose of home visits; see Eck (1997, 98 n. 79); cf. D'Arms (1970, 48–9) = (2003, 57–8) on senatorial recesses and visits to villas in the letters of Cicero. Pliny must ask for official leave to depart the environs of Rome when acting as the prefect of Saturn or curator of the Tiber and its banks; cf. 3.4.2, 3.6.6, 5.14.9, 10.8.

14. The Laurentine villa is characterized as a winter residence in contrast to the Umbrian villa's summer (9.40); but the reality of Pliny's seasonal visits to each was likely determined by the hunting and agricultural calendar: see Rossiter (2003).

15. 8.1.1 *quidam ex meis aduersam ualetudinem feruentissimis aestibus contraxerunt*; 8.1.2 *exasperatis faucibus puluere sanguinem reiecit.* (For the villa of 8.1 as likely the Tifernum property, see Sherwin-White (1966, 448).) The size of Pliny's entourage no doubt protected him from the low-level banditry that affected contemporary travellers along the same route; for banditry on the via Flaminia, cf. 6.25, Shaw (2000, 387), Patterson (2006, 47–8), more generally Laurence (1999, 177–86); for Pliny's frequent journeys throughout Italy, see Cova (1999); for Pliny's route from Rome to the Umbrian villa, cf. 1.4.1 (quoted later) and see Appendix 2.

16. Highet (1957, 83).

17. 5.6.7–15 *regionis forma pulcherrima. imaginare amphitheatrum aliquod immensum, et quale sola rerum natura possit effingere. lata et diffusa planities montibus cingitur,*

montes summa sui parte procera nemora et antiqua habent. frequens ibi et uaria uenatio. inde caeduae siluae . . . sub his per latus omne uineae porriguntur, unamque faciem longe lateque contexunt . . . quarum a fine . . . arbusta nascuntur. prata inde campique, campi quos non nisi ingentes boues et fortissima aratra perfringunt . . . palus nulla, quia deuexa terra, quidquid liquoris accepit nec absorbuit, effundit in Tiberim. medios ille agros secat . . . magnam capies uoluptatem, si hunc regionis situm ex monte prospexeris. neque enim terras tibi sed formam aliquam ad eximiam pulchritudinem pictam uideberis cernere. . . . uilla in colle imo sita prospicit quasi ex summo: ita leuiter et sensim cliuo fallente consurgit, ut cum ascendere te non putes, sentias ascendisse. a tergo Appenninum, sed longius habet; accipit ab hoc auras quamlibet sereno et placido die . . . magna sui parte meridiem spectat.

18. On ways of seeing in 5.6, see Chinn (2007), Spencer (2010, 125–34).
19. See Pretzler (2007, 57–72).
20. On the history of attempts to locate Pliny's Umbrian villa, see Du Prey (1994, 74–81), Braconi (1999b, 21–3).
21. *Italia Illustrata* 3.3; on Biondo Flavio, see White (2005).
22. Extracts from Lazzari's manuscript are transcribed at Braconi and Uroz Sáez (2001, 212–3 n. 3).
23. On the excavations of Pliny's villa near San Giustino, see Appendix 2.
24. See the summary of Gibson and Morello (2012, 230).
25. On the brick stamps bearing the Elder's initials (CPS), see Uroz Sáez (2008, 130, 142 Figs. 17, 18); cf. Gibson and Morello (2012, 221–5) for a reading of Pliny's luxury villa against the lifestyle and preferences of the Elder.
26. On brick stamps attesting the prior ownership of M. Granius Marcellus, see Braconi (1999b, 34–5), Uroz Sáez (1999a, 46), Uroz Sáez (1999b, 192–3, 195), Braconi and Uroz Sáez (2008, 111–19), Uroz Sáez (2008, 124–131). If, as seems likely, the Plinii inherited the villa from Marcellus, the Younger's 'maternal connections become rather grand, far grander than those of any contemporary writer' (Champlin (2016, 120)). The statues that got Marcellus into trouble on a treason charge under Tiberius (Tac. *Ann.* 1.74.3) may well surface in the temple of the imperial cult funded by Pliny at Tifernum, to which he transferred inherited statues of former emperors from his nearby villa; cf. 3.4.2, 4.1, 10.8. For the full argument, see Champlin (2001, 122–3) = (2016, 110–11), (2016, 119–20); cf. Chp. 8 n. 57.
27. The identity of Gallus is uncertain (Whitton (2013, 222–3)), but Domitius Apollinaris from Vercellae in the Transpadana was consul in 97 C.E. (see Chp. 7 n. 33).
28. For a list of features at the two villas in narrative order, see Tanzer (1924, 44, 108); on the number of spaces mentioned, see Riggsby (2003, 170). For an outline of the Laurentine tour, see Whitton (2013, 221–2). On the similarity in narrative structure between the two villa letters, see Gibson and Morello (2012, 213–14). On the tendency of Pliny's style of narration to produce floor plans that are challenging to reconstruct, see Du Prey (1994, 8–9, 21, 26), Riggsby (2003, 169–70).
29. For literary, cultural, and architectural guides to Pliny's villas, see (e.g.) Tanzer (1924), Förtsch (1993), Bergmann (1995) = (2016), Riggsby (2003), Spencer (2010, 113–34), Gibson and Morello (2012, 200–33), Whitton (2013, 218–55), Dewar (2014, 51–67),

all with further references to a very extensive literature. For the gardens of Pliny's villas in their literary and social contexts, see Hartswick (2018), Myers (2018), and Gleason and Palmer (2018). For modern and early-modern attempts to imitate or reconstruct Pliny's villas, see Du Prey (1994), (2018); Miziotek (2016).

30. On the close connection between house and owner in Roman thought, see Envoi n. 26.

31. For the prominence given to Comum and the reasons for it, see Chp. 7.

32. 4.1.4 is quoted in Chp. 7.

33. On the inheritance of estate and local patronage from the Elder, see Sherwin-White (1966, 265). For Pliny as civic patron of Tifernum and other communities, including the province of Baetica, see Nicols (2014, 131–47). Calpurnius Fabatus, another native of Comum related by marriage to Pliny, also owned an estate in Umbria near Ameria in the south of the region (8.20.3.)

34. See Bonomi Ponzi (1999, 8); for recent excavations in the town, see Migliorati (2008).

35. The statues which Pliny transferred from his nearby estate to the temple (10.8.9) may be connected with M. Granius Marcellus; see earlier n. 26. The later construction of another building is implied by the discovery in the town of a testamentary inscription for Pliny: cf. CIL 11.5934, Champlin (2001, 123) = (2016, 111–12).

36. For Tifernum and environs as the likely setting of 7.30, 8.2, 9.39, see Sherwin-White (1966, 439–40, 449, 523). Complaints of over-enthusiastic locals swarming a visiting grandee go back to Cicero (e.g. Att. 2.14.2).

37. On the dates and number of Pliny's marriages, see Chp. 5 nn. 32, 166.

38. Pompeia Celerina appears at 1.4, 3.19, 6.10, and 10.51; for an overview of her life, see Shelton (2013, 259–266); cf. Carlon (2009, 106, 119–123). She owned, perhaps inherited, the villa at Alsium just north of Rome that had once belonged to Pliny's guardian Verginius Rufus of Milan (6.10; cf. Chp. 4 n. 121): further evidence of links between elites in northern and central Italy; see Champlin (2001, 126–7) = (2016, 115–16).

39. Pompeius Catellius Celer has regularly been assumed to be the father of Pompeia Celerina (e.g. Syme (1968a, 144) = RP 2.709; RP 7.509–510, 554; Raepsaet-Charlier (1987, 507, no. 626)), but he has been doubted more recently by Salomies (1992, 118–119). For likely Umbro-Etruscan origins for Catellius Celer, perhaps Volsinii, see Syme (1980, 18–19, 55–56; 1985, 348 n. 144). Pompeia Celerina's ancestors appear also to have owned property in Interamna Nahars (Terni), in the valley below Narnia; see Champlin (2001, 127 n. 25) = (2016, 117 n. 25).

40. See Raepsaet-Charlier (1987, 507–508, nos. 626–7) referring to CIL 11.1735; cf. Shelton (2013, 97, 259–260).

41. See Syme (1980, 57), Scheid (1983).

42. On Pompeia, Bittius Proculus, and a nexus of Umbrian and Sabine landowners, see Patterson (2006, 272–273); cf. Patterson (2008) on the broader urban history of the area.

43. Syme (1980, 57), who notes, among possible ancestors, 'an obscure senator of 43 B.C.' (Cic. Fam. 12.30.7); cf. Syme RP 7.509–10 on the social ambitiousness of Pliny's match.

44. See Chp. 5 on the Certus action. On Proculus, see Chp. 5 n. 152.
45. 1.4.1 *quantum copiarum in Ocriculano, in Narniensi, in Carsulano, in Perusino tuo, in Narniensi uero etiam balineum!*
46. For Pliny's route to Tifernum on the via Flaminia, see Appendix 2. On the Roman road system in Italy more generally, see Laurence (1999).
47. Cf. Chp. 5 n. 165.
48. E.g. 4.6, 5.6, 5.18, 9.15, 9.36. Book 8 of the *Letters* has a claim to being Pliny's Umbrian book. Here Pliny includes his famous description of the source of the Clitumnus river near Hispellum (8.8), reports news of devastating floods along the length of the Tiber (8.17), and tells of a recent visit to the estates of father-in-law near Ameria (8.20)—not to mention activities on unidentified estates that are most plausibly identified as Pliny's Tifernum holdings (8.1, 8.2, 8.15).
49. But for Calpurnia's first appearance at 4.1 as an over-writing of 'Venuleia', see Chp. 7 n. 95. Calpurnia, however, makes no appearance at the Laurentine villa, despite the prominence of other men's wives at *their* villas (3.1.5, 5.18.1, 7.3). Calpurnia enjoys a presence at her family's Campanian residence (6.4, 6.30): Umbria and the *ager Laurens* are evidently reserved for Pliny himself.
50. Cf. Chp. 7 and see Gibson (2020).
51. In addition to the properties of Pompeia Celerina in the towns mentioned, Champlin suggests Umbrian domiciles or property for: Octavius Rufus (1.7, 2.10, 7.25) in Carsulae; Erucius Clarus (1.16) in Spoletium; Corellius Rufus (1.12, 4.17) in Hispellum; Passenus Paulus (6.15, 9.22) in Asisium; Terentius Iunior (7.25, 8.15) in a farm near Perusia; and Iavolenus Priscus (6.15) in Iguvium; see Champlin (2001, 124–7) = (2016, 113–18) for arguments and inscriptional and prosopographical evidence.
52. *CIL* 11.5272, with Alföldy (1999c).
53. See Champlin (2001, 123–4, 127) = (2016, 112, 118).
54. Cf. esp. Hor. *Ep.* 1.7, 8, 10, 14.
55. The Umbrian estate is specifically named in many instances as the venue for the letters cited later in this chapter, but just as often an Umbrian venue is to be inferred by cross-reference to other letters or from the specified season; see Sherwin-White (1966) ad loc., Duncan-Jones (1982) = (2016).
56. Cf. 5.18, 7.30.4–5, 8.15, 9.16, 9.36.
57. Cf. 9.10.2–3, 9.15.1–2.
58. Cf. 9.10.2, 9.15, 9.32.
59. Cf. 5.6.46, 8.1, 8.16, 9.20, 9.36.4.
60. Cf. 5.6.46, 5.18, 9.10, 9.36.6; cf. 1.6. For hunting as a particularly Trajanic activity, cf. *Paneg.* 81, Jones (1978, 120).
61. Cf. 7.25, 8.15, 9.36.4.
62. On the temple of imperial cult in Comum, see Chp. 3; on the imperial priesthood at either Comum or Vercellae, see Chp. 7 n. 136; on the augurship at Rome, see Chp. 5; cf. also 3.6 on Pliny's dedication of a statue in the temple of Jupiter at Comum to mark his consulship.
63. See Chp. 8; cf. Ando (2007, 443) on instances of other religious problems encountered in Bithynia involving the application of Roman religious law to the provinces.

64. 9.39 (on the Ceres temple) occurs within a run of letters with strong connections to the Umbrian villa (9.36, 9.37 with Sherwin-White (1966, 519); 9.40), although 9.39 itself contains only vestigial hints of an Umbrian setting (Sherwin-White (1966, 522–3)). Nevertheless, the riverside setting described at 9.39.5–6 fits the Campo di Santa Fiora near San Giustino well, and the discovery there of a likely temple and porticoes complex encourages understanding the Ceres temple as located at the Umbrian estate; see Appendix 2; cf. Braconi (2001) on possible links between the (now vanished) church of Santa Fiora and Pliny's Ceres.

65. 9.39.2 *multae res aguntur, multa uota suscipiuntur, multa redduntur; sed nullum in proximo suffugium aut imbris aut solis.* (The phrase *multae res aguntur* might equally refer to a market or fair; see Scheid (1997, 248–50).) Scheid (1997, 242–6, 253–5) offers detailed analysis of the cult of Ceres described in 9.39. See de Cazanove (2007, 53–6) on the fate of local Italian cults in Roman Italy, and Várhelyi (2010, 107–21) on the evidence for senatorial practice of religion outside Rome.

66. On the source of the Clitumnus and shrine, see Appendix 2. For the literary tradition surrounding the site and Pliny's divergences from it, see Sherwin-White (1966, 456–8). For a detailed analysis of the Clitumnus shrines and cult as described by Pliny, see Scheid (1997, 246–7, 250–2, 255–6).

67. 8.8.7 *studebis quoque: leges multa multorum omnibus columnis omnibus parietibus inscripta, quibus fons ille deusque celebratur.* (For Voconius Romanus, see Chps. 5, 8.) The *inscripta* might equally refer to graffiti; see Scheid (1997, 250–1). For Pliny's ultimately respectful attitude to the inscriptions at the shrine, see Beard (2001, 39–40, 44); on inscriptions bearing vows at a shrine in the larger Roman religious context, see Belayche (2007, 280–5).

68. 8.8.2–6 *modicus collis adsurgit, antiqua cupressu nemorosus et opacus. hunc subter exit fons et exprimitur pluribus uenis sed imparibus, eluctatusque quem facit gurgitem lato gremio patescit, purus et uitreus, ut numerare iactas stipes et relucentes calculos possis. inde non loci deuexitate, sed ipsa sui copia . . . impellitur . . . adiacet templum priscum et religiosum. stat Clitumnus ipse amictus ornatusque praetexta; praesens numen atque etiam fatidicum indicant sortes. sparsa sunt circa sacella complura, totidemque di. . . . nam praeter illum quasi parentem ceterorum sunt minores capite discreti; sed flumini miscentur, quod ponte transmittitur. is terminus sacri profanique.*

69. On Lake Vadimon, see Appendix 2.

70. Gibson (2015) argues that Pliny uses the flooding Tiber of 8.17 to express pessimism about Trajan's reign; cf. Chp. 5. On the literary texture of 8.17, see Rocchi (2015).

71. For Pliny's emphasis on the views from the various rooms of his villa, see Whitton (2013, 229); cf. Spencer (2010, 114–20). It was only during Pliny's lifetime that it had become permissible to write in praise of luxury residences, although Pliny himself avoids the costly indoor ornaments highlighted by his contemporary Statius; see Gibson and Morello (2012, 211–12). On Roman maritime villas, see Marzano (2018).

72. 2.17.5 *triclinium satis pulchrum, quod in litus excurri . . . fractis iam et nouissimis fluctibus leuiter adluitur . . . ita a lateribus a fronte quasi tria maria prospectat . . . siluas et longinquos respicit montes;* 2.17.11, 12 *calida piscina mirifica, ex qua natantes mare*

adspiciunt . . . cenatio quae latissimum mare longissimum litus uillas amoenissimas possidet; cf. also 2.17.21, 27.

73. See Du Prey (1994, 21). The view from the villa out to the sea is characteristically reversed by architects and artists who have generally preferred to depict the Laurentine villa *from* the sea (as in Fig. 6.3).

74. Hoffer (1999, 29); cf. the Comum villa of Caninius Rufus in 1.3 (Chp. 7). The assertion of no lands attached to the villa at 4.6.2 is contradicted to a degree by 2.17.28 (Whitton (2013, 253)).

75. Cf. 9.40, with reference to 9.36. For Pliny's regimen in context, see Gibson and Morello (2012, 116–23); cf. Chp. 4 on the rather different work ethic of the Elder.

76. The suburban villa was central to literature and politics in Cicero's time (D'Arms (1970, 50–1, 61) = (2003, 58–60, 70–1), Agache (2008)), but the latter aspect is played down in Pliny's epistolary picture (Gibson and Morello (2012, 232)). There are hints of a Laurentine social life at 2.17.9, 5.6.45; see Whitton (2013, 234, 238).

77. Cf. 5.2, 7.4.3–6; and 1.9, 1.22.11, 2.2.

78. 4.6.1–2 *Tusci grandine excussi, in regione Transpadana summa abundantia, sed par uilitas nuntiatur: solum mihi Laurentinum meum in reditu. . . . ibi enim plurimum scribo, nec agrum quem non habeo sed ipsum me studiis excolo; ac iam possum tibi ut aliis in locis horreum plenum, sic ibi scrinium ostendere.*

79. Riggsby (1998, 93) = (2016, 244). For the turn inwards and Pliny's lack of sympathy with it, see Chp. 2. For further examples of Pliny's turn inwards / cultivation of the self, cf. 1.9.4–7, 5.3.2, 6.10.5, 9.3.3, Riggsby (1998, 83–93) = (2016, 234–44).

80. *Conf.* 3.4.7 *exhortationem . . . ad philosophiam . . . ille uero liber mutauit affectum meum . . . non enim ad acuendam linguam, quod uidebar emere maternis mercedibus, cum agerem annum aetatis undeuicensimum iam defuncto patre ante biennium, non ergo ad acuendam linguam referebam illum librum, neque mihi locutio sed quod loquebatur persuaserat.*

81. For Augustine's reading practices and the effect on him of reading, see Brown (2000, 256–66), O'Donnell (2005, 120–6); for the effect of reading the Platonic volumes (including perhaps Plotinus), see Brown (2000, 85–92). A change in Augustine is implied by *mutauit affectum meum* (O'Donnell (1992, II.166)).

82. See Gibson (2014) for a survey of Pliny's reading and admired literary greats; cf. Gibson (2018) for the contrast with Plutarch.

83. 6.21.1 *sum ex iis qui mirer antiquos, non tamen (ut quidam) temporum nostrorum ingenia despicio*; see Gibson (f'coming) for the reference here to Tac. *Dial.* 15.1. Tacitus takes up the debate again at *Ann.* 3.55.5; see Woodman and Martin (1996, 408–13).

84. 7.30.4 *cum lego, ex comparatione sentio quam male scribam*; 7.9.15 *aiunt enim multum legendum esse, non multa.*

85. For Pliny on his own literary career (including poetry), see Gibson and Steel (2010); cf. Chp. 1 for Pliny's poetry, and Chp. 5 n. 57 for imperial favour for literary skills.

86. On *constantia* and getting it right first time, cf. Chps. 1, 4.

87. See Dobbin (1998, 88–98) on Arr. *Epict. diss.* 1.4.

88. Tac. *Agr.* 4.3 *memoria teneo solitum ipsum narrare se prima in iuuenta studium philosophiae acrius, ultra quam concessum Romano ac senatori, hausisse, ni prudentia matris incensum ac flagrantem animum coercuisset*; see Woodman and Kraus (2014, 99–101) on this passage.

89. For style and character, the *locus classicus* is Sen. *Ep.* 114.

90. Whitton (2013, 20–8)—from whom the quotation here is drawn—offers a brilliant analysis of Pliny's epistolographical style.

91. See Brown (2000, 261–2).

92. 1.9.5–6 *nulla spe nullo timore sollicitor, nullis rumoribus inquietor: mecum tantum et cum libellis loquor. o rectam sinceramque uitam! o dulce otium honestumque ac paene omni negotio pulchrius! o mare, o litus, uerum secretumque mouseion, quam multa inuenitis, quam multa dictatis!*

93. 5.6.45–6 *altius ibi otium et pinguius eoque securius: nulla necessitas togae, nemo accersitor ex proximo, placida omnia et quiescentia, quod ipsum salubritati regionis ut purius caelum, ut aer liquidior accedit. ibi animo, ibi corpore maxime valeo. nam studiis animum, uenatu corpus exerceo. mei quoque nusquam salubrius degunt.*

94. Cf. earlier in this chapter for the limited cultivation of 'the self' evident in 1.9.5–6.

95. Sorabji (2006, 1–20) provides a succinct overview of modern views: for some 'the self' is a metaphysical question: 'what sort of self can be supposed to exist?' For others ethical or historical: what 'personae . . . people have had at different times in Western history'. There is a divide between those who see 'the self' as signifying primarily 'what it is to be a human being', and those who concentrate on what it is to develop an individual *persona*. Others insist that 'the self' is the result of a grammatical mistake: 'my self' is not a thing like 'my house'; or that instead of the self, there exists 'only an embodied stream of consciousness', or that there are at best only 'short term' selves. For select modern accounts of the history of the self and the individual, see Morris (1972), Carrithers, Collins, and Lukes (1985), Taylor (1989), Seigel (2005); cf. Lee (2009, 45, 102) on biography and the true self.

96. The idea of a true self is raised already in Homer's *Odyssey*, where Odysseus encounters the *eidolon* of Heracles in Hades, but where 'he himself' is said to be enjoying 'festivities with the immortal gods' (Sorabji (2006, 34, 40)). For an overview of ancient philosophical opinion on which aspect of the individual was to be privileged as the self, see Sorabji (2006, 32–53); cf. Habinek (2016) on broader Roman ideas of the self.

97. Cic. *Red. Sen.* 1.1 'You have reunited parents with children and children with parents; you have given back to us honour, position, wealth, a most splendid *res publica*. You have given back to us that sweetest of all human possessions, our *patria*; in sum, you have given back to us ourselves'.

98. Relevant here is the Ciceronian / Panaetian theory of the individual's four constituent *personae*: the rational *persona* imposed by Nature on all humans; one's own individual *persona* or character; the *persona* imposed by circumstance; and the profession of one's choosing (*Off.* 1.105–25); cf. Gill (1998), Sorabji (2006, 43, 45).

99. Hor. *Epist.* 1.10.8–9 *uiuo et regno, simul ista reliqui | quae uos ad caelum effertis rumore secundo*; cf. also Sen. *Ep.* 104.6–7, where Seneca declares of time spent in his

country villa, 'The result is that I am fully myself again now' (*repetiui ergo iam me*), where the reference is to restoration of physical and mental health.

100. For Horace and the country as a place for reading, writing, and ethical study, cf. Hor. *Epod.* 2, *Sat.* 2.6, *Ep.* 1.4, 1.10, 1.14, 1.18.104–12, 2.2.65–80; Riikonen (1976), Mayer (1994, 46–7), Whitton (2014, 21).

101. On 1.10, see Chp. 8; cf. Chp. 5 for Pliny and philosophy.

102. Cf. Arr. *Epict. diss.* 3.15.9–12: note that Epictetus here refers explicitly to the Euphrates who gives Pliny the advice on philosophy in 1.10. (I owe this observation to Michael Hanaghan.)

103. Minucius Felix *Octavius* 2–3. Epigraphical and literary evidence attest to the attraction of Greek scholars, sophists, and philosophers to the Laurentine shore in the early imperial age; the philhellenic Hadrian owned a beloved villa further down the same coast at Antium; see Purcell (1998a, 26–7) = (1998b, 17–18).

104. Cf. Aug. *Conf.* 9.23–6, Brown (2000, 121–4).

105. Whitton (2014, 24–8) notes that the close thematic relationship between Pliny and Horace has been underestimated: both share an unresolved tension between city and country life, with extensive overlaps between texts connected to that theme: e.g. 1.3 and Hor. *Ep.* 1.4; 7.26 and Hor. *Ep.* 1.4; 2.8 and *Ep.* 1.10; and particularly 1.9 and Hor. *Sat.* 2.6; cf. also Spencer (2010, 26, 119–20) on Pliny, Horace, and landscape.

106. On Pliny's relationship with Comum, see Chp. 7 and earlier in this chapter. For the Plinian privileged self, see also Envoi.

107. On Pliny as a landowner, see esp. Kehoe (1988), (1989), (1993); also de Neeve (1990), (1992), Andermahr (1998, 384–6), Sherwin-White (1966, 520–2). On aspects of the Roman agrarian economy, see further Bowman and Wilson (2013), Kehoe (2006), Witcher (2016), with references to earlier literature. As de Neeve (1992, 343–4) points out, Pliny may be typical of his class, but he does not provide 'independent evidence for economic conditions in Italy as a whole': the Umbrian estate may well be exceptional; cf. Kehoe (1989, 587).

108. See Duncan-Jones (1982, 17–27) = (2016, 90–100); cf. Chp. 7 on Pliny's extensive donations to Comum.

109. Cf. 5.13.8–10, Sherwin-White (1966, 343).

110. On the factors influencing this elite mentality, see Kehoe (1993, 220–6).

111. Cf. 2.4.3, 6.32.1, Talbert (1984, 54–66), Kehoe (1993, 214–5).

112. Cf. 3.19.8, Duncan-Jones (1982, 21) = (2016, 93–4).

113. See Chp. 8 for the depredations of governors in their provinces.

114. For the value and income of Pliny's estates, including the Umbrian estate, cf. 3.19.7, 10.8.5, Duncan-Jones (1982, 18–21) = (2016, 91–4). Note, however, the important methodological caveats offered by de Neeve (1990, 380–2), (1992, 337).

115. On these two types of viticulture and their importance for understanding the history of the local landscape, see Braconi (2008, 89–93, 99–101).

116. Cf. 1.20.16 on diversification of crops (in a metaphorical context; see Braconi (2008, 99–100) and 3.19.4 on diversification of estates. There is no room here for that other great Mediterranean staple, the olive tree: the region was too temperate for the production of olive oil (5.6.4)

117. It is an assumption that what Pliny's eye lights upon is his own estate near San Giustino rather than the countryside around Tifernum in general; cf. the cautionary remarks of de Neeve (1992, 336).

118. For centuriation in the valley, the influence of the Granii Marcelli (see earlier in this chapter), and the likely shape of Pliny's estate, see Braconi (2008, 94–8), also Braconi (2003); cf. Lo Cascio (2003) on the broader Italian economic context.

119. Cf. 4.6.1, 8.2, 8.15, 9.16, 9.20.2, 9.28.2; cf. 5.6.27–9 for views of vineyards from the Umbrian villa. For assumptions that all these letters refer to the Tifernum estate, see later in this chapter.

120. See Vidal (2008, 222–4).

121. See Vidal (2008, 224–31), and cf. Pliny, *HN* 14.37, Juv. 7.121–2 for the poor reputation of wine from the area in antiquity.

122. On trade down the Tiber to Rome, see Patterson (2006, 62–6); on the navigability of the Tiber, see Rice (2018, 200–1).

123. See Vidal (2008, 227–8).

124. See Braconi and Uroz Saez (2008, 114–16).

125. 3.19.7 *nec ipse usquam uinctos habeo nec ibi quisquam*; for the assumption that 3.19 refers to the vicinity of the Umbrian estates, see Sherwin-White (1966, 257), Duncan-Jones (1982, 20) = (2016, 92). In 3.19.7, Pliny does contemplate buying slaves for his tenants (see Duncan-Jones (1982, 24) = (2016, 97) on these enslaved persons); cf. Chp. 7, Envoi for Pliny's slaves elsewhere.

126. See Kehoe (1989, 557, 576–8). Pliny speaks consistently of *rustici* (7.30.3, 9.15.1, 9.20.2), *conductores* (7.30.3), *coloni* (9.36.6), and of leasing (9.37.1 *locandorum praediorum*, 10.8.5 *agrorum . . . locatio*); cf. also 5.14.8 (Comum). For five-year leases, cf. 9.37.2, 10.8.5.

127. See de Neeve (1992, 339, 341), Kehoe (1988, 17–18, 29–30). Letter 3.19 (see n. 125) assumes tenant ownership of enslaved persons as normal.

128. See de Neeve (1992, 342–3), more broadly Kehoe (2007, 93–130).

129. 9.36.6 *datur et colonis, ut uidetur ipsis, non satis temporis, quorum mihi agrestes querelae litteras nostras et haec urbana opera commendant*; cf. 7.30.3, 9.15.2, also 5.14.8 (Comum). See Kehoe (1988, 20–1) for the ideology behind such sentiments.

130. See Kehoe (1988, 19, 23–9), (1993, 227–31). Typically, Pliny considers buying a second property rather than investing in the one he already owned (3.19); see Kehoe (1988, 22–3). Pliny also thinks of buying this property, not because he has spare cash to invest, but because it is adjacent to an estate he currently owns; see Kehoe (1993, 218–9).

131. Owners normally provided the equipment necessary to make a tenancy productive (e.g. wine presses and storage facilities: Kehoe (1988, 18)), but they were not required to take any interest in *how* the land was cultivated, so long as the rent was met (Kehoe (1988, 21–2)). On the financial risk borne by tenants, see Kehoe (1988, 36–7).

132. See Kehoe (1988, 31–8), de Neeve (1992, 341–2).

133. There are significant methodological problems with the reconstruction of any story. We do not know what Pliny is not telling us. The relative chronology of Pliny's

individual letters on his farms, particularly in Books 7–9, are a matter of guesswork. And while it is likely that most of the letters cited below belong to Pliny's Umbrian rather than Transpadane holdings, this is a matter of inference rather than certainty. For the issue of the estate to which 3.19 refers, see earlier.

134. 10.8.5 *continuae sterilitates cogunt me de remissionibus cogitare.*

135. Cf. 8.15, 9.16, 9.20, 9.28.2; cf. 8.17 on the flooding of the Tiber.

136. On Pliny's risk-avoiding strategy of selling the crop in advance, and the rebate scheme driven by the need to retain the goodwill of the *negotiatores*, see Kehoe (1989, 559–74).

137. See Kehoe (1989, 574–86).

138. 9.37.2 *rapiunt etiam consumuntque quod natum est, ut qui iam putent se non sibi parcere.*

139. On Pliny's introduction of sharecropping, see Kehoe (1988, 38–42), de Neeve (1992, 340–1).

7

Return to Comum

The great Comum inscription (in Milan)

Como's proximity to powerful Milan made the town vulnerable in the strife between Italian city states endemic in the Middle Ages. Among spoils of war taken
away from Como to Milan in the tenth century was an impressive 3-metre-long
tablet of Roman marble.[1] It was cut up into six pieces. In 950 C.E., four of its
fragments were used to shape the sarcophagus of Lothar, nominal king of Italy,
in the basilica of St Ambrose in Milan.[2] The large pieces contained carefully incised letters. On inspection, they constituted the testamentary inscription that is
the source for much of our knowledge of Pliny's career and, importantly, of his
civic building projects in Comum (*CIL* 5.5262). The text of the four fragments
was recorded and the inscription pieced together by scholars in the fifteenth
and sixteenth centuries. Then the fragments disappeared. One piece of about
87 x 85 centimetres reappeared in the basilica at some point between 1858 and
1864. Its ancient frame had been chiseled off and its surface disfigured by four
dowel holes—introduced for the uses the fragment had been put to since original dismemberment. The sole surviving portion formed the original top left-
hand corner of the inscription, beginning with Pliny's name. Today it can be
found fixed into the wall in a portico within the atrium of St Ambrose's handsome Romanesque church (Fig. 7.1).[3] Satisfaction is to be had in the marble
fragment's final resting place: the proximity of the inscription and the remains
of St Ambrose are a physical reminder of a literary relationship. The body of St
Ambrose is preserved, and on display, in the crypt of the church. This fourth-
century bishop of Milan, mentor of St Augustine in the city,[4] arranged his correspondence on the Plinian model into nine books of 'private' letters and one book
of 'official' communications: the first clear sign of a revival of interest in Pliny's
Letters, after two centuries of neglect, and one century after the resurgence of his
Panegyricus.[5]

Pliny's inscription records all the offices he held in Rome, beginning with
the prestigious posts of consul and augur, descending in chronological order
for the remaining offices.[6] The eight-line catalogue is followed by seven lines
documenting a rich programme of buildings and donations for Comum, from
latest to earliest. The whole is written in the unabashed mode characteristic of
Roman municipal epigraphy: self-effacement and understatement were not

Man of High Empire. Roy K. Gibson, Oxford University Press (2020). © Oxford University
Press.
DOI: 10.1093/actrade/9780199948192.001.0001

Figure 7.1. Sole surviving fragment of the great Como inscription in the atrium of the church of Sant' Ambrogio in Milan. *Photo by C. Delaney.*

virtues in this culture.[7] The presentation of the inscription strongly suggests that Pliny himself composed this memorial of lifetime and testamentary gifts to Comum, prior to his own death:[8]

C (aius) Plinius L(uci) f(ilius) Ouf(entina tribu) Caecilius [Secundus co(n)s(ul)]
augur legat (us) pro pr(aetore) prouinciae Pon[ti et Bithyniae pro]
consulari potesta[te] in eam prouinciam e[x senatus consulto ab]
Imp(eratore) Caesar(e) Nerua Traiano Aug(usto) German[ico Dacico p(ater) p(atriae) missus]
curator aluei Tiberis et riparum et [cloacarum urbis]
praef(ectus) aerari Saturni praef(ectus) aerari mil[itaris pr(aetor) trib(unus) plebis]
quaestor Imp(eratoris) seuir equitum [Romanorum]
trib(unus) milit(um) leg(ionis) [III] Gallica[e in prouincia Syria Xuir stli]
tib(us) iudicand(is) therm [as ex HS ---] adiectis in
ornatum HS CCC [--- et eo amp]lius in tutela[m]
HS CC t(estamento) f(ieri) i(ussit) [item in alimenta] libertor(um) suorum homin(um) C
HS |XVIII| LXVI DCLXVI rei [p(ublicae) legauit quorum in]crement(a) postea ad epulum
[pl]eb(is) urban(ae) uoluit pertin[ere item uiuu]s dedit in aliment(a) pueror(um)
et puellar(um) pleb(i) urban(ae) HS [D item bybliothecam HS ? et] in tutelam bybliothe
cae HS C(milia)

Gaius Plinius Caecilius Secundus, son of Lucius of the tribe Oufentina, consul: augur: praetorian commissioner with proconsular power for the province of Pontus and Bithynia, sent to that province in accordance with the senate's decree by the emperor Caesar Nerva Trajan Augustus, victor over Germany and Dacia, the Father of his country: curator of bed and banks of the Tiber and sewers of Rome: prefect of the treasury of Saturn: prefect of the military treasury: praetor: tribune of the people: quaestor of the emperor: commissioner for the Roman knights: military tribune of the third Gallic legion in the province of Syria: magistrate on board of ten: left by will public baths at a cost of . . . and an additional 300,000 sesterces for furnishing them, with interest on 200,000 for their upkeep . . . and also to his city capital of 1,866,666 sesterces to support a hundred of his freedmen, and subsequently to provide an annual dinner for the people of the city . . . Likewise in his lifetime he gave 500,000 sesterces for the maintenance of boys and girls of the city, likewise . . . sesterces for a library and also 100,000 for the upkeep of the library . . .[9]

CIL 5.5262

The earliest endowment to Comum recorded here is the library. Its construction can be dated to the mid-90s C.E. under Domitian, and its dedication under Nerva to the late 90s C.E.. The latest endowment is the baths whose donation was specified in Pliny's will, perhaps in 112 C.E. or just after.[10] This period will be the main focus of the present chapter: from a year or two before the death of Domitian in 96, when Pliny had already achieved the office of praetor in Rome, to the period of Pliny's governorship of the province of Pontus-Bithynia c.110–12 C.E., when the baths in Comum were perhaps already being built.

An earlier chapter covered Pliny's childhood in Comum, before he began his public career in Rome. It is immediately apparent from the inscription that it was only as an adult and successful senator that Pliny returned to Comum to erect the civic amenities characteristic of high empire. He had undertaken no building in Comum since the completion of the temple of the imperial cult perhaps begun by his father and dedicated in the late 70s C.E. This long gap in his civic generosity raises questions: how often did the adult Pliny come back to his distant hometown, how closely involved was he with its affairs? Return will be made to these questions later in this chapter. The opportunity to play gracious praetorian and consular benefactor provided relief from senatorial infighting at Rome. In his hometown, Pliny's record could be openly and honestly stated. No need to play with words on an inscription recording gifts or to omit mention of the prefecture of the treasury of Saturn. Even the removal of Domitian's name from the record of Pliny's quaestorship had been mandated by Nerva's senate.[11]

Pliny was not alone in the beautification of Comum. Around 105 C.E., learning of the dedication of a colonnade by his grandfather-in-law, Pliny writes

'I rejoice . . . our native place is flourishing' (5.11.2).[12] This golden age of civic munificence would not be matched for ambition in Como until the Renaissance. Around 1460, no longer at war with Milan and keen to boost local pride, Como saw the start of construction of a new marble cathedral on the site of an earlier basilica. The statues of the Elder and Younger Plinii were fixed on the west front of the building two decades later.[13] An imposing church was central to the Christian conception of a town. The Roman idea of a proper core for a town extended far beyond a temple: an urban grid, forum, senate house, baths, colonnades, theatre or amphitheatre, and library.[14] Thanks in part to Pliny, Roman Comum possessed the full set early in the second century.

The inscription in the basilica of St Ambrose also reveals that Pliny provided by will or during his lifetime sums for the upkeep and ornamentation of the baths and library. He added a larger donation for the welfare of his freed slaves, designed to revert in time to funding an annual civic feast in Comum, plus funds for an alimentary scheme for the support of freeborn children in the town.[15] Further substantial gifts to individuals from Comum are recorded elsewhere,[16] also to the town itself in the form of donations of money,[17] and the funding of a *rhetor* to finish the education of the town's elite young males.[18] 'Pliny was outstanding in the extent of his public generosity', in the estimate of an authority: he is the largest public donor documented in imperial Italy, at least where the value of the gifts is known.[19]

If our knowledge of donations by others elsewhere is far from complete, and the discovery of new inscriptions is likely to revise the picture, it is still hard not be impressed by the scale of Pliny's adult munificence. He was a very wealthy man.[20] Even so, Pliny was not the richest man of his generation: an observation that needs to be understood in the context of ancient material disparities between elite and masses that easily dwarf our own.[21] His childlessness played a role in his generosity.[22] Pliny had no direct descendants for whom family wealth must be preserved. Equally important was the desire to win credit with successive emperors: wealthy senators were expected to lavish funds on their birthplaces or on town to which they acted as patrons. Love of home might dovetail neatly with advancement in the later stages of an adult career.

In the remainder of this chapter, Pliny's civic munificence is set within the broader context of the contemporary rise of the Transpadana to prominence as a region. Pliny's extensive adult network in the area is also traced. There follows a focus on two important connections established with Comum in the period between the mid-90s C.E. and Pliny's death: the erection by Pliny of major buildings in the town and a new marriage contracted with Calpurnia of Comum, after the end of the marriage to Pompeia Celerina's daughter (discussed in the previous chapter).[23] This pair of public and private 'initiatives', it will emerge, are closely connected in time and perhaps in broad intent. Questions will be asked about the reality behind the proud façade of intense personal investment in Comum, and about the nature and quality of Pliny's relationship with the town and the portrait of civic harmony he offers. The chapter concludes by looking at the individuality of Pliny's views of the landscape of lake Como and at the care Pliny took to ensure his posterity in Comum.[24]

The acme of Transpadana

In Cicero's dialogue *On the Laws*, set in his birthplace of Arpinum 62 miles/100 kilometres south-east of Rome, the author had raised the question of regional loyalty and national identity:

> I think that . . . all natives of Italians towns have two fatherlands, one by nature and the other by citizenship . . . we consider both the place where we were born our fatherland, and also the city into which we have been adopted. But that fatherland must stand first in our affection which, under the name of the commonwealth [*rei publicae*], is the common country of us all. . . . I shall never deny that my fatherland is here, though my other fatherland is greater and includes this one within it.[25]

Cicero, De Legibus. 2.5

In a contest between Arpinum and Rome, this new man understands that Rome demands greater loyalty and devotion. Like Cicero, Pliny was born into a family with local ties stronger than those felt by senatorial dynasties established at Rome. He was well placed to understand potential conflicts in loyalty. Yet, nearly a century and half after Cicero, Pliny displays no consciousness that Rome must take precedence.[26] Comum is hailed as Pliny's 'delight' (1.3.1) before Rome is even mentioned in the *Letters*. Crushed under the administrative burdens of the prefect of the Treasury of Saturn at Rome, Pliny yearns for the fishing, hunting, and studious quiet offered by Caninius Rufus' villa overlooking Lake Como, like a sick man longs for baths and wine (2.8).[27]

Pliny's domestic self-assurance has a precise historical context: his career coincided with a golden age for the elites of Comum and the Transpadana, and with a time of urban prosperity and growth for the privileged classes in Italy and across the Mediterranean. In the western half of the empire, the roots of this flourishing could be traced back to Augustus and his reorganization of the provinces around a century before. Each province came to consist of a complex of interlinked *ciuitates* or self-governing municipalities, where each *ciuitas* was made up of an urban centre with its own precisely defined rural hinterland. The intention was to centralize: any villages or smaller communities in the area were subordinated to the town.[28] It was expected that each town would have a monumental centre comprising some or all of the architecture that Comum would come to possess by the time of Pliny's death. Revenue for the community was provided by local taxes and the lease of public land. This income was supplemented by substantial contributions expected from town councillors, as likely from Pliny's father in Comum.[29] The urban centre in turn became the focal point for the administration of justice, the upkeep of roads, and the provision of hospitality to visiting dignitaries.

Stable local elites arose in the newly prosperous urban centres of the western empire. The Transpadana, not a part of Italy until the 40s B.C.E, bore a closer resemblance to these municipalities than to longer established communities in the Italian peninsula. Comum, refounded as Novum Comum in the era of Julius Caesar, had a head start. Its walls, urban grid and monumental centre made it a model of urbanization for export to the western provinces.[30] By the time of Pliny's youth, the moment had arrived for the Transpadana to supply Rome with senators and consuls in numbers. Its acme was brief: the high point coincides roughly with Pliny's departure for Pontus-Bithynia.[31] Between 70 and 110 C.E., fully five men from the region achieved the rare honour of a repeated consulship.[32] Two of this elite group, Vestricius Spurinna and Verginius Rufus of Mediolanum, are family friends of Pliny, the former his guardian. Friends and correspondents from the Transpadana also achieved the consulship in the years around Pliny's own of 100 C.E.: Domitius Apollinaris of Vercellae (97 C.E.), Metilius Nepos of Novaria (103), and Minicius Fundanus of Ticinum (107).[33] Pliny's elderly patron, Corellius Rufus of Laus Pompeia, had achieved his consulship in 78 C.E.[34]

The Transpadana was joined in its energetic production of senators and consuls by three western regions. Narbonensis in southern Gaul, the urbanized eastern coast of the huge northern Spanish province of Tarraconensis, and the southern Spanish province of Baetica—all saw signal success at Rome for their elite males in this period.[35] Syme ventures a comparison between the four, from an Olympian height. The Transpadane luminaries, unlike their Narbonesian counterparts, are 'not a group, only a collection', somewhat isolated as individuals, with 'few kinsfolk . . . on record'. Their alleged lack of wider connections is given explanation: 'local affinities' counted for much with the Transpadanes; 'Not so adventurous as western aristocrats, they were not so wealthy either'.[36] Yet Pliny reflects the animation and confidence of the northerners at their regional peak. Several friends from Bergomum are prominent in his networks.[37] When added to the hometowns of Pliny's consular friends and patrons, Bergomum and its fellows can be seen to form a ring around Mediolanum (Map 1): from Comum in the north, through Novaria and Vercellae in the west and Ticinum and Laus Pompeia in the south, round to Bergomum in the east. This is the heart of 'Pliny country'.[38] Pliny labels an equestrian friend from Bergomum as 'an ornament to my native district' (7.22.2 *ornamentum regionis meae*). The ring can be extended. Over one hundred people receive communications from Pliny in the *Letters*, and numerous acquaintances are mentioned in passing. By far the biggest single grouping of correspondents and friends belongs to the Transpadana.[39] Their regional homes can be traced further east from Mediolanum to Brixia and Verona.[40] These two cities were already acknowledged by Catullus as closely tied (67.34). After this point, Pliny's connections in the east begin to dwindle; in the west, no friends can be positively identified in the country beyond Vercellae.[41] There are few truly grand names in this circumscribed regional assemblage of friends, the fundament of the correspondence. Pliny is quite unconcerned to highlight any connections he might have had with Rome's old aristocratic families.[42] It is part of his purpose to put this northern network on display: a confirmation in writing of the flourishing of the Transpadana. But only he would have precise knowledge of the regional identities of every one of his correspondents. Roman and local elites were too large in the aggregate and too scattered for everyone to know everyone else.

Pliny does not make a show of the kind of intense one-on-one friendships that Augustine's *Confessions* and letters feature between their author and old friends from home in North Africa, such as Alypius and Nebridius. Augustine was 'an imperialist in his friendships', according to his modern biographer.[43] Pliny was not. Some friends *are* particularly treasured by Pliny,[44] including Atilius Crescens: 'He is the one whom I cherish . . . with my whole heart. Our towns are separated by one day's journey only. Our love for each other began—and this is the most fervent kind of love—when we were mere youths' (6.8.2).[45] Crescens is evidently from Bergomum or Mediolanum.[46] Significantly, he receives no direct communication in the published *Letters*. No one would claim that Tacitus, himself likely from Narbonensis, was a confidant to Pliny in the mould of Atticus, Cicero's own most favoured correspondent.[47] Pliny is at his best when sitting at the centre of an extended network of correspondents: his talent in friendship is perhaps for the general rather than the particular.

Building Comum

The municipal golden age on the Roman model would not last forever in the western high empire. Even the wealthy Numidia of Augustine, rich on trade and a fertile agricultural hinterland, was showing signs of civic inertia in the late fourth century. In Hippo, the second port of Africa, there had been no spending on major civic projects in the forum for around a century before the start of Augustine's ecclesiastical tenure in the 390s. Funds were now spent on enlarging churches or on decorations for urban homes and country villas. Venues for public entertainment began to fall out of use.[48] Classical civic culture was starting to wither, and not only because of a shift in focus towards the church. In some parts of the empire, an increasingly oppressive imperial bureaucracy had diminished the fiscal resources available to cities. Local town councilors found ways of shirking long-standing demands to beautify and entertain towns.[49] The picture of shrinkage in trade and civic activity is not uniform for every city. Modern historians dispute, acrimoniously, whether the process represents 'decline' or 'transformation'.[50] The answer to that question depends on the relative value placed on what was both lost and gained in the shift from classical to Christian city.

Pliny symbolizes an earlier culture of industrious civic dedication. His library and baths made significant additions to Comum's civic infrastructure and cityscape. The cost of the library was recorded on one of the two fragments of the inscription that were lost from Milan even before the Renaissance. That cost might be recovered, or so Mommsen thought, by subtracting the other lifetime donations recorded on the inscription from the sum of 1.6 million sesterces recorded as the total of Pliny's gifts to Comum up to 105–6 C.E. (5.7). The figure of 1 million sesterces for Pliny's library makes it the most expensive public building financed by a private citizen known in the Roman world. It presumably cost less.[51] Even so, with an upkeep donation of 100,000 sesterces, it was a very substantial structure. A candidate for the library was located in 1999 just outside Como's city walls, to the immediate west on the junction between viale Varese and via Benzi (Map 3).[52] This large building appears to have been part of a deliberate building programme. It is placed in near symmetry with another large complex of around the same date just outside the eastern walls of Comum. Between them they created two extra-urban spaces which provided civic life in Comum with new western and eastern poles.[53] This site to the east is a large bath complex, first discovered in 1971 between viale Lecco and via Dante, but not fully excavated until 2006–8 (Map 3).[54]

The dangers of positivism are obvious: Pliny's association with these two sites is possible, not proven. What can be emphasized is that Pliny tells us nothing whatever about the architecture or appearance of his baths and library in the correspondence. In a letter marking the dedication of his library in Comum, Pliny reports a speech recently given in Comum before the town council (1.8). His focus is on the alimentary scheme which accompanied the dedication,[55] with barely a word on the library itself. There might be an explanation for Pliny's silence on the baths. They were likely promised to the town while he was still alive: the sum mentioned for their decoration and upkeep is in addition to the original monies set aside for the complex. Perhaps the baths were begun too late for inclusion in the private *Letters*—whose latest datable references belong to c. 109 C.E.[56] Yet there are no specific details elsewhere in the correspondence about any other building in Comum, aside from the portico erected by his grandfather-in-law (5.11.2). Pliny's apparent lack of interest in Comum's city-scape will reappear later in this chapter.

Marriage to Calpurnia of Comum

Pliny's programme of dedications and donations was accompanied by a second decisive action designed to link him more firmly to Comum. In 97 or 98 C.E., not long after the formal opening of his library and announcement of a local alimentary scheme in Comum, Pliny contracted a union with Calpurnia. The swift transition from the deceased 'Venuleia' to a new bride would not necessarily be perceived as hasty. Laws from the Augustan era encouraged quick remarriage by senators like Pliny, for the propagation of children.[57] Despite the social cachet of his earlier marriage and the sure prospect of his promotion to the consulship, Pliny now refrained from a prestigious match: Calpurnia was the daughter of a family of wealthy local landowners. There was no definite career advantage in marrying her—other than proving to emperors that this promising new man had no ambition to insinuate himself into an established senatorial dynasty. All of Rome had seen the devastation wreaked by Domitian on powerful family groupings. Calpurnia of Comum, it will soon emerge, nevertheless possessed invaluable symbolic importance for Pliny at an important moment in his career.

Pliny was in his mid-thirties, she was two decades younger. The gap in years between them was not unusual.[58] Both of Calpurnia's parents were dead (4.19.1, 8.11). Her grandfather had served in the army at equestrian rank, and been somehow implicated in a plot against Nero, only to escape punishment 'by virtue of relative insignificance' (*quasi minores*, Tac. *Ann.* 16.8.3).[59] Calpurnius Fabatus confined his service thereafter to Comum (*CIL* 5.5267). His resources were extensive. Estates in Campania and Umbria (6.30, 8.20.3) and Comum allowed him to fund the portico applauded by Pliny. Complex ties in Comum encouraged the union between Pliny and his granddaughter Calpurnia. Pliny's own mother had been a close friend of Calpurnia Hispulla, adored aunt of Pliny's new wife (4.19.7). Calpurnia herself may have been cousin of Corellia Hispulla—a daughter of Pliny's mentor Corellius Rufus and a niece of that sister of Corellius who was the dearest friend of Pliny's own mother (7.11.3).[60] A sister-in-law of Corellius perhaps stood as grandmother to Calpurnia and wife of Calpurnius Fabatus.[61] Fabatus was not among Pliny's admired Transpadane mentors of senior years. He reacts angrily to Pliny's sale of land in the Comum area at below market-value to Corellia, sister of Corellius Rufus (7.11, 7.14).[62]

Cicero's letters offer a relatively full portrait of his marriage to, and eventual divorce from, the resourceful, influential, and financially independent Terentia.[63]

Pliny allows us to see rather less.[64] Calpurnia and her family are prominent in Pliny's affections and attention, but the factual content of the marriage is low. Most of the events in their shared life have been canvassed in previous chapters. Pliny and Calpurnia travel together from Rome to Comum to see families and estates (5.14.8), visiting Tifernum in Umbria along the way (4.1). She reads and values Pliny's published works, attends his recitations modestly concealed from view, and even sets his verse to the lyre (4.19). Taken ill, Calpurnia convalesces at her family's villa in Campania (6.4, 6.30). Pliny writes to say how desperately he misses his absent wife (7.5), but is delighted to hear she is consoled by the presence of Pliny's writings, although he still misses the charm of her conversation (6.7). Ignorant of her pregnancy, Calpurnia suffers a miscarriage: her grandfather is expected to be angry and disappointed (8.10); her aunt Calpurnia Hispulla, it is understood, will be concerned for her niece's health (8.11).[65] In due course, Calpurnia accompanies her husband on his tour of duty in Pontus-Bithynia (10.120–21).[66]

Pliny's evident desire to promote the image of a perfect union is partly inspired by the imperial family. Just as his adoption was deliberately played up for the sake of suggesting resonances with the adoption of the new emperor by Nerva,[67] so the *concordia* that Pliny attributes to his marriage (4.19.5) echoes the idealized picture that Trajan consciously promoted of his union with Plotina. Pliny duly eulogizes that marriage in the speech of thanks for his consulship. Plotina is 'unswerving in her devotion' to her husband (*Paneg.* 83.6) and models her behaviour on his (*Paneg.* 83.8).[68] Calpurnia is praised for her ardor for her husband ('she loves me', 4.19.2) and for devoting herself to activities likely to highlight Pliny's literary and rhetorical accomplishments (4.19.2–4, 6.7.1–2).[69] This is a traditional Roman marriage founded not on mutual understanding, but on the expectation that a wife can make a success of the union if she focuses on her husband's interests.[70] Pliny, at least, does not claim to have 'moulded' Calpurnia, despite the praise offered to Trajan for his shaping of Plotina (*Paneg.* 83.7). The honour of fashioning Pliny's wife is attributed to Calpurnia Hispulla (4.19.6).

Calpurnia's agency in her marriage cannot be missed. Pliny reports that it not his 'time of life or his body' that his wife loves, but 'his fame' (*non . . . aetatem meam aut corpus . . . sed gloriam diligit*, 4.19.5). 'Calpurnia was an astute girl', argues Jo-Ann Shelton; 'she assuaged [Pliny's] fear by convincing him that he need not worry about their age difference because his renown was more appealing to her than a youthful body'.[71] If the marriage seemed rewarding to Pliny, it was because Calpurnia created the reality or illusion of success. He, in turn, decorates their relationship with intense motifs borrowed from Roman love elegy (6.4, 6.7, 7.5). These artfully raise his relationship above Roman epistolary literature's other famous married couples: Cicero and Terentia, and Ovid and the wife depicted in *Letters from Pontus*.[72] The hint of infatuation with a wife

is something new in Latin literature, whatever the reality behind the love letters for Calpurnia.[73] Ultimately, Pliny entertains very traditional expectations
of Calpurnia as spouse. What is novel is his willingness to assert the personal
satisfactions of conventional marriage.[74]

Pliny, Comum, and Calpurnia: behind the façade

Pliny's buildings, donations, and marriage to Calpurnia appear to confirm significant financial, personal, and emotional investment in Comum. Questions
remain. How often did he actually come back? It was one thing to keep in touch
with fellow northerners by letter. Journeys to and from the Transpadana were
major events. His estates near Tifernum were 150 Roman miles from the capital (10.8.6), and took around five days to reach.[75] At a distance from Rome
just under three times that, Comum required serious advance planning as a
destination.[76] Pliny's time was constricted by duties in court and senate. As
Saturnian prefect he must write to Trajan himself, on the frontiers of empire
in Pannonia, to gain special permission for absence from Rome for thirty
days to attend to pressing matters on the Umbrian estates (10.8). One recent
critic has found it possible to argue that Pliny made only one trip to Comum
in the period between the assassination of Domitian and departure for Pontus-
Bithynia. Most would argue for at least two or more. He cannot have returned
home very often.[77]

There are no recorded donations to Comum between the likely dedication
of the temple of the imperial cult in the late 70s C.E. and the opening of the
library around twenty years later.[78] Was Pliny absent from the town for the
whole of that period? Perhaps not. Yet these decades overlap to a significant
degree with the period of marriage to 'Venuleia' and Pliny's installation in the
senatorial networks of Umbria and Etruria. There is a clear correlation between
Pliny's suddenly re-awakened investment in Comum and a desire to gain imperial favour in Rome during the run from praetor in the 90s C.E. to consul in
100 C.E. and onwards to further prestigious posts.[79] (It will be suggested later
that marriage to Calpurnia of Comum, at a felicitous moment in the years of
transition between the regimes of Domitian and Nerva-Trajan, brought added
symbolic advantages.)

Under the Flavian emperors, it was the fashion for wealthy senators to build
amphitheatres in towns connected to them by patronage.[80] This imperial dynasty had built the Colosseum for the entertainment of the people directly
on top of the ruins of Nero's private pleasure palace and gardens. There are
subterranean traces of an amphitheatre or theatre in Comum.[81] This structure
has nothing to do with Pliny. Averse even to attending the Circus Maximus in

Rome (9.6), Pliny did not find the financing of gladiatorial games in Comum to his taste (1.8.10). The Flavians, however, were more enthusiastic restorers and re-stockers of libraries in Rome than their successors.[82] Planning and construction of the library in Comum appear to have begun in the last years of Domitian. What better way to bring together Pliny's literary tastes and desire to maintain imperial favour after his praetorship of 93–4 C.E.? The erection of the library just before Domitian's death caused no embarrassment to Pliny under the new regime, whatever later sensitivities he might have had about his record of political success in Rome.[83] A library also told the people of Comum what sort of person its benefactor was.[84] Ancient literacy levels were well below those normal in modern societies: this was not a gift to all the people of Comum, as games might have been.[85]

Pliny's alimentary scheme for the children of Comum is even more clearly linked to a bid for imperial favour. Announced on the occasion of the dedication of the library at Comum (1.8), the alimentary scheme was evidently meant to gain credit with Nerva or Trajan just as the push for the consulship began in earnest.[86] Designed to encourage the free population of the town to bear children (1.8.10–11), the project's impact on the *plebs urbana* of Comum was ultimately symbolic. The donated capital of 500,000 sesterces is substantially larger than any known sum given previously in this way, and brought in about 30,000 sesterces a year, according to an innovative financial scheme of Pliny's own devising (7.18). It would benefit as few as 175 children a year, out of around 7,000 free children in total.[87] One scholar is right to emphasize the need for Pliny to 'deflect [local] resentment from below by means of munificence'.[88] As a major local landowner, he would expect to collect rents ranging from one-third of agricultural produce to two-thirds. The complaints of the farmers in Comum (5.14.8) were no less vocal than those on his estates in Umbria.[89]

Marriage to Calpurnia was part of the broad programme of purposeful reinvestment in Comum. Pliny could hardly choose the moment of his previous wife's death. Her demise early in the reign of Nerva presented an opportunity all the same. The new union gave Pliny a new start in a new era. Marriage to 'Venuleia' had provided him with a place in the aristocratic networks of central Italy and a long history of her family's service to the Flavians.[90] Calpurnia reinforced ties to the virtuous north and offered the fresh slate of a young Transpadane bride with no ancestors in the Flavian senate. One was easier to trumpet abroad than the other. Umbria could not lend Pliny a distinctive moral identity. The region possessed a reputation for agricultural prosperity, as Catullus's characteristic remarks on a 'fat Umbrian' suggest (*pinguis Vmber*, 39.11).[91] The lands immediately east of the upper Tiber, in general, have neither strong presence nor especially memorable ethical character in Roman writing before the age of Pliny.[92]

Calpurnia brings the aura of the Transpadana into her husband's life. A symbolic link between a female character and a nation, race, or region was not unfamiliar in either life or literature. Serrana Procula, grandmother of Pliny's young Transpadane friend Minicius Acilianus, is hailed as 'model of sobriety' (*seueritatis exemplum*, 1.14.6) even to the inhabitants of the famously austere north-eastern Italian town of Patavium. In Vergil's *Aeneid*, Creusa, Dido, and Lavinia are linked to respective homes in Troy, Carthage, and Italy and to the values and historical associations of those regions.[93] Creusa, the wife of Aeneas who dies during the sack of their city, encapsulates the Trojan past that Aeneas leaves behind; the youthful Lavinia, offered in marriage to Aeneas upon arrival in Italy, symbolizes the new identity that the hero is expected to embrace. Italy is presented as the original homeland of the Trojans.[94] Calpurnia plays Lavinia to the Creusa of Pliny's deceased earlier wife. 'Venuleia' lives on in Pliny's life as a ghost, her spectre detectable only in the background to Pliny's Umbrian life.[95]

Writing to Calpurnia Hispulla to provide assurances of the success of the match, Pliny praises his wife for her 'remarkable quickness, remarkable thriftiness (*summum . . . acumen, summa frugalitas*, 4.19.2). Such *frugalitas* was, on Pliny's account, a distinctively Transpadane virtue: the Brixia of Minicius Acilianus had been praised for it.[96] Pliny worries that his northern bride, gone to convalesce in Campania, has received some personal or moral damage from the notorious pleasures of the region.[97] Comum and Calpurnia even seem to coalesce in Pliny's thinking. The desire expressed by Pliny for his native region in the letter to Caninius Rufus (2.8) anticipates in structure, tone, and conception the love expressed for the absent Calpurnia (7.5).[98] It is perhaps serendipity that in her first and last appearances in Pliny's record of his life, Calpurnia is travelling home towards Comum (4.1, 10.120–1). But the pull towards the Transpadana that Calpurnia symbolizes is not deceptive.

Pliny's final donation to Comum, that of the baths, can be linked to the need to adapt to changing imperial fashions. Trajan, ever mindful of the need to distance himself from Domitian, set to work with his Greek architect Apollodorus on a set of magnificent baths in the first of his great series of projects at the heart of Rome.[99] He set a fashion for senators to do the same in their towns. This trend would continue well into the second century as the building of amphitheatres in the earlier Flavian mode continued to decline. In Pontus-Bithynia, Pliny would urge Trajan's own example on the emperor. The public baths in Prusa were 'mean and old', and the citizens regarded the funding of a new set as a priority: 'This is a work which is demanded both by the importance of the city and the glory of your reign' (10.23.1–2).[100] Trajan, keen to keep expenditure by the cities of the province in check, agreed, so long as no special taxes were enforced (10.24). The citizens of Comum might count themselves lucky that the splendour of Trajan's reign was enhanced at the expense of their leading son.

Trouble in Comum

Pliny could not return to Comum very frequently. There is a hiatus of two decades in his record of donations to the town. The reawakening of investment in Comum can be linked to the desire to gain imperial credit at key stages in Pliny's career. Marriage to Calpurnia helpfully re-oriented Pliny's image towards the virtuous north. Yet he is not lacking in sentiment for his landed estates near Comum. He is willing to sell Corellia 'anything she liked' from his northern estates, except for what he had inherited from his mother and father, 'for I could not part with these even to Corellia' (7.11.5). The farms inherited from Pliny's mother cause trouble, but 'they delight me as coming from my mother' (2.15.2). It is part of Pliny's bond with Verginius Rufus, the man who showed him the affection of a parent, that 'our towns were neighbouring, our estates and properties joined each other' (2.1.8).[101] Here is emotional investment in land, its owners, and the interconnections between them.[102] There are no happy memories, however, of time spent on northern estates with his parents, and not one of his Transpadane properties receives the intimate, detailed, and warm descriptions lavished on his villas in Umbria and the Laurentine shore.[103] Good memories from younger years attach to Tifernum and its early adoption of Pliny as patron (4.1.4).

As suggested in the previous chapter, Pliny deliberately overplays his distant hometown at the expense of Umbria. E. J. Champlin has persuasively argued that the estate near Tifernum ultimately appears more suited to Pliny's tastes and more expressive of his interests.[104] Comum is a source of agricultural wealth and concomitant trouble.[105] In Umbria private pursuits are paramount, interrupted as they are by business matters. Comum is a place of duty: Pliny is the public man, a great benefactor and powerful friend.[106] In Umbria, nearby Tifernum places its demands on Pliny, but on his estate he is free to concentrate on the production of the writings that he believed were his one path to longevity. Life is more vividly recreated there. In Comum, Caninius Rufus aside (1.3, 8.4), there are no aspiring litterateurs to share Pliny's interests.[107] No sign of a *need* among the elite of the area for the library that Pliny bestowed at such great expense.

Was Comum the place of civic harmony and domestic flourishing that the Pliny suggests? He later presents Trajan with a portrait of endemic civil chaos among the cities of Pontus-Bithynia: citizens who spend too much or not enough on their towns, wasteful and extravagant civil projects, needless distributions of cash, excessively competitive town councilors.[108] In Prusa, the handing over of a finished library to the town by its most internationally famous son, the orator Dio, provokes the eruption of a legal dispute so brutal that Pliny refers it to Trajan for arbitration (10.81). In Comum, the worst that Pliny expects to face for his library and alimentary scheme are grumbles about self-advertisement or that he has not donated gladiators instead (1.8).[109] Civic discord in the eastern half of the empire was unwelcome, but it might ultimately 'justify' the rule of Greeks by Romans. There was less gain to be had from dwelling on such troubles in the enterprising Transpadana. Was there discord and competition within the elite of the town—as so very evidently in the cities of Pontus-Bithynia? Were there other local benefactors to rival Pliny?[110] Who paid for the construction of the theatre or amphitheatre that appears to be contemporary with his own building works in the town?[111] Who funded a recently discovered temple of Trajanic date in the town?[112] Were relations between the decurion class and lower orders of Comum healthy?[113] Did there exist rivalry with Milan, as in the Middle Ages, despite Pliny's picture of Transpadane harmony?[114]

Hints of trouble emerge. In a letter of advice to Caninius Rufus on a mooted legacy to Comum, Pliny asks: 'Suppose you pay the amount to the municipality? It is to be feared that it may be squandered. Suppose you give land? Being public land, it will be neglected' (7.18.1).[115] Such fears are realized, not in Comum, but of course later in Prusa, where Pliny reports to Trajan on the current desolate state of a property bequeathed to the city in the reign of the emperor Claudius (10.70). The only worries in Comum are unrealized ones, as in Pliny's reflections on the potential for civic corruption in his funding of the *rhetor* at Comum (4.13.6). Broader worries about the stability of finances among Italian towns eventually led to the emergence of *curatores rei publicae*: officials of high social rank tasked by the emperor with supervising or investigating the finances of a community not their own. Four curators are attested for Comum, including one P. Clodius Sura from Brixia, appointed by Hadrian to supervise the affairs of the city (*CIL* 5.5126), after playing the same short-term role at nearby Bergomum under Trajan.[116] If such figures intervened in Comascan affairs in Pliny's lifetime, they have left no trace in the correspondence. Imperial interventions in the financial affairs of the cities are confined to the Greek cities of Pontus-Bithynia.

Pliny and Lake Como

It is time to turn our gaze beyond the town of Comum and try to capture something of Pliny's individuality away from the concerns and affairs of the municipality. As in Rome, the townscape did not catch Pliny's eye. He is attracted by the sights outside the city, around Lake Como. Writing to literary friend Caninius Rufus, he asks:

> What news of Comum, your delight and mine? What of that most charming of suburban villas? What of that portico, where it is always spring time? What of that most shady of plane groves? What of the canal with its green and enameled banks? What of the lake lying below at your service?[117]

Letters 1.3.1

This villa is situated outside the walls of Comum, overlooking the lake, and encapsulates the things that appeal to Pliny's eye.[118] These are not the mountains or the lake itself, but a villa complex designed to take best advantage of its natural position. Rufus' artificial canal (*euripus*) takes precedence over the lake below that is described as 'at the service' of the villa as if the latter were the lake's owner (*seruiens lacus*).[119] The grove comes loaded with its own symbolic allusions to philosophy and the opening scene in Plato's *Phaedrus* of Socrates under a plane tree.[120] Underlying Pliny's own description is a celebration of human triumph over a physical environment that has been made to serve the varied needs of an elite lifestyle as the owner moves from walking through bodily exercise to bath, dinner, and rest: 'What of the exercising ground uniting softness with solidity? What of that bath room which always catches the full sun on his way round? What of those dining rooms for large company and those for small? What of the resting-chambers for day and for night?' (1.3.1).[121]

Chekhov longed for the wide-open spaces of the steppe or the acacia trees of his birthplace on the Black Sea, according to his biographer.[122] Pliny is thrilled by the thought of a luxury villa with a view over water and all the amenities of the traditional Graeco-Roman 'pleasant place' (*locus amoenus*): water, shade, grass. This is a preference for suburban light and shade over the awe-inspiring vistas of the Romantic sublime or their ancient equivalents—the natural environments of Homer and the Dionysiac landscapes of poetry and wall paintings.[123] Out on the water, conversely, Pliny's attention is directed towards an arresting residence on shore: 'I was sailing on our lake Como [*Larium nostrum*] when an elderly friend pointed out to me a villa with a room projecting over the lake' (6.24.2).[124] The villa embodies the interaction of art with nature, and comes with a memorable human story attached: an elderly couple from Comum jumped from the projecting room to their deaths in the lake below after discovering the mortal nature of the husband's illness. A spring on the shore of lake Como, preserved today at the modern Villa Pliniana near Torno,[125] is miraculous on account of the intervention of human artifice. 'Three times a day it is increased and diminished in volume by a regular rise and fall', thanks to being 'enclosed in a small grotto made by hand' (4.30.2).[126] Pliny picnics there, as if the site were an outdoor *triclinium* ('dining room').

Pliny himself owned spectacularly sited villas on the lake. He gives special attention to a contrasting pair called 'Tragedy' and 'Comedy': the former named for its commanding position overlooking the lake, as if on the high boots of a tragic actor; the latter named for its site on the edge of the lake, as if wearing the low slipper associated with comic actors (9.7). They enjoy views of the lake appropriate to the lofty detachment or everyday engagement of their genres: 'One enjoys a nearer, the other a more extended view of the lake; one, with a gentle curve, embraces a small bay, the other, situated on a lofty summit, separates two small bays from each other' (9.7.4).[127] Pliny is not really concerned to make us more familiar with the spectacular scenery of lake Como. The site of neither villa has been convincingly identified.[128] His ultimate purpose here is to play a multilayered literary game. Lake Como becomes the venue for general expression of his own cultural interests, and Tragedy and Comedy are vehicles for engaging specifically with Ovid's contest between virtue and vice.[129] Added comments on the relative opportunities offered by the two villas for observing or participating in fishing on the lake mark Pliny's oblique, and only, engagement with the activities of the common people of Comum (9.7.4), other than on his own farms (5.14.8).[130]

Celebrity and posterity in Comum

A sense of the occasion accompanying Pliny's return visits to Comum as praetor or consul can be gleaned from an account given of arrivals in an Umbrian town: 'Tifernum Tiberinum . . . while I was still little more than a boy, adopted me for its patron . . . It celebrates my visits to it, is pained at my departure, and rejoices in the honours paid me' (4.1.4).[131] It was not usual at this period for senators to become the official patron of their hometown.[132] The honour of being Comum's patron was reserved at the time for the addressee of the Tifernum letter, Pliny's grandfather-in-law—as is known from the old man's funerary statue base preserved in Como's archaeological museum (*CIL* 5.5267).[133] Pliny must be more circumspect in portraying his reception at Comum. It was a rather more substantial town than Tifernum. Throughout the correspondence Pliny is careful to offer exaggerated respect for the local senate despite his vastly superior status as a senator and consul (1.8, 5.7, 7.18). He avoided the public assemblies that clearly still took place in Comum (1.8.17), as he would also in Pontus-Bithynia during his later stint there as governor.[134] Glimpses of celebrity can be gained from details of visits from local worthies and their sons to pay respects (4.13.3) and of time spent 'with my wife's grandfather, and her aunt, with friends long missed' (5.14.7).[135]

Several inscriptions from Comum honouring Pliny have been found.[136] The most revealing was recovered as recently as 1971 at the western perimeter of Como's old town, in the area between viale Varese, via Cinque Giornate, and via Volta. It too is on display in the Museo Archeologico:

C(aio) Plinio L(uci) f(ilio) Ouf(entina tribu) Caecilio Secundo co(n)s(uli) M(arcus) Cassius Comic(us)

   To the consul C. Plinius Caecilius Secundus, son of Lucius of the Oufentina tribe, [dedicated by] M. Cassius Comicus

AE (1972, 212)

The dedicant, Cassius Comicus, is otherwise absent from the epigraphical record at Comum and from Pliny's own writings, although the house (*gens*) of the Cassii is well attested across northern Italy.[137] The inscription, which takes the form of a low 1-metre-squared base and presumably once held a statue of Pliny himself, has two unusual features: the dedicant is an individual rather than a community; and, alone among surviving inscriptions to feature Pliny, this one mentions only his consulship. This is a private dedication.[138] Perhaps the statue was set up by Cassius Comicus in Pliny's own villa in Comum, by way of thanks for some benefaction, or it may have been part of a gallery of Comascan worthies assembled by Cassius or his family at some later date.[139] Pliny was a significant figure in Comum. The dedication he had himself set up to mark his consulship in the town's most important temple confirmed it (3.6).

Pliny took care to cement his status and long-term connections with Comum in other ways, both during his lifetime and for posterity. His testamentary inscription records a generous fund for the support of one hundred of his freedmen in the town.[140] It is understood that the beneficiaries were to be freed at the time of their owner's death. Any enslaved persons who worked the fields of his northern estates would not be included.[141] The grant of freedom and support to a relatively large number in Comum can be linked to a concern for the longevity of Pliny's name in his native region. Its success is embodied in the most visually impressive of all inscriptions preserved in the archaeological museum of Como: a handsome 1.75-metre-tall monument erected by C. Plinius Calvos in the later second century (*CIL* 5.5300).[142] Put up by its freedman dedicator while still alive, the inscription records the names of Plinius Calvos' family and the civic success of both himself and his freeborn son-in-law in reaching office on the city council. The inscription supplies the names of Plinius Calvos' former owners, Plinius Tharsa, and Plinia Verecunda. It is likely that these were among the original group of slaves freed by Pliny himself. There are around thirty further attestations of the name Plinius on inscriptions in northern Italy, eighteen from the Comum area alone. The prevalence of certain *praenomina* ('first names') suggests that a good proportion belong to the freedmen of the great Plinii.[143]

From Comum to the east

By these means, Pliny would eventually secure in Comum the posterity for which he had aimed also in his great testamentary inscription. But at the end of the first decade of the second century, before that inscription had been put on display, Pliny himself stood on the verge of one final crowning appointment to a senator's career: the governorship of a significant province. Before that moment, as the great inscription records, he had achieved the offices of quaestor, praetor, and consul, in addition to the curatorship of the bed and banks of the Tiber, and the prefecture of two of Rome's treasuries, not to mention a prestigious priesthood. He also owned significant estates near Rome, Comum, and in Umbria, and had donated large sums of his vast patrimony to the support and beautification of communities in northern and central Italy. He had been married at least twice, but had no children. In addition, Pliny was one of Rome's greatest living courtroom orators, as well as the nephew of the distinguished author of the *Natural History* and himself the composer of well-received literary works, including poetry, speeches, and the *Letters*. An impressive set of activities and achievements for a new man. But would he prove entirely equal to a challenge outside Rome and away from Italy, the governorship of Pontus-Bithynia?

Notes

1. For the original size of the marble tablet, see Eck (1997, 99 n. 80), Alföldy (1999c, 227), Krieckhaus (2006, 216): it was perhaps 3 metres x 1.6 metres in total.
2. On the medieval fate of Pliny's inscription, see Alföldy (1999c, 222) with reference to the older accounts of Mommsen in *CIL* 5 and Calderini (1945).
3. A church has stood on the site since the late fourth century, although its Romanesque form, including the atrium, is due to rebuilding works which started in the ninth century, and took their current form largely in the late eleventh and early twelfth centuries.
4. On the Milan of Augustine and Ambrose, see Lane Fox (2015, 181–92), Gwynn (2017).
5. On Ambrose's letters and their relationship with Pliny, see Zelzer (1989), Liebeschuetz (2005, 32–8), Gibson (2012, 59, 68–9), Nauroy (2017, 148–50).
6. See Birley (2000a, 5) on the order of presentation of information in the inscription.
7. See Gibson (2003).
8. Eck (1997, 98–9): 'the inscription, although it was set up after Pliny's death, does not directly name anyone as responsible for carrying this out. It must in fact have been Pliny himself, since he is named in the nominative'.
9. *CIL* 5.5262 = Alföldy (1999c). The text here is reproduced from Krieckhaus (2006, 216) following Alföldy's reconstruction. For a summary of debates on aspects of the inscription, see Krieckhaus (2006, 44–7), also Gibson and Morello (2012, 270–3), Roncaglia (2018, 84–6). On the function of Roman career inscriptions, see Eck (2009).
10. On dates for the library, see later in this chapter; for the date of Pliny's death, see Envoi.
11. For Pliny's play with words in the *Panegyricus* on his Domitianic record, his omission of the prefecture from his record, and the *damnatio memoriae* of Domitian enjoined by senatorial decree, see Chp. 5.
12. 5.11.2 *gaudeo . . . patria nostra florescit.*
13. See Chp. 1.
14. See Edmondson (2006, 251–3, 260–72).

15. See later in this chapter. The size of the fund for the civic feast is the largest known in Italy: see Duncan-Jones (1982, 29 n. 88) = (2016, 103 n. 88); cf. 7.18, where Pliny advises Caninius Rufus on donations for an annual civic feast at Comum, in part to draw attention to his own earlier alimentary scheme (Sherwin-White (1966, 422)).

16. For donations to individuals in Comum, cf. 1.19 (with imperial encouragement: Duncan-Jones (1982, 28 with n. 77) = (2016, 101 with n. 77)), 6.3, 6.25; cf. Duncan-Jones (1982, 28–9) = (2016, 101–103) on Pliny's benefactions to individuals more generally.

17. See Patterson (2006, 169–76) for civic cohesion as one of the aims of such donations and distributions. In 5.7 Pliny declares his intention to pay to Comum out of his own resources a sum of money which a deceased friend, Saturninus, had left to the town in a will that was not legally valid; see Duncan-Jones (1982, 25–6) = (2016, 97–9) on the complicated details of the case. This letter includes the information: 'I have given 1,600,000 sesterces to the town out of my own money, so surely I ought not to grudge it this 400,000, little more than a third of my unexpected inheritance' (5.7.3). Advice is given in 7.18 on how to make an effective testamentary gift to Comum.

18. See Chp. 3 on the provision of a *rhetor* for Comum.

19. Duncan-Jones (1982, 32) = (2016, 106), with discussion and context at (1982, 30–2) = (2016, 104–6). For an overview of all Pliny's recorded donations, see Duncan-Jones (1982, 25–32) = (2016, 97–105); on Pliny's concept of *liberalitas*, see Manuwald (2003, 203–8).

20. See Chp. 6 nn. 108–9.

21. See Duncan-Jones (1982, 17–19) = (2016, 89–91), who estimates that Pliny was perhaps worth 'twice the sum of HS 8 million that contemporary sources sometimes indicate as an appropriate capital for a senator'.

22. See Chp. 5 on Pliny's childlessness.

23. See also Chp. 5 for the death of Celerina's daughter.

24. The title of this section borrows that of Syme, *RP* 7.635–46. For overviews of Pliny's adult relationship with Comum, see also Gasser (1999, 186–213), Krieckhaus (2006, 31–50).

25. Cic. *Leg.* 2.5 *ego mehercule . . . omnibus municipibus duas esse censeo patrias, unam naturae, alteram ciuitatis . . . nos et eam patriam dicimus, ubi nati, et illam <a> qua excepti sumus. sed necesse est caritate eam praestare <e> qua rei publicae nomen uniuersae ciuitatis est . . . ego hanc meam esse patriam prorsus numquam negabo, dum illa sit maior, haec in ea contineatur.*

26. On Pliny and the concept of *duae patriae*, see Krieckhaus (2004), also Gasser (1999, 216–28); cf. Newlands (2012, 157–9) on Statius and Naples and Rome, and Madsen (2009, 79–81) on the experience of Greek senators.

27. On Pliny as prefect of the Treasury of Saturn in 2.8, see Sherwin-White (1966, 156); cf. Spencer (2010, 121–2) on the Vitruvian context for Pliny's metaphors of sickness, also later in this chapter for parallels with desire for Calpurnia. For the villa of Caninius Rufus, see later in this chapter.

28. On the Augustan reorganization of *ciuitates* and early imperial urbanization in the western provinces, see Edmondson (2006, 254–5), also Dondin-Payre

and Raepsaet-Charlier (1999), Laurence, Esmonde Cleary, and Sears (2011); cf. Bispham (2007a), Berry (2016) on the earlier history of municipalization and urbanization in Italy.

29. See Edmondson (2006, 272–3, 275–7).

30. See Edmondson (2006, 260), with reference to the works of Ward-Perkins (1970) and Zanker (2000).

31. See Syme, *RP* 7.639.

32. There were five iterated consulships: Vibius Crispus of Vercellae; Rutlius Gallicus and Atilius Agricola of Augusta Taurinorum, i.e. Turin (see Syme, *RP* 7.620–34 on this pair); Verginius Rufus of Mediolanum (see Chp. 4 n. 121); and Vestricius Spurinna (precise domicile unknown: Syme, *RP* 7.543; on Spurinna, see Chp. 4 n. 121). On the whole group of five, see Syme (1958, 643–4), *RP* 7.640–3.

33. For Domitius Apollinaris, see Syme, *RP* 7.588–603, Mratschek (2018); for Minicius Fundanus, see Syme, *RP* 7.603–19; cf. Chp. 5. The identification of Metilius Nepos as the addressee of 2.3, 3.16, 4.26 is controversial; see Birley (2000a, 71–2).

34. On Corellius Rufus, see Hoffer (1999, 141–59), Gibson and Morello (2012, 127–31); on his origin, see Syme (1958, 616), *RP* 7.508–9, 640–1; McDermott (1971, 86–8), Birley (2000a, 51–2). Other local consuls include Baebius Macer of Comum (103) and Cornelius Priscus of Patavium (104?).

35. See Syme (1969, 201) = *RP* 2.742; *RP* 7.638–9; cf. the Elder's Pliny's admiration for the local elites of Narbonensis at *HN* 3.31, with the commentary of Syme (1969, 224) = *RP* 2.763.

36. Syme, *RP* 7.645.

37. Friends from Bergomum include Atilius Crescens (on whom see later), Cornelius Minicianus (3.9, 4.11, 7.22, 8.12: further information in Birley (2000a, 52)), and Maesius Maximus (3.20, 4.25: further information in Birley (2000a, 70)).

38. 'Pliny country' is Syme's memorable conceptualization of Pliny's home networks: evoked best at Syme (1968a, 136) = *RP* 2.696; his other evocations of Pliny country are catalogued at Birley (2000a, 17 n. 37); cf. Roncaglia (2014) on the coherence of Pliny's networks in 'Pliny country'.

39. See Birley (2000a, 17).

40. Friends include Minicius Acilianus, Minicius Macrinus (Brixia); Sentius Augurinus, Vibius Maximus (Verona); see Birley (2000a).

41. See Syme (1968a, 136) = *RP* 2.696.

42. Syme (1969, 233) = *RP* 2.771 opines: 'the Plinian company is a genuine assemblage, from consular down to small friends at home. The large nucleus is local and regional, and it can be circumscribed . . . Nor was Pliny at pains to solicit illustrious names. In fact, no descendant of Republican or Augustan consuls is on the list'; cf. Sherwin-White (1966, 69).

43. Brown (2000, 50, 52–3, 56–7). Augustine would also herald the end of traditional thinking by holding the deeply anti-classical view that friends might be an obstacle to achieving virtue; see Nawar (2015).

44. Special friends of Pliny carry very subtle markers of particular friendship in the *Letters*: see Gibson and Morello (2012, 139–68) on Calestrius Tiro, Voconius

Romanus, Cornutus Tertullus, Septicius Clarus, and Tacitus; cf. Chp. 5 for Tiro, Romanus, and Tertullus in Rome with Pliny.

45. 6.8.2 *hunc ego . . . artissime diligo. oppida nostra unius diei itinere dirimuntur; ipsi amare inuicem, qui est flagrantissimus amor, adulescentuli coepimus.* On Pliny and Crescens, see Gibson and Morello (2012, 143–4), Gibson (f'coming) on 6.8.

46. Syme (1985a, 332–3) = *RP* 5.449–50 takes 6.8.2 to specify a domicile for Crescens in the Transpadana; but Champlin (2001, 124–5) = (2016, 113–14) prefers Umbria— as part of a more general reorientation of contested identifications in Pliny to the region of his estates near Tifernum.

47. On the quality of the friendship between Pliny and Tacitus, see Griffin (1999, 146–56) = (2016, 364–75), also Gibson and Morello (2012, 161–8); on their literary relationship, see Chp. 5 n. 6; on Tacitus' origin, see Birley (2000b, 233–4).

48. On Hippo in the fourth century, see Brown (2000, 183–7), O'Donnell (2005, 12–15), Lane Fox (2015, 411–13), Sterk (2017).

49. On the evidence and causes of civic inertia and decay in the cities of the late empire, see Liebeschuetz (2001, 29–103); on the shirking of curial duties by town councillors in late antiquity, see Liebeschuetz (2001, 104–36); cf. Lane Fox (2015, 378–81) on Augustine's solution to his obligations to Thagaste.

50. See Ward-Perkins (1997). For 'transformation', see Brown (1978); decline is unambiguously espoused by (e.g.) Liebeschuetz (2001, 29, 414–15).

51. On the cost of the library, see Mommsen (1869, 100–1 with n. 6), Duncan-Jones (1982, 27) = (2016, 100); both the calculations and relative cost are disputed by Dix (1996, 91–4).

52. See Appendix 2.

53. See Caporusso (2002, 17–18).

54. See Appendix 2; cf. Roncaglia (2018, 76–9) for Pliny's donation of baths within a northern Italian context.

55. See later in this chapter.

56. For the likely promise of the baths while Pliny was still alive, see Duncan-Jones (1982, 30–1) = (2016, 104–5). For benefactions in the context of the constant need for maintenance and restoration of baths, see Patterson (2006, 156–7).

57. For the date of the marriage to Calpurnia and the Augustan marriage laws, see Chp. 5 n. 166.

58. E.g. the wife of Pliny's teacher Quintilian was considerably younger than her husband; cf. Quint. *Inst.* 6 *praef.* 4–13, Shelton (2013, 101–2). On the pressures contributing to the early marriage of elite women, see Caldwell (2015).

59. For Fabatus' equestrian career, see Sartori (1994, 35–6) on *CIL* 5.5267.

60. On Pliny's relationship with Calpurnia Hispulla, cf. 4.19, 5.14.18, 8.11, 10.120.2, 10.121, Shelton (2013, 112–14, 255–9); with Corellia Hispulla, cf. 3.3, 4.17, Shelton (2013, 203–11); cf. also 1.12.3, 9.

61. On family ties between the Corellii and Calpurnii, see Syme (1985a, 347) = *RP* 5.465–6; *RP* 7.509–10; see earlier n. 34 on Corellius Rufus from Laus Pompeia.

62. Calpurnius Fabatus receives more letters than anyone in the collection other than Tacitus: cf. 4.1, 5.11, 6.12, 6.30, 7.11, 7.16, 7.23, 7.32, 8.10; cf. 4.19.2, 5.14.8,

8.20.3, and the record of his death at 10.120. He is memorable within largely because of apparently peremptory behaviour towards Pliny; he is also made to appear somewhat stingy towards Comum, at least by implicit comparison with Pliny (Sherwin-White (1966, 339)); cf. Gibson and Morello (2012, 63–5), Gibson (f'coming) on 6.12, 6.30.

63. Cf. esp. Cic. *Fam.* 14, Treggiari (2007).

64. On the social contexts for the Calpurnia cycle and on the historical marriage it portrays, see esp. Shelton (1990) = (2016), (2013, 93–136); Carlon (2009, 157–75), also Hindermann (2013), Centlivres Challet (2013).

65. See Shelton (2013, 125–7).

66. See Chp. 8. For Calpurnia's virtual absence from Pliny's villas, other than those owned by her own family, see Chp. 6 n. 49.

67. See Chp. 2.

68. *Paneg.* 83.6 *quam constanter . . . ipsum te reueretur*; see Shelton (2013, 103–7) for the parallel between the marriages of Pliny and Trajan.

69. 4.19.2 *amat me.* On the terms of praise offered in 4.19, see esp. Carlon (2009, 158– 65), Shelton (2013, 102–3, 111–15).

70. See Shelton (2013, 120–1, 128–9) *contra* the analysis of Foucault (1986, 160–1), also Shelton (2013, 113–14) on 'moulding' a wife.

71. Shelton (2013, 120–1); cf. Shelton (2013, 111–12) on the agency of Calpurnia in her marriage.

72. On the literary ambitions of the Calpurnia sequence and its relation to elegy, Cicero and Ovid's exile poetry, see Guillemin (1929, 138–41), de Verger (1997–8), de Pretis (2003), Carlon (2009, 166–79), Hindermann (2010), Gibson and Morello (2012, 99–101), Shelton (2013, 122–4), Baeza-Angulo (2016), (2017); Gibson (f'coming) on 6.4, 6.7.

73. Cf. Shelton (2013, 121–4).

74. Cf. Shelton (1990, 186) = (2016, 184).

75. On the time taken to reach the Umbrian estates, see Chp. 6 n. 12.

76. A figure of around fifteen days to Comum is significantly below the estimate of Scheidel and Meeks (orbis.stanford.edu): 'The fastest journey from Roma to Comum in September takes 21.4 days, covering 605 kilometers', assuming 'private' travel of 22 miles/36 kilometres per day.

77. Champlin (2001, 122) = (2016, 110) argues for one trip to Comum during the time of the *Letters*. The evidence is set out by Sherwin-White (1966, 345), who tries to establish likely frequency of visits home based on references in 4.1, 4.13, 4.30, 5.14, 6.1, and 6.18. Severe problems of interpretation remain.

78. See Sherwin-White (1966, 103).

79. See Chp. 5 for Pliny's progress along the *cursus honorum* in Rome.

80. See Patterson (2006, 151–2, 155).

81. See Chp. 3.

82. See Dix (1996, 90–1), Tucci (2013).

83. On the Domitianic construction and Nervan dedication of Pliny's library, see Hoffer (1999, 94); Sherwin-White (1966, 103, 105–6) suggests a Domitianic date for

both. For Pliny's sensitivities about his political record in the last years of Domitian, see Chp. 5.

84. See Dix (1996, 98).

85. Did the library house at its core the Elder Pliny's 160 notebooks, 105 volumes of literary works, and the reading of thousands of volumes that allegedly went into the 37 books of the *Natural History* (3.5.3–6, 8–19; *HN* praef. 17)? Was it a venue for public recitations of Pliny's own works or those of Caninius Rufus (1.3, 2.8, 3.7, 6.21, 8.4, also 7.25 and 9.38), or schoolroom for the *rhetor* whom Pliny would partly fund (4.13)? Was it ultimately the resting place for Pliny's ashes, a function known for other libraries, and did it find room on its façade for the inscription that would go to Milan? On the possible uses of the Comum library, see Dix (1996, 88–9, 97). On Roman public libraries as very much *public* venues (not just places for the *cognoscenti* to peruse scrolls), see Nicholls (2013, 261–7, 274–6). On libraries as tombs, see Dix (1996, 89–90, 101 n. 16); cf. the case in Prusa encountered by Pliny (10.81, with Williams (1990, 129–30)). Pliny's testamentary inscription was meant for very public display; see Eck (1997, 99), (2001, 234–5); for the façade of Roman public libraries as places for saturation advertisement of family status and achievements, see Nicholls (2013, 267–74).

86. See Hoffer (1999, 94).

87. On the relative size of the alimentary donation and the number of children it would reach, see Duncan-Jones (1982, 27) = (2016, 100–101), Hoffer (1999, 95–6), Roncaglia (2018, 79–80). On alimentary schemes in Italy more generally, see Woolf (1990), Kehoe (1997, 78–87), Purcell (2000, 430–1), with further references.

88. Hoffer (1999, 98).

89. See Chp. 6.

90. See Chp. 6 on 'Venuleia' and her family.

91. Cf. Prop. 1.22.9–10, Ov. *Ars* 3.303, Pers. 3.74, Athen. 12.526f., Fordyce (1961, 186–7).

92. See the overview of Syme (2016, 272–6) on the little attention given to Umbria by Vergil and Livy, prior to the increased prominence of the region in Pliny the Elder (*HN* 3.112–114) and Silius Italicus (e.g. *Pun.* 4.544, 8.456–69). Umbria plays only a relatively small part in the poetry of Propertius of Assisi (1.21–2, 4.1.63–6, 121–30). Pliny does attribute good health, longevity, and 'old stories and talk of men of the past' (*fabulas ueteres sermonesque maiorum*) to the people of the region (5.6.5–6). See in more detail Gibson (2020).

93. See Cairns (1989, 151–76) on the evanescent Lavinia (who shares some characteristics with Calpurnia as she is presented by Pliny.).

94. For geography and nationalism more generally in the *Aeneid*, see Cairns (1989, 109–28).

95. See further Gibson (2020). Note that Calpurnia first appears in the *Letters* en route to Comum via Tifernum Tiberinum, bypassing the Umbrian villa that Pliny and 'Venuleia' presumably once shared (4.1): the new wife symbolically overwrites her predecessor.

96. See Chp. 3 n. 23 on 1.14.4. Pliny attributes *frugalitas* elsewhere to himself (2.4.3), Atilius Crescens of Bergomum or Mediolanum (6.8.5), his own freedman Zosimus

(5.19.9), and Titius Aristo (1.22.4): a 'small municipal man' (Syme (1985a, 351–2 = *RP* 5.469–70)); cf. more generally 2.6.6. In the *Panegyricus, frugalitas* is attributed to Trajan (41.1, 49.5) and also used more generally (3.4, 44.8, 88.6). On the *frugalitas* of Calpurnia, see also Carlon (2009, 159–60), Shelton (2013, 111–12).

97. See Chp. 4 on 6.4.2.

98. See Gibson (2020) on the shared language of distress, desire, and illness, and the shared deployment of the language of love poetry.

99. See Chp. 5.

100. 10.23.1–2: *sordidum et uetus . . . quod alioqui et dignitas ciuitatis et saeculi tui nitor postulat*; cf. 10.70–1.

101. 7.11.5 *quod uellet . . . his enim cedere ne Corelliae quidem possum*; 2.15.2 *delectant . . . ut materna*; 2.1.8 *municipia finitima, agri etiam possessionesque coniunctae*.

102. See Spencer (2010, 120–1).

103. See Shelton (2013, 194).

104. The arguments summarized in this paragraph are those of Champlin (2001) = (2016).

105. Cf. 2.15.2, 4.6.1, 5.14.8, 7.11, 7.14.

106. Cf. esp. 2.5.

107. Plinius Paternus of Comum also receives letters on literary matters (4.14, 9.27); see later in this chapter for this presumed relation of Pliny's.

108. See Jones (1971, 119), citing 10.17b–18, 37–40, 43–4, 58.1, 81, 110.2, 113, 116–17.

109. Pliny is perhaps alluding here to the contemporary construction of an amphitheatre in nearby Mediolanum; see Roncaglia (2018, 83–4).

110. The *Letters* are rich in their record of other donors to Comum, but all are connected to Pliny by ties of family or *amicitia*; cf. 1.8.5 (the *parentes* of Pliny), 5.7 (Saturninus), 5.11 (Calpurnius Fabatus), and Caninius Rufus (7.18).

111. See Chp. 3.

112. On possible traces of a Trajanic-era temple found in the Piazza Cacciatori delle Alpi, see Sacchi (2013, 157).

113. For the literary and inscriptional record for the various orders of Roman Comum (*populus, magistratus, ordo decurionum*), see Luraschi (1999d, 472–7); cf. the analysis of the same record for Comum by national categories, from senator to slave, at Luraschi (1999d, 482–5).

114. For contemporary links and rivalries between Comum and Mediolanum, see Roncaglia (2018, 83–4, 86).

115. 7.18.1 *numeres rei publicae summam: uerendum est ne dilabatur. des agros: ut publici neglegentur.*

116. On *curatores* for Comum, cf. *CIL* 5.8291, 5.5126, and see Luraschi (1999d, 481). Recent research has tended to downplay the role of such *curatores* in controlling finances, and emphasized the supportive function of such figures; see the detailed account of Roncaglia (2018, 65–9). On such *curatores* more generally, see Purcell (2000, 424–7), Cooley (2016b, 126–7), with further references.

117. 1.3.1 *quid agit Comum, tuae meaeque deliciae? quid suburbanum amoenissimum, quid illa porticus uerna semper, quid platanon opacissimus, quid euripus uiridis et gemmeus, quid subiectus et seruiens lacus?*

118. See Appendix 2 for parallels with the Roman-era 'via Zezio' villa in Como.

119. See Sherwin-White (1966, 92). There may be an echo here of Catull. 31.12–13 *salue, o uenusta Sirmio, atque ero gaude | gaudente*, 'Greetings, delightful Sirmio and enjoy your master's joy'.

120. On the Hellenic symbolism of *euripus* and plane tree, a possible engagement with the *euripus* of Cic. *Leg.* 2.2, and on the letter's Catullan language (*deliciae, mollis*), see Spencer (2010, 65–9, 121–2); cf. Hartswick (2018, 80–81) and Myers (2018, 263–4) on philosophical gardens.

121. 1.3.1 *quid illa mollis et tamen solida gestatio, quid balineum illud quod plurimus sol implet et circumit, quid triclinia illa popularia illa paucorum, quid cubicula diurna nocturna?* Pliny writes to Caninius again in 2.8 about the lakeside Comum villa, emphasizing the productivity of the environment both for food and for literary activity. For this typical emphasis on productivity rather than beauty, cf. 2.15, 5.14.8. Elsewhere, Pliny makes reference to a published speech delivered originally on behalf of Comum, containing 'descriptions of places, which will be rather numerous in this book' (*descriptiones locorum, quae in hoc libro frequentiores erunt*, 2.5.5). The speech is almost certainly 'a civil suit about municipal property' (Sherwin-White (1966, 151)): the likelihood of descriptions of lakes and mountains appears distant.

122. See Bartlett (2004, 22, 44, 49).

123. Contrast the description of Lake Como and its surrounding mountains in the sixth-century *Variae* 11.14 of Cassiodorus. On the *locus amoenus* vs. the Romantic sublime, and the natural environments of mystery and danger hinted at in Homer, associated with Dionysus (and reflected in ps. Longinus' *On the Sublime*), see Spencer (2010, 2–3, 11, 19–20, 136–7), with further references. On Roman villas in northern Italy, see Brogiolo and Arnau (2018).

124. 6.24.2 *nauigabam per Larium nostrum, cum senior amicus ostendit mihi uillam, atque etiam cubiculum quod in lacum prominet*; see Gibson (f'coming) on this letter.

125. See Appendix 2.

126. 4.30.2 [*fons*] *excipitur cenatiuncula manu facta . . . ter in die statis auctibus ac diminutionibus crescit decrescitque*; see Spencer (2010, 122–3) on the role of artifice in the scene.

127. 9.7.4 *haec lacu propius, illa latius utitur; haec unum sinum molli curuamine amplectitur, illa editissimo dorso duos dirimit.*

128. See Appendix 2.

129. See Spencer (2010, 123–4), and Gibson and Morello (2012, 203–10) on 9.7 and Ov. *Am.* 3.1.

130. A *collegium nautarum Comensium* is attested by *CIL* 5.5295 (a guild of boat transporters on the lake); cf. Roncaglia (2018, 86–7). For local archaeological finds associated with fishing, see De Agostini (2006, 79–81); for a survey of broader economic activity in Roman Comum as revealed by inscriptions, see Luraschi (1999d, 485–90).

131. 4.1.4 *Tiferni Tiberini . . . me paene adhuc puerum patronum cooptauit . . . aduentus meos celebrat, profectionibus angitur, honoribus gaudet*; see Chp. 6 for Pliny's relationship with this Umbrian town.

132. See Nicols (2014, 145–6).

133. *CIL* 5.5267 *flam(en) diui Aug(usti) patr(onus) munic(ipi)*.

134. Pliny speaks of 'interposing the entrance and the walls of the council chamber between myself and that very populace in whose interests I was acting, so as not to incur any appearance of currying their favour' (1.8.17). The absence of further reference to public assemblies suggests his avoidance was normal; cf. Chp. 8 for Pliny in Pontus-Bithynia. Dio of Prusa, by contrast, dealt with both local council and the popular assembly in his hometown in Bithynia; see Jones (1978, 96–9), Salmeri (2000, 69–74).

135. 5.14.8 *eram cum prosocero meo, eram cum amita uxoris, eram cum amicis diu desideratis*.

136. *CIL* 5.5263, 5264, 5667, *AE* (1972, 212). On *CIL* 5.5263–4 and *AE* (1972, 212), see further Krieckhaus (2006, 41–2), with texts reprinted at (2006, 216–7). It is not clear whether *CIL* 5.5667, recording a local priesthood in the cult of the divine Titus (and today held in the Brera museum in Milan), was originally set up in Vercellae or Comum; see Duncan-Jones (1982, 19 n. 14) = (2016, 91 n. 14), Krieckhaus (2006, 39–40, 217), also Mratschek (2018, 210) on links here with Domitius Apollinaris of Vercellae. *CIL* 5.5263 was built into the south wall of the cathedral of Como, at the behest of Benedetto Giovio; *AE* (1972, 212), as noted immediately in what follows, is on display in the town's archaeological museum.

137. On the Cassii of northern Italy, of whom Comicus may have been a freedman or the son of a freedman, see Alföldy (1999d, 330–1); cf. Krieckhaus (2006, 42 n. 48).

138. See Krieckhaus (2006, 41–2 with n. 49).

139. On the significance of the findspot of *AE* (1972, 212), see Krieckhaus (2006, 42 n. 47); on the function of the statue of Pliny, see Krieckhaus (2006, 42), Sartori (1994, 36).

140. Pliny's bequest to his freedmen of 1,866,666 sesterces would have provided monthly income comparable to (and mostly more generous than) other alimentary payments mentioned in the *Digest* of Roman law; see Duncan-Jones (1982, 29–30) = (2016, 102–104).

141. See Chp. 6 n. 125 for the issue of Pliny's use of enslaved labour on his estates.

142. See Sartori (1994, 23–4) on *CIL* 5.5300; cf. Chp. 3 on offices available to local elites.

143. Aside from the brick stamps found on Pliny's Umbrian estates (Chp. 6, Appendix 2), there are around sixty-seven epigraphic attestations of the name Plinius, largely from Italy and most from the first to third centuries C.E. Of these fully thirty-two are from northern Italy, eighteen from the Comum area alone. Those from further south show more consistent levels of high status. A good proportion of inscriptions from the Comum area may then belong to freedmen of the great Plinii, as the prevalence of the *praenomina* Publius or Caius may also suggest; see Bacchiega (1993, 273–4). For a full analysis of the data and complete listing and texts of all the relevant inscriptions, with tabular analysis of the names, see Bacchiega (1993). The Plinius Paternus of Comum who is the addressee of 1.21, 4.14, 8.16, 9.27, and attested by inscription at *AE* (1916, 116)—on display in the Museo Archeologico in Como—may well be a 'kinsman of Pliny's mother's family' (Birley (2000a, 78–9);

cf. Bacchiega (1993, 273 n. 17). *CIL* 5.5521 M. Plinius Sab[. . .] (from Bellagio) is a *quattuoruir iure dicundo* identified by Syme, *RP* 7.510 n. 104 with the addressee of 9.21, 24. Aside from Pliny's wives, and two freedmen, and a *lector* mentioned in the *Letters* (5.19, 7.11, 8.1: two of these are independently witnessed on inscriptions as Plinius Zosimus (in Greek) and Plinius Hermes: *IGRR* 1.332, *CIL* 14.1474; cf. also Plinia Chreste, attested by inscription near the Umbria villa site), other familial relations of Pliny include: Calvina (2.4.2) and Antonia Maximilla (10.5.2, 10.6.1). For other more distant relations, including the suggestion of links to Pliny's patrons Corellius Rufus and Vestricius Spurinna, see Birley (2000a, 4).

8

Pontus-Bithynia

A new start

On 17th September, around 110 C.E.,[1] Pliny arrived as governor in the province of Pontus-Bithynia, modern north-west Turkey. He was now almost fifty years old: his consulship lay a full decade behind him. The thread of Pliny's political life can be picked up from his years in Rome, where the period after Trajan's return from Dacia in 107 C.E. had seen the onset of pessimism in the senator.[2] Pliny's time in Pontus-Bithynia apparently unveils a newly energized man focused on considerable responsibilities as legal authority and imperial representative in the province. It also reveals a man whose sensibilities, up till now so keenly concentrated on the Italian peninsula, are now required to adjust to a rather different geographical and political zone.[3]

If Rome brought to light a political survivor and talented orator, and life at villas in Umbria and the Laurentine shore suggested a warm man of humane interests,[4] Pliny emerges with rather less overall credit from his stint as provincial governor. A history of prior involvement at Rome with Bithynian delegations shows a figure happy, as most senators were, to privilege the interests of the senate over aggrieved claims from the governed.[5] Pliny's subsequent letters to Trajan from Pontus-Bithynia offer a portrait of an upright man who performs his gubernatorial tasks with a probity lacking in predecessors. He also appears rigid and high-handed, not least during encounters with prominent Greeks and with an early Christian community on the Black Sea coast—the first recorded in the ancient world outside Jewish and Christian sources. A concern for the civic health of communities in Pontus-Bithynia, plain enough already in his mature relationship with Comum,[6] is everywhere in evidence.

Pontus et Bithynia

Pliny's province was made up of two formerly separate regions (Map 2).[7] Bithynia had been 'bequeathed' to the Romans in their relentless expansion eastwards by its last king Nicomedes IV in the 70s B.C.E. It was an urbanized region and encompassed a large area around the sea of Marmara, stretching nearly

Man of High Empire. Roy K. Gibson, Oxford University Press (2020). © Oxford University Press.
DOI: 10.1093/actrade/9780199948192.001.0001

186 miles/300 kilometres due east from Byzantium (modern Istanbul) and over 62 miles/100 kilometres south. Pontus—'the sea' in Greek—was an extended coastal strip of some hundreds of miles/kilometres backed by mountain ranges rising steeply almost from the southern shore of the Black Sea. It had fewer substantial towns. Formerly a part of the extensive Black Sea power base of Mithridates VI Eupator, terror of Roman Asia Minor during the 60s B.C.E., the region had been joined to Bithynia as part of a strategic dissolution of the latter's kingdom. Reorganization since pacification by Pompey the Great had worked to separate Pontus from its Anatolian hinterland and reduce it to the coastal strip that Pliny inherited as governor.[8] The official name of the province was *Pontus et Bithynia*. Pliny treats the former as a mere adjunct of the latter.[9]

Bithynia is not Aegean or Mediterranean Turkey. The landscape of the area today, with its green rolling hills and wooded mountains rising high above fertile valleys, resembles the coast of northern Spain along the bay of Biscay. The summers are muggy and the winters rainy and largely cool. On the Pontic coast, northerly and westerly winds blowing off the Black Sea onto mountain ranges produce winters that are persistently damp. The extreme cold of the Balkans is avoided; the months from June to August are humid. This is a different climate from the one Pliny knew in central Italy.

Elite Romans knew the Pontic coast was an exotic locale. Cold, deep, and stormy by comparison with the Mediterranean, the Black Sea possessed a Greek name that was an obvious euphemism: Euxine, 'the hospitable'. Both its southern and northern shores were by tradition home to Amazons; the inhabitants of Crimea practised human sacrifice; while Colchis in the east gave birth to Medea. In his poetry of exile, Ovid complained of conditions of near-barbarism on western fringes. Arrian of Nicomedia, pupil of Epictetus and compiler of his teacher's *Discourses*, wrote a *Circumnavigation of the Euxine* for the emperor Hadrian in the generation after Pliny. The work is filled with colourful details of places, rivers, and tribes within and beyond the outposts of Hellenism around the Black Sea.[10] In the generation after Arrian, Lucian tells the story of the miraculous new cult of Asclepius that grew up at Abonuteichus on the southern coast of the Black Sea.[11] A Roman governor allegedly paid a visit to the oracular shrine and its charlatan prophet Alexander (Lucian, *Alexander* 27). Pliny's Pontus is comparatively featureless: 'No forests and wild shores, no historic sites or crumbling temples, no strange uncivilised peoples appear.'[12] Roman governors rarely exhibit the taste for the alien or exotic that has come to be associated with more recent imperial functionaries. The Christians of Pontus would provide the sole imaginative challenge to Pliny during his tenure in the province.

Arrival in the east

A mid-September landing in Pontus-Bithynia was somewhat later than Pliny had anticipated. He did arrive in time to celebrate the emperor's birthday on the next day (10.17a). By serendipity, Trajan's birthday coincided with the date on which Domitian had been assassinated, just fourteen years before.[13] Pliny's voyage out from Italy had taken perhaps fifty days or more.[14] The letter he sent back to Trajan to announce arrival in Pontus-Bithynia would hardly take less, particularly if the emperor was in one of his residences outside Rome.[15] An earlier missive to the emperor, written en route, told of delays encountered in reaching the province:

> Because I feel sure, sir, that you are interested, I am reporting to you that, together with all my entourage, I have reached Ephesus by sea after 'rounding Malea', despite being held up by opposing winds. Now I propose to make for my province, by coastal vessels part of the way, by carriages for the rest. Just as the excessive heat is an impediment to a land journey, so the Etesian winds oppose continuous navigation.[16]
>
> *Letters* 10.15

Pliny briefly switches to Greek to record his successful transit of Malea (*hyper Malean*), as if only the native language could convey the significance of the ancient equivalent of rounding Cape Horn. Malea is the most easterly of the great peninsulas at the southern tip of the Peloponnese, gateway to the Aegean, traditionally beset by storms and winds. Trajan, or perhaps a member of secretarial staff writing on his behalf,[17] replied in the courteous tones expected of an avowedly personal relationship between governor and emperor: 'You were right to report to me, my dearest Secundus. For I do feel concern about what kind of journey you are having on the way to the province' (10.16.1).[18] Pliny would only receive this reply well into the first year of his term in Pontus-Bithynia.

The voyage across the Aegean, to or from Asia, was apt to produce contemplation or spark imagination. Writing to Cicero over 150 years before, a distinguished correspondent had told how 'on my way back from Asia, sailing from Aegina towards Megara, I began to gaze at the landscape around me.'[19] The sight of formerly great cities on the Saronic gulf, now in ruins, induced reflection on human limitations: 'Check yourself, Servius, and remember that you were born a mortal man.' Byron would remember this letter, famous for its severe 'consolation' of Cicero on the death of his only daughter, in a replica voyage across the Aegean: 'I lay reclined | Along the prow, and saw all these unite | In ruin, even as he had seen the desolate sight' (*Childe Harold* 4.44). Around a decade before Servius wrote to Cicero, Catullus had apparently described his journey home by fast sailing yacht to Lake Garda in northern Italy from the very province to which Pliny was now travelling as governor. Catullus had spent the winter of 57–6 B.C.E. in the entourage of the governor of Bithynia, Gaius Memmius, patron of the Epicurean poet Lucretius.[20] Literary governors liked to bring protégés in their retinue: Pliny may well have brought Suetonius with him to his province.[21] The arrival of spring awakened Catullus's thoughts of leaving Nicaea, a leading Bithynian city, for Ephesus and Pergamum in the south (Catull. 46.4–6)—two famous cities that Pliny would pass through on his own way north along Asia by land and sea (10.17a.1). The alleged voyage back would eventually take Catullus from the Black Sea shore of Pontus-Bithynia through the Cyclades to the Adriatic (Catull. 4.6–13). The route, narrated in the Catullan poem by the yacht itself, is designed to remind readers of the enchanted Argo and the perilous return journey of Jason and the Argonauts from Colchis.[22] Pliny could hardly match Catullus and Servius for invention or rumination in his own sober gubernatorial report of travels to the emperor. He was not to be completely outdone. The Homeric heroes Menelaus and Odysseus had rounded cape Malea in the reverse direction, travelling homewards from Asia. Unlike Pliny, they had done so without preserving 'all their entourage'.[23] Whether Trajan cared for the passing allusion to the *Odyssey*, marked for him by the shift into Greek, is unknown.

Pliny reported an immediate start on his mission to Trajan: 'I have written to you about this, sir, at the very moment of my arrival' (10.17a.4). The business that awaited appears firmly prosaic: 'I am examining the expenditures, revenues and debtors of the state of Prusa'. But the task was fraught with the danger of inflaming local sensitivities. The process of investigation revealed its own necessity: sums of public money were 'being kept in their possession by private persons', not to mention 'wholly unlawful outlays' (10.17a.3).[24] Governors had the formal right to inspect a city's accounts and building projects.[25] No one expected them to exercise it systematically. Dio, leading citizen of Prusa and orator of repute, had indicated as much with a speech to his town assembly a few years previously. Speaking to the gathering immediately prior to the appearance there of Pliny's gubernatorial predecessor, Varenus Rufus, Dio reminded the inhabitants of Prusa that various persons had public funds in their possession, 'some through ignorance, some otherwise'.[26] An effort would have to be made to recover the funds, 'yet not with hatred or wrangling' (*Or.* 48.9). No one seems to have expected Rufus to apply himself to this incendiary initiative. Such complacency would hardly survive Pliny's arrival:[27] in Prusa he would soon be seeking the whereabouts of missing furniture and decorations bequeathed with a house to the town (10.70.4).

Early years in the east: lifelong connections

This was not Pliny's first stint in the Greek-speaking part of empire. Nearly three decades earlier, perhaps a few years after the accession of Domitian in 81 C.E., Pliny arrived in the Roman province of Syria to take up the post of military tribune with the legion III Gallica.[28] The unit was perhaps based at Samosata on the west bank of the Euphrates, modern south-east Turkey. Service as officer in the military was no longer a prerequisite for entry to the senate. New men tended to take up the post anyway. Pliny could add it to the first minor post he had recently gained in Rome. The tribunate offered experience of the army, although only the Rhine and Danube legions, where the Elder Pliny had served in the 40s and 50s C.E., offered any realistic prospect of military action. Pliny's tribunate was served at legionary headquarters.[29] Instructed to audit the accounts of the cavalry and infantry divisions, he discovered an 'extensive and filthy rapacity of certain parties' (7.31.2) that neatly anticipates his mature experience as governor of an eastern province.[30] Writing several decades later, Pliny implies that he also encountered shocking standards of military discipline among the Syrian legions (8.14.7). Domitian was no doubt to blame, somehow.

Pliny's period in Syria evidently made a deep impression on him: he returns repeatedly to memories of his time there.[31] Men encountered in Syria recur as objects of concern thirty years later, including a former prefect of cavalry (7.31), a chief centurion (10.87), and fellow military tribune Calestrius Tiro (7.16.1).[32] Pliny would serve in Rome as *quaestor Augusti* with Tiro, and later take the centurion, now well advanced in years, to Pontus-Bithynia as trusted advisor. Hellenic high society in Syria also had something to offer. Lifelong relationships with two philosophers, Artemidorus and Euphrates, were begun there. With the first Pliny attests 'the closest bonds of friendships' (3.11.5) already in Syria; of Euphrates there he writes, 'I knew him intimately, and visited him at home, and laboured to gain his affection' (1.10.2).[33] Artemidorus, as Pliny himself tells us, would later marry the daughter of Musonius Rufus, well-connected Stoic philosopher to Rome's upper classes (3.11.5, 7);[34] Euphrates married into the family of a *prouinciae princeps*—a leading citizen of Syria (1.10.8). Both philosophers eventually came to Rome and would suffer banishment at the hands of Domitian after the treason trials of 93 or 94 C.E. Pliny, it will be remembered, takes care to underline his visit at the time to Artemidorus, accompanied by full praetorian motorcade.[35] The return of Euphrates to the capital after the assassination of Domitian is ostentatiously heralded by Pliny.[36]

With Euphrates now back in Rome, Pliny emphasizes how much the advice of the philosopher was valued during his stint as Prefect of the Treasury of Saturn—the post which guaranteed the consulship.[37] He found the office 'as highly irksome as it is important', with its duty to 'countersign petitions, make up accounts' (1.10.9). Complaints to Euphrates elicited the consoling response that it was 'a function, and indeed the noblest function of philosophy, to conduct public affairs' (1.10.10). Pliny responded by praising the affability (*comitas*) of Euphrates, and the fact that he 'attacks vices, not individuals; the errant he reforms rather than punishes' (1.10.7).[38] This sounds like the discourse of a tame or socially ambitious Greek intellectual: an un-philosophical Roman is being told what he wants to hear.[39] Another view suggests itself. In a short treatise with the awkward title *That a philosopher ought to converse especially with men of power*, Plutarch advises against the sort of philosophical frontal assaults that Epictetus, also a pupil of Musonius Rufus, evidently wished to inflict on *his* Roman audiences.[40] There was to be no 'pitching camp in the ears' of famous men and leaders 'with inopportune sophistical disquisitions' (*Mor.* 778b). Epictetus wistfully remembers his time in Rome, prior to exile under Domitian, and the opportunities available for approaching men of consular rank to ask searching questions—up to the point the consul might 'raise his fist and land a blow on you' (Arr. *Epict. diss.* 2.12.24).[41] According to Plutarch, the philosopher should be 'glad to converse and spend his leisure' with leading Romans *only when they wished it*. The goal was clear: powerful Romans could be made 'more just, more moderate, and more eager to do good' (*Mor.* 778f).[42] Such may have been the ultimate aim of Euphrates in interaction with Pliny, soon to be consul and—it could be presumed—eventually governor of a province.

Soon after the return of Euphrates to Rome, Pliny greets the arrival in the capital of Isaeus, a master of Hellenic 'display' speaking (2.3). This 'admiration for Isaeus' declamation', in the estimate of one critic, 'is exceptional as a Roman celebration of Greek rhetoric'.[43] Pliny, it might appear, was ready to embrace the efflorescence of Hellenic rhetoric, culture, and philosophy that had already begun to make itself felt in Rome: a high empire renaissance known to modernity as the Second Sophistic.[44] He was not. The link between Euphrates, Artemidorus, Isaeus, and Pliny's enthusiasm for the trio is Syria: all three were from the province that left their mark on the young military tribune. Greeks from beyond Syria are treated somewhat differently. Plutarch from Chaeronea in the old heartlands of continental Greece is completely ignored, despite strong connections to some of Pliny's own closest friends.[45] Dio of Prusa, another associate of Musonius Rufus, is apparently unrecognized by Pliny when they meet in Bithynia (10.81). Both Greeks visited Rome for lengthy periods on several occasions: Dio would arrive at the head of a Prusan delegation to Trajan not long after Isaeus' visit, perhaps in the year of Pliny's consulship (100 C.E.).[46] Pliny was capable of worse than silence. Around 106 C.E. he would declare of the leader of a Bithynian delegation at Rome, 'In most Greeks, as in him, volubility takes the place of eloquence', adding 'mere loquacity is the gift of many, and of highly impudent individuals in particular' (5.20.4–5).[47] The Greek in question, Fonteius Magnus, was in the capital to undertake a prosecution of a former governor: Pliny's partisan defence of the corrupt Roman official would provide an uncomfortable prelude to his own turn as governor of Bithynia.

The Elder Pliny had been more thoroughly ambivalent and even antagonistic towards Greeks, their philosophy, and particularly their doctors.[48] The Younger's own attitudes to contemporary Hellenes are characterized by partial embrace, partial hostility, and silence.[49] Alongside continuing affection for friends of high birth and culture acquired in Syria, and evident admiration for classical Greek oratory and literature, Pliny maintains a correspondence with a handful of high-ranking senators of eastern origin: Hellenes do not suffer complete exclusion.[50] The exchange of epistles with eminent men from Africa or Baetica, Spain's southern province, is likewise meagre.[51] Thanks to the Elder Pliny's long career of military and imperial service, the Younger was perhaps better connected in northern and western regions of empire than in east or south.[52] Yet the success of correspondents such as Catilius Severus and Cornutus Tertullus in gaining the senate and even the consulship—the latter alongside Pliny in 100 C.E., the former in the year of Pliny's arrival in Bithynia—is part of the explanation for this maintenance of distance from oriental senators. The western provinces of empire, long the recipient of imperial attention from Augustus onwards, had provided senators from its elite families for several generations. Pliny had every reason to be comfortable with this. He would attempt to gain from Trajan a place in the senate for his old friend Voconius Romanus from northern Spain (10.4).[53] It was under the more eastward-looking Flavians that an influx of Hellene senators had begun; under Trajan it had become well established.[54] Prior to that, ambitious men of eastern origin had generally preferred careers in home cities with more settled environments and more absorbing local politics than those in the west. The incursion did not go unnoticed. Around 106–7 C.E. Pliny reports a rise in the price of land around Rome. The reason? Trajan has compelled candidates for senatorial office to invest a substantial part of their wealth in Italian real estate:

> . . . he has ordered them to invest a third part of their fortunes in real estate, deeming it disgraceful, as indeed it was, that those who sought honours should look upon Rome and Italy, not as their country, but as a kind of inn or hostelry, as if on their travels. There is consequently a rush of candidates; they are bidding against each other for the purchase of whatever they hear is for sale . . .[55]
>
> *Letters* 6.19.4–5

Pliny does not spell out the origin of senators now compelled to treat Rome as something more than a hotel. Contemporary readers would understand.

Bithynia comes to Rome

If Pliny's formal arrival in Pontus-Bithynia early in the second decade of the century had been preceded by earlier experience of the east, he also had intimate knowledge of the internal politics of the province some years before he set foot there. The playing out of Bithynian affairs in Rome's highest courts was somewhat trying for the future governor. It was ultimately perhaps more alarming for the soon-to-be governed.[56]

Pontus-Bithynia had an unattractively long history of corrupt Roman administration. One of Pliny's own probable ancestors, Granius Marcellus, former owner of the Umbrian villa, had been arraigned for extortion in the province, alongside the rather more serious charge of treason against the emperor Tiberius. (The incident is related by Tacitus in language which recalls the language of Pliny.[57]) Pontus-Bithynia emerges as the narrow winner in a list of provinces with the highest number of known prosecutions of governors for maladministration between Augustus and Trajan.[58] That aggrieved provinces could prosecute governors in Rome for injuries suffered during tenure must count as one of the most remarkable features of Roman imperialism.[59] The Bithynian experience in the capital, as recorded by Pliny, shows how difficult it was for provinces to secure any meaningful form of redress.

Iulius Bassus, the recently returned governor of Pontus-Bithynia, was patently guilty. Not even Pliny, leading member of the defence team in the senate, disputed that. Bassus' origins perhaps lie in the local nobility of Pergamum.[60] Generally aloof from Hellene senators, Pliny could at least extend himself to defending such men against the eastern provincials they governed. Bassus had been proconsul of Pontus-Bithynia c. 100–1 C.E., and in the following year found himself on the receiving end of a charge of extortion 'with criminal savagery' (saeuitia). The nub of the matter was simple: did the 'certain objects' (quaedam) that Bassus received from local notables during his tenure count as 'gifts' (munera), as the former governor insisted, or 'plunder and rapine' (furta ac rapinas), as the prosecution retorted?[61] Bassus, Pliny declared, was a 'simple and unsuspecting man' (simplex et incautus, 4.9.6). That may be doubted: he was a man of advanced years and great political experience.[62] There remained one inconvenient fact: 'The law forbids even presents being accepted' (4.9.6). In his report of the trial, Pliny is reduced to labeling Theophanes, the lead prosecutor for the Bithynians, as a 'firebrand' (fax, 4.9.3), criticising his 'consummate impudence' in daring to claim time to speak beyond nightfall after two 'men of consular rank as well as of eloquence' had spoken before him (4.9.14).[63] What is more remarkable is that the Bithynian prosecution stayed united against Bassus, and did not splinter into local factions that might sabotage prosecution of a governor.[64]

If convicted, Bassus would suffer *infamia* and forfeit his standing as senator. At sentencing two proposals were made: either enforce the law rigorously with all its penalties, or mitigate the effect by preserving Bassus' senatorial status once the case for financial restitution to the province had been assessed by judicial committee (4.9.16–17).[65] The senate could be relied on to defend one who, like Bassus, had suffered exile under Domitian (4.9.2). The softer proposal prevailed, to Pliny's delight (4.9.16–18). As so often in Rome's highest court, the law's penalties were subject to modification by vote.[66] Evidence and prescripts of law were of less importance than the birth, alleged virtues, and the political record of the defendant. In fact, a majority of the senate was in favour of now prosecuting Theophanes under the very law that had been used to indict Bassus—although the consuls declined to pursue this action (4.9.20–1). It is not until a decade after the trial that we learn of a decree that had formed part of the senate's settlement, unmentioned by Pliny at the time. The news comes from Pliny's own hand, in a letter to Trajan: all of Bassus' judicial decisions (*acta*) in Bithynia had been rescinded, and 'the senate had given to all those who had been the subjects of any of his decisions the right of trying the matter afresh' (10.56.4).[67] Whatever else the senate thought of the Domitianic exile, it clearly had little confidence in his integrity.

Augustine's misgivings as a teacher of rhetoric might now ring in the ears: 'in all honesty I taught them trickery . . . so that, when the occasion required, they could act on behalf of a guilty man' (*Conf.* 4.2.2).[68] We can only make a guess about what Bithynians might think of a future governor who defended Bassus, and celebrated that defence in published works—although no one in the Hellenic half of empire will have read the *Letters*, much less the revised courtroom speech that Pliny planned to publish (4.9.23).[69] What happened next cannot have improved matters.

Varenus Rufus acted as governor of Pontus-Bithynia a few years after Bassus, perhaps in 105–6 C.E.[70] Like Bassus, he was subsequently indicted by Bithynian representatives for extortion 'with *saeuitia*': this ancillary charge, dropped during the course of the Bassus action, would remain in the Rufus case.[71] The trial of Rufus before the senate took place over a considerable period of months.[72] The action began with a declaration by the Bithynians of their intention to call witnesses against Rufus from the province. A debate in the senate followed, during which Rufus, supported by Pliny, gained permission to seek out his own witnesses (5.20.). The request was highly irregular; its grant shocking and inflammatory.[73] Pliny admits the lack of precedent (5.20.7). A bitter clash ensued at the next meeting of the senate, where a body of senators sought to have it revoked (6.5). The occasion provoked a masterful and diversionary lament from Pliny over poor standards of behaviour in the contemporary senate, particularly amongst junior members. Varenus' request for witnesses may well seem equitable, 'but equity is not usually observable in the senate's proceedings', in the judgement of a modern authority; 'The true motive was surely partiality to a senator'.[74] Frustrated, the Bithynians approached the consuls and even made contact with Trajan, absent from Rome on campaign on Dacia. The emperor, mindful of his need to respect the independence of the senate, referred the Bithynians back to the senate. The august body confirmed its original irregularity (6.13).[75]

At this point, local politics made a decisive intervention. Bithynia's provincial council (*koinon*) consisted of representatives from every eligible city in the region.[76] It was deeply divided over the prosecution of Varenus Rufus. The faction in favour of action evidently prevailed at first. Its delegation had arrived in Rome some months earlier headed by the Fonteius Magnus whose volubility would be derided by Pliny. The opposing faction now appeared in the capital, fronted by one Polyaenus and bearing a fresh decree from the council to the effect that the prosecution must be halted (7.6). The party of opposition had clearly prevailed in the absence of its rivals.[77] Fonteius fought on, demanding that the consuls compel the former governor to produce the accounts of his administration (7.6). The affair disappears from record with the news that Trajan, now returned from Dacia at last, is undertaking to discover whether the province really does wish to pursue the serious matter of withdrawing a prosecution (7.10). The original accuser would be exposed to the charge of *calumnia*, 'malicious prosecution'.[78]

Pliny prepares to go east

In his public speeches to the great urban centres of Bithynia, Dio of Prusa repeatedly warns against rivalries within and between cities: they weaken communities and make them ripe for exploitation by Roman governors.[79] The provincial rivalries of Bithynia were now only too obvious to Pliny. What the Bithynians learned of Pliny was equally discouraging. Here was a consular orator willing to promote gross irregularities in defence of two recent governors of (at best) dubious reputation. In the Rufus case, Pliny may well have endeared himself to the Polyaenus faction; but the Fonteius faction can only have been further alienated.

What made Trajan think that Pliny was the right appointment? Unlike others of his rank, such as Tacitus, Pliny had acquired no experience as praetor either of command of a legion or of provincial government.[80] Yet he was to be governor of a region with a recent troubled history, in which he had been directly involved in a manner likely to inflame local factions. Did Pliny's newly acquired knowledge of internal politics outweigh any considerations of how his presence might antagonize internal cliques? Or had Trajan simply come to trust him? Whatever else his political record might show, Pliny gave every impression of being responsible, competent, industrious, and rich enough to be free from the temptation of bribery. Perhaps his lack of experience was part of his attraction in the context of Pontus-Bithynia.[81]

Other questions remain. Why did it take Pliny so long to achieve this appointment, a decade after the consulship? Earlier promotion had been rapid: he had become consul at the early age of 38 or 39.[82] Sir Ronald Syme, always keen to immerse Pliny's career in quantities of cold water, could somehow sense that 'the alert young orator did not excite the enthusiasm of all the military men' around Trajan, such that 'the provincial command may have seemed slow in coming'.[83] Others have pointed to the disparity between the limited range of gubernatorial posts open to consulars and the large number of ex-consuls produced each year in the decade 101–10 C.E.[84] As with Rome's priestly colleges, competition for places was intense.[85]

What is clear is that Pliny developed a growing interest in the idea of provincial government.[86] Calestrius Tiro disappears as a correspondent of Pliny's for nearly a decade, after a first letter dating to 97–8 C.E. (1.12). He is greeted on his return in 106–7 C.E. with marked enthusiasm (6.1). A probable reason is soon apparent: Tiro, currently of praetorian rank, has been allotted the governorship of Baetica in southern Spain (6.22.1, 7; 7.16.3).[87] Pliny advises his friend on gubernatorial matters on two occasions. First, a governor must choose his staff carefully: a recent case, heard at Rome before Trajan with Pliny present as member of an advisory body (consilium), featured a governor accused of extortion by a member of his own retinue (6.22).[88] It was not unusual for provincials to accuse a governor, quite shocking for the indictment to come from the circle of trusted assistants. In this case, the assistant was found to be using the accusation to divert attention from his own extortionary activities. Pliny no doubt went on to choose his own retinue for Pontus-Bithynia with care: hence the enlisting of the old centurion from Syrian days. His wife Calpurnia would also accompany him.[89]

Pliny later praises Tiro for reports of his handling of local notables: he has followed the sound course of showing due respect to the powerful, while keeping an appropriate distance from 'inferiors' (9.5).[90] There is implied recognition of the need to avoid stoking in the province the kind of elite factionalism that Pliny had done little to dampen down during the trial of Rufus at Rome.[91] In the event, Pliny's letters to Trajan from Pontus-Bithynia reveal almost nothing of his interactions with local elites, except where contact is forced on him by serious disputes among leading men of Prusa (10.58, 81).[92] Distance was required of him.[93] The governed had different expectations. Even the upright Plutarch, in an essay aimed at local Greek elites, had opined that the politician 'should always have a friend among the men of high station', because 'the Romans themselves are most eager to promote the political interests of their friends' (Mor. 814c).[94] The sentiment had evidently been over-interpreted by Bassus and Rufus.

Plutarch can scarcely have been shocked by Pliny's desire to reinforce local inequalities in a province. One of the few attractions of Roman rule for a member of the Greek elite was the restriction imposed on 'the mob'.[95] Plutarch, for all that he was ignored by Pliny, can only have positively approved of the latter's advice to a second friend, Maximus, newly designated 'special commissioner' (*corrector*) for Plutarch's home region of Achaia (8.24). Here, in the elegant summary of Syme, Pliny 'reminds Maximus how noble is his task and how delicate—Hellas is the home and mother of arts, letters, and civilized life; he must honour the great past of the Greeks, their history and their fables, not infringing dignity, freedom, or even vanity'.[96] Such privileges were emphatically *not* to be extended to the province in which Maximus had served with distinction as quaestor some years before:

> . . . you must the more earnestly strive that you be not reputed to have acted with greater courtesy, integrity and judgement in a distant province than in a nearer one; among those who are servile rather than among freemen.[97]
>
> *Letters* 8.24.9

That 'distant province' filled with the 'servile' (*seruientes*) was in fact Bithynia (8.24.8).[98] Despite Pliny's earlier willingness to acknowledge, and disparage, the characteristic 'Greekness' of a Bithynian representative, that disposition evaporates here. The inhabitants of the province are not to be compared to the Hellene freemen (*liberi*) of old Achaia. It can be added that Maximus appears to have visited Epictetus, resident in Nicopolis on the west coast of Greece, on the journey out to Achaia. Maximus, an Epicurean, would be given a full dressing down by the Stoic.[99] Doubt would be cast on his integrity: 'How did you come to be a judge? Whose hand did you kiss? . . . Who did you send gifts to?' (Arr. *Epict. diss.* 3.7.31).[100]

Pliny took the attitudes expressed to Maximus with him to Pontus-Bithynia: the correspondence with Trajan contains barely an acknowledgement of the Greekness of the inhabitants.[101] His stance anticipates the Pan-Hellenic union that Hadrian would found early in the third decade of the century in Athens: the cities of Bithynia would not meet the new definition of Hellene.[102] Greeks colonies had long ago been founded on the sea coasts of both Bithynia and Pontus. Most Bithynians, Greek in language, culture, and tradition, were related to the inhabitants of Thrace on the far side of the Bosphorus.[103] Inhabitants of Pontus-Bithynia also had little exposure to or interest in Rome, its history, or language. Few possessed Roman citizenship.[104] Pliny would perhaps speak in Greek to his subjects, but his view of them would be firmly Roman: the social order of the province is conceived in Roman terms, and the fundamental laws of the province are assumed to be those put in place at the moment of incorporation into the Roman empire. Centuries of Hellenistic precedent are ignored. The majority of those actually named by Pliny are junior Roman officials working alongside Pliny, plus a few grandees from Bithynian cities bearing names that suggest Roman citizenship.[105] One could hardly guess from his account that Bithynia was beginning to supply Rome with senators, or that the region would produce a disproportionately large number of writers and intellectuals in relation to its size and importance. The Transpadana might struggle to compete.[106] Ultimately, nevertheless, what mattered to Pliny, as to any provincial governor, was the distinction between citizen and non-citizen. Any sense of ethnic difference from or between the inhabitants of Pontus-Bithynia might be of less significance.

The cities of Pontus-Bithynia

The major cities of Bithynia that would absorb most of Pliny's time were Nicomedia (modern Izmit), Nicaea (Iznik), and Prusa (Bursa) (Map 2).[107] Each was a centre for assizes.[108] Byzantium was yet to attain the importance that it would acquire by the age of Augustine after re-foundation as Constantinople. Nicomedia and Nicaea had obvious advantages over other cities in the region, since each stood at the head of a major overland route to the east.[109] There was no undisputed provincial capital, however, no governor's palace for Pliny to reside in: he would have to keep on the move between these and other cities, hearing cases and inspecting accounts.

Prusa in the far south of the province, site of Pliny's arrival in Bithynia, occupies a dramatic position on a terrace on the lower slopes of the far western end of the Olympus mountain range that rises to a height of well over 2000 metres. Further north, Nicaea sits at the far eastern end of a large inland lake and is approached by road from the east down a long and fertile valley that is overlooked by steep hills to north and south. Impressive Roman walls still circuit the town today (Fig. 8.1), and the theatre Pliny feared might have to be demolished owing to subsidence is standing in good part still (10.39–40). Nicomedia likewise sits at the far eastern end of a body of water, but here on the northern shore of a long inlet from the sea of Marmara at its narrowest. The city's hills rise up steeply from the shore.[110] The ancient site is famously praised by Augustine's contemporary Libanius, after the city had been devastated by an earthquake, tsunami, and fire, starting on 24th August 358 C.E.: the same (traditional) date as the eruption of Vesuvius almost three centuries before.[111] Libanius lauds the promontories which embraced the sea, the city which 'ascended the hill by four colonnades extending the whole length', and tells of the hush which gripped his band of travellers on the road from Nicaea after 'we had passed through the intricate windings of the hills' and Nicomedia suddenly became visible in the far distance (Or. 61.7).[112]

Figure 8.1. Roman city gate in Nicaea (Iznik). The impressive Roman walls that still encircle the town belong to the later second and early third centuries C.E.; the city gates preserve earlier material. *Photo by C. Delaney.*

Pliny's lack of response to a cityscape is evident in his accounts of Comum and Rome: his eye is drawn instead to villas, landscape, and water. Municipal problems in the towns of Bithynia change Pliny's focus; here he must deal with baths, libraries, theatres, aqueducts, temples, sewers, and gymnasia.[113] A new urban focus emerges, although Pliny's failure to take an interest in a panoramic city view remains. Nor is there reference to Trajan's own contemporary *grands projects* in Rome, despite cues from the emperor (10.18.3, 10.40.3). Landscape disappears almost completely in Bithynia: to remark on it might disturb the image of hard-working governor and emperor. As for the region's country villas, if Pliny spent his time dining there with the locals, as he clearly had done in Syria, such things were best left unmentioned. An eye for water remains.[114] Alongside reports of his journey by boat to his province (10.15–17a) and those bath-houses and aqueducts, Pliny shows particular interest in a lake some distance to the east of Nicomedia (10.41–2, 61–2). He planned to connect the city to the lake by canal, to ease the transport of marble, grain, and wood in the region. Much interest is shown in the relative levels of city and lake, and the risk of draining the latter by building the connecting canal. The locals who were to supply the labour to construct the 18-mile/29-kilometre canal (10.4.2) might be forgiven some apprehension.[115]

In Pontus, three cities would also take up most of Pliny's time: Amastris, Sinope, and Amisus (Map 2).[116] It was here, somewhat surprisingly, rather than in more urbanized Bithynia, that Pliny would encounter a community of Christians. The most westerly town of the three, Amastris, appears to have been the centre for assizes. A road connected the cities of the Pontic coast, but travel by sea was undoubtedly more efficient. Overall, the distances in Pontus-Bithynia were not small by ancient standards: between Nicaea in the not-quite far west to Amisus in the far east lay over 560 miles/900 kilometres of travel.[117] The rigours imposed on Pliny and his company were challenging. His health had already suffered on the long journey out from Italy (10.17a.1).[118]

Rome and the provinces

Before homing in on Pliny's activities and interventions in the cities of Pontus-Bithynia, it is worth pausing briefly to reflect on the ideology of Roman imperial administration and how the inhabitants of empire experienced its reality. Unsurprisingly, the subject is highly controversial.

Was Roman government of empire minimalist in both objectives and achievements? Did it possess neither the ability nor even interest to establish imperial policy for the dissemination of Roman civic or religious practices and the institutions of urban life? Or was it the purpose of empire, in Vergil's notorious formulation, 'to institute law in addition to peace' (*pacique imponere morem, Aen.* 6.852)?[119] The military resources committed by Rome to absorbing or invading and then pacifying alien territory were massive on any reckoning. Once apparent stability had been achieved, unimpressive resources were allotted to the daily practice of government. By Pliny's time, perhaps as few as 160 elite officials were sent in any given year to govern the tens of millions of subjects in the empire. The core staff attached to these officials was small. And away from military areas on the boundaries of empire, the presence of the army in a province might be limited. Most of the mundane business of local government, including policing, was officially delegated to local elites and authorities.[120]

Official Roman presence was undeniably minimal, but the tools of potential Romanization were everywhere in evidence: the spread of the cult of the emperor; the imposition of a census for taxation purposes; the administrative centralization of a province around its major cities; the division of arable land into huge rectilinear grids and the building of roads, harbours, and aqueducts; the encouragement of cities to request privileges in tax and civic status; the participation of cities in a system of direct official correspondence with the emperor; the availability of Roman citizenship to local elites; and even the encouragement of cultural practices such as bathing and dining.[121] On one view, these interventions worked to foster a consensus within provincial elites about the efficacy and value of the Roman imperial system itself. The empire experienced extraordinary and largely unparalleled success in co-opting its subjects and making them 'insiders'.[122] Nor was the process uni-directional—in the case of Greece, at least. 'In contrast to the expectations of contemporary colonial theory', writes Simon Goldhill, 'the politically and militarily dominant Rome found itself speaking the cultural language of the colonized'.[123] Elite Romans were expected both to speak Greek and to be conversant with Hellenic literature. Roman literature was widely acknowledged to be derivative from Greek. More surprisingly, perhaps, the Hellenic east produced nothing like a literature of resistance to the Roman colonizers. The greatest critics of the imperial system were all Roman: Ovid, Lucan, and Tacitus. Those who died, like the 'Stoic opposition' of Pliny's era, were often senators. Greek writers challenged Rome's authority largely by cultivating their own resplendent literary history.[124]

There is an alternative to this picture of mostly peaceful integration. 'Even at the height of empire', observes Emma Dench, 'Roman power was thinly stretched, coexisted with competing systems of power and authority, and fostered opportunism on the part of local states and groups'.[125] Endemic banditry within the provinces of empire and the constant threat of war inside and beyond northern and eastern frontiers point to larger pressures and sources of dissatisfaction with the status quo. As for allegedly settled provinces, Dench insists that we think through 'the consequences of the degree to which functions of state were delegated to, or more often simply assumed by, local agencies and institutions within the Roman empire'.[126] The result is an edgier and more precarious empire than hitherto envisaged by many scholars.

In the pages that follow, evidence will be found for cities happy to operate inside an imperial culture and its legal systems and to compete for civic honours and privileges from Rome. Evidence will also be found of alienation, endemic opportunism, and of the willingness of local agents to operate without reference to Roman jurisdiction.[127]

Pliny's 'mission' in Pontus-Bithynia

As governor, Pliny had at his disposal only the usual skeleton staff of Roman civil and military functionaries,[128] in addition to the small entourage he brought with him from Italy.[129] Cities were expected to run their internal affairs, finance construction, collect taxes, maintain roads, and deal with petty justice. The time would come, only a century later, when provincial elites would gradually prove less willing to take on these roles, amidst the turbulent economic and military conditions of the third century. The cumulative effects on the infrastructure of Augustine's Hippo by the fourth century have already been glimpsed.[130] Such a future could hardly be guessed. At the beginning of the second century, from a Roman viewpoint, the 'problem' in Bithynia was an excess of prosperity, at least among the elite.[131] Rivalries between cities appeared to be fuelling overspend on prestigious building projects by local city councils—where, in turn, competition between rich members of councils was provoking factional conflict within cities.[132] Hence Pliny's haste on arrival to examine the accounts of the city of Prusa.

The standard duties of a provincial governor were to maintain religious, civil, and military order, act as judge in criminal and civil cases, and forward to the emperor petitions from individuals, groups, and cities.[133] The collection of taxes and the supervision of imperial property were normally delegated elsewhere.[134] Such routine business required constant communication with the emperor, despite the lengthy delays in time required for correspondence to receive an answer from Trajan.[135] To an extent that will appear remarkable or even astonishing, 'government at a distance, by means of letters', in the words of Fergus Millar, 'was simply the standard mechanism through which the Roman Empire worked'.[136] Rather than formulating general policies for imposition on empire, emperors characteristically spent their time *reacting* to quite specific issues raised by governors and the cities for which they had responsibility.[137] No matter was too small for Trajan's attention, it would seem. Even while on campaign in faraway Dacia, he had found time to deal with an inheritance dispute between private claimants of modest social status, finally resolving it upon return to Rome (6.31.8).[138] What messy reality, one wonders, lay behind this optimistic façade.

It is to this practice of government by correspondence that we owe the existence of Book 10 of Pliny's letters. And thanks to Book 10 we know more about Pliny's time in Pontus-Bithynia than any other gubernatorial stint in the history of the Roman empire—more even than Cicero's reluctant term as governor of Cilicia in modern south-west Turkey in 51 B.C.E.[139] The bulk of the book is taken up by an alternating series of mostly short queries or reports from Pliny and replies from Trajan on a vast range of topics: from the use of public slaves to guard prisoners, at the outset of Pliny's probable intended three-year tenure (10.19), to rewards for athletes returning home in triumph from international competitions, towards the end of that tenure (10.118).[140] Unlike Cicero, Pliny would not spend his time longing for Rome or yearning for news from home.

It is not clear whether Pliny himself put the book together for publication, or whether the work of selecting and organizing the material for inclusion fell to another after Pliny's own death at some point before Trajan's demise in 117 C.E.[141] It has recently been made clear, against earlier scholarly consensus, that the letters themselves, even if materially revised by Pliny or another, *do* in fact resemble the norm for correspondence between governor and emperor in high empire.[142] There may be significant omissions in the kinds of issues that Pliny is willing to raise with Trajan: some unpalatable topics, as will become evident, are simply never discussed. But, far from offering a portrait of a fussy and nervous governor lacking in initiative or responsibility, the correspondence of Book 10 offers some clue to expected patterns of behaviour.[143] Gone are the playfulness, the erudition, and anxious self-revelation of Books 1–9. The Pliny of Book 10 is all work and no play: unremittingly sober, deferential, and even stern in his communications with Trajan, he concentrates strictly on matters of state.[144] The emperor in turn is even briefer and more direct, albeit inclined to focus on what interests *him*. He is also occasionally testy.[145] Significantly, Trajan is notably more willing than his correspondent to respect local custom and avoid the knee-jerk imposition of Roman law and technical expertise.[146] The widely travelled emperor possessed broader views and sympathies than the Italian senator.

Alongside routine duties, governors had specific *mandata* ('instructions') issued for their tenure by an emperor. Interpretation of these *mandata* required further communication with the emperor. Pliny alludes to his own set of imperial instructions on several occasions. They evidently contained directives on military discipline (10.22, 10.30), the rights of exiles (10.56.1), the issue of donations from civic funds (10.110–11), and on prerogatives of association among provincials (10.96).[147] It was in connection with the last issue that the fire-brigades of Nicomedia and the Christians of Pontus would come to Pliny's attention. The most significant of his *mandata* is reiterated in an early letter from Trajan: 'Above all . . . you must closely examine the public accounts, for that they as well as other things are in a state of confusion is quite clear' (10.18.3).[148] With a long-standing concern for the beautification and health of the public finances of Comum, Pliny was no doubt well placed to take control of this issue.[149] He examined the accounts and finances of at least nine cities.[150]

A curiosity about Pliny's role remains. Well over a century before, Augustus had divided Rome's provinces into those under his direct control and 'public' provinces nominally under the control of the senate. Pontus-Bithynia fell into the latter category. The great Comum inscription affirms that Pliny was 'praetorian commissioner with proconsular power for the province of Pontus and Bithynia, sent to that province in accordance with the senate's decree by the emperor Nerva Trajan Augustus'.[151] Pliny is a special imperial appointment in a senatorial province: the first known for Pontus-Bithynia. Some have seen here evidence of an imperial mission to the province, with Trajan clearly concerned about the state of public finances.[152] Support is apparently forthcoming from the *mandata* that Pliny received, and from the encouragement that Trajan offered when a city questioned Pliny's right to inspect the accounts (10.47–8). Yet, as the testimony of Dio suggests, it was a standard right for governors to ask to see accounts.[153] (Pliny was simply more conscientious than his predecessors in doing what he had been asked.) More persuasive is the view that Trajan had come to a greater appreciation of the strategic importance of Pontus-Bithynia than his predecessors.[154] The focus of empire was already beginning to shift north and eastwards. This broad area of empire had come to Trajan's attentions during his campaign in Dacia. Rome had long-term concerns with the security of the far eastern border of the empire. Armies were already beginning to pass through Asia Minor en route to the east along more northerly routes. Trajan himself would depart Rome in 113 C.E. for war against Parthia. If recent gubernatorial stints suggested that an increasingly important province was being governed by men of low personal probity, Pliny perhaps seemed like a solution—whatever the Bithynians themselves might think. Governors of Pontus-Bithynia would be regularized as imperial appointments from the reign of Marcus Aurelius onwards.[155]

Delays in the mail: the problem of government by correspondence

The letters of Book 10, unlike those of Books 1–9, are apparently arranged by systematic chronology according to date of letter sent by Pliny.[156] The more than one hundred missives exchanged by Pliny and Trajan may not represent a complete record of the gubernatorial correspondence: gaps and cross-references perhaps point to omitted epistles.[157] The linear ordering of the letters allows an overview of Pliny's movements around the province in the three calendar years of his posting—although it is not evident how far certainty extends. What seems clear is that, in the first year of his tenure, Pliny was permanently on the move between the major urban centres of Bithynia (10.15–89), with repeat visits paid in particular to Prusa and Nicomedia. He appears not to have entered Pontus until his second year (10.90–121); the cities of Bithynia do not reappear after this point.[158]

The editorial system in Book 10 of immediately appending replies from Trajan to Pliny's original creates an illusory system of 'problem submitted' by governor and then 'resolved' by emperor. At some point in the second calendar year of his tenure Pliny wrote to request that the people of Iuliopolis, in the far south-east of the province on the border with Galatia, be granted a legionary centurion, just like Byzantium on the border with Thrace in the far north-west: 'They lie at the edge of Bithynia, and provide passage for many persons who travel through it' (10.77.3).[159] By the time Pliny received a reply some months later, he was probably several hundred kilometres away in Pontus on the Black Sea coast. Such delays of time and space do not appear conducive to the smooth functioning of imperial government.[160]

It is hardly too much to say that an abyss threatens to open beneath our feet. Did Pontus-Bithynia and other provinces around the empire suffer from perpetual planning blight? 'The governor will get back to you when he eventually hears from Rome' fails to convince or inspire as a basis for effective jurisdiction. We are close now to Dench's 'edgy' and 'precarious' empire, where the functions of state *must* be routinely assumed by local agencies. As for Pliny, was it understood that he generally made decisions on the spot and took the risk of hoping for retrospective approval? (Pliny's urgent supply of travel passes to Calpurnia at the very end of Book 10, without first waiting to hear from Trajan, perhaps lifts the veil on such practice.) In that case, the scenario of request submitted and resolution received must have seemed pure artifice to the first readers of Book 10 of the *Letters*. If Pliny did in fact wait for Trajan's replies before acting, then his reputation as an energetic problem solver appears severely compromised. In either case, Book 10 takes on the appearance of propaganda for governor, or emperor, or both.

On the road in Pontus-Bithynia

Problems of infrastructure and overspend dominate Pliny's initial engagement with Prusa, Nicaea, and Nicomedia.[161] He seems unaware that Roman imperial government was minimalist in its aims. In the first city, Pliny uncovers irregularities in the financing of public building projects (10.17a, b), writes to Trajan to support the construction of a new bath-house to replace the current one which is 'squalid and old' (*sordidum et uetus*, 10.23.1), and discovers existing structures to be in a state of disrepair (10.70). At Nicomedia, a planned aqueduct is causing problems: large sums of public money have been spent on two unsuccessful attempts at completion. Pliny proposes to Rome a resurrection of the project (10.37). An exasperated Trajan, eventually, replied: 'God be my witness' (*medius fidius*), Pliny needed to get to the bottom of who was responsible for the waste of money (10.38).[162] More happily, a new forum is being built in the town, and requires the emperor's permission for the relocation of an ancient temple of the Great Mother (10.49). Meanwhile in Nicaea a publicly funded theatre is already beginning to subside and a rebuilt gymnasium strikes Pliny as 'ill-planned and rambling' (*incompositum . . . et sparsum*, 10.39.4). Similar municipal problems would emerge in Pontus: an aqueduct in Sinope (10.91), the eyesore of an uncovered sewer in Amastris (10.98), and the recovery of public funds at Amisus (10.110).[163] Later readers of the published Book 10 back in Comum, furnished with a library to the west of their town walls and a new set of baths to the east, might be supposed to find themselves blessed by the private munificence of Pliny and a town council apparently united in his praise.[164]

Not all of the problems Pliny encountered would fit comfortably on the agenda of a modern council meeting: the legal status of men formerly banished from a city (10.56); a philosopher accused of evading a prior condemnation to the mines (10.58); free children exposed at birth and raised as enslaved persons now claiming their freedom (10.65). The strange story of a fugitive slave claiming that he had escaped from foreign captivity in Parthia after capture in Dacia (10.74) contains one of the few hints of the trouble brewing in the east and the campaign Trajan was planning there.[165]

Throughout, one asks, how did Pliny's record of defending previous governors and effectively taking sides in disputes between regional factions affect those he dealt with? Did critics of Varenus Rufus find their cities singled out for particularly close scrutiny of accounts? Did Prusa feel itself unfairly treated by comparison with Nicomedia, or Nicaea think that other cities were getting more support? How fresh were the memories of local elites when cases involving the revocation of the judicial decisions of Iulius Bassus came to trial before Pliny (10.56)? Pliny studiously avoids any acknowledgement of his prior experience in Rome of Bithynian matters. No notice at all is taken of the provincial council.

There are clear signs of antagonized sections of the Bithynian elites, and indications of opposition to local elites from below and of broader discontent with Roman rule. It was perhaps while in Claudiopolis in the far east of Bithynia that Pliny heard of a great fire in Nicomedia.[166] The conflagration was so great, in Pliny's report, in part because of 'the inactivity of the people', who 'stood around, idle and motionless spectators of so great a disaster', not to mention the lack of 'any apparatus at all for fighting fires' (10.33.2).[167] Pliny requests the importation of a western practice to the Hellenic east: the formation of a *collegium fabrorum* ('guild of workmen', 10.33.3) of up to 150 members to serve as a fire brigade.[168] He was fully aware that his *mandata* contained an explicit ban on the formation of societies (*hetaeriae*, 10.96.7). Whatever Pliny did or did not do while waiting for a reply, some months later the emperor refused: 'let us recall that that province of yours, and particularly those cities, are subject to trouble from associations of this description' (10.34.1).[169] Trajan refreshes Pliny's memory of what the trial of Varenus Rufus had revealed: endemic factionalism.[170] A fire brigade might evidently be mobilized by a local politician against a rival on the city council. Pliny had perhaps already inflamed these rivalries.

Equally, a *collegium* might become an instrument of class war within a city. Endemic class strife is just visible in an issue raised by Pliny in connection with membership of local town councils: was it permissible to enroll those under thirty in the councils if they had already held one of the lesser magistracies in the town (10.79)?[171] Membership of the council was normally reserved for those over thirty, but lesser magistracies, normally a prerequisite for entry to the council, could be held through co-option from the age of twenty-two.[172] Consistent with advice to Tiro on preserving hierarchies in Baetica, Pliny makes it clear he agrees with local motivation to reinforce status boundaries: whereby 'it is far better that the sons of honourable men should be admitted to the senate-house than that commoners should be' (10.79.3).[173] Trajan concurs, but draws the line at admitting those below the age of thirty who have not held a magistracy (10.80). 'It is the earliest direct evidence', a modern commentator adds, 'of that cleavage between *honestiores* [the honourable] and *plebeii* or *humiliores* [the lowly] that set the social pattern of the later empire'.[174] The distinction would eventually pass into law. The Romans, after all, depended on the wealthy to run the towns of the empire: it was in their interest to grant local elites a monopoly of prestige.[175] Time would have its revenge when these elites became personally liable for local tax burdens.

Pliny might well ingratiate himself with the wealthy by establishing precedents in their favour, but there is plenty of evidence that towns had been getting along just fine without interference from governors or reference to Roman jurisdiction. Early in his tenure, the governor makes a shocking discovery:

> In most cities, and notably at Nicomedia and Nicaea, certain men who had been condemned to forced labour, or to the arena and to punishments similar to these, are performing the duties and functions of public slaves, even to the point of drawing the yearly emolument of the public slave. On hearing of this, I pondered long and hard about what I should do.[176]
>
> *Letters* 10.31.2

Men sentenced to the mines or to the delayed death sentence of the gladiatorial arena were guilty of serious crimes.[177] On investigation, the decrees of condemnation were soon located, but 'there were no proofs which could establish that they were freed' (10.31.4). Further enquiries proved fruitless (10.31.4). Associates entered pleas for the condemned: 'they had been released by orders of proconsuls or their deputies' (10.31.5). Pliny is inclined to believe these testimonies on the perhaps naïve basis that it is 'unbelievable that anyone should have ventured to do this without authority' (10.31.5).[178] In fact, as a recent critic suggests, 'local solutions' had evidently been found for local problems, to the extent that 'cities could expect their decisions to be unnoticed even for decades'.[179] Some of the condemned men had grown old in their commuted service as public slaves (10.31.3). Trajan ruled that those whose condemnations were less than ten years old must serve their original sentences (10.32): a more severe ruling than Pliny had perhaps anticipated (10.31.3). Did the inevitable delay in the emperor's reply and Pliny's probable presence elsewhere allow for a new fudging of the issue in Nicaea and Nicomedia?

Beyond Pliny's incredulity can be sensed a local elite largely united in their determination to minimize the effects of Roman rule. Apparent accommodation to imperial systems might have shallow roots. In *Political Precepts*, Plutarch condemned fellow Greeks who are 'unwilling to occupy an inferior position among their fellow-citizens', act to 'call in those who are mightier; and as a result senate, popular assembly, courts, and the entire local government lose their authority' (*Mor.* 815a). By inviting 'the sovereign's decision on every decree, meeting of a council, granting of a privilege, or administrative measure', citizens of the eastern half of empire were in effect forcing 'their sovereign to be their master more than he desires' (*Mor.* 814f).[180] The inhabitants of Nicomedia and Nicaea were perhaps not as high-minded in their intentions as Plutarch clearly desired. Yet they had found a way of strengthening local structures by dealing with the outcomes of due legal process in a way that suited their cities—and without continually bringing in the Roman authorities.[181]

Yet for all the indirect resistance to Roman interference, Bithynia remains a place where problems can be uncovered by determined questioning—at least according to Pliny's account. No matter how obfuscatory or vague the locals might be, the facts can be established and a concise summary offered to Trajan. Can it really have been so straightforward? What has been left out of Pliny's letters to Rome? Greg Woolf offers a catalogue of possibilities based on Cicero's experience in Cilicia:

> The governor at loggerheads with his procurator, the civic squabbles that cannot be resolved because the truth is obscure or the protagonists too well connected in Rome, the Roman troublemakers whose connections in the capital make them invulnerable to gubernatorial regulation, the governor accused of peculation or cruelty, the governor embarrassed by the behaviour of his family and entourage, the atrocities perpetrated in remote hinterlands by soldiers, publicans or imperial freedmen . . . who must nevertheless be supported in the name of Rome.[182]

Such problems, hardly amenable to government by correspondence, would be unlikely to keep Pliny in good odour with Trajan.

If Calpurnia or any member of his entourage behaved improperly through frustration, fatigue, bad weather, or boredom, we never hear of it. Wives were deemed liable alongside their husbands for any harm they might personally inflict on a province.[183] Pliny had been involved in a prosecution for such culpability around a decade previously (3.9.19).[184] The scandal of adultery involving imperial staff and their families in the provinces was hardly unknown (6.31.4–6).[185] It is entirely unclear how Calpurnia, still only in her mid-twenties, spent her time in Pontus-Bithynia. Could she speak Greek? Her presence alongside

Pliny is revealed only in the final two letters of Book 10, where she is encountered travelling back home to comfort her aunt Calpurnia Hispulla on the death of old Calpurnius Fabatus. It is a matter of speculation whether her willingness to return alone without Pliny indicates family piety or relief at quitting the province.[186]

Meeting the future in Bithynia: Pliny and Dio of Prusa

In Pontus-Bithynia Pliny encountered the future in its near and distant forms. In Bithynia he met an expert rhetorician who symbolizes, as hinted earlier, the growing confidence of the Second Sophistic. In Pontus Pliny encountered a bizarre religious cult. The first movement would continue to shape Greek cultural life well into the third century and influence the Latin west: its potency is coincident with high empire. After the turbulence of the latter part of the third century, a new culture would begin to emerge: the majority of the Greek and Latin classics of the fourth century and later would be written by Christian authors. The Christians encountered by Pliny in Pontus, who run the full spectrum from the 'obstinate' to the long lapsed, are the forerunners of this distant age of energetic renewal. If Pliny sensed the cultural confidence of Dio of Prusa, he could hardly guess that in a much further future Christians would erect his own statue on the walls of Como cathedral. Pliny ignored whatever he knew of Dio and his reputation, and pursued the dissolution of the Christian sect in accordance with Trajan's *mandata*. A traditionalist and a Ciceronian in his religious and cultural habits, Pliny was hardly predisposed to an interest in either Christianity or the Second Sophistic.

The messy politics of Bithynia, previously glimpsed at the trial of Varenus Rufus in Rome, take centre stage with the appearance of Dio before Pliny. The opportunism which the Roman imperial system fostered in its subject cities is on full display. Just before shifting attention to Pontus, Pliny wrote to Trajan from Nicaea to report the origin of a long-running legal matter: 'While I was employed in public business in my own lodging at Prusa under Olympus, sir, being about to leave the same day, Asclepiades, a magistrate, announced that an appeal had been lodged . . .' (10.81.1).[187] Dio, the man under accusation in Prusa, was of course a celebrity in Bithynia.[188] An energetic member of the local elite, he had a reputation throughout the eastern half of empire as public speaker, counsellor, and intellectual. He had travelled widely and spoken at Olympia and the great communities of the east, including Alexandria, Tarsus, Rhodes, and Athens, not to mention the major cities of Bithynia.[189] Dio had perhaps had personal contact with successive emperors from Vespasian onwards, and acquired the prestige of personal exile by Domitian and recall by Nerva.[190] He later authored a famous set of orations *On Kingship* that have usually been understood as aimed at Trajan. Later antiquity found fit to place these at the head of his preserved corpus of around eighty separate works.[191]

That he could be prosecuted by his rivals in their shared hometown of Prusa at all was a direct result of a privilege gained by Dio in his leadership of a civic embassy to Trajan.[192] The right of hosting assizes conferred both honour and economic benefits on a city. Prior to Dio's embassy, cases involving citizens at Prusa were heard at a nearby city, perhaps Apamea on the sea of Marmara, which enjoyed its own prestige as the only Roman colony in the province. (Not even here was Latin spoken.[193]) Criticism of Dio began as soon as he returned to Prusa from Rome. The story is murky in its details and can be pieced together with little confidence from scattered references in the public speeches of the accused. Dio had apparently 'failed' to have his hometown granted the status of a free city, exempt from routine interference from governors.[194] He had already conceived the plan of building a portico in the town using his own money, public funds, and the contributions of local subscribers. It would be a tribute to his public generosity and an attempt to beautify the town.[195] Despite its magnificent mountainside location, Prusa was less impressive than its Bithynian rivals: Pliny would comment on eyesores and lack of facilities (10.23, 70). There was opposition to the portico from city rivals, accusations of destroying landmarks in the town, allegations of embezzlement and default amongst subscribers. With the project incomplete and unrest in the city, a proconsul intervened, possibly Varenus Rufus. Dio perhaps entered into an alliance with Rufus, resulting in the exile or even death of some rivals. The affair rumbled on, now involving a library connected to the portico.[196] Two local politicians, Claudius Eumolpus and Flavius Archippus, began voicing suspicion of peculation and demanded that Dio produce accounts. A new accusation was added: Dio had buried his wife and son in the precincts of the structure in the presence of a statue of Trajan.[197] A capital penalty was mandatory for this treasonous act.

Pliny now became embroiled. The details are mundane, the evidence of civic friction forceful.[198] Pliny attempted to try the matter first in Prusa and, when this proved impossible, at Nicaea. He made his own inspection of the contested site in Prusa (10.81.7). In Nicaea the case was bedevilled by delays: 'Eumolpus began to apply for an adjournment on the grounds he was not fully prepared, while Dio in response demanded that the case should be heard. Many things were said . . .' (10.81.4). Pliny asked both parties to supply memoranda on their side of the case: these were to be sent on to Trajan with a request for advice on how to proceed. Dio complied; nothing emerged from his accusers despite a wait of 'very many days' (10.81.6).[199] When he eventually replied, Trajan dismissed the portion of the case relating to the statue, and insisted Dio be made to produce accounts for the public work (10.82).

It is remarkable that Pliny betrays no familiarity with Dio and expects none from Trajan: all the Prusan figures in the letter are introduced as if for the first time.[200] Is a point being made? Even the internationally famous Dio can expect subjection to Roman rule. The emperor shows no flicker of recognition. The partial success of Dio's embassy to Trajan and aspiration to the role of imperial counsellor on display in the 'kingship' orations ostensibly point to a more intimate relationship. It may well be that Dio accompanied Trajan to the frontier at the outset of the first Dacian war.[201] A later generation's understanding of the relationship is encapsulated, over one hundred years later, by an image in the Greek writer Philostratus of the emperor in a triumphal chariot turning to Dio beside him: 'What you are saying I do not know, but I love you as myself'.[202] Yet the partial failure of Dio's embassy perhaps indicates imperial disaffection with Prusa and its affairs.

Such is the reported encounter between two great writers of the Trajanic age, east and west, Hellene and Roman, accused and arbitrator. Was there more friendly intercourse than Pliny can report in an official letter to Trajan? Pliny's more general aloofness from Greeks suggests perhaps not. The pair had much in common. Accomplished public speakers, each contributed through published works to a golden age of prose in western and eastern halves of the empire.[203] Both were intensely interested in the welfare of home communities, with a shared preference for the benefaction of magnificent new buildings rather than games.[204] (If Pliny faced similar opposition within the town council of Comum, it is hidden from us.) The year of Pliny's consulship and Dio's embassy to Trajan gave rise to the *Panegyricus* and perhaps to the orations *On Kingship*. A joint sensitivity to imperial ideology is showcased.[205]

The two also had much to divide them. Dio's love of Prusa is a symptom of his lack of interest in Rome; Pliny's concern for Comum sits alongside his political investment in the imperial capital. It is evident from Dio's writings he had no interest in Latin culture, and his knowledge of Roman political institutions matched his lack of concern with their operation. His vision of empire was based on the Hellenistic practice of a monarch's recruitment of *philoi* or advisers from amongst the elite of his territories; the orations *On Kingship* make no mention of senators.[206] Dio, careful to avoid outright defiance, had a clear sense of the superiority of Greek culture and history.[207] The integration with Rome that his own career displayed, and that he sought for his city through the request of privileges from the emperor—both perhaps masked a more fundamental opportunism. Pliny's view of servile Bithynians, distant from the old Greek heartlands, has already been aired. It was Dio's stated policy to try to minimize the involvement of Roman governors in local Hellenic affairs.[208] Plutarch shared his view. But in published speeches Dio had been severely critical of the behaviour of certain governors.[209] It was precisely such men whom Pliny had defended in Rome. These attitudes were hard to keep out of the room.

Meeting the future in Pontus: the Christians of the Black Sea

It has been estimated that by the middle of the second century C.E., around forty years after Pliny's tenure in Pontus, there were less than fifty thousand Christians resident in the entire Roman empire. A good proportion of even this small number lived in Rome.[210] The new religion took root most quickly in the coastal cities of the eastern Mediterranean, and from there spread to the hinterlands of Asia Minor, evidently reaching Pontus well before 110 C.E. According to the *Acts of the Apostles*, Paul had devoted much of his third missionary journey to Asia Minor, travelling through Galatia and Phrygia in central Anatolia before settling for three years at Ephesus on the Aegean coast. The *First Epistle of Peter*, traditionally dated to the 60s C.E., is explicitly addressed to the faithful in various Asian provinces, including Pontus and Bithynia. Apocryphal *Acts of Andrew* of a later age narrate the miracles of the apostle Andrew in both parts of Pliny's future province.[211] Christians, nevertheless, here as elsewhere, formed a tiny minority of the broader population:[212] a percentage that initially sits uneasily with Pliny's insistence on the 'infection of this cult' throughout the towns, villages, and countryside (10.96.9). Perhaps he was overly reliant on estimates of local 'informers' whose testimony he initially took seriously (10.96.4–5). Asia Minor, along with the Greek province of Achaia, acted as an important nursery for the new religion all the same. The cities of Ephesus and Pergamum hosted important communities.[213]

By the time Pliny arrived in Pontus, the last gospel had been completed perhaps just over a decade previously, and the *Acts of Apostles* were at most twenty-years old, although the epistles of Paul had been circulating for over half a century.[214] How much of this Christian literature had reached Pontus is unclear. Pliny would eventually learn a little about the practices of this novel *superstitio*: pre-dawn meetings on set days, antiphonal singing of a 'hymn to Christ as if to a god' (*carmenque Christo quasi deo*, 10.96.7), the taking of oaths not to commit theft or adultery or break faith, and a communal meal later on the same day (10.96.7). It must remain an open question whether these practices reflect beliefs that would be recognized as 'orthodox', according to the Nicene creed formulated at the church Council in the Bithynian city of Nicaea in 325 C.E.[215]

It was not curiosity that drove Pliny to find out about Christian practice.[216] By the time their hymns and shared meals had come to light, Pliny had already executed a number of practitioners. Accusations against the group quickly expanded in the wake of the executions. Only then was an investigation of the cult's activities deemed necessary. The questioning of two enslaved women under torture confirmed other reports of the innocuous practices of the Christians (10.96.8). Pliny was disgusted: 'nothing but a depraved and extravagant cult' (10.96.8).[217] But the situation was spinning out of control. It was time to write to Trajan for confirmation of procedure so far, even if Trajan's reply could not be expected for months.

Each line of Pliny's letter and Trajan's eventual response (10.97) has been queried for evidence of early Christian practice and Roman policy towards the spread of the new religion. The letters have been over-taxed: demands have been placed on these short documents that their substance can hardly bear.[218] They are particularly valued by reason of apparent primacy in the chain of Roman evidence that leads to the great age of persecution in the third century. The letters in reality yield no principles of governmental policy towards Christianity. The fate of the Black Sea cult, as James Corke-Webster has argued, simply illustrates the brutal realities of imperial government for the vast majority who lacked Roman citizenship.[219] Members of the elite like Dio of Prusa could demand trial in Rome as citizens. The rest were exposed to harassed governors whose main imperial directive was to maintain order.[220] This is the context in which the epistles on the Christians of Pontus ought to be read: a specific one-off response by Trajan to a local situation encountered by an overworked Pliny and his skeleton staff. The irregularities in sentencing at Nicomedia and Nicaea elicited a similar reply from the emperor (10.31–2).[221]

Misunderstanding of the epistles begins early with the first recorded readers of the *Letters*, deep in an age that had otherwise ceased to read the literature of the era of Domitian, Trajan, and Hadrian. With their focus on the pre-Ciceronian age, the literary men of the second and third century Latin west had one eye on the Second Sophistic of the eastern half of empire, which was busying itself with the canonization of the works of Greece's classical age six centuries before. The general revival of Pliny's *Letters* would not begin till the mid-fourth century.[222] Well before this moment, prior even to the revival of the *Panegyricus* in the late third century, Tertullian of Carthage made use of Pliny's 'Christian' letters in his *Apology* of around 197 C.E. As part of a sarcastic attack on the confusion of Roman responses to Christianity, he mockingly insisted that the epistles enshrined universal principles of procedure. Gubernatorial correspondence was conceived, in fact, as specific to a single province with no validity in principle beyond the death of a reigning emperor. Tertullian's bitter distortion of the correspondence would be recycled into something more fully positive by Eusebius of Caeserea in his early-fourth century history of the church: Trajan's injunction that Christians 'should not be sought out' (*conquirendi non sunt*, 10.97.2) was now cited as evidence that Christians had enjoyed legal protection under this 'best' of emperors.[223]

The situation in Pontus is best understood by focusing on the injunctions from Plutarch and Dio that fellow Hellenes not involve Romans unnecessarily in local affairs. The reality that they knew only too well featured elite factions competing in opportunistic appeals to imperial authority, and local populaces thrusting legal petitions on governors during hard-pressed visits for town assizes. Papyrological evidence suggests that 1,084 petitions were addressed to the prefect of Egypt in the course of a two-day visit to Arsinoë in 209 C.E.[224] Pontus was hardly so densely populated. Yet Pliny did not arrive there until the second year of his tenure. He did not go looking for offenders: 'they were brought before me as being Christians' (ad me tamquam Christiani deferebantur, 10.96.2). Papyrological documentation again suggests local petitions had little sense of legal principle: they were often speculative or unscrupulous. The language Pliny uses to describe the charge contains legal terminology, but it fails to offer specifics.[225] That there was no imperial standing charge against Christians will hardly have bothered locals.[226] The probable context for the accusations emerges towards the end of Pliny's report: 'temples which just now were almost abandoned have begun to be thronged . . . and the flesh of sacrificial victims, for which until recently very few buyers were to be found, to be sold far and wide' (10.96.10).[227] Pliny's actions against Christians had evidently restored a local status quo whose earlier upset likely impelled vindictive petitions for prosecution.

What were the defendants charged with 'as being Christians'? Perhaps no one was very clear on this point.[228] The sect had a poor reputation as troublesome. Tacitus reports that already in Rome during Nero's day Christians were 'resented for their outrages' (per flagitia inuisos, Ann. 15.44.2). In Pontus there appear to have been implications of 'guilt or, if you will, error' (culpae suae uel erroris, 10.96.7): at a much later stage in the process former Christians insist under questioning that the sum total of guilt consisted of gatherings and communals meals (10.96.7). It is these meetings that seem to have formed the basis of Pliny's initial suspicion of the group. His mandata contained a clearly stated ban on such private associations (10.96.7). Elite Romans needed little encouragement, in any case, to entertain suspicions of lower-class co-operatives. The turbulence created by political clubs in the final years of the Republic had not been altogether forgotten.[229] Pliny asked those brought before him to deny their Christianity, or affirm it three times (10.96.3). It was not their actual beliefs that concerned Pliny, who apparently knew little about them at this stage. It was something else: 'I was in no doubt that, whatever it might be that they were admitting to, their stubbornness and unyielding obstinacy certainly ought to be punished' (10.96.3).[230] Impudence itself might be enough to indicate guilt.[231]

With that, the executions began (10.96.3).[232] Non-citizens were taken away for capital punishment, citizens were marked down for sending on to Rome for trial (10.96.4). This is the reality of Roman imperial justice: 'Pliny has adopted what is essentially a shoot-first policy because he is dealing with a small number of troublesome non-citizens who have affirmed their membership of a sketchy association.[233] Flooded with petitions in a situation of obvious unrest, a governor had an easy way to rid his province of the bothersome or unsavoury. There is no reason to believe that the Christians of Pontus were a special case. Presumably other non-citizens across Pontus-Bithynia received similar treatment from Pliny, as they would from any Roman governor across the empire.[234] The only difference is what happened next.[235]

Pliny expected the matter to end there. The success of the initial accusations actually provoked more across a wider area (10.96.4): 'an anonymous pamphlet containing the names of many persons was posted up' (10.96.5);[236] others were identified 'by an informer' (*ab indice*, 10.96.6). The governor implies proliferation is normal: 'through the very course of dealing with the matter, as usually happens, the charge spread widely' (10.96.4).[237] This is belied by his willingness to use anonymous accusations and the services of an informer. Trajan will later criticize him for it (10.97.2). At this point, with Christians already executed, Pliny devises a test.[238] Those accused in the anonymous pamphlet are given the opportunity to discharge themselves by paying homage to a statue of Trajan and cult-images of the gods and by cursing Christ (10.96.5). Pliny evidently has some superficial knowledge of the monotheistic cult. No deeper investigation has yet taken place. At least his earlier suspicions are confirmed: Christians are troublemakers. Did Pliny feel some relief that Christians failed his test and provided retrospective justification for the death sentences handed out earlier? One thing is clear: when he wrote his report to the emperor, 'Pliny was encouraging Trajan to read back the later Christians' refusal to sacrifice into his initial interactions with them'.[239] The governor's skills as courtroom orator, not to mention his willingness to play with words in pressurized situations, return to the fore.[240]

Pliny moved on to those accused by an informer: this group is apparently made up of those who have recanted their faith, some as much as two decades previously (10.96.6). They too are given a chance to discharge themselves. When the recanters insist that no crimes were committed even when they were Christians, Pliny finally learns more in detail about the cult. Here the details of antiphonal singing and the taking of oaths against wrongdoing finally emerge (10.96.7). The torture of the two enslaved persons provides confirmation (10.96.8). Christians appear not to be guilty of whatever criminal activity Pliny had vaguely suspected them of at the very start of the investigation. The situation is now dangerous. Those endangered include 'many persons of every age, of every rank, of both sexes' (10.96.9).[241]

It is only at this point Pliny writes to Trajan: the account of his actions previously quoted is part of a retrospective 'up-to-now' narrative addressed to the emperor. He begins by expressing his doubt, uncertainty, and ignorance (10.96.1).

He does not know 'whether it is the name itself [of Christian], if it is free from crimes, or the crimes associated with the name which are being punished' (10.96.2).[242] This is the query of a man conscious that belated discoveries about the nature of Christian activities throw doubt on the first executions. Even if the letters have been edited prior to publication, it cannot be quite concealed that the successful test of demanding homage to Trajan and the gods was only devised at a late stage. Pliny was fully aware of the propensity for Bithynia to prosecute its governors. What if some of the Roman citizens sent from Pontus for trial turned out to be well connected in the capital? Two cases of financial misconduct in which Pliny had been involved as prosecutor in the early years of Trajan's reign included aggravating accounts of violent gubernatorial behaviour. Marius Priscus the governor of Africa had, in Pliny's own words, 'taken bribes for the condemnation, and even the murder, of innocent persons' (2.11.2).[243] The governor of Baetica, Caecilius Classicus, had behaved 'in a manner no less brutal than squalid' (*non minus violenter quam sordide*, 3.9.2).[244] The *saevitia* attached to the charges against Iulius Bassus and Varenus Rufus was fresh in the memory. Pliny's premature actions, of course, involved only non-citizens. There was still his reputation for justice and moderation to think of. The recent advice to Maximus to avoid gubernatorial 'arrogance and severity' (*absit superbia asperitas*, 8.24.5) perhaps now rang hollow.

Pliny needed Trajan to confirm in writing that his procedure so far had been correct. A reply arrived some months later. By then Pliny had presumably already made a provisional decision about the Christians of Pontus and moved on to try different cases in a new venue. In eighty-three words the emperor provided reassurance for the past and guidance for the future. The former was welcome. The latter might be superfluous in the light of whatever Pliny had done in the interval between query and reply. Trajan's opening offered emphatic endorsement: 'My dear Secundus, you followed the procedure which you ought to have followed, in examining the cases of those who were prosecuted before you as Christians' (10.97.1). Pliny was now safe from any unwelcome developments after his return to Rome. Next, Trajan, somewhat belatedly, de-escalates the situation: Christians 'should not be sought out' (10.97.2); and 'pamphlets posted up without an author's name ought to have no place in any criminal charge. For they both set the worst precedent and are not in keeping with the spirit of our age' (10.97.2).[245] A characteristically ad hoc response: the rampant proliferation of charges is now to be halted. If there is a determination to hold Pliny to the high standards of the emperor's reign, there is no question, here or elsewhere in Book 10, of asking Pliny to reverse an action already undertaken.[246] The governor had made it easy for the emperor by emphasizing 'stubbornness and unyielding obstinacy'. As for Christianity, Trajan appears ignorant or uninterested. If non-citizens show allegiance through homage to the gods, they can go free; those who do not may be executed (10.97.2). Trajan dodges the question whether it is the name or the associated crimes that are being punished. His feelings on private associations are clear elsewhere.

Epilogue

Christians are no different from any other group of troublesome locals disturbing the peace of a province. The historical significance of Pliny's encounter with them, in some sense, is rather slight. His career did not culminate in a date with destiny. It is the relationship with Trajan that remained paramount for Pliny.[247] Christians take up no more than two letters in a book containing over 120. The first readers of Book 10 were doubtless not especially struck by their appearance.

'Looking back to the roots of the movement', comments one writer on early Christianity, 'it has often proven difficult for scholars, especially those who are insiders to the Christian tradition, to avoid thinking of its development as inevitable, and to understand early historical data as trending towards what Christianity eventually became'.[248] So it must be for the Christians of Pontus. Christianity grew only rather slowly over the next two centuries, despite its geographical spread. In 300 C.E., on the eve of Constantine's edict of toleration, Christians perhaps comprised nearer to 5 per cent than 10 per cent of the empire's population.[249] The fate of Christians on the southern coast of the Black Sea appears mixed. Writing in the later second century, the Greek satirical author Lucian records Alexander, prophet of the miraculous new cult of Asclepius, complaining that 'Pontus was full of atheists and Christians' (*Alex.* 25). He encouraged his followers to expel the latter from his rites (*Alex.* 38).[250] By the early third century, their numbers may have been rather fewer.[251]

As for Pliny, his general conduct in Pontus-Bithynia was no doubt moderate and restrained by Roman standards of provincial government. Failings appear excusable, or at least comprehensible, in a context of overload on an inexperienced individual. The summary execution of Christians, and presumably others whose fates we cannot recover, retains its power to shock all the same. Pliny appears out of his depth, like the Elder Pliny at Vesuvius. Was it typical, all the same, of imperial treatment of non-citizens? Probably. Pliny is untypical only in leaving an extensive gubernatorial record. In other respects, he was a clear improvement, in so far as we can judge, on the likes of Iulius Bassus and Varenus Rufus. He hardly seems a candidate for receiving 'gifts' from local elites or committing acts of extortion 'with savagery'. His apparent lack of interest in the culture, traditions, and identity of his subjects is unattractive, by modern standards. Overall, a mixed record for a man whose real strengths lay in senate, courtroom, and the written word.

Notes

1. The exact dates of Pliny's gubernatorial stint are disputed: some scholars (e.g. Sherwin-White (1966, 80–1), Millar (2004b, 38) = (2016, 435)) argue for 109–11; others (e.g. Syme (1985b) = *RP* 5.478–89) for 110–12; and yet others for 111–13; the evidence is set out by Birley (2000a, 16–17).
2. See Chp. 5.
3. Cf. Woolf (2015, 148).
4. See Chp. 6.
5. For a concise summary of the pressures acting on senators in these cases, cf. Potter (2006b, 16–17), 'trials raised questions not only of proper moral behaviour, but also of the standing of the [senate] as a whole'.
6. See Chp. 7.
7. For a history of the broader region in which the Roman province of Pontus-Bithynia is located, see Williams (1990, 10–11), Madsen (2009, 27–40); cf. Marek (2003, 181–3, Karte I–IV) for a useful visual representation of boundary changes in the area from Hellenistic times to high empire. For a brief history of Asia Minor as a whole under Trajan, see Magie (1950, 593–610).
8. On the processes of Hellenization, urbanization, and Romanization specifically in Pontus in the context of wider developments in central Anatolia, see Mitchell (1993, 80–99).
9. On Pliny's Pontus as a coastal strip and his treatment of it, see Millar (2004b, 39) = (2016, 435–6), Mitchell (1993, 61–2) with map 3 (opposite p. 40).
10. See Rood (2012) on the *Circumnavigation* ('Periplus') of Arrian.
11. See Jones (1986) on Lucian's *Alexander*.
12. Woolf (2006a, 106) = (2016, 460).
13. Cf. Pliny *Paneg.* 92.4, Suet. *Dom.* 17.2, Williams (1990, 88).
14. Millar (2004b, 40–1) = (2016, 436–7) estimates two months for a journey from Sinope in the far east of Pliny's province to Rome; Scheidel and Meeks (orbis.stanford.edu) produce various estimates for Rome to Prusa, depending on route, cost, and method of transport, ranging from thirty-seven to fifty-two days. Pliny was delayed by winds and was likely travelling with his wife (see later in this chapter).
15. E.g. at Centumcellae (6.31).
16. *Quia confido, domine, ad curam tuam pertinere, nuntio tibi me Ephesum cum omnibus meis hyper Malean nauigasse quamuis contrariis uentis retentum. nunc destino partim orariis nauibus, partim uehiculis prouinciam petere. nam sicut itineri graues aestus, ita continuae nauigationi etesiae reluctantur.* For Cicero's account of his six- to seven-week gubernatorial journey from Brundisium to Ephesus in summer 51 BCE (en route to Cilicia), cf. Cic. *Att.* 5.9–13, Tempest (2014, 151–3).
17. On the old controversy over whether Trajan could have written all of the replies to Pliny, and to all his other governors across the empire, see the summary of Sherwin-White (1966, 536–46) and the sensible remarks of Noreña (2007, 251–2): we don't know and we can't tell, but all the letters are written 'as if' from Trajan, and were certainly read as such once in circulation.

18. 10.16.1 *Recte renuntiasti, mi Secunde carissime. pertinet enim ad animum meum, quali itinere prouinciam peruenias.* On Trajan's need to create the impression of a personal (but not necessarily intimate) friendship with his governors, and to dissociate himself from the lofty and distant Domitian and foster the ideal of partnership with the senate, see Noreña (2007, 252–60).

19. Cic. *Fam.* 4.5.4 *ex Asia rediens cum ab Aegina Megaram uersus nauigarem, coepi regiones circumcirca prospicere ... 'uisne tu te, Serui, cohibere et meminisse hominem te esse natum?'* Servius Sulpicius Rufus writes to Cicero in 47 B.C.E., en route from Samos to Rome; see Scourfield (2013) for the place of the letter within the broad tradition of ancient consolation. Servius' letter is remembered also by Sterne (*Tristram Shandy* V.3).

20. On Catullus and Memmius in Bithynia, see Konstan (2007, 72, 75, 81–2), Braund (1996).

21. See later in this chapter.

22. On biography, allegory, and metaphor in Catullus 4, see Fitzgerald (1995, 104–10), Young (2011), Fordyce (1961, 96–9); on the yacht as the Argo, see Hornsby (1963).

23. On Pliny and the journeys of Menelaus and Odysseus around Malea (Hom. *Od.* 3.286–92, 9.74–6; cf. *Od.* 1.5–9 on the return of Odysseus *without* his men), see Gibson and Morello (2012, 262 n. 58); cf. Gibson and Morello (2012, 259–63) on possible interactions with Ovid's journey out to the Black Sea in *Tristia* 1.

24. 10.17a.4 *haec tibi, domine, in ipso ingressu meo scripsi*; 10.17a.3 *nunc rei publicae Prusensium impendia, reditus, debitores excutio ... multae enim pecuniae uariis ex causis a priuatis detinentur; praeterea quaedam minime legitimis sumptibus erogantur.*

25. Cf. Dio *Or.* 48.2, Jones (1978, 99), (1971, 121); see also Talbert (1980, 425, 428–30).

26. For the suggestion that first two letters attributed to Dio of Prusa are genuine and addressed to Varenus Rufus, see Jones (2015).

27. Cf. *Or.* 47.19, 48.3, 9 for the complacency of Dio of Prusa (on whom see later).

28. The identity of Pliny's legion is known from the great Comum inscription (*CIL* 5.5262: quoted in Chp. 7). For the office of military tribune, see Talbert (1984, 14), Sherwin-White (1966, 269, 441–2).

29. For Pliny's service in the office—perhaps obtained for him by a Transpadane governor of Syria, T. Atilius Rufus—see Syme, *RP* 7.552–3, Birley (2000a, 7–8). On the Elder Pliny's service in Germany, see Chp. 4, Healy (1999, 5–6).

30. 7.31.2 *magnam quorundam foedamque auaritiam.* On the Syrian legions as habitually non-active, despite Pliny's implied accusations, cf. Tac. *Ann.* 12.12, 13.35.

31. Cf. 1.10.2, 3.11.5, 7.4.3, 7.16.1, 7.31.2, 8.14.7, 10.87.1.

32. Prefect of cavalry Claudius Pollio: see Syme, *RP* 7.553; chief centurion Nymphidius Lupus: see Williams (1990, 133–4); Tiro: see Chp. 5.

33. 3.11.5 *arta familiaritate complexus sum*; 1.10.2 *penitus et domi inspexi, amarique ab eo laboraui.*

34. The Stoic Musonius Rufus (Sherwin-White (1966, 244), Thorsteinsson (2010, 40–54)), father-in-law of Artemidorus, had perhaps spent a period of banishment from Rome in Syria (Thorsteinsson (2010, 42), Shelton (2013, 159–60)) and had also taught Dio of Prusa (see n. 46 later).

35. See Chp. 5 on 3.11.

36. 1.10 on Euphrates belongs to an early date under Trajan, c. 98 C.E., but within Book 1 of the *Letters* is evidently meant to mark the return of the philosophers (Hoffer (1999, 120–1)). On Euphrates of Tyre, another pupil of Musonius, see Sherwin-White (1966, 108–9), Shelton (2013, 160–1).

37. See Chp. 5.

38. 1.10.9–10 *officio, ut maximo sic molestissimo . . . subnoto libellos, conficio tabulas . . . adfirmat etiam esse hanc philosophiae et quidem pulcherrimam partem, agere negotium publicum*; 1.10.7 *insectatur uitia non homines, nec castigat errantes sed emendat.*

39. See Hoffer (1999, 119–40).

40. On the dating of Plutarch's work (*Maxime cum principibus*) to the reign of Trajan, see Zecchini (2002, 196–7). Epicetus attended the lectures of Musonius Rufus while still enslaved (Arr. *Epict. diss.* 1.9.29) and refers approvingly to Euphrates (3.15.8, 4.8.17); see Envoi n. 14 for his life and works.

41. On Epictetus' memories of bearding men of consular rank in Rome, see Arr. *Epict. diss.* 2.12.17–25.

42. On the non-specific vocabulary for 'ruler' (and similar terms) used by Plutarch, capable of application to a range of figures from local aristocrats up the emperor himself, see Roskam (2002).

43. Whitton (2013, 89). On Isaeus and his origin in Syria (and role as educator of Hadrian), see Whitton (2013, 89–90, 91).

44. For a brief introduction to the Second Sophistic and its issues, see Whitmarsh (2005) and, in rather more detail, the essays collected in Richter and Johnson (2017). For the reaction of writers in Latin to this renaissance, see Habinek (2017).

45. See Chp. 5 n. 73, Gibson (2018). On the greater social prestige of Syria, as opposed to the backwaters of old Greece, see Jones (1971, 46, 61).

46. On Dio's associations with Musonius, see Moles (2005, 120–1); on his visits to Rome, see Bekker-Nielsen (2008, 120–5); on his encounter with Pliny in Prusa, see later in this chapter.

47. 5.20.4–5 *est plerisque Graecorum, ut illi, pro copia uolubilitas . . . loquentiam . . . multis atque etiam impudentissimo cuique maxime contigit.* On Pliny's involvement with the Fonteius Magnus case, see later in this chapter. See also Woolf (2006b) on Pliny's expression of hostility to Greek games in the Roman colony of Vienne in southern France (4.22).

48. Cf. Pliny *HN*. 24.4–6, 26.11, 29.13–28; Nutton (1986), Beagon (2005, 50–1), Griffin (2007), Doody (2011, 124–6).

49. See Gibson (2014, esp. 205–10) on Pliny's admiration for Homer, Aeschines, and Demosthenes in the context of a general preference for contemporary literature; cf. 10.5–7, 10–11 for the Younger's more positive attitude to Greek doctors. On Pliny's general attitude to Greek culture, see Galimberti Biffino (2007).

50. The handful of high-ranking Hellenes addressed in the *Letters* includes: Catilius Severus of Apamea in Bithynia (1.22, 3.13, 9.22: Apamea was a Roman military colony); Cornutus Tertullus of Perge in Pamphylia (7.21, 7.31: mentioned also in 2.11, 2.12, 4.17, 5.15, 9.13; *Paneg.* 90–1; cf. Chp. 5 n. 171); and Quintilius Valerius Maximus of Alexandria Troas (8.24). On their origins, see Syme (1985a, 329–30,

355-6) = *RP* 5.446-7, 473-4; Salomies (1992, 51, 65-6), Birley (2000a, 44, 64, 84), Gibson and Morello (2012, 154-7); see also later on Maximus. Pliny's friends Sosius Senecio and Pompeius Falco (see Chp. 5) used to be claimed for the Greek east, but are generally no longer so; see Birley (2000a, 80-1, 90).

51. See Syme (1985a, 351-9) = *RP* 5.469-77 for a useful review of notable categories of absentees / near absentees from Pliny's list of correspondents. For Pliny's otherwise strong links with Baetica, see Chp. 5 and later in this chapter.

52. For Pliny's showcase of Transpadane correspondents and the north-western service and connections provided by the Elder Pliny, see Chps. 4, 7, Syme (1985a, 343-5, 348-9) = *RP* 5.460-3, 466-7.

53. On the probable failure of Pliny's petition on behalf of Romanus in 10.4, see Syme (1960, 364) = *RP* 2.480 = (2016, 70-1); the matter is disputed by Sherwin-White (1966, 565-6).

54. On the early entry of western elites into the senate, and the later arrival of easterners under the Flavians and Trajan, see Salmeri (2000, 55-63), Madsen (2009, 59-81). Plutarch regretted the departure of local dignitaries—including Bithynians—from their native cities to Rome; cf. *Mor.* 470c, Madsen (2009, 72-5).

55. 6.19.4-5 *eosdem patrimonii tertiam partem conferre iussit in ea quae solo continerentur, deforme arbitratus (et erat) honorem petituros urbem Italiamque non pro patria sed pro hospitio aut stabulo quasi peregrinantes habere. concursant ergo candidati; certatim quidquid uenale audiunt emptitant.* For a register of senatorial families known to have owned property in the vicinity of Rome (including many non-Italian families), see Andermahr (1998, 44-53); cf. Patterson (2006, 210) for the identification of groups of villas on the periphery of Rome (on the via Latina and at Tivoli) as the properties of wealthy senators from overseas.

56. For an overview of the Bassus and Varenus cases, see Talbert (1980, 413-17). Procchi (2012) devotes a short monograph to the Bassus case.

57. For the trial in 15 C.E. of Granius Marcellus (on whom see Chp. 6 n. 26), cf. Tac. *Ann.* 1.74, with Woodman (2009, 35) on Tacitus' echo of letter 10.8.

58. There are seven known prosecutions of governors of Bithynia in the period (with five on record for Asia, Baetica, Crete, and Cyrene and Africa); see Brunt (1961, 224-7).

59. For the system of prosecution of governors under the empire, see Brunt (1961), with addenda in Brunt (1990, 487-505), and Talbert (1984, 480-87); cf. Chp. 5 on the prosecution of Baebius Massa. For a suggestion that provincial corruption rose under Nerva and Trajan after the collapse of the authoritarian regime of Domitian, see Jones (1971, 119).

60. On Bassus and his high birth (4.9.4), see Sherwin-White (1966, 274-5), Birley (2000a, 63-4).

61. On the legal technicalities and processes of the trial, as outlined in 4.9, see Sherwin-White (1966, 274, 278).

62. Cf. 4.9.1-2, 22, Brunt (1961, 202).

63. 4.9.6 *lex munera quoque accipi uetat*; 4.9.14 *impudentissime . . . duos et consulares et disertos*; cf. Brunt (1961, 217): 'It was the height of impudence for a Greekling and a subject to answer a Roman and a consular'.

64. See Brunt (1961, 216-17) on the remarkable unity of the Bithynian prosecution team.

65. On penalties for conviction and procedures for passing the case to assessors after due process in the senate, see Brunt (1961, 196–7, 199–200).

66. On the fluctuation of penalties at the discretion of the court, see Brunt (1961, 201, 212, 217).

67. 10.56.4 *sciebam acta Bassi rescissa datumque a senatu ius omnibus, de quibus ille aliquid constituisset, ex integro agendi.*

68. See Chp. 5.

69. The question of imperial Greek knowledge of Latin literature remains open to refinement of answers; see Goldhill (f'coming). It is possible that even Plutarch, who visited Rome, knew prominent Romans, and had every reason to read Latin historical sources for his Roman biographies, lacked wide reading in the field; cf. Plut. *Demosth.* 2.2, Jones (1971, 76–7, 81–7), Van Hoof (2010, 91 nn. 33–4), Stadter (2015, 130–48).

70. On the date of Rufus' trial, see Syme (1985e, 240–2) = *RP* 5.496–8. Little is known about this governor of Pontus-Bithynia outside his appearances in Pliny and the forty-eighth oration of Dio of Prusa.

71. See Sherwin-White (1966, 274).

72. Pliny devotes five full letters to his prominent role in the defence of Rufus (5.20, 6.5, 6.13, 7.6, 7.10): it receives more attention than any other trial in the correspondence. Did Pliny, compiling the later books of his letters towards the end of the first decade of the second century, highlight these reports for inclusion once he knew he was under consideration for Pontus-Bithynia?

73. See Sherwin-White (1966, 352, 354), Talbert (1980, 415) on the irregularity of the request for witnesses.

74. Brunt (1961, 219).

75. On 6.5 and 6.13, see Gibson (f'coming).

76. On the provincial councils of both Bithynia and Pontus, see Sherwin-White (1966, 407), Williams (1990, 8), with further references; Pliny (significantly) makes no mention of either during his own tenure as governor. On the role of councils in bringing charges against governors (almost certainly *not* their envisaged function), see Brunt (1961, 212–3); on the temptation they created for governors to side with a particular city so as to ensure the votes they controlled in the event of a motion to prosecute him, see Jones (1978, 88).

77. On the context for the divisions and interventions of the council in the Rufus case, and the happiness of Rufus to prolong his trial so as to exploit those divisions, see Sherwin-White (1966, 352, 407), Brunt (1961, 213–4).

78. See Sherwin-White (1966, 408).

79. See Brunt (1961, 214) on Dio's warnings to Nicomedia in *Or.* 38.33–7, to Prusa in *Or.* 48.7, and to Nicaea in *Or.* 39.4.

80. On levels of provincial experience expected in senior senators, see Talbert (1980, 417–19); on likely praetorian commands acquired by Tacitus, see Birley (2000b, 235),

81. On the bad reputation presumably acquired by Pliny in advance of his appointment to Pontus-Bithynia, see Talbert (1980, 416); on Pliny's lack of experience as perhaps a

point in his favour, see Talbert (1980, 420). Bekker-Nielsen (2008, 65–6) suggests that Pliny was chosen out of respect for senatorial sensibilities in the context of a transfer of a senatorial province to the emperor.

82. See Chp. 5.

83. Syme (1958, 83).

84. See Williams (1990, 14–15) (a pupil of Sherwin-White, it can be noted). On a sustained investment by both Syme and Sherwin-White in disagreement over the career and promotions of Pliny and Tacitus, see Griffin (1999, 144–5) = (2016, 361–2); cf. Whitton and Gibson (2016, 38–9).

85. See Chp. 5.

86. See Syme (1958, 80–1).

87. On Tiro, see Chp. 5. A series of letters tracks Tiro's progress up through Italy en route to Baetica via Comum: 7.16, 23, 32. Pliny had his own strong contacts with Baetica as a patron of the province (1.7, 3.4.4, 7.33.4; see Chp. 5)—despite the lack of Baetican correspondents (see earlier).

88. On the complicated accusation of the governor Bruttianus in 6.22, see Gibson (f'coming); cf. Sherwin-White (1966, 382) on the horror raised by 'improper' accusations of governors by staff.

89. The exact composition of Pliny's staff in Pontus-Bithynia is unknown beyond the centurion Nympidius Lupus (mentioned earlier) and Calpurnia (10.120–1). Candidates for inclusion are: Voconius Romanus (9.28.4, with Syme (1958, 80–1), (1985b, 183) = RP 5.488): disputed by Sherwin-White (1966, 80)), and Suetonius (10.94: with Syme (1958, 779)), Sherwin-White (1966, 689–90); cf. also 10.51 on the transfer of the kinsman of his (former) mother-in-law, Pompeia Celerina, to his province, likely to an equestrian officer's post (Williams (1990, 108)). Pliny was aware that a governor's non-official agents, including members of his family, were liable to prosecution for corruption in a province; see later in this chapter.

90. Syme (1958, 80) is at his acidic best on Pliny's reinforcement of structural inequalities in Roman provinces: 'Were Pliny himself denied scope for the exercise of sound principles in government, it would have been highly regrettable'. But for Pliny's sentiments on (in)equality as part of a Roman cultural package, see Dench (2018, 95–8).

91. On 9.5 and examples known to Pliny of governors who did provoke factionalism (2.11.8, 3.9.3, 4.9.5), see Sherwin-White (1966, 484).

92. See later in this chapter on the Prusan dispute.

93. See Talbert (1980, 427), citing 9.5, Tac. Agr. 9, Callistratus Dig. 1.18.19 pr.

94. Plut. Political Precepts; on Plutarch's political treatises, see Jones (1971, 110–21).

95. On the attraction of Roman rule to Plutarch and the latter's approval of the free status given to Achaia under Nero, see Jones (1971, 120).

96. Syme (1958, 80); cf. Syme (1958, 85), (1985a, 329–30) = RP 5.446–7. On the mission of Maximus in Achaia, see Sherwin-White (1966, 478–9).

97. 8.24.9 magis nitendum est ne in longinqua prouincia quam suburbana, ne inter seruientes quam liberos . . . humanior melior peritior fuisse uidearis.

98. On the broader Roman rhetoric of the provinces as slaves to Rome, see Lavan (2013, 73–123).

99. On the addressee of 8.24 as Quintilius Valerius Maximus and likely identical with the Maximus who visits Epictetus (against the reservations of Sherwin-White (1966, 479–80)), see Syme (1985a, 329–30) = *RP* 5.446–7, Millar (1965, 142–3) = (2004d, 108–9), Birley (2000a, 84). To complicate matters, this Maximus was likely from Alexandria Troas in Asia.

100. Millar (1965, 145) = (2004d, 113) underlines the contrast between Epictetus' cynicism over the qualifications of Maximus and Pliny's endorsement of the same man's track record at 8.24.8.

101. On the occluded Greekness of Pliny's province, see Woolf (2006a, 102) = (2016, 456): 'Trajan at one point (10.40) opines *gymnasiis indulgent Graeculi* ["these Greeklings are addicted to gymnasia"] and a few Greek institutions are mentioned in passing—*threptoi* (65) and *eranoi* (92)—but in general the specificity of the Bithynians' situation is played down'.

102. See Spawforth and Walker (1985), Madsen (2009, 121). On broader issues of Greek ethnicity, culture, and identity in the period, see Dench (2017).

103. On the origin of the Bithynians and the gradual depression of Thracian names in the epigraphical record, see Corsten (2006), noting the qualification of Bekker-Nielsen (2008, 97–8); cf. Sherwin-White (1966, 623) on the non-Greek names of villages in the area of Nicomedia.

104. On Bithynians, Rome, Latin, and citizenship, see Madsen (2009, 83–4, 87–90 99ff.). Nevertheless, the advertisement on inscriptions (in Greek) of closeness to Roman power appears to be an approved marker of prestige; see Madsen (2009, 90–6),

105. See Woolf (2006a, 99–101) = (2016, 451–3).

106. On Bithynian praetors and consuls, starting first with those of Italian ancestry (such as Pliny's friend Catilius Severus), but soon moving onto those with a more obviously Hellenic background (Madsen (2009, 64–79)), culminating in the consulships and gubernatorial stints of such Greek intellectuals as Arrian of Nicomedia (120–130s C.E.) and Cassius Dio of Nicaea (early 200s C.E.), see Madsen (2009, 119–26); cf. Bekker-Nielsen (2008, 110–14) on such careers in the context of political careers at local and regional level. In addition to the latter pair and Dio of Prusa, the province also produced further intellectuals in (e.g.) Asclepiades of Prusias (first century B.C.E.) and Memnon of Heraclea (second century C.E.).

107. On the rivalrous relationship between Nicomedia, Nicaea and Prusa—where Nicomedia had formerly been the royal capital of Bithynia and claimed the title of 'mother' or 'first' city (and was also the meeting place of the Bithynian council)—see Jones (1978, 67–8), Bekker-Nielsen (2008, 15–16, 47–8). Cf. Levick (1979, 121), Madsen (2009, 52–3) on the later history of claims to leading status in the province, up to the Council of Chalcedon in 451 C.E. On ancient remains in the modern towns, see Appendix 2.

108. See Williams (1990, 11–13).

109. For major roads in Bithynia, see Marek (2003, 183, Karte V).

110. On the sites, foundations, landscapes, urban environments, and political institutions of Nicomedia, Nicaea, and Prusa, see Bekker-Nielsen (2008, 21–6, 31–3, 49–57, 61–87); cf. Jones (1978, 1–2) on Prusa, and Marek (2003, 80) for a map of Nicomedia and hinterland.

111. See Chp. 4 n. 25 for this traditional date (and attempts to revise it).

112. On Libanius and Nicomedia, see Watts (2014, 41–8).

113. Cf. e.g. 10.23–4, 37–40, 49–50, 70, 81, 90–1, 98–9.

114. See Chp. 3 for Pliny and water.

115. On the Nicomedian canal, which was never built (and would in fact have drained the lake), see Sherwin-White (1966, 621–5, 646–8), Williams (1990, 102–3, 115–16).

116. On Pliny's absorption in these three Pontic towns and the role of Amastris as the centre for assizes, see Sherwin-White (1966, 531–2), Williams (1990, 11–13).

117. On the vast distances of the province of Pontus-Bithynia and the problems for imperial communication, see Millar (2004b, 40) = (2016, 436–7).

118. On the threat to Pliny's health provided by Pontus-Bithynia and later imperial instructions for governors to look after their health, see Talbert (1980, 421).

119. I borrow here the succinct formulation of Ando (2006, 192).

120. See Ando (2006, 179–82, 191–2) on provincial officials, their staff, and the delegation of government and policing in the provinces.

121. On these features of Roman government and acculturation, see the short survey by Ando (2006) and the more detailed studies of Woolf (1998) and Ando (2000).

122. For a survey of the history of debate on the workings of Roman imperialism, see Dench (2018, 1–17, 155–9).

123. Goldhill (f'coming).

124. See Goldhill (f'coming). On the literary contours of the Second Sophistic, see later in this chapter and earlier n. 44. On the extent to which Greek orators and philosophers of the era challenged Roman rule, see Bowie (2009).

125. Dench (2018, 157).

126. Dench (2018, 158–9).

127. For recent approaches to east-west relations of the period, see the essays collected in Madsen and Rees (2014), with references to earlier literature.

128. For an estimate of the size of the permanent Rome presence in Bithynia in the context of dependence on local elites, see Levick (1979, 122–3).

129. In addition to personal assistants and family members (see earlier in this chapter), Pliny was entitled by his proconsular authority in the province (Alföldy (1999c, 229), Birley (2000a, 5–6): see the restoration of the Great Comum inscription in Chp. 7) to a motorcade of lictors. Alföldy (1999c, 240) and Noreña (2007, 243) assume six lictors; Cotton (2000, 233–4), Eck (2001, 226–9), and Vervaet (2007, 131–2) prefer twelve.

130. See Chp. 7.

131. An 'excess' of elite prosperity was a factor in the Bithynian 'problem' for Roman government (Sherwin-White (1966, 527), Madsen (2009, 25–6)), but civic rivalry was also a sign of the local energy required to make the empire function (Levick (1979, 122–3). Nevertheless such prosperity, even among the elite, should not be exaggerated: Spain was far richer in natural resources (Madsen (2009, 76–9)).

132. Cf. 10.17b, 34, 37, 39–40, 58–60, 81–2, 93; Levick (1979, 119–20). For Dio on inter-city rivalry, see Talbert (1980, 426–8), Jones (1978, 83–94).

133. On Pliny's ordinary duties as governor, see Sherwin-White (1966, 82), Millar (2004b, 39) = (2016, 435). Specifically on the assize system—which took up so

much of Pliny's time—see Ando (2006, 189–91). On the operation of Roman law and jurisdiction within provinces, see Richardson (2016).

134. See Ando (2006, 179–80, 186–88), with reference to earlier studies.

135. On delays in Pliny's correspondence with Trajan, see earlier and Millar (2004b, 28–35) = (2016, 424–31); cf. Corcoran (2014, 203–6) for instances of difficulties caused elsewhere by delayed imperial correspondence.

136. Millar (2004b, 34) = (2016, 431). For a general overview of Roman state correspondence, see Corcoran (2014).

137. See Williams (1990, 15–16), Millar (2004b) = (2016), both with further references. Millar (1977) is the classic expression of a case for imperial government as essentially reactive.

138. On the legal case and context of 6.31.8, see Millar (2004b, 34) = (2016, 430); Gibson (f'coming).

139. On Cicero in Cilicia, see Rawson (1983, 164–82), Tempest (2014, 151–60); cf. Woolf (2015, 144, 146).

140. 10.1–14 contains Pliny's earlier personal correspondence with Trajan, during the latter's absence from Rome on the frontiers; while 10.15–121 contains gubernatorial correspondence with Trajan from Pontus-Bithynia. On the former, see Millar (2004b, 29, 32–4) = (2016, 425, 428–31), Seelentag (2004, 62–212), Hoffer (2006), Noreña (2007, 241–2), Woolf (2015, 140–3).

141. For assumptions of another, such as Suetonius, as editor of Book 10, see Syme (1958, 660), Williams (1990, 4); for newer arguments that Pliny himself put the book together, see Stadter (2006) (cf. Stadter (2015, 179–87)), Noreña (2007), Woolf (2006a) = (2016). For the critical contexts for these disagreements, see Woolf (2015), Whitton and Gibson (2016, 43–7). Harries (2018) argues that Pliny assembled Book 10 in competition with collections of legal opinions circulated by experts in the law under the title of *epistulae*.

142. See the important contribution of Lavan (2018), against the consensus of Stadter (2006), Woolf (2006a), and Noreña (2007).

143. Against Pliny as nervous and fussy governor, see Williams (1990, 15–16), with further references. Corcoran (2014, 182) observes that Pliny 'seems to have troubled the emperor far less than Symmachus did' during his tenure as Urban Prefect in the late fourth century. But see Talbert (1980, 421–3) for possible signs of inexperience in Pliny.

144. On stylistic, intertextual, and other differences between Book 10 and its predecessors, see Gamberini (1983, 332–76), Noreña (2007, 250–1, 267), Coleman (2012), Whitton (2013, 29 n. 170), (2019, Chp. 11).

145. Trajan's tone with Pliny can be hard to judge (Sherwin-White (1966, 539–42), Woolf (2015, 134)), but some detect an impatience or worse with Pliny that suggests the book was not put together with Pliny's hand or approval (e.g. Coleman (2012, 233–5)): cf. 10.38, 40, 82, 117. For Trajan's inclination to focus on his own interests at the expense of Pliny's queries, see Williams (1990, 100–1) on 10.38, 40.

146. For Trajan as more inclined than Pliny to avoid automatic imposition of Roman norms or to override local practice, cf. 10.17–18, 37, 39–40, 49–50, 61–2, 68, 84, 93, 109, 113, Levick (1979, 123), Dench (2018, 32–3).

147. Pliny's *mandata* do not survive independently, but at least some can be reconstructed from the letters and others may be inferred; see Millar (2004b, 38–9) = (2016, 435), Sherwin-White (1966, 81, 589–91), Talbert (1980, 422); cf. 10.32.1 (on the scandal of those condemned to the mines or the arena found in service as public slaves), 10.117 (on shaping the habits of the province and ensuring permanent tranquillity).

148. 10.18.3 *rationes . . . in primis tibi rerum publicarum excutiendae sunt; nam et esse eas uexatas satis constat.*

149. See Chp. 7.

150. Pliny appears to have examined the accounts of Prusa, Nicomedia, Nicaea, Claudiopolis, Byzantium, Apamea, Sinope, Amastris, and Amisus; see Noreña (2007, 244 n. 16). Cf. Williams (1990, 11–13) for a useful review of all the towns mentioned by Pliny in the province.

151. See Chp. 7. The portion of the text reporting the imperial appointment in Bithynia is positioned immediately after Pliny's name and status as consul and augur, and takes up fully three lines of the inscription. In the parallel Hispellum inscription (*CIL* 11.5272), by contrast, the text after consulship and augurate reverts to the beginning of Pliny's career, so that the Bithynian post appears (in rather smaller letters) at the very end of the text; see Alföldy (1999c, 243).

152. The argument for a special mission to Pontus-Bithynia focused on public finance has been made most forcibly by Talbert (1980); scepticism is expressed by Woolf (2006a, 101) = (2016, 454), and implicitly by Noreña (2007, 243–4). Levick (1979, 119–21) provides evidence that many of the administrative and financial abuses tackled by Pliny were, in fact, long-standing either in the east or throughout the empire.

153. See earlier in this chapter.

154. See Levick (1979, 125–8).

155. On the history of imperial representation in, and government of, Pontus-Bithynia, see *OCD*[4] s.v. Bithynia, Levick (1979, 129–30).

156. For the chronological ordering of Book 10, see Millar (2004b, 39–40) = (2016, 436–7), with table at (2004a, 42–6) = (2016, 439–41) setting out the likely dates and locations at which Pliny wrote the letters, together with indications of which letters from Pliny received no reply from Trajan. In the ancient world, official or contractual letters are usually dated, but private letters often are not; see Appendix 1. Dates have apparently been removed from the 'official' correspondence of Pliny's tenth book.

157. A positivistic Sherwin-White (1966, 533–5) is forced to concede omissions—even without taking into consideration his own highlighting of eight missing cities whose financial records Pliny likely reviewed (Sherwin-White (1966, 532–3)). Williams (1990, 3–4) offers a renewed argument for completeness, and Woolf (2015, 134) a counter-argument.

158. Woolf (2006a, 107 n. 21) = (2016, 454 n. 21) expresses scepticism about the detailed reconstruction of Pliny's travels by Sherwin-White (1966, 529–33).

159. 10.77.3 *sunt enim in capite Bithyniae, plurimisque per eam commeantibus transitum praebent.*

160. See Millar (2004b, 38–41) = (2016, 435–38), Woolf (2015, 146). Trajan's response was negative: 'we shall be burdening ourselves with a precedent: for more cities . . . will seek the same help' (10.78.2 *onerabimus nos exemplo; plures enim . . . idem petent*).

161. For a fuller chronological account of the business encountered by Pliny during his tenure, see Madsen (2009, 17–22).

162. See Bracci (2011, 177–8), Coleman (2012, 230–31) on this colloquial phrase.

163. There are further infrastructure problems in Claudiopolis in the construction of a new set of baths (10.39).

164. See Chp. 7 for Pliny's gift of a library and set of baths to Comum.

165. Pliny, as ever, is sparing in his reference to Trajan's foreign wars: he preferred a *ciuilis princeps*; see Chp. 5 n. 161.

166. Pliny in Claudiopolis: 10.33.1, 10.39.5, Sherwin-White (1966, 606).

167. 10.33.2 *inertia hominum . . . otiosos et immobiles tanti mali spectatores perstitisse . . . nullum denique instrumentum ad incendia compescenda.*

168. See Williams (1990, 98). On Roman *collegia* and the history of their modern study, see Perry (2006).

169. 10.34.1 *meminerimus prouinciam istam et praecipue eas ciuitates eius modi factionibus esse uexatas.*

170. Sherwin-White (1966, 609–10) provides a useful summary overview of the evidence for local factions in the speeches of Dio of Prusa, esp. *Or.* 40.8–15, 43.6–7, 11; 45.7–10, 50.3.

171. On class and factional strife in Bithynia as the context for 10.79–80, see Jones (1978, 90–1, 100–1), Levick (1979, 120).

172. For the technicalities behind the local Pompeian and Augustan laws on council membership and lesser magistracies, see Sherwin-White (1966, 669–71), Madsen (2009, 34–40).

173. 10.79.3 *quia sit aliquanto melius honestorum hominum liberos quam e plebe in curiam admitti.* Sherwin-White (1966, 673) points out that, in context, this 'is given not as Pliny's own statement . . ., but as his consultants' notion, though Pliny seems to accept it as valid'.

174. Sherwin-White (1966, 673). On social status and legal privilege in the practice of Roman law, see Taylor (2016).

175. See Levick (1979, 123–4).

176. 10.31.2 *in plerisque ciuitatibus, maxime Nicomediae et Nicaeae, quidam uel in opus damnati uel in ludum similiaque his genera poenarum publicorum seruorum officio ministerioque funguntur, atque etiam ut publici serui annua accipiunt. quod ego cum audissem, diu multumque haesitaui, quid facere deberem.*

177. See Sherwin-White (1966, 603), Williams (1990, 96).

178. 10.31.4 *nulla monumenta quibus liberati probarentur*; 10.31.5 *iussu proconsulum legatorumue dimissos . . . credibile erat neminem hoc ausum sine auctore.*

179. Madsen (2009, 55).

180. On the context for Plutarch's advice, see Jones (1971, 113); cf. Jones (1971, 116–18) for concord here with the advice of Dio of Prusa—whom Plutarch elsewhere

implicitly criticizes for absence from his native Bithynia (*Mor.* 470c). For parallels between problems in Greek cities encountered by Pliny and those that vexed Plutarch in his political treatises, see Jones (1971, 119).

181. The determination of Apamea (10.47–8) to preserve its traditional right as a Roman colony of freedom from the inspection of its accounts by a governor (Sherwin-White (1966, 629–31)) belongs in the same vein of low-level resistance to Roman rule; cf. Talbert (1980, 432–4). On the fragmented nature of intellectual opposition to Roman rule in Pontus-Bithynia and elsewhere in the Greek world, see Madsen (2006), (2009, 103–7).

182. Woolf (2006a, 103) = (2016, 457); cf. Woolf (2015, 145–7), contrariwise, on the lack of routine and repetitiveness in the letters of Book 10.

183. Cf. Ulpian *Dig.* 1.16.4.2, Sherwin-White (1966, 234–5), Carlon (2009, 193–4), Shelton (2013, 163).

184. See Carlon (2009, 191–6), Shelton (2013, 162–7) on the trial of Caecilius Classicus, former governor of Baetica, and his wife Casta.

185. For charges of adultery between the wife of a military tribune and a centurion in 6.31.4–6, see Carlon (2009, 201–4), Shelton (2013, 173–5).

186. For speculation on how Calpurnia spent her time in the province, see Shelton (2013, 133–6).

187. 10.81.1 *Cum Prusae ad Olympum, domine, publicis negotiis intra hospitium eodem die exiturus uacarem, Asclepiades magistratus indicauit adpellatum me . . .*

188. Pliny refers to Dio with the hybrid Greco-Roman name Cocceianus Dion (10.81.1). He is known to history as Dio of Prusa or Dio 'Chrysostom' ('Golden Mouth'): so named by later antiquity in recognition of his eloquence as writer and orator and also to distinguish him from his probable relation, Cassius Dio of Nicaea, imperial historian of the early third century. Dio's full name may have been Titus Flavius Cocceianus Dio: an indication that his Roman citizenship was acquired under the Flavians through the patronage of the future emperor Cocceius Nerva; but the matter is disputed: see Jones (1978, 6–7), Salmeri (2000, 66 n. 67, 89 n. 176), with further references. For short accounts of Dio's life and works, see Swain (2000a, 1–10), Madsen (2009, 107–19), Bekker-Nielsen (2008, 119–40), Jackson (2017); for a full scale biography, see Jones (1978); cf. Moles (1978).

189. See Salmeri (2000, 77–83).

190. See Jones (1978, 14–16) for possible imperial contacts; for the exile and recall of Dio, see Jones (1978, 45–6, 51).

191. Internal evidence is lacking for the address of the kingship orations to Trajan; see Swain (2000b, 42–3), Whitmarsh (2005, 60–3). On the orations themselves, see Jones (1978, 115–23), Moles (1990), Swain (2000b, 45–6), and Whitmarsh (2001, 156–57), with further references.

192. See earlier in this chapter on Dio's embassy. On the same embassy Dio appears to have acquired further economic boosts for Prusa: the admission of 100 new members to the local council (each of whom would have to pay a substantial entrance fee), and perhaps the right for the city to issue its own coinage; see Jones (1978, 67–8, 107–9), Salmeri (2000, 68).

193. See Salmeri (2000, 54 n. 6).

194. See Jones (1978, 54, 109).

195. On Dio's concern to beautify Prusa, see Salmeri (2000, 68), Jones (1978, 5–6).

196. For full accounts of the long-drawn-out portico affair, see Jones (1978, 54, 111–14), Salmeri (2000, 67–8). It is not clear whether the portico associated with the library is new or identical with the older structure; see the divergent opinions of Sherwin-White (1966, 676), Jones (1978, 114), Salmeri (2000, 68 n. 73).

197. A fragmentary inscription from ancient Prusa may well derive from the funerary monument for Dio's wife and son; see Salmeri (2000, 89 n. 176).

198. For factionalism in Prusa and Bithynia in the first decade of the second century, see Jones (1978, 99–103).

199. 10.81.4 *Eumolpus tamquam si adhuc parum instructus dilationem petere coepit, contra Dion ut audiretur exigere. dicta sunt utrimque multa . . .*; 10.81.6 *plurimis diebus.*

200. On the apparent lack of familiarity with Dio, see Swain (2000b, 43), Salmeri (2000, 91 n. 189). On the puzzling nature of the reported encounter between Pliny and Dio, see Billault (2015).

201. For speculation on greater intimacy of Dio with Trajan, including the journey to Dacia, see Jones (1978, 52–3), Salmeri (2000, 89–91): the latter notes Dio's lack of enthusiasm for the Dacian campaign (Salmeri (2000, 86 n. 162)).

202. Philostratus *Vit. Soph.* 1.7.488; cf. Jones (1978, 11), Salmeri (2000, 91 n. 189).

203. Dio, like Plutarch, was ultimately more interested in civil life than literature for its own sake (Salmeri (2000, 61 n. 33)); Pliny stands out for a distinctive interest in modern literary affairs (Chp. 6 n. 83).

204. See Chp. 7 and Jones (1978, 110–11).

205. For parallels between the *Panegyricus* and the kingship orations, see Jones (1978, 116–20), who nevertheless argues against those who have seen references to Pliny in Dio (cf. Moles (1990, 301–2)).

206. On Dio, Prusa, and his lack of interest in Rome, see Salmeri (2000, 55–63, 69); on his lack of knowledge of Roman institutions and his Hellenistic vision of empire, see Salmeri (2000, 89–91). But for the possibility of Dio's engagement with Vergil, see Moles (2017).

207. See Salmeri (2000, 86–8).

208. Cf. *Or.* 48.1–3, Salmeri (2000, 64, 74–6).

209. See Swain (2000b, 45), who criticizes Jones (1978) for somewhat smoothing the matter over.

210. For the difficulties of making such estimates, see Trombley (2006, 306–9) on the figures produced by Stark (1996).

211. See Trevett (2006, 323).

212. See Trombley (2006, 308–9), with reference to Mullen (2004, 83–132).

213. For the early history of Christianity in Asia Minor, see Trevett (2006).

214. For a brief outline of the development of early Christianity and its practices and doctrines, see the Christian-focused account of Snyder (2013) and the Roman-focused account of Fredriksen (2006). The assumption that Pliny encountered the

Christians in Pontus is an inference from the ordering of the letters of Book 10 (see earlier).

215. For a positivistic account of what can be known about Pontic Christian practices from Pliny's description, see Sherwin-White (1966, 702–8); for a more skeptical approach, see Harrill (2006), with reference to earlier literature.

216. The reading that follows of 10.96–7 is greatly indebted to Corke-Webster (2017a), also (2017b).

217. 10.96.8 *nihil aliud . . . quam superstitionem prauam et immodicam*. For elite Roman attitudes to 'acceptable' and 'unacceptable' religion, see Várhelyi (2010, 163–7).

218. The bibliography on these letters is vast, easily matching that on the letters on Pliny's villas and Vesuvius. The foundational items for modern scholarship are Sherwin-White (1952) = (1966, 772–87), (1964); De Ste Croix (1963), (1964); and Barnes (1968). For a selection of recent items on a range of confessional, procedural, and contextual matters, see Muth (1982), Fishwick (1984), Johnson (1988), Williams (1990, 138–44), Reichert (2002), Thraede (2004), Peper and DelColgiano (2006), all with further references. Earlier bibliography is surveyed by Aubrion (1989, 338–40).

219. For an important estimate that, prior to the general grant of citizenship in 212 C.E., only 15 to 33 per cent of the empire's subjects possessed citizenship, see Lavan (2016).

220. For the directive to maintain order in a province, cf. Ulpian *Digest* 1.18.13 pr.

221. See earlier in this chapter and Corke-Webster (2017a, 395).

222. For the rejection of 'silver age' Latin literature in the second and third centuries, see Cameron (2011, 399–420); for the influence of the Second Sophistic on this rejection, see Cameron (2011, 399–400); for the revival of Pliny's *Letters* in the mid-fourth century, see Cameron (2016); for the revival of the *Panegyricus*, see Chp. 5 n. 179.

223. For distortions introduced by the sarcastic denunciations of Tertullian (*Apol.* 2.6–9) and the *Ecclesiastical History* of Eusebius (3.21.1–4.3.1), see Corke-Webster (2017b); cf. Corke-Webster (2017a, 397–404) on the validity and scope of imperial rescripts.

224. For the reflection in Pliny of the Arsinoë situation (*P.Yale* 1.61, 1.5–7: Lewis (1981, 120–1), Horstkotte (1996), Kelly (2011)), see Corke-Webster (2017a, 377–8).

225. See *OLD* s.v. *defero* 9a for the use of the verb to signify 'denounce' in legal contexts, and *OLD* s.v. *tamquam* 7 for the use of the term in contexts of legal and other allegations. See also Reichert (2002, 244).

226. On the likely absence of contemporary legal provisions against Christians, see Corke-Webster (2017a, 380–1), with further references.

227. 10.96.10 [sc. *constat*] *prope iam desolata temple coepisse celebrari . . . passimque uenire <carnem> uictimarum, cuius adhuc rarissimus emptor inueniebatur*. On the emptying of temples as a motive for prosecution, see Sherwin-White (1966, 709); cf. Millar (1973, 152–3) = (2004e, 303–4) on Pliny's concern for the flourishing of cults.

228. On the difficulty of reconstructing the charge against the Christians on the basis of Pliny's text, the absence of any evidence for a standing charge against the sect, and

Pliny's lack of concern with the beliefs of the Christians, see Corke-Webster (2017a, 380–83).

229. See Sherwin-White (1966, 608–9).

230. 10.96.3 *neque enim dubitabam, qualecumque esset quod faterentur, pertinaciam certe et inflexibilem obstinationem debere puniri.*

231. On the assumed connection between impudence and guilt in the Roman courtroom, see Meyer (2016, 279–80); cf. Sherwin-White (1966, 699).

232. 10.96.3 *perseuerantes duci iussi,* 'those who persisted I ordered to be led away', where *duci* is to be understood as 'led away to execution'; cf. Seneca *de Ira* 1.18.3–6, *OLD* s.v. *duco* 4b, Sherwin-White (1966, 698).

233. Corke-Webster (2017a, 383).

234. Pliny's friend Minicius Fundanus would encounter trouble with Christians in Asia around a decade later and receive a reply from Hadrian similar to the one Pliny soon received from Trajan; cf. Justin Martyr *Apol.* 1.68.1–10, Eusebius *Hist. Eccl.* 4.8.6–4.9.3, Corke-Webster (2017a, 399–400). Perhaps Tacitus ran into similar problems during his stint as proconsul also in Asia around 112–13 C.E. (Birley (2000b, 236)).

235. For the fuller argument summarized from here to the end of the chapter, see the excellent Corke-Webster (2017a, 384–97).

236. 10.96.5 *propositus est libellus sine auctore multorum nomina continens.*

237. 10.96.4 *ipso tractatu, ut fieri solet, diffundente se crimine plures species inciderunt;* cf. Johnson (1988, 419–20) on 'denouncers' in Pontus-Bithynia.

238. See Fishwick (1984) on Pliny's test.

239. Corke-Webster (2017a, 385).

240. Cf. Chp. 5 for earlier manifestations in Rome.

241. 10.96.9 *multi enim omnis aetatis, omnis ordinis, utriusque sexus.* On Roman judicial torture, see Pölönen (2004).

242. 10.96.2 *nomen ipsum, si flagitiis careat, an flagitia cohaerentia nomini puniantur.*

243. 2.11.2 *ob innocentes condemnandos, interficiendos etiam, pecunias accepisset.*

244. On the trials of Priscus and Classicus, see Chp. 5 nn. 167–8; cf. Corke-Webster (2017a, 389–93) on the broad context of the exposure of a governor and his reputation to adverse action, including the Priscus and Classicus trials.

245. 10.97.1 *actum quem debuisti, mi Secunde, in excutiendis causis eorum, qui Christiani ad te delati fuerant, secutus es;* 10.97.2 *conquirendi non sunt;* 10.97.2 *sine auctore uero propositi libelli <in> nullo crimine locum habere debent. nam et pessimi exempli nec nostri saeculi est.*

246. On the disinclination to reverse judicial decisions, see Sherwin-White (1966, 637); cf. Corke-Webster (2017a, 393–7) on the context and characteristics of Trajan's response.

247. Cf. Corke-Webster (2017a, 397).

248. Snyder (2013, 192–3). Yet there remains no doubt of the ability of Christianity to touch hearts and minds of all sections of society more deeply than the structures of the Roman empire could; cf. Brown (2000, 490–1).

249. See Trombley (2006, 306–7), with reference to further literature.
250. See Sherwin-White (1966, 694) for further contemporary references to Christianity in Pontus.
251. See Trevett (2006, 314, 318) on the dearth of material evidence and the testimony of Gregory Thaumaturgus.

Envoi

The death of Pliny

Book 10 of the *Letters* ends with the news that Calpurnius Fabatus has died. Calpurnia has been provided by Pliny with official transport passes (*diplomata*) to speed her to Comum (10.120). Trajan replies to confirm that Pliny was correct to act without first requesting permission: 'You were right to feel confidence in my attitude, dearest Secundus' (10.121).[1] To many, this seems an abrupt closure to the book: evidence, no less, of Pliny's death soon after the penning of his final letter.[2] It is observed that Pliny celebrates Trajan's accession day of the 29th of January twice in the course of the book (10.52, 102), and not a third time. Death occurred then around 112 C.E., the year of the dedication of Trajan's magnificent forum, and one year before war with Parthia and the dedication of his column.

Abruptness is a matter of taste and judgement. How could one end correspondence with an emperor?[3] No successor is known for Pliny, at any rate, in Pontus-Bithynia until around 113–14 C.E. This would be Cornutus Tertullus from Perge in Asia, Pliny's colleague in the consulship.[4] Time enough for Pliny to compile Book 10 in the final year of his tenure in the province? What is clear is that Pliny predeceased Trajan: the great Comum inscription implicitly refers to the emperor as still living.[5] Trajan would die in the summer of 117 C.E. at Selinus on the south coast of Turkey en route to Rome after his triumph against the Parthians. His ashes would be buried at the base of his column in Rome.[6] Pliny's testamentary memorial was in Comum. We do not know when, where, or how he met his end. His health was no doubt weakened by two or three years of constant travel. Perhaps he died on the arduous return journey from Bithynia to Italy. Plinys's lifespan of just over fifty years was not a short one, by ancient standards.

Judging Pliny: Cicero, Tacitus, Epictetus, and Augustine

As a senator in the Italy of high empire, Pliny the Younger lived a life rich in personal privilege, political event, and even drama. He has left clear traces in the history of architecture, helped to shape our understanding of early Christianity, and particularly of the traumatic event on the bay of Naples in 79 C.E., and influenced the learned letter-writers of Renaissance and early modern Europe.[7] His *Letters* continue to be read and studied, and have enjoyed a strong literary revival over the last two decades in academic circles.[8] Like most prominent Romans, however, Pliny does not sustain across his life a record to admire. His misleading lack of clarity in connection with his political record at Rome is hardly a biographical high point. The treatment of non-citizens, exemplified in the summary punishment handed out to the Christians of Pontus, surely mocks the personal ideal of eschewing gubernatorial severity and arrogance.

Ancient figures demand our interest, but there are few enough who offer uncomplicated inspiration. Not long after Giovanni de Matociis authored his biographical notice on the Plinii, based on a manuscript of the *Letters* at the cathedral in Verona,[9] Petrarch discovered Cicero's *Letters to Atticus* in the same library in 1345.[10] Joy soon turned to disappointment. The orator and philosopher of the political speeches and philosophical dialogues stands revealed in his correspondence as an 'impulsive and unhappy old man'. Or so Petrarch wrote in a disappointed epistle belatedly addressed to Cicero himself (*Rerum Familiarum* 24.3). A tradition of disillusion with Cicero's weaknesses and failures as a politician and man stretches back to antiquity itself.[11] Had we the *Letters* of Tacitus, he too would disappoint: a more thoroughly compromised record of senatorial ambition would likely be open to view. He can be admired largely thanks to the evasive reticence about self and career that his name encapsulates.[12] Augustine the man can be admired fully only by turning a blind eye to his talent for partisan hostility. 'A man who could go forty-three years from conversion to his grave when one or another polemical work was *not* on his plate', in the estimate an eminent biographer, 'and who can be shown . . . to have picked every fight he got into, must surely be thought to be part of the problem, not part of the solution'.[13]

Perhaps the only figure who might draw full admiration from among the quartet of ancient characters who have accompanied Pliny through this biography is Epictetus.[14] An exact contemporary of Pliny, born into slavery in the Hellenic half of the empire, Epictetus was brought to Rome by Epaphroditus, freedman and former secretary of the emperor Nero. Allowed while still enslaved to attend the lectures of Pliny's acquaintance Musonius Rufus,[15] Epictetus achieved his freedom and became himself a teacher of philosophy in the imperial capital. This was not a society impressed by social mobility, least of all where it involved enslaved Greeks. By the time he suffered banishment under the emperor Domitian, along with all other philosophers then in Rome, Epictetus had evidently achieved enough of a reputation to found a school in exile. He moved to Nicopolis on the west coast of Greece—the city established over a century before by the emperor Augustus to commemorate the defeat of Mark Antony at the battle of Actium. Epictetus' ethical teachings were recorded there and later published by his pupil Arrian. These make for uncomfortable reading at times. They contain 'often severe comments on the inability of more materially fortunate people to handle themselves with dignity and equanimity'; here, suggests a modern commentator, Epictetus' 'slavish origins, chronic ill health, exile and probably precarious income are experiences to keep in mind'.[16] He remained fully convinced of the emptiness of a life of public ambition. Epictetus' teachings also suggest a life devoted to his students, often expressed with a wonderfully dark sense of humour glimpsed occasionally in this biography. Towards the end of his life Epictetus adopted a child that would otherwise have been exposed to die as unwanted, and finally took a partner to help raise the infant.

This is a life to admire. There are very few to parallel it in the ancient world. Yet these bare facts represent almost the entirety that is known about Epictetus the man. We know his world view in great detail, thanks to Arrian's *Discourses*, but lack the narrative framework within which it arose. He evidently declined to publish his own writings. The first half of his life was distinctly challenging. The years of teaching at Nicopolis may not have been very much more exciting in external events than that of a modern academic. The life of Epictetus is not one that gets us quite close enough to circles of Roman power, to a sense of how things worked—or at least fitted together. A senatorial life in high empire is bound to be messy, compromised, and filled up to the brim with its own sense of entitlement. Yet it commands attention. Such is the life of Pliny the Younger.

Pliny's privileged self

It would be ungenerous to leave Pliny there. I return to an issue raised in an earlier chapter. Pliny presents the apparently humane individual who flourishes in Umbria or by the Laurentine shore as his privileged or cherished self. He urges others to join him in the Laurentine experience: 'you too must at the first opportunity abandon this city din, this pointless bustle, these quite foolish toils, and devote yourself to your studies or to leisure' (1.9.7). How are we to respond to the person who devotes time to reading and writing, and rejoices in the absence of urban compromise and grind? 'I hear nothing, I say nothing, which one need be ashamed of hearing or saying ... I censure no one except myself' (1.9.5).[17]

There is some value in taking the Umbrian and Laurentine Pliny seriously—at least for a moment. Pliny has suffered more than most from biographical 'encapsulation', above all at the hands of the master of the art, Sir Ronald Syme. The ten pages that Syme devotes to boiling down Pliny's life to its essence in his 1958 work on Tacitus relish the irony and innuendo of their own capture of the man.[18] Pliny is dismissed as a disingenuous time-server and arch careerist who lacked the integrity that Syme projected onto Tacitus. Pithy judgements of the man become harder to make when other locations in his life are awarded equal space with Rome.[19] Even on his own account, he is not a monolith of *constantia* across all the regions with which he is associated. Each area brings out a distinctively different aspect of his person, at least as he presents it to us. There are overlaps and continuities between the senator in Rome, public man in Comum, and governor of Pontus-Bithynia. Equally there are contrasts between the litterateur of humane interests in Umbria or by the Laurentine shore, and the consul who plays with words in the capital and privileges the interests of the senate over restitution for the provinces, or the official who dispenses harsh and summary justice in Pontus. Comum brings out the solicitous, if rather traditional, husband, and alerts us to the impressive scale of Pliny's civic generosity. Umbria reveals the roots of that wealth in the labour of tenant farmers and enslaved persons, but also highlights Pliny's flexibility in trying to engineer solutions to his problems as a landowner. A religious sensibility, unexpressed in other locations, emerges here too. Rome adds further layers. Not only can we see the popular courtroom orator at work, but we hear Pliny express a covert pessimism about the 'best' of emperors that both anticipates and matches Tacitus. Each locale also displays a different way of 'seeing things'. What Pliny sees in each region is an expression of individuality.[20]

Part of the purpose in scattering Pliny across his venues in this biography has been to avoid standard encapsulations of the man. One influential source for summation of Pliny in Anglophone countries can be traced back to the large number of commentaries on his 'Selected Letters' produced for secondary school pupils. Written in the late nineteenth and early twentieth centuries, many were used right up until a few decades ago. The prefatory material of the select commentaries characteristically includes comment on Pliny *als Mensch* ('as a man').[21] Writing in 1871, Church and Brodribb found that Pliny could not be acquitted of 'excessive vanity and self-consciousness'. In his 1915 edition, G. B. Allen conceded 'a certain vanity and priggishness', alongside 'a tendency to take credit for good actions, a lack of the sterner virtues'. 'Prig'—denoting a self-righteous or self-consciously precise person—becomes a dominant note. The editor of the 1915 Loeb Classical Library edition of Pliny added 'want of humour' to the base provided by priggishness and vanity. In 1937 H. McNeill Poteat moved the summation from introduction to main text by printing letter 9.34 in his edition with the heading 'Priggish affectation, personified'.[22] The last two systematic attempts in English to evaluate Pliny as a man do not escape the tractor-beam of the p-word. Betty Radice and A. N. Sherwin-White did much to advance Pliny's reputation and establish his study at the secondary and tertiary level in Anglophone countries.[23] Even they can only tone down or qualify earlier judgements: Sherwin-White allows 'an accidental appearance of priggishness'; Radice asserts Pliny 'is an intelligent man, sensible, honest and pleasant even when he may seem over-conscientious or a little priggish'.[24]

Prig has long fallen out of use. The essence of the criticism lives on. Such encapsulation produces a one-dimensional Pliny. He is reduced to a single feature of his discourse that in any case needs to be understood within an ancient culture that placed little value on modesty, and allowed very generous leeway to self-praise and the desire to set others an example.[25] There is another Pliny: one represented above all by the Umbrian and Laurentine estates. That a dwelling should be representative and symbolic of its owner was axiomatic in Roman thought.[26] Educated artists of the nineteenth and early twentieth centuries were fully aware of this. They did not produce paintings and drawings of homes fit for a vain and tiresome careerist. Images of both residences produced by K. F. Schinkel and W. Stier, beginning in the 1830s and 40s, engage closely with the details and atmosphere of Pliny's great villa letters.[27] In the estimate of Pierre Du Prey, historian of Pliny's influence on architects and artists, Schinkel's drawings highlight the 'four cardinal characteristics' of the residences: 'to see and be seen; room to breathe; openness and movement; house and garden'. Schinkel responds to the 'easygoing amorphousness' of the Umbrian villa (Fig. 6.4), and captures in his Laurentine plan 'the onrushing, wavelike motion of Pliny's prose' (Fig. 6.3). Stier was directly inspired by the letters to a 'freedom from constraint . . . a certain looseness . . . and a rational lack of orderliness' in his representation of the two residences. Schinkel, Du Prey concludes, 'revealed his understanding of Pliny's innermost aspirations for artistic fulfilment in an inspiring ambience'.[28]

This is heady stuff. The drawings are also the product of artists who spent decades of their lives reading and thinking about Pliny quite as intently as the schoolroom commentators. Schinkel, Stier, and the numerous artists and architects who joined them in the project of imagining the villas were responding to the self that Pliny wanted to privilege in Umbria and the *ager Laurens*. Critics, historians, and biographers of Pliny have been slow to follow the opportunity up, in part because Pliny broadcasts a message about the overriding importance of Comum. This message confuses or discourages a focus on other regions. Artists knew better. Modern drawings of Pliny's residences in Comum are vanishingly rare.[29]

Not every modern artist, however, is so admiring of Pliny or his society as were Schinkel and Stier. Treuttel, Garcias, and Treuttel used their 1982 reconstruction of Pliny's villas to highlight the unjust social base on which his residence and wealth were built.[30] Unlike most artists, they placed the *pars rustica* of the villa in very close proximity to the residential quarters. They added a motto to their drawings, pairing *Otium cum Dignitate* ('leisure with due dignity') and *Labor cum Flagello* ('labour with the whip'). Treuttel, Garcias, and Treuttel point unmistakably towards some shadowy figures who accompany Pliny throughout his life or live alongside him in each of his locales, but who never quite come into focus in Rome, Umbria, Comum or any other location.[31]

Pliny perhaps owned as many as five hundred enslaved persons, not to mention his responsibility for a substantial number of freedmen.[32] Slavery underpinned the life of all citizens of any substance in the early empire, and would continue to do so in Augustine's day. Among the 5 million words that survive from the pen of the African saint, no separate work or sermon is devoted to the topic of slavery. Two recently discovered letters show him dealing with problems of the trade in his diocese (*Ep.* 10*, 24*).[33] Enslaved persons otherwise receive largely incidental attention, as in Pliny.[34] The latter thought he was a humane slave-master by the standards of his day. The reality is beyond recovery. Seneca, often lambasted as a hypocrite, was perhaps more honest in confessing his struggles to live up to his ideals in the restraint of emotions when dealing with enslaved persons (*Ben.* 3.27.2–3, *Ep.* 123.1–2).

A final word

If we were to let a former enslaved person, Epictetus, have the final word on Pliny, he would remind us to take a holistic approach to a person. External events cannot be controlled, he would insist, but internal responses are a different matter. The sphere of what is 'up to us' is our chief concern: individual moral choice in reaction to an external event is key.[35] No room here for a distinction between a man potentially compromised by events at Rome or in Pontus-Bithynia, who yet experiences true human flourishing at a country villa.[36] Pliny, of course, joins the general run of humanity in failing to impress Epictetus.

What do I think of Pliny? It would be unwise to let myself down in front of Epictetus. Nor can I live up to the philosopher's standards. My thoughts return to the answer given two decades ago by Stanley Hoffer, in the epilogue to an important monograph, *The Anxieties of Pliny the Younger*: 'To answer honestly, I should also ask what I think of myself, for modern life, especially academic life, is disconcertingly similar to Pliny's in many ways. Cultivating circles of "friends" and patronage relationships for mutual benefit . . . publishing for symbolic capital, living off the labours of others . . .'[37] To these parallels we might add the experience of living under 'regimes' with whose motivations and operations we might disagree, yet whose decisions we ultimately enact. There are some 'basic distinctions', of course, as Hoffer goes on to point out: Pliny owned hundreds of enslaved persons, and unhesitatingly executed the bothersome in his province. Yet these are perhaps 'essentially the flaws of [Pliny's] position in upper-class society'.[38] A fundamental similarity cannot be denied. If classicists readily criticize Pliny and continue to love Vergil, this is in part because the poet is strange, exotic, unknowable, and was probably not very much like a modern academic. And the sins of Vergil's early advocacy of monarchy and the murderous Julian house as the solution to Rome's

troubles are pardoned, out of consideration for the undoubted genius of his poetry. Pliny is a lesser talent with a vastly better documented life. He is more pettily
compromised, more like us, less readily forgiven.

What remains for *me* is the intense interest of the ancient society that Pliny
records and encapsulates so compellingly. Study of his *Letters* and of the communities and landscapes he inhabits has brought sustained pleasure. The deliberate
and artistic economy of his language, so unusual for Latin prose, has been no
small part of that joy.

Notes

1. 10.121.1 *merito habuisti, Secunde carissime, fiduciam animi mei.*
2. See (e.g.) Sherwin-White (1966, 82), Vidman, *PIR*[2] P 490 (pp. 207–8), Williams
   (1990, 13). For a more open mind on the issue, see Noreña (2007, 270–1), Whitton
   (2011), Gibson and Morello (2012, 270), Woolf (2015, 149).
3. In one minor respect, the Calpurnia letters offer a sense of closure to the collection,
   with their reassertion of a family connection which bulked large in the later books of
   the nine-volume correspondence. The evocation of a Catullan journey home from
   Pontic Amastris (Catull. 4.13) to the lakes of northern Italy also reverses, in thematic
   terms, the journey out to Bithynia (10.15–17b).
4. See Sherwin-White (1966, 82, 84), Birley (2000a, 64).
5. See Chp. 7 for the text of the inscription.
6. See Bennett (2001, 201–4).
7. On Pliny and architecture, see Du Prey (1994); on Christianity and Vesuvius,
   see Chps. 4, 8; for Pliny's influence on Renaissance and early modern culture, see
   Whitton and Gibson (2016, 3–11). Further influences are adumbrated at Gibson and
   Morello (2012, 301–2).
8. Pliny's academic fortunes began to recover with the publication of Ludolph (1997)
   and Hoffer (1999), followed by Castagna and Lefèvre (2003), Morello and Gibson
   (2003), Marchesi (2008), etc.; cf. Whitton and Gibson (2016) for an overview of
   Pliny's critical fortunes.
9. See Chp. 1.
10. See Marsh (2013, 306–7).
11. For the tradition of disappointment with Cicero, e.g. on the issue of self-praise, cf.
    Sen. *Dial.* 10.5.1, Quint. *Inst.* 11.1.17–18, 11.1.15, 22; Plut. *Mor.* 541a, Gibson (2003,
    240–1).
12. Cf. Woodman (2012, 280) on Tacitus' deployment of a unique version of the 'divided
    self' at Tac. *Agr.* 3.2 'survivors not only of the others but even of ourselves' (*non modo
    aliorum sed etiam nostri superstites*): '[Tacitus] was perhaps . . . hoping that his im-
    agistic brilliance would distract attention from the uncomfortable fact that his suc-
    cessful political career . . . would have involved him in constant public speaking as a
    mouthpiece of the administration'; cf. Woodman and Kraus (2014, 90–1).

13. O'Donnell (2005, 110).

14. For the biography and intellectual context of Epictetus, see Dobbin (1998, xi–xxiii), Long (2002, 7–17), also Millar (1965) = (2004d). The latter rightly remarks on the value of Epictetus as a foil to the 'values and aspirations' cherished by Pliny in particular and his society in general.

15. On Musonius Rufus and Pliny, see Chp. 8.

16. Long (2002, 11).

17. 1.9.7 *tu quoque strepitum istum inanemque discursum et multum ineptos labores, ut primum fuerit occasio, relinque teque studiis uel otio trade*; 1.9.5 *nihil audio quod audisse, nihil dico quod dixisse paeniteat . . . neminem ipse reprehendo, nisi tamen me.*

18. See Syme (1958, 75–85). Syme's gift for biographical encapsulation is evident in papers on Plinian associates (e.g. (1969) = *RP* 2.742–73 on the Elder Pliny; *RP* 7.603–19 on Minicius Fundanus), quite as much as in brief asides in the grand manner of a Victorian novelist: e.g. 'From the overvalued Calestrius Tiro, it will be a relief to turn briefly to half a dozen consuls . . .' (*RP* 7.566). For Syme, Pliny, and Tacitus, see Chps. 1 n. 21, 7 n. 47, 8 n. 84.

19. Pliny hardly avoids encapsulating others, above all in his obituary letters, e.g. 1.12 (Corellius Rufus), 2.1 (Verginius Rufus), 3.5 (the Elder Pliny), 3.7 (Silius Italicus), 3.21 (Martial).

20. On vision and individuality, see Spencer (2010, 6–8).

21. On the age of selected letters in Plinian scholarship, see Whitton and Gibson (2016, 12–13, 19). For the nineteenth-century tradition of evaluating the author *als Mensch*, see Beard (2002, 115).

22. The quoted judgements from commentators are taken from: Church and Brodribb (1871, xiv), Allen (1915, 6), Hutchinson (1915, I.xv), and McNeill Poteat (1937); cf. Prichard and Bernard (1872, 6–8), Mayor (1880, 4), Duff (1906, xix–xx). Most commentators produce positive judgements to balance the negative: e.g. Allen (1915, 6), 'these defects are easily excused when compared with the sincerity, the kindness, the invariable good temper and good taste, the consideration for other people'; cf. Cowan (1889, xxvi–xxvii), Merrill (1903, xxxv). On 'want of humour', a response was forthcoming from Thompson (1942), who also took on McNeill Poteat's judgement. The age of such prefatory assessments has passed: Pliny's latest commentator, Whitton (2013), offers no character judgements of any sort.

23. For the contributions of Radice and Sherwin-White to the study of Pliny, see Whitton and Gibson (2016, 16–19).

24. See Sherwin-White (1969, 84), Radice (1975, 121). Sherwin-White adds, charmingly: 'We see his weaknesses as a man, and some of his weaknesses are the unpopular ones' (1969, 89–90).

25. See Gibson (2003); cf. Fitzgerald (2018) on how Pliny negotiates a world filled with various forms of insincerity.

26. See Bodel (1997, 5–6, 13) on Sen. *Ep.* 12.1, 86; Henderson (2003, 120–4); Leach (2003, 154) on Cic. *Off.* 1.138–4; Myers (2005, 105–6) on Cato *Agr.* 4.45; cf. Métraux (2014) for an overview.

27. For Schinkel's drawings of the Umbrian villa: see Du Prey (1994, 14–15, 20–1, 33–4, 108–12, 289–90, 292–3); of the Laurentine villa: see Du Prey (1994, 14–15, 26–7, 39, 108–9, 113–14, 118–19, 289–90). For Stier's drawings of the Umbrian: see Du Prey (1994, 205–11); of the Laurentine: see Du Prey (1994, 196, 198–205).

28. See Du Prey (1994, 14, 21, 27, 210, 288).

29. For a rare drawing of a Comum villa, see Du Prey (1994, 7).

30. See Du Prey (1994, 227–31).

31. Even the freedmen of Comum achieve prominence through inscriptional record rather in than the *Letters*; see Chps. 6 and 7 for some further details on Pliny's slaves and freedmen.

32. For an estimate of the total number of enslaved persons owned by Pliny, see Duncan-Jones (1982, 24–5) = (2016, 96–7).

33. For a very brief overview of Augustine on slavery, see Mary (1954); on slavery in *Ep.* 10*, 24*, see McLynn (2012, 317–18).

34. Cf. e.g. 1.4, 1.21, 3.14, 3.19, 4.10, 5.19, 6.28, 7.16, 7.29, 7.32, 8.1, 8.6, 8.14, 8.16, 8.19, 9.21, 9.24, 10.19, 10.31, 10.65, 10.74, 10.96. On further aspects of slavery in Pliny, see Yuge (1986), Bonelli (1994), Hoffer (1999, 45–52), Gonzalès (2003, 109–249), Carlon (2009, 119–21), Lefèvre (2009, 181–94), Williams (2006).

35. For Epictetus on what 'is up to us' and moral choice, see Dobbin (1998, 65–78) on Arr. Epict. *diss.* 1.1.

36. The picture of unsullied life at the Laurentine may look a little more tarnished, in any case, when set against political events in the years preceding the ostensible composition date of 97 C.E. for 1.9; see Hoffer (1999, 111–18).

37. Hoffer (1999, 227).

38. Hoffer (1999, 227).

APPENDIX 1

Timeline

Events during Pliny's lifetime are catalogued in what follows, with some artificiality, according to three categories: major political events; events in Pliny's life and career; and events in Pliny's 'circle' (very broadly conceived). Many dates are necessarily provisional.

Dates from 96 C.E. onwards can be read against the broad time periods covered by the individual books of Pliny's letters—although establishing these dates raises problems of methodology. In the ancient world, official or contractual letters are usually dated, but private letters often are not (White (1986, 5–8)). Cicero is the only major exception to the latter tendency (White (2010, 75–6)); cf. Sarri (2017, 121–2) on the gradual disappearance of dates even from private letters preserved on papyri. No Plinian letter carries a formal date, not even the correspondence with Trajan in Book 10. Nevertheless, a minority of letters within each book offer rough indications of apparent date of initial composition. It is an assumption that these letters establish broad parameters for the remaining items in a book (Gibson and Morello (2012, 19–20, 51–2)), although the further assumption that Pliny revised his letters before publication, perhaps even wrote a proportion as independent literary artefacts, introduces a significant degree of uncertainty. Letters in Books 1–9, nevertheless, appear to exhibit a chronological progression across the collection as a whole, although not within individual books (except where Pliny is narrating the same event across two or more letters). Book 10 alone—which seems to follow seamlessly in time from Book 9—may preserve an internal chronological ordering.

Bearing these difficulties in mind, the generally accepted dates for Pliny's individual books must remain provisional: Book 1 (97–8); 2 (97–100); 3 (101–2); 4 (103–5); 5 (105–6); 6 (106–7); 7 (107); 8 (107–9); 9 (107–9); 10 (109/10–111/12). On principles and problems in the dating of the letters, see further Sherwin-White (1966, 27–41), Syme (1958, 660–4), (1985b) = RP 5.478–89. As for publication, Bodel (2015) speculates that Pliny began circulating individual books in instalments from c. 100 C.E. onwards, with a (revised?) edition of the first four books, accompanied by a new fifth book, issued c. 106–7. Books 6–8 then followed in 108–9, with Book 9 compiled before departure for Pontus-Bithynia c. 110. Earlier accounts assume a publication date of no earlier than 106 for the first instalments of Pliny's letters; see Gibson and Morello (2012, 19 n. 42).

Particular uncertainty or controversy over dating is marked by the use of 'c.' or '?'. The question-mark sign is not used to query matters of fact. P. = Pliny the Younger.

DATE		EVENTS	
Approx. Year	Political	In Pliny's Life	In Pliny's 'Circle'
c. 58	Nero emperor since 54.		Birth of Tacitus; Elder Pliny finishes last in series of military tours in Germany: meets future emperor Titus (?).

DATE		EVENTS	
Approx. Year	Political	In Pliny's Life	In Pliny's 'Circle'
61–2		Birth of P.	
68–9	Death of Nero (68); civil war, brief reigns of Galba, Otho, and Vitellius (68–9), accession of Vespasian (69).		Ambiguous role of Verginius Rufus during insurrection against Nero in 68; Silius Italicus consul in 68 and Verginius consul in 69.
c. 70			Birth of Suetonius
Before 76		Death of P.'s father; appointment of Verginius Rufus as P.'s guardian; P. dedicates temple of imperial cult in Comum (before 79).	Elder Pliny holds series of equestrian procuratorships, including Hispania Tarraconensis (73–4?); 'dramatic' date of Tacitus' *Dialogus* (c. 75).
c. 77		P. studying in Rome with Quintilian.	Elder Pliny's *Natural History* finished; Corellius Rufus consul (78).
79	Accession of Titus.	Probable testamentary adoption of P. by Elder Pliny.	Death of Elder Pliny during eruption of Vesuvius while commanding fleet at Misenum.
80–81	Great plague in Rome (80); accession of Domitian (81).	P. receives *latus clauus*; first appears in court as advocate (for Iunius Pastor?); coopted as *patronus* of Tifernum Tiberinum; marries for first time?	Tacitus *quaestor Augusti* (81?).
c. 82		P. appointed *decemvir stlitibis iudicandis* (?).	
c. 84–7	Dacian war (85–8).	P. *tribunus militum* in Syria for one, two, or three years.	Tacitus *tribunus plebis* (85?); Martial begins to publish epigrams (86).
c. 87–8	Domitian celebrates centenary of secular games (88).	P. *seuir equitum Romanorum*.	Tacitus praetor (88).
c. 89	Domitian proclaims edict against philosophers.	P. enters senate as *quaestor Augusti* either now or in 90, alongside Calestrius Tiro.	

DATE		EVENTS	
Approx. Year	Political	In Pliny's Life	In Pliny's 'Circle'
91–2	Domitian on campaign along the Danube (92).	P. *tribunus plebis* either in 91 or in 92.	Publication of *Thebaid* of Statius (91–2).
93–4	Trials of Baebius Massa, then of members of the 'Stoic opposition': Herennius Senecio, Helvidius Priscus, Arulenus Rusticus; Domitian expels philosophers from Rome.	P. praetor either in 93 or in 94; in tandem with Herennius Senecio, P. undertakes public prosecution of Baebius Massa.	Statius begins to publish *Siluae*.
94–6	Domitian expels philosophers from Italy (94/95?).	P. *praefectus aerari militaris*, either 94–6 or 95–7 (?).	Publication of Quintilian's *Institutio Oratoria* (95–6?).
96	Assassination of Domitian (Sept. 96); accession of Nerva.	Probable date of earliest *Letters*; death of P.'s wife (daughter of Pompeia Celerina) now or in 97.	Deaths of Statius and Quintilian (?).
97	Increasing unrest with Nerva; riot of Praetorian guard, adoption of Trajan (Oct.?).	P. attempts prosecution of Publicius Certus; dedicates library and announces alimentary scheme in Comum; marries Calpurnia now or in 98 (?); suffers serious illness.	Verginius Rufus consul for third time, but dies the same year; Tacitus consul at time of funeral (Nov.?); Vestricius Spurinna governor of Germania Inferior; suicide of Corellius Rufus (?).
98	Death of Nerva (Jan. 98); accession of Trajan.	P. *praefectus aerari Saturni* with Cornutus Tertullus, for two years (?); gains *ius trium liberorum* from Trajan; in tandem with Tacitus begins lengthy public prosecution of Marius Priscus.	Vestricius Spurinna consul for second time; Tacitus publishes *Agricola* and *Germania* (?); Martial leaves Rome.
c. 99	Trajan finally enters Rome as emperor (autumn).	P. undertakes public prosecution of Caecilius Classicus on behalf of province of Baetica; his estates near Tifernum suffer from series of poor harvests (98–9).	

DATE		EVENTS	
Approx. Year	Political	In Pliny's Life	In Pliny's 'Circle'
100	Trajan *consul ordinarius*.	P. *consul suffectus* with Cornutus Tertullus (Sept.–Oct.); publishes *Panegyricus* (?).	Iulius Frontinus consul for second time.
101			Death of Silius Italicus (?).
102	First Dacian war (begins 101): Trajan absent from Rome.	P. undertakes defence of Iulius Bassus, governor of Pontus-Bithynia, in the senate.	Tacitus publishes *Dialogus* (?); Martial's last book of epigrams.
c. 103		P. finally achieves co-option as augur in succession to Iulius Frontinus.	
104–6	Second Dacian war 105–6: Trajan again absent from Rome until early 107.	P. *curator aluei Tiberis et riparum et cloacarum urbis*; builds temple of imperial cult in Tifernum (c. 104).	Tacitus returns to Rome (104/105) possibly after governing consular province; death of Regulus (105?).
106–7		P. undertakes defence of Varenus Rufus, governor of Pontus-Bithynia in the senate, and acts for Attia Viriola in the Centumviral court.	
108–9		Further poor harvests at Pliny's Tifernum estates (?).	Tacitus publishes *Histories* (?).
109/10– 111/12	Dedication of Trajan's forum (112).	P. governor of Pontus-Bithynia.	Tacitus governor of Asia (112–13).
113	Parthian war; dedication of Trajan's column.	Death of Pliny? Testamentary donations to Comum, including baths.	
115			Tacitus writing the *Annals*.
117	Death of Trajan; accession of Hadrian.		

Guide to Pliny's Italy and Bithynia

Visits to literary locations have a history in Anglophone cultures (Booth (2016, 1–58)) that is nearly as long as attempts to raise theoretical objections against the practice (Watson (2006)). Any attempt to follow in Pliny's footsteps risks the accusation of taking literally what may be literary metaphor. No one has yet argued that Pliny never travelled to Pontus-Bithynia, in the way that critics once took seriously the idea that Ovid's exile to the Black Sea was a poet's metaphor for alienation from Rome (Woolf (2015, 144)). Some believe Pliny's villas are largely works of fiction, exercises in the construction of the Plinian self (Bergmann (1995, 407–10) = (2016, 203–7))—no matter what the brick stamps marked CPCS found on the Campo di Santa Fiora in Umbria might suggest. As in the case of Pliny's elegiac sojourn on a Mediterranean isle (7.4.3), I think that the *Letters* do two things simultaneously here: they both suggest the data of Pliny's life *and* use that data as a metaphor. *Letters* 1.4.1 mentions travel through Ocriculum, Narnia, Carsulae, and Perusia in what looks like a route to the Umbrian villa. Equally the same passage might represent a retracing of the scenes of military action that brought the Flavian house to power in 69 C.E. (Hoffer (1999, 52–3)). The political metaphor enriches rather than negates the literal journey. The literal is privileged in this brief 'guide' to Pliny's Italy and Bithynia.

On the perennial problem of reconciling archaeological remains with ancient written accounts of the same sites, see Hall (2014). For orienting maps of the sites discussed in what follows, see Maps 1, 2.

Comum and lake Como

See Roncaglia (2018) for a history of northern Italy from the bronze age to late antiquity. For a map of relevant Roman finds in Como, see Map 3. There are excellent guides to the Como archaeological museum by De Agostini (2006) and to its epigraphical collection by Sartori (1994).

Museo Archeologico, Como

The extensive museum is housed in Palazzo P. Giovio at Piazza Medaglie d' Oro 1 in the old town. Most of the Comum inscriptions mentioned in Chapters 3 and 7 are currently housed in a series of rooms on the ground floor, near the ticket office. Further finds relating to the Comum of Pliny's era are held in the 'Sezione romana' of the main museum. These include four finely decorated marble bases discovered in 1971 on the junction between viale Varese and via 5 Giornate (De Agostini (2006, 56–8), Luraschi (1999d, 463–4, 497–500), Scarfi (1993)). Originally designed to support pillars or the columns of a colonnade, these marble bases and their sculpted reliefs might provide suitable decoration for a library or a gymnasium. The proximity of the possible site of Pliny's library on viale Varese is no more than suggestive, however, and the marble bases may be of a later date.

Roman Como

Library: excavations in 1999 immediately to the west of Como's old town, on the junction between viale Varese and via Benzi, turned up a suburban quarter of around 6,000 square metres, bisected by an ancient suburban road connecting the centre of Comum with the main road to north and south. The findings have all now been reburied in the vicinity of the local government offices of the Regione Lombardia. Three separate complexes were uncovered at the site: a cemetery plot, an impressively large public building, and a smaller building that was either a wayside inn or, more racily, a brothel. The public building is square-shaped, with sides of 66 metres, and equipped with porticoes around an internal courtyard of 46 x 46 metres. It was initially thought this might building might be a candidate for Pliny's library, but it is now generally dated to the later second century C.E. Only the foundations beneath floor level remain. The structure might well represent the headquarters of a local guild (*collegium*) or a temple of the imperial cult; see De Agostini (2006, 27–8, 45–8), Caporusso (2002) and, in more detail, Caporusso (2000), *Extra Moenia I* (2004). The later second century complex was built over an earlier structure containing a portico and central apse (Sacchi (2013, 158, 161–5)). This older building remains a candidate for Pliny's library.

Baths: a large bath complex, immediately to the east of Como's old town, was first discovered in 1971 between viale Lecco and via Dante. It was not fully excavated until 2006–8 (Jorio (2011)). Extensive ruins, which represent only the lower service-floor of the magnificent original complex, are today tastefully preserved underneath a raised modern building within sight of the town's cathedral. They appear to date from the second half of the first century C.E. to around the end of the third century C.E. Nothing remains to connect the baths with an identified public benefactor. If these are the baths mentioned in Pliny's will (see Chp. 7), then he is to be associated with the second phase of building in the complex, that is his contribution was to a pre-existing structure (Jorio (2011, 52)). Possible traces of another set of baths were found in the garden of the archaeological museum in Como (De Agostini (2006, 45), Luraschi (1999d, 470)).

Suburban villa: a villa was discovered in the environs of Como in 1975, a short but steep walk up the lower slopes of the Brunate ridge to the immediate east of the town, at the intersection between via Zezio and via T. Grossi. The excavations are partially visible in the grounds of a primary school. Dating to the end of the first century C.E., the villa occupied three levels on the slopes, including working or residential buildings and, on a higher level, a covered portico (De Agostini (2006, 49–52), Luraschi (1999f, 543–60)). Well situated in antiquity to offer a good view of the lake, the residence's position offers both relief from summer heat and shelter from the winter winds on the lake: one step below the eternal springtime of the villa of Caninius Rufus (1.3; see Chp. 7). There is nothing to connect the via Zezio villa directly with the one belonging to Caninius Rufus, although there are parallels with Pliny's description.

Lake Como

Comedy and Tragedy: despite a long history of investigation (Allain (1901–2, III.vii–xvii, lxxxvii–cii, 505–16); Du Prey (1994, 3–14)), the sites of Pliny's villas on Lake Como (9.7) have never been convincingly identified (Gibson and Morello (2012, 210–11)).

A tradition going back to Benedetto Giovio, author of the inscriptions underneath the statues of the Plinii in Como, locates Tragedy on the high promontory above Bellagio, in the grounds of the modern Villa Serbelloni Gardens (guided tours available) and Comedy on the curving shore of the village of Lenno on the western side of the lower left fork of the lake (Map 1 inset A; Gibson and Morello (2012, 200–1), Giovio (1982, 232–3)). Lenno is clearly visible from the grounds of the villa gardens. For B. Giovio and his archaeological researches around lake Como, see Zimmerman (1995, 4–5, 291–2 n. 9); for the strong association also of his brother P. Giovio with Plinian 'sites' on the lake, see Du Prey (1994 5–6), Zimmerman (1995, 161, 188–9), Lauterbach (1996, 132–6).

Fons Plinianus: the miraculous spring mentioned in 4.30 (Du Prey (1994, 6)) is preserved in the grounds of the modern Villa Pliniana, now a luxury hotel, near Torno on lake Como (Map 1 inset A).

Umbria

Syme (2016, 272–336) provides an engaging evocation of the Roman history and topography of the region, with bibliographical updates provided by his editor F. Santangelo at Syme (2016, 378–82). A fuller picture, with emphasis on the period up to Augustus, is offered by Harris (1971) and Bradley (2000). (The information on the Umbrian villa below is lightly adapted from Gibson and Morello (2012, 228–30).)

The route to the Umbrian villa

The evidence, such as it is, for Pliny's route to the Umbrian villa is reviewed by Sherwin-White (1966, 92–3, 456). The various branches of the via Flaminia are surveyed by Syme (2016, 282–9), with bibliographical updates from his editor F. Santangelo at Syme (2016, 379). For orientation, see Map 1.

Hints that Lake Vadimon and Ameria (8.20) are new to Pliny suggest that he perhaps did not habitually take the via Amerina via Tuder (modern Todi) to the Umbrian villa, but preferred the via Flaminia; cf. 1.4.1 (cited in Chp. 6). This road left the Tiber valley on its journey north from the capital at Ocriculum (Otricoli) and climbed steadily upwards to the spectacular hilltop town of Narnia (Narni), ancestral home of the emperor Nerva and site of a famous Augustan bridge that joined the two heights of the town (Mart. 7.93). After Narnia the via Flaminia split into two parallel branches. The more easterly branch took the traveller down past the valley town of Interamna Nahars (Terni), up once more into the foothills of the Apeninnes, and across to the hill-town of Spoletium (Spoleto). The journey becomes easier thereafter with the descent of the road onto the long valley floor, past the source of the Clitumnus river and Hispellum (Spello) on the valley's eastern side. There are clues that Pliny may have more routinely travelled on the western branch of the via Flaminia that took him past Carsulae (near San Gemini), since 8.8 implies a belated first visit by Pliny to the source of the Clitumnus. This westerly route was the old military road which stuck more consistently to high ground after crossing the valley north of Narnia. It joined the other branch of the via Flaminia just below Hispellum. Pliny left the via Flaminia just before Hispellum and travelled northwards towards Perusia. After Perusia the Tiber valley narrows markedly, before widening again beyond Tifernum Tiberinum.

Umbrian villa and museum near San Giustino

The likely site of Pliny's Tifernum villa lies north of Città di Castello in the area of the Comune di San Giustino, next to the hamlet of Pitigliano on a site including a large raised area known until the nineteenth century simply as 'Colle' (Braconi (1999b, 22), Du Prey (1994, 74–7)), and fields a little below known locally as the Campo di Santa Fiora (see Figs. 6.1, 6.2; Braconi (2001)). Initial archaeological findings at the site were given authoritative publication in 1999 under the editorship of Paolo Braconi and José Uroz Saéz (summarized in English by Marzano (2007, 110–14, 150–1, 736–7)). Over fifty roof tiles and other masonry bearing Pliny's initials (CPCS) were uncovered on the Campo di Santa Fiora (Uroz Sáez (1999a)); around one hundred more would be added to this total in the final phase of the excavations which lasted into the early years of the new century (Uroz Sáez (2008)).

Buildings belonging largely to the agricultural and productive part of the villa were uncovered at first, mostly in a very poor state of preservation (Braconi (1999b, 24–36)). By the 1970s agricultural activity had drastically lowered the level of the site, apparently destroying much that had been preserved into the twentieth century; the remains that may be seen there today are mostly from beneath the ancient floor level (Braconi (1999a, 20), (1999b, 23–4)). Later work revealed a further substantial structure in front of the previous excavations a little further down the incline, apparently a temple and portico complex—probably that described by Pliny in 9.39 (Braconi and Uroz Sáez (2001), Braconi and Uroz Sáez (2008, 114–17)). From the excavations, it is clear that the part of Pliny's estate which has been discovered is the *pars rustica*. The residential part of the villa, the *pars urbana*, in all likelihood lies further up the slope on top of Colle Plinio, inside the grounds of the magnificent walled estate belonging to the Marchesi Cappelletti (Fig. 6.2; Braconi and Uroz Sáez (2008)). But of excavation inside these walls, where local oral tradition insists on the existence of underground remains (Braconi and Uroz Sáez (2001, 216 n. 12), Braconi and Uroz Sáez (2008, 106)), there is no realistic possibility.

The Museo della Villa di Plinio in Tuscis is hosted at the Villa Magherini Graziani in the nearby village of Celalba. It contains finds from the site and reconstructions of the estate in its setting in the upper Tiber valley. The museum is usually open at the weekend, but it is advisable to make contact before visiting.

Clitumnus/Le fonti del Clitunno

The source of the river Clitumnus, described by Pliny in 8.8, is situated between Spoleto and Trevi, next to Campello sul Clitunno. The site is privately owned, but open to the public. The current atmospheric layout (Fig. 6.5), including the plantations of trees, is largely a nineteenth century creation. The force of the flow of the water has been much reduced since antiquity by successive earthquakes. Gilbert Highet offers an evocative account of a visit in the 1950s, when the site was not formally open (Highet (1957, 95–102)).

The small temple (Tempietto del Clitunno) which lies less than a kilometre north along the road from the Fonti is *not* that mentioned by Pliny as originally housing the cult statute of Clitumnus himself (8.8.2–6: quoted in Chp. 6). Despite the impressively classical appearance of the structure, itself partly the product of the re-use by its builders of Roman columns and entablatures, this is in fact a church built in the sixth or seventh centuries during an early classicizing phase in the region; see Emerick (2014).

Vadimon/Lago Vadimone

Lake Vadimon lies on the west bank of the Tiber, just over the border from Umbria (Map 1). Greatly reduced since antiquity, this 'lake' is perhaps the hardest to find and least rewarding of all Plinian sites. It lies in the Tiber valley between Attigliano and Orte, immediately west of a small train station: Stazione di Bassano in Teverina. Navigation to the site is best made by use of Google Earth/Maps or similar. See Sherwin-White (1966, 471–3), Saylor (1982), Ash (2018, 129–40, 143–4) on the historical traditions surrounding the lake and the literary techniques Pliny uses to describe it in 8.20.

Rome and environs
Esquiline and Forum Romanum

Alone among his major residences, Pliny's home on the Esquiline receives no description of either layout or prospect. He mentions it only once (3.21.5), although it features also as the implied point of departure for short journeys in the city (e.g. 1.5.8, 5.9.1, 8.21.2–3). The house was presumably the scene also for various literary recitals to friends (Johnson (2010, 47–8); cf. Chp. 5). It was no doubt unwise to lavish too much attention on one's house in Rome; better to avoid any hint of competition with the current occupant of the Palatine hill and to concentrate on country villas (Bodel (1997, 7, 18–20, 31–2), Woodman and Martin (1996, 127)).

Thanks to Martial 10.20 (discussed in Chp. 5) and the survival of the relevant portion of the Severan marble plan of Rome, Pliny's house can be located with some confidence immediately to the east of the Porticus Liviae in a large *domus* (V 607) in the vicinity of the modern Piazza S. Martino ai Monti (Rodríguez Almeida (1987, esp. 421–3), Carandini (2017, I.331, II.tab. 126 n .27)). The enormous baths of Trajan, which Pliny never mentions, were less than 200 metres from his house.

The Curia Iulia and Basilica Iulia, scenes of Pliny's actions in senate and courtroom, lay in the Forum Romanum, less than a mile downhill from the Esquiline house. For overviews of the early imperial Forum Romanum see Coarelli (2007, 43–101), Carandini (2017, I.168–78, II.tab. 40, 41, 269).

Laurentine villa

This stretch of coast has been subject to repeated excavation for almost three centuries. Visiting a possible site for Pliny's villa in the late eighteenth century, the Polish Count Potocki remarked, 'These ruins were already altogether neglected and are now underground for the second time. What exists of them is better suited to mark the location of the house than to give the slightest idea about it' (Miziotek (2016, 73)). In 1838, the French architect L. P. Haudebourt encountered in the area 'such confusion among the debris' of previous excavations that he judged it 'fruitless' to attempt to restore Pliny's villa (Haudebourt (1838, 60–61)).

Pliny's reference to two roads that can be taken towards the coast (2.17.2) narrows the location of his villa to a particular stretch of the shore road running south of Ostia (Ricotti (1984, fig. 3), Lauro and Claridge (1998, 40: fold out Plate 1); cf. Map 1 in this volume). A reference in the same letter to a village said to be within one house of Pliny's own villa (2.17.26) appears to specify a settlement known to contemporaries as the *uicus Augustanus* or *uicus Laurentium* (Ricotti (1987, 123)). Modern excavation has focused on two sites just to the north and south of the ancient village. The first is the 'villa di Plinio' (also known as 'la Palombara'), open to the public in the Castelfusano estate. Surveys have yielded no links with Pliny (Ramieri (1995), de Franceschini (2005, 260–4), Buonaguro, Camardo, and Saviane (2012), Camardo, Buonaguro, Civitelli, and Saviane (2012), Gibson and Morello (2012, 230–1)). The second is the 'Villa Magna' in the vicinity of Grotte di Piastra inside the presidential estate of Castelporziano. The 'discovery' of Pliny's Laurentine villa at this site was announced to the Anglophone world by Ricotti (1987, 182–4); cf. excavation reports, based on modest digs: Ricotti (1983 [non vidi], 1984, 1985, 1988). Aside from the problem of the dates of what has been excavated (Lauro and Claridge (1998, 47)), the contrast between the fulsome reconstructions of Ricotti (e.g. (1985, fig. 2)), and the map produced by Lauro and Claridge (1988, 45 fig. 11) of exiguous actual discoveries, tells its own story; cf. de Franceschini (2005, 265–7).

For a summary in English of excavations along this stretch of coast as whole, see Marzano (2007, 306–9, 312–29); cf. the project report on 'The evolution of Rome's maritime façade' (H. Rendell and A. Claridge) maintained by the Archaeology Data Service (http://archaeologydataservice.ac.uk: accessed November 2018).

Alsium/Ladispoli

In 6.10 Pliny records a visit to Alsium on the coast north of Rome (Map 1)—former home of his deceased guardian Verginius Rufus, before ownership passed to his mother-in-law Pompeia Celerina. Alsium lies today in the vicinity of the modern villages of Ladispoli, Palo, and Marina di S. Nicola. In ancient times the site accommodated the villas of Rome's elite (Cic. *Mil.* 54, *Fam.* 9.6.1, *Att.* 13.50), including a residence of Marcus Aurelius, where the emperor received letters from Fronto (*de Feriis Alsiensibus*); see Marzano (2007, 8, 388–9, 419–21) for extensive known villa sites in the area.

Centum Cellae/Civitavecchia

In 6.31 Pliny tells of his summons to serve on a council of assessors at the imperial villa overlooking the new port of Centum Cellae (Civitavecchia), some miles north of Alsium (Map 1). Pliny's description of the port acts as a metaphor for the bulwark provided by Trajan (Saylor (1972)); he draws heavily on a passage from *Aeneid* 1 in his description of the harbour (Guillemin (1929, 118)). His report also corresponds well to modern reconstructions of the Trajanic harbour (Marconi (1998, 202–3)): eighteenth century drawings show a port with a breakwater and two moles at the harbour entrance recognizable from Pliny's description. The modern port is much changed, not least on account of action during the Second World War; but the modern structures have been built directly over the ancient (Marconi (1998, 201–3)). For a helpful diagram showing the relation between the ancient and modern structures, see Bastianelli (1954, 38); cf. also the analysis of Caruso (1998, 35–7). Begun around 107 C.E., the port would host a detachment of the western imperial fleet at Misenum governed some decades before by the Elder Pliny. It is the first deep water harbour on the coast north of Rome after the Trajanic Portus itself at the mouth of the Tiber (Rice (2018, 210–13)). Its importance to Trajan is signalled by the presence of baths, an aqueduct, and the extension of the via Aurelia (Marconi (1998, 203–5), Caruso (1998, 35)).

An earlier generation of excavators identified Trajan's villa at Centum Cellae with a site on the Belvedere hill, about 1 kilometre inland near the Capuchin monastery in Civitavecchia (Bastianelli (1954, 60–1, fig. 5)). However, it is clear from Pliny's own words that it looked directly over the harbour (6.31.15). More likely it lies somewhere in the vicinity of the modern duomo di S. Francesco, directly above the port (Marconi (1998, 197–201)). The name Centum Cellae probably refers to the presence in the area of many scattered 'cells' or (poor man's) 'cubicles' (Marconi (1998, 208–9)).

Bay of Naples

For a useful general overview of Roman archaeology of the bay of Naples, see Keppie (2009). A blog maintained by P. Foss (https://quemdixerechaos.com: accessed Nov. 2018) offers an excellent guide to the landscape and archaeology of Pliny's Vesuvius letters. Foss (f'coming) will provide an authoritative account of a full range of topics relating to the Plinii and the Vesuvian eruption. For general orientation, see Map 1 inset B.

Cape Misenum/Miseno

Misenum is at the northern tip of the bay of Naples. The plateau on top of cape Miseno can be reached by path on the seaward side, from via del Faro. On clear days, Vesuvius and the whole of the bay of Naples are visible to the east. It was from here that the Elder Pliny first had proper sight of the eruption cloud. Few traces of buildings have been found on the plateau (Keppie (2009, 60)). Immediately to the northwest can be seen lago Miseno ('Mare Morto'); see Figure 4.2. The lagoon formed the inner harbour that was home to the western imperial fleet commanded by the Elder Pliny (D'Arms (1970, 80–82, 136–7) = (2003, 85–7, 135)). Nothing remains of the harbour other than the huge underground reservoir which provided the large contingent of sailors with water. This reservoir, a central feature of Robert Harris' 2003 novel *Pompeii*, is located on via Piscina Mirabile in Bacoli. The admiral's residence lay on the low ground immediately to the north of cape Miseno, perhaps near the *sacellum* of the *Augustales* on via Sacello di Miseno (Chp. 4 n. 17). Pliny the Younger and his mother appear to have fled Misenum along the route of via Lido Miliscola towards Monte di Procida, rather than through Bacoli towards the high ground above Baiae (Chp. 4 n. 97); see Figure 4.2.

Stabiae/Castellammare di Stabia

The Elder Pliny took shelter in a villa at Stabiae at the southern end of the bay of Naples during the eruption, and later died on the beach while waiting for escape by sea. Castellammare di Stabia sits on what is effectively the ancient beach, while ancient Stabiae itself was situated along the edge of the Varano hill, just above the modern town; see Figure 4.3. Stabiae was in reality a collection of luxury villas strung out across the low cliff, placed there in order to take advantage of the views across the bay. The entrance to two impressive villas, Villa Arianna and Villa San Marco, can be found on via Passeggiata Archeologica on Varano hill, with views to Vesuvius immediately north. On the villas and their owners, see Zarmakoupi (2014, 54–74), Howe (2018), with maps at Zarmakoupi (2014, 56), Howe (2018, 98); on ancient Stabiae and its recovery, see Camardo and Ferrara (2001) and the essays in *In Stabiano* (2004).

Bithynia

For general orientation, see Map 2. Distances by modern road from Istanbul: Izmit/ Kocaeli (64 miles/104 kilometres); Iznik (86 miles/140 kilometres); and Bursa (95 miles/ 154 kilometres).

Nicomedia /Izmit /Kocaeli

Remains of the beautiful ancient city of Nicomedia are few and somewhat scattered in modern Izmit/Kocaeli. The Archaeological and Ethnographical museum and its extensive gardens, located on İstasyon Caddesi in the Kozlu area of the town, have significant holdings, particularly in ancient statuary, building materials, inscriptions, sarcophagi, glassware, and jewellery. For imperial Nicomedia, see Madsen (2009), Bekker-Nielsen (2008); cf. Marek (2003). Lake Sapanca, which Pliny planned to connect to Nicomedia by canal, is located 18 miles/29 kilometres to the east of the modern town.

Nicaea/Iznik

A rather isolated and atmospheric lakeside town, Iznik contains extensive and impressive ancient remains. The Hellenistic grid pattern of the streets largely survives. The walls which still encircle the town belong to the later second and early third centuries C.E., although the city gates preserve earlier material (see Fig. 8.1), including, apparently, decorations from the city's theatre. This theatre, which attracted Pliny's attention (10.39–40), and is located at the south-western corner of the town, has been recently re-excavated and restored. The town's well-endowed archaeological museum appears to be open currently only by appointment. For imperial Nicaea, see Madsen (2009), Bekker-Nielsen (2008); cf. Marek (2003).

Prusa/Bursa

Bursa is today a busy commercial centre situated dramatically on the lower slopes of the ancient mount Olympus range. The ancient city was situated on the Hisar plateau at the centre of the old city, where Greco-Roman materials can be seen recycled into the later architecture. The town's ancient archaeological museum is located in the Kültür Parki. It has good holdings in statuary and coins. The famous hot springs that fed the Roman baths which caused Pliny some problems (10.23), feature in numerous hotels to the west of the old town. For imperial Prusa, see Madsen (2009), Bekker-Nielsen (2008); cf. Marek (2003).

Bibliography

Adams, J. N. 2003. *Bilingualism and the Latin Language*, Cambridge.

Agache, S. 2008. 'La villa comme image de soi (Rome antique, des origines à la fin de la République)', in P. Galand-Hallyn and C. Lévy (eds.), *La villa et l'univers familial dans l'Antiquité et à la Renaissance* (Paris), 15–44.

De Agostini, I. N. 2006. *La sezione romana del museo archeologico di Como*, Como.

De Agostini, I. N. 2013. 'Como romana. Le testimonianze archeologiche', in Luraschi (ed.) 2013a: 105–29.

Alföldy, G. 1983. 'Ein Tempel des Herrscher-Kultes in Comum', *Athenaeum* 61: 362–73 = 1999b.

Alföldy, G. 1999a. *Städte, Eliten, und Gesellschaft in der Gallia Cisalpina. Epigraphisch-historische Untersuchungen*, Stuttgart.

Alföldy, G. 1999b. 'Ein Tempel des Herrscher-Kultes in Comum', in id. 1999a: 211–19 = 1983.

Alföldy, G. 1999c. 'Die Inschriften des jüngeren Plinius und seine Mission in Pontus und Bithynia', in id. 1999a: 221–44 = *Acta Antiqua Academiae Scientiarum Hungaricae* 39: 21–44.

Alföldy, G.1999d. 'Die Eliten im römischen Norditalien: Senatoren aus den *regiones* IX, X, und XI', in id. 1999a: 259–341 (originally published as id. 'Senatoren aus Norditalien, Regiones IX, X und XI', *Tituli* 5: 309–68).

Allain, E. 1901–2. *Pline le Jeune et ses héritiers*, 4 vols., Paris.

Allen, G. B. 1915. *Selected Letters of Pliny*, Oxford.

Andermahr, A. M. 1998. *Totus in Praediis: Senatorischer Grundbesitz in Italien in der frühen und hohen Kaiserzeit*, Bonn.

Anderson, P. W. S. (dir.). 2014. *Pompeii*, Lionsgate Summit Entertainment.

Ando, C. 2000. *Imperial Policy and Provincial Loyalty in the Roman Empire*, Berkeley.

Ando, C. 2006. 'The administration of the provinces', in Potter (ed.), 177–92.

Ando, C. 2007. 'Exporting Roman religion', in Rüpke (ed.), 429–45.

Ando, C. 2016. 'The changing face of Cisalpine identity', in Cooley (ed.), 271–87.

Ash, R. 2003. ' "Aliud est enim epistulam, aliud historiam . . . scribere" (*Epistles* 6.16.22). Pliny the historian?', *Arethusa* 36: 211–25.

Ash, R. 2013. 'Drip-feed invective: Pliny, self-fashioning, and the Regulus letters', in A. Mamodoro and J. Hill (eds.), *The Author's Voice in Classical and Late Antiquity* (Oxford), 207–32.

Ash, R. 2018. 'Paradoxography and marvels in post-Domitianic literature', in König and Whitton (eds.), 126–45.

Aubrion, E. 1989. 'La "Correspondance" de Pline le Jeune: problèmes et orientations actuelles de la recherche', *Aufstieg und Niedergang der römischen Welt* II.33.1.304–74.

Augoustakis, A. 2015. 'Campanian politics and poetics in Silius Italicus' *Punica*', *Illinois Classical Studies* 40: 155–69.

Bablitz, L. 2007. *Actors and Audience in the Roman Courtroom*, Abingdon and New York.

Bablitz, L. 2011. 'Roman society in the courtroom', in Peachin (ed.), 317–34.

Bablitz, L. 2016. 'Roman courts and private arbitration', in Du Plessis, Ando, and Tuori (eds.), 234–44.

Bacchiega, S. 1993. 'Gli altri Plinii', in Sena Chiesa et al. (eds.), 269–90.

Baeza-Angulo, E. 2016. 'Deleite y tormento. El amor de Plinio y Calpurnia (*Epist.* 6.7)', *Agora: Estudos Clássicos em Debate* 18: 121–40.

Baeza-Angulo, E. 2017. 'Plinius exclusus (*Ep.* 7.5)', *Philologus* 161: 292–318.

Baltussen, H. 2010. 'Marcus Aurelius and the therapeutic use of soliloquy: an interdisciplinary approach', in B. Sidwell and D. Dzino (eds.), *Emotion, Power and Status in Late Antiquity: Papers in Honour of R. F. Newbold* (Piscataway, NJ), 39–57.

Baraz, Y. 2012. 'Pliny's epistolary dream and the ghost of Domitian', *Transactions of the American Philological Association* 142: 105–32.

Barnes, T. D. 1968. 'Legislation against the Christians', *Journal of Roman Studies* 58: 32–50.

Bartlett, R. 2004. *Chekhov: Scenes from a Life*, London.

Bartsch, S. 1994. *Actors in the Audience: Theatricality and Doublespeak from Nero to Hadrian*, Cambridge, MA.

Bartsch, S., and D. Wray (eds.). 2009. *Seneca and the Self*, Cambridge.

Bastianelli, S. 1954. *Centumcellae (Civitavecchia), Castrum Nouum (Torre Chiaruccia)*, Rome.

Bauman, R. A. 1974. *Impietas in Principem: a Study of Treason against the Roman Emperor with Special Reference to the First Century*, Munich.

Beagon, M. 2005. *The Elder Pliny on the Human Animal. Natural History Book 7*, Oxford.

Beagon, M. 2011. 'The curious eye of the Elder Pliny', in Gibson and Morello (eds.), 71–88.

Beard, M. 2001. 'Writing and religion: ancient literacy and the function of the written word in Roman religion', in *Literacy in the Roman World* (*Journal of Roman Archaeology* Supplementary Series 3, Ann Arbor): 35–58.

Beard, M. 2002. 'Ciceronian correspondences: making a book out of letters', in T. P. Wiseman (ed.), *Classics in Progress* (London), 103–44.

Beard, M. 2008. *Pompeii: the Life of a Roman Town*, London.

Beard, M. 2013. *Confronting the Classics: Traditions, Adventures, and Innovations*, London.

Becker, A. H. 2014. 'Augustine's *Confessions*', in M. Di Battista and E. O. Wittman (eds.), *The Cambridge Companion to Autobiography* (Cambridge), 23–34.

Bekker-Nielsen, T. (ed.). 2006. *Rome and the Black Sea Region: Domination, Romanisation, Resistance*, Aarhus.

Bekker-Nielsen, T. 2008. *Urban Life and Local Politics in Roman Bithynia: the Small World of Dion Chrysostomos*, Aarhus.

Belayche, N. 2007. 'Religious actors in daily life: practices and related beliefs', in Rüpke (ed.), 275–291.

Bennett, C. 1988. 'The conversion of Vergil: the *Aeneid* in Augustine's *Confessions*', *Revue des Études Augustiniennes* 34: 47–69.

Bennett, J. 2001. *Trajan: Optimus Princeps*, 2nd edition, London.

Bergmann, B. 1995. 'Visualising Pliny's villas', *Journal of Roman Archaeology* 8: 406–20 = Gibson and Whitton (eds.) 2016: 201–24.

Bernstein, N. W. 2008. 'Each man's father served as his teacher: constructing relatedness in Pliny's *Letters*', *Classical Antiquity* 27: 203–30.

Bernstein, N. W. 2009. '*Cui parens non erat maximus quisque et uetustissimus pro parente*: parental surrogates in imperial Roman literature', in Hübner and Ratzan (eds.), 241–56.

Berriman, A., and M. Todd. 2001. 'A very Roman coup: the hidden war of imperial succession', *Historia* 50: 312–31.

Berry, J. 2016. 'Urbanization', in Cooley (ed.), 293–307.

Billault, A. 2015. 'L'image de Dion Chrysostome dans le correspondence de Pline le jeune (*Ep.*, 10.81–82)', in Devillers (ed.), 239–44.

Birley, A. R. 1997. *Hadrian: Restless Emperor*, London.

Birley, A. R. 2000a. *Onomasticon to the Younger Pliny. Letters and Panegyric*, Munich [2000a: 1–17 reprinted as 'Pliny's family, Pliny's career', in Gibson and Whitton (eds.) 2016: 51–66].

Birley, A. R. 2000b. 'The life and death of Cornelius Tacitus', *Historia* 49: 230–47.

Bisel, S., and J. Bisel. 2002. 'Health and nutrition at Herculaneum: an examination of the human skeletal remains', in Jashemski and Meyer (eds.), 451–75.

Bispham, E. 2007a. *From Asculum to Actium. The Municipalization of Italy from the Social War to Augustus*, Oxford.

Bispham, E. 2007b. 'Pliny the Elder's Italy', in E. Bispham, G. Rowe, and E. Matthews (eds.), *Vita Vigilia Est: Essays in Honour of Barbara Levick* (*BICS* Supplement 100, London), 41–67.

Blackman, D., and B. Rankov. 2014. *Shipsheds of the Ancient Mediterranean*, Cambridge.

Boas, H. 1938. *Aeneas' Arrival in Latium*, Amsterdam.

Bodel, J. 1995. 'Minicia Marcella: taken before her time', *American Journal of Philology* 116: 453–60.

Bodel, J. 1997. 'Monumental villas and villa monuments', *Journal of Roman Archaeology* 10: 5–35.

Bodel, J. 2015. 'The publication of Pliny's letters', in Marchesi (ed.), 13–108.

Bonelli, G. 1994. 'Plinio il Giovane e la schiavitù', *Quaderni Urbinati di Cultura Classica* 48: 141–48.

Bonneau, D. 1971. *Le fisc et le Nil: incidences des irregularities de la crue du Nil sur la fiscalité foncière dans l' Egypte grecque et romaine*, Paris.

Bonomi Ponzi, L. 1999. 'Introduzione storico-topografica', in Braconi and Uroz-Sáez (eds.), 9–17.

Booth, A. 2016. *Homes and Haunts: Touring Writers' Shrines and Countries*, Oxford.

Borgongino, M., and G. Stefani. 2001–2. 'Intorno alla data dell'eruzione del 79 d.C.', *Rivista di Studi Pompeiani* 12/13: 177–215.

Bowie, E. 2009. '*Quid Roma Athenis*? How far did imperial Greek sophists or philosophers debate the legitimacy of Roman power', in G. Urso (ed.), *Ordine e sovversione nel mondo Greco e Romano* (Milan), 224–40.

Bowman, A. K., P. Garnsey, and D. Rathbone (eds.). 2000. *The Cambridge Ancient History*, vol. 11 (2nd edition), Cambridge.

Bowman, A. K., and A. Wilson (eds.). 2013. *The Roman Agricultural Economy: Organization, Investment, and Production*, Oxford.

Bracci, F. 2011. *Plinio il Giovane. Epistole. Libro X*, Pisa.

Braconi, P. 1999a. 'Introduzione', in Braconi and Uroz-Sáez (eds.), 19–20.

Braconi, P. 1999b. 'La villa di Plinio a San Giustino', in Braconi and Uroz-Sáez (eds.), 21–42.

Braconi, P. 2001. 'La pieve "vecchia" di San Cipriano e la villa *in Tuscis* di Plinio il Giovane', in *Umbria cristiana. Dalla diffusione del culto al culto dei Santi* (Spoleto), vol. 2: 737–47.

Braconi, P. 2003. 'Les premiers propriétaires de la *villa* de Pline le Jeune *in Tuscis*', *Histoire et Sociétés Rurales* 19.1: 37–50.

Braconi, P. 2008. 'Territorio e paesaggio dell'alta valle del Tevere in età romana', in Patterson and Coarelli (eds.), 87–104.

Braconi, P., and J. Uroz-Sáez (eds.). 1999. *La villa di Plinio il Giovane a San Giustino: primi risultati di una ricerca in corso*, Perugia.

Braconi, P., and J. Uroz-Sáez. 2001. 'Il tempio della tenuta di Plinio il Giovane "*in Tuscis*", *Eutopia* n.s. I.1–2: 203–17.

Braconi, P., and J. Uroz-Sáez. 2008. 'La villa di Plinio il Giovane a San Giustino', in Patterson and Coarelli (eds.), 93–108.

Bradley, G. 2000. *Ancient Umbria: State, Culture, and Identity in Central Italy from the Iron Age to the Augustan Era*, Oxford.

Bradley, K. R. 1991. *Discovering the Roman Family: Studies in Roman Social History*, New York and Oxford.

Braund, D. 1996. 'The politics of Catullus 10: Memmius, Caesar, and the Bithynians', *Hermathena* 160: 45–57.

Brogiolo, G. P., and A. C. Arnau. 2018. 'Villas in northern Italy', in Marzano and Métraux (eds.), 178–94.

Brown, P. 1978. *The Making of Late Antiquity*, Cambridge, MA.

Brown, P. 2000. *Augustine of Hippo: a Biography*, 2nd edition, Berkeley and Los Angeles.

Brunt, P. A. 1961. 'Charges of provincial maladministration under the early principate', *Historia* 10: 189–227.

Brunt, P. A. 1990. *Roman Imperial Themes*, Oxford.

Brunt, P. A. 2013. *Studies in Stoicism*, edited by M. Griffin, A. Samuels, and M. H. Crawford, Oxford.

Buckley, E. 2018. 'Flavian epic and Trajanic historiography: speaking into the silence', in König and Whitton (eds.), 86–107.

Buonaguro, S., C. Camardo, and N. Saviane. 2012. 'La villa della Palombara (cd. villa di Plinio) a Castelfusano (Ostia). Nuovi dati dale campagne di scavo 2007–2008', in C. Angelelli (ed.), *Amoenitas II* (Rome), 65–85.

Buraselis, K. 2000. *Kos between Hellenism and Rome*, Philadelphia.

Burridge, R. A. 2004. *What Are the Gospels?: a Comparison with Graeco-Roman Biography*, 2nd edition, Grand Rapids, Michigan.

Burton, P. 2001. *Augustine: the Confessions*, New York, London, Toronto.

Cairns, F. 1989. *Virgil's Augustan Epic*, Cambridge.

Calderini, A. 1945. 'Note epigrafiche Mediolanensi I', *Epigraphica* 7: 111–22.

Caldwell, L. 2015. *Roman Girlhood and the Fashioning of Femininity*, Cambridge.

Camardo, C., S. Buonaguro, E. Civitelli, and N. Saviane. 2012. 'I pavimenti della c.d. villa di Plinio a Castel Fusano (Roma)—campagna di scavo 2008', *Atti del XV Colloquio Associazione Italiana per lo Studio e la Conservazione del Mosaico*, 395–409.

Camardo, D. 2013. 'Herculaneum from the AD 79 eruption to the medieval period', *Papers of the British School at Rome* 81: 303–40.

Camardo, D., and A. Ferrara (eds.). 2001. *Stabiae: dai Borbone alle ultime scoperte*, Castellammare di Stabia.

Cameron, A. D. 2011. *The Last Pagans of Rome*, Oxford.

Cameron, A. D.2016. 'The fate of Pliny's *Letters* in the late empire', in Gibson and Whitton (eds.), 463–81.

Caporusso, D. 2000. 'Como—I rinventimenti archeologici di viale Varese', *Rivista archeologica dell' antica provincia e diocese di Como* 182: 227–34.

Caporusso, D. (ed.). 2002. *Ritrovare i Comenses: archeologia urbana a Como*, Como.

Carandini, A. (ed). 2017. *The Atlas of Ancient Rome: Biography and Portraits of a City*, 2 vols., Princeton and Oxford.

Carey, S., and H. Sigurdsson. 1987. 'Temporal variations in column height and magma discharge during the 79 A.D. eruption of Vesuvius', *Geological Society of America Bulletin* 99: 303–14.

Carlon, J. M. 2009. *Pliny's Women: Constructing Virtue and Creating Identity in the Roman World*, Cambridge.

Carpenter, H. 1977. *J. R. R. Tolkien: a Biography*, London.

Carrithers, M., S. Collins, and S. Lukes (eds.). 1985. *Categories of the Person: Anthropology, Philosophy, History*, Cambridge.

Caruso, I. 1998. 'Traiano, Plinio ed il porto di Centumcellae', *Rivista di Cultura Classica e Medioevale* 40: 33–9.

Cary, P. 2000. *Augustine's Invention of the Inner Self: the Legacy of a Christian Platonist*, Oxford.

Casson, L. 1995. *Ships and Seamanship in the Ancient World*, Baltimore.

Castagna, L., and E. Lefèvre (eds.). 2003. *Plinius der Jüngere und seine Zeit*, Munich and Leipzig.

Catanaeus, I. M. (G. M. Cattaneo). 1506. *C. Plinii Caecilii Secundi Epistolarum libri novem . . . cum enarrationibus Ioannis Mariae Catanaei*, Milan.

De Cazanove, O. 2007. 'Pre-Roman Italy, before and under the Romans', in Rüpke (ed.), 43–57.

Cellarius, C. (C. Keller). 1693. *C. Plinii Secundi Epistolae et Panegyricus: recensuit ac nouis Commentariis illustrauit, etiam Indicibus Plenioribus tum rerum, quam Latinitatis: et tabulis geographicis auxit Christophorus Cellarius*, Leipzig (2nd edition, 1700).

Centlivres Challet, C.-E. 2008. 'Not so unlike him: women in Quintilian, Statius, and Pliny', in F. Bertholer, A. Bielman Sánchez, and R. Frei-Stolba (eds.), *Egypte-Gréce-Rome: les différents visages des femmes antiques* (Bern), 289–319.

Centlivres Challet, C.-E. 2011. 'Pliny the nephew: youth and family ties across generations and genders', in M. Harlow and L. Larsson Lovén (eds.), *Families in the Roman and Late Antique World* (London), 7–22.

Centlivres Challet, C.-E. 2013. *Like Man, Like Woman: Roman Women, Gender Qualities, and Conjugal Relationships at the Turn of the First Century*, Vienna

Chadwick, H. 2001. *Augustine: a Very Short Introduction*, Oxford.

Champlin, E. 2001. 'Pliny's other country', in M. Peachin (ed.), *Aspects of Friendship in the Graeco-Roman World (Journal of Roman Archaeology* Supplement 43: Portsmouth, RI), 121–8 = Gibson and Whitton (eds.) 2016: 107–20.

Champlin, E. 2012. 'Seianus Augustus', *Chiron* 42: 359–86.

Champlin, E. 2016. 'Pliny's other country', in Gibson and Whitton (eds.), 107–20.

Chinn, C. M. 2007. 'Before your very eyes: Pliny *Epistulae* 5.6 and the ancient theory of ekphrasis', *Classical Philology* 102: 265–80.

Church, A. J., and W. J. Brodribb. 1871. *Select Letters of Pliny the Younger*, London.

Ciapponi, L. A. 2011. 'Plinius Caecilius Secundus, Gaius', in V. Brown, J. Hankins, and R. A. Kaster (eds.), *Catalogus Translationum et Commentariorum*, vol. 9 (Washington DC), 73–152.

Claridge, A. 1997–98. 'The villas of the Laurentine shore', *Rendiconti della Pontificia Accademia Romana di Archaeologia* 70: 307–17.

Claridge, A. (f'coming). 'Thomas Ashby nell'Ager Laurens. Appunti e carte topografici inediti nell'archivio della British School at Rome', in Lauro (ed.).

Clark, A. (2007). 'The city in epistolography', *Oxford University Research Archive*, https://ora.ox.ac.uk/objects/uuid:ce2ad6d6-5093-4c12-b5b1-fab38e4a826c.

Clark, G. 1995. *Augustine Confessions Books I–IV*, Cambridge.

Clark, G. 2004. *Augustine: the Confessions*, Exeter.

Clark, G. 2015. *Monica: an Ordinary Saint*, Oxford and New York.

Clarke, J. R. 2018. 'The building history and aesthetics of the "Villa Poppaea" at Torre Annunziata: results from the Oplontis Project 2005–14', in Marzano and Métraux (eds.), 75–84.

Clarke, J. R., and N. K. Muntasser (eds.). 2014. *Villa A ("of Poppaea") at Torre Annunziata, Italy. Vol. 1: the Ancient Setting and Modern Rediscovery*, New York.

Clifford, J. 1978. '"Hanging up looking glasses at odd corners": ethnobiographical prospects', in D. Aaron (ed.), *Studies in Biography* (Cambridge, MA), 41–56.

Cline, S., and C. Angier. 2013. *Life Writing: a Writers' and Artists' Companion*, London.

Coarelli, F. 2007. *Rome and Environs: an Archaeological Guide*, Berkeley, Los Angeles, London.

Coleman, K. M. 2012. 'Bureaucratic language in the correspondence between Pliny and Trajan', *Transactions of the American Philological Association* 142: 189–238.

Collins, A. W. 2009. 'The palace revolution: the assassination of Domitian and the accession of Nerva', *Phoenix* 63: 73–106.

Como fra Etruschi e Celti: la città preromana e il suo ruolo commerciale (Società Archeologica Comense: Como, 1986).

Connolly, J. 2011. 'Rhetorical education', in Peachin (ed.), 101–18.

Connors, C. 2015. 'In the land of the giants: Greek and Roman discourses on Vesuvius and the Phlegraean fields', *Illinois Classical Studies* 40: 121–37.

Conybeare, C. 2016. *The Routledge Guidebook to Augustine's Confessions*, London and New York.

Conybeare, C. 2017. 'Review essay: towards a hermeneutics of laughter', *Journal of Late Antiquity* 10: 503–14.

Cooley, A. E. (ed.). 2016a. *A Companion to Roman Italy*, Malden, MA and Oxford.

Cooley, A. E. 2016b. 'Italy during the high empire, from the Flavians to Diocletian', in Cooley (ed.), 121–32.

Corbeill, A. 2007. 'Rhetorical education and social reproduction in the republic and early empire', in Dominik and Hall (eds.), 69–82.

Corbier, M. 1974. *L'aerarium Saturni et l'aerarium militare: administration et prosopographie sénatoriale*, Rome.

Corcoran, S. 2014. 'State correspondence in the Roman empire', in K. Radner (ed.), *State Correspondence in the Ancient World: From New Kingdom Egypt to the Roman Empire* (Oxford), 173–210.

Corke-Webster, J. 2017a. 'Trouble in Pontus: the Pliny-Trajan correspondence on the Christians reconsidered', *Transactions of the American Philological Association* 147: 371–411.

Corke-Webster, J. 2017b. 'The early reception of Pliny the Younger in Tertullian of Carthage and Eusebius of Caesarea', *Classical Quarterly* 67: 247–62.

Corsten, T. 2006. 'The role and status of the indigenous population in Bithynia', in Bekker-Nielsen (ed.), 85–92.

Cotton, H. M. 2000. 'Cassius Dio, Mommsen, and the quinquefascales', *Chiron* 30: 217–34.

Courtney, E. 1993. *The Fragmentary Latin Poets*, Oxford.

Cova, P. V. 1999. 'I viaggi di Plinio il Giovane', *Bollettino di Studi Latini* 29: 136–40.

Cova, P. V. 2001. 'Plinio il Giovane contro Plinio il Vecchio', *Bollettino di Studi Latini* 31: 55–67.

Cowan, J. 1889. *Pliny's Letters Books I and II*, London.

Cribiore, R. 2009. 'The education of orphans: a reassessment of the evidence of Libanius', in Hübner and Ratzen (eds.), 257–72.

D'Arms, J. 1970. *Romans on the Bay of Naples*, Cambridge, MA.

D'Arms, J. 2000. 'Memory, money, and status at Misenum: three new inscriptions from the *collegium* of the Augustales', *Journal of Roman Studies* 90: 126–44 = id. 2003: 439–73.

D'Arms, J. 2003. *Romans on the Bay of Naples and Other Essays on Roman Campania*, Bari.

De Ligt, L. 2012. *Peasants, Citizens, and Soldiers: Studies in the Demographic History of Roman Italy 225 BC–AD 100*, Cambridge.

Dench, E. 2017. 'Ethnicity, culture, and identity', in Richter and Johnson (eds.), 99–114.

Dench, E. 2018. *Empire and Political Cultures in the Roman World*, Cambridge.

Devillers, O. (ed.). 2015. *Autour de Pline le jeune en homage à Nicole Méthy*, Bordeaux.

Dewar, M. 2014. *Leisured Resistance: Villas, Literature, and Politics in the Roman World*, London.

Dickey, E. 2012–15. *The Colloquia of the Hermeneumata Pseudodositheana*, 2 vols., Cambridge.

Dickey, E. 2016. *Learning Latin the Ancient Way: Latin Textbooks form the Ancient World*, Cambridge.

Dickson, K. 2009. 'Oneself as others: Aurelius and autobiography', *Arethusa* 42: 99–125.

Dix, T. K. 1996. 'Pliny's library at Comum', *Reading & Libraries* 31: 85–102.

Dobbin, R. 1998. *Epictetus, Discourses Book 1*, Oxford.

Dominik, W. 2007. 'Tacitus and Pliny on oratory', in Dominik and Hall (eds.), 323–38.

Dominik, W., and J. Hall (eds.). 2007. *A Companion to Roman Rhetoric*, Oxford and Malden, MA.

Dondin-Payre M., and M.-Th. Raepsaet-Charlier (eds.). 1999. *Cités, municipes, colonies. Les processus de municipalisation en Gaule et en Germanie sous le Haut-Empire romain*, Paris.

Doody, A. 2011. 'The science and aesthetics of names in the *Natural History*', in Gibson and Morello (eds.), 113–29.

Duff, J. D. 1906. *P. Plini Caecili Secundi Epistularum liber sextus*, London.

Duncan-Jones, R. P. 1982. *The Economy of the Roman Empire*, 2nd edition, Cambridge ['The finances of a senator', pp. 17–32, reprinted in Gibson and Whitton (eds.) 2016: 89–106].

Eck, W. 1974. 'Beförderungskriterien innerhalb der senatorischen Laufbahn, dargestellt an der Zeit von 69 bis 128 n. Chr', *Aufstieg und Niedergang der römischen Welt* 2.1: 158–228.

Eck, W. 1979. *Die staatliche Organisation Italiens in der hohen Kaiserzeit*, Munich.

Eck, W. 1997. 'Rome and the outside world: senatorial families and the world they lived in', in B. Rawson and P. Weaver (eds.), *The Roman Family in Italy: Status, Sentiment, Space* (Oxford), 73–99.

Eck, W. 2001. 'Die grosse Pliniusinschrift aus Comum: Funktion und Monument', in A. Bertinelli and A. Donati (eds.), *Varia Epigraphica. Atti del Colloquio Internazionale di Epigrafia, Bertinoro, 8–10 giugno 2000* (Faenza), 225–35 (= *Epigrafia e Antichità* 17).

Eck, W. 2002. 'An emperor is made: senatorial politics and Trajan's adoption by Nerva in 97', in G. Clark and T. Rajak (eds.), *Philosophy and Power in the Graeco-Roman World: Essays in Honour of Miriam Griffin* (Oxford), 211–26.

Eck, W. 2009. 'There are no *cursus honorum* inscriptions. The function of the *cursus honorum* in epigraphic communications', *Scripta Classica Israelica* 28: 79–92.

Eck, W. 2010. *Monument und Inschrift: Gesammelte Aufsätze zur senatorischen Repräsentation in der Kaiserzeit*, Berlin.

Eco, U. 1990. 'A portrait of the Elder as a Young Pliny', in *The Limits of Interpretation* (Bloomington, IN), 123–36 = Gibson and Whitton (eds.) 2016: 185–200.

Edmond, M. 2017. *The Expatriates*, Wellington.

Edmondson, J. 2006. 'Cities and urban life in the western provinces of the Roman empire 30 BCE—250 CE', in Potter (ed.), 250–80.

Edwards, C. 1997. 'Self-scrutiny and self-transformation in Seneca's *Letters*', *Greece & Rome* 44: 23–38 = 2008, in J. G. Fitch (ed.), *Oxford Readings in Classical Studies: Seneca* (Oxford), 84–101.

Ellmann, R. 1982. *James Joyce*, revised edition, Oxford.

Emerick, J. J. 2014. 'The Tempietto del Clitunno and San Salvatore near Spoleto: ancient Roman imperial columnar display in medieval contexts', in Reeve (ed.), 41–71.

· *Extra Moenia I.* 2004. 'Ricerche archeologiche nell'area suburbana occidentale di como romana', *Rivista archeologica dell' antica provincia e diocese di Como* 186.

Fear, T. 2005. 'Propertian closure: the elegiac inscription of the liminal male and ideological contestation in Augustan Rome', in R. Ancona and E. Greene (eds.), *Gendered Dynamics in Latin Love Poetry* (Baltimore), 13–40.

Ferraro, A. 2004. 'History of the Stabiae settlement', in *In Stabiano: Exploring the Ancient Seaside Villas of the Roman Elite* (Castellammare di Stabia), 35–43.

Fielding, I., and C. E. Newlands (eds.). 2015. *Campania: Poetics, Location, and Identity, Illinois Classical Studies* 40: 85–205.

Fishwick, D. 1984. 'Pliny and the Christians: the rites *ad imaginem principis*', *American Journal of Ancient History* 9: 123–30.

Fitzgerald, R. 1961. *Homer. The Odyssey*, New York.

Fitzgerald, W. 1995. *Catullan Provocations: Lyric Poetry and the Drama of Position*, Berkeley and Los Angeles.

Fitzgerald, W. 2016. *Variety: the Life of a Roman Concept*, Chicago and London.

Fitzgerald, W. 2018. 'Pliny and Martial: dupes and non-dupes', in König and Whitton (eds.), 108–25.

Fitzgerald, W., and E. Spentzou (eds.). 2018. *The Production of Space in Latin Literature*, Oxford.

Fordyce, C. J. 1961. *Catullus: a Commentary*, Oxford.

Förtsch, R. 1993. *Archäologischer Kommentar zu den Villenbriefen des jüngeren Plinius*, Mainz.

Foss, P.W. 2017. 'Translating Pliny's letters about Vesuvius, pt. 11. The elements torn asunder', https://quemdixerechaos.com/2017/04/14/translating-plinys-letters-about-vesuvius-pt-11-the-elements-torn-asunder/ (accessed July 2018).

Foss, P.W. (f'coming). *Pliny and the Destruction of Vesuvius*.

Foster, R. 1997. *W. B. Yeats: a Life. I: the Apprentice Mage 1865–1914*, Oxford and New York.

Foster, R. 2003. *W.B. Yeats: a Life. II: the Arch-Poet 1915–39*, Oxford and New York.

Foucault, M. 1986. *The Care of the Self*, New York (trans. R. Hurley) = *The History of Sexuality*, vol. 3.

Franceschini, M. de (2005). *Ville dell'agro romano*, Rome.

Fredriksen, P. 2006. 'Christians in the Roman empire in the first three centuries CE', in Potter (ed.), 587–606.

Fredriksen, P. 2012. 'The *Confessions* as autobiography', in Vessey (ed.), 87–98.

Fuhrer, T. 2018. 'Carthage-Rome-Milan: "*Lieux de passage*" in Augustine's *Confessions*', in Fitzgerald and Spentzou (eds.), 195–214.

Fulkerson, L. 2013. *No Regrets: Remorse in Classical Antiquity*, Oxford.

Galimberti Biffino, G. 2007. 'Pline et la culture grecque', in Y. Perrin (ed.), *Neronia VII. Rome, l'Italie et la Grèce* (Brussels), 285–301.

Gamberini, F. 1983. *Stylistic Theory and Practice in the Younger Pliny*, Zürich and New York.

Gardner Coates, V. C. 2011. 'Making history: Pliny's letters to Tacitus and Angelica Kauffmann's *Pliny the Younger and his Mother at Misenum*', in Hales and Paul (eds.), 48–61.

Gardner Coates, V. C. 2012. 'Pompeii on the couch: the modern fantasy of "Gradiva"', in Gardner Coates, Lapatin, and Seydl (eds.), 70–77.

Gardner Coates, V. C., K. Lapatin, and J. L. Seydl (eds.). 2012. *The Last Days of Pompeii: Decadence, Apocalypse, Resurrection*, Los Angeles.

Gasser, F. 1999. *Germana Patria. Die Geburtsheimat in den Werken römischer Autoren der späten Republik und der frühen Kaiserzeit*, Stuttgart and Leipzig.

Geisthardt, J. M. 2015. *Zwischen Princeps und Res Publica. Tacitus, Plinius, und die senatorische Selbstdarstellung in der Hohen Kaiserzeit*, Stuttgart.

Gibbon, E. 1776–88. *The History of the Decline and Fall of the Roman Empire*, London = 1994, ed. D. Womersley, Harmondsworth, 3 vols.

Gibson, B. J., and R. D. Rees (eds.). 2013. *Pliny the Younger in Late Antiquity, Arethusa* 46.2.

Gibson, R. K. 2003. 'Pliny and the art of (in)offensive self-praise', *Arethusa* 36: 235–54.

Gibson, R. K. 2011. 'Elder and better: the *Naturalis Historia* and the *Letters* of the younger Pliny', in Gibson and Morello (eds.), 187–206.

Gibson, R. K. 2012. 'On the nature of ancient letter collections', *Journal of Roman Studies* 102: 56–78.

Gibson, R. K. 2014. 'Suetonius and the *uiri illustres* of Pliny the Younger', in Power and Gibson (eds.), 199–230.

Gibson, R. K. 2015. 'Not dark yet . . . : reading to the end of the nine-book collection', in Marchesi (ed.), 185–222.

Gibson, R. K. 2018. 'Pliny and Plutarch's practical ethics: a newly rediscovered dialogue', in König and Whitton (eds.), 402–21.

Gibson, R.K. 2019. 'Pliny on the Nile: *Panegyricus* 29–32', *MAIA* 71: 447–66.

Gibson, R. K. 2020. 'Calpurnia of Comum and the ghost of Umbria: marriage and regional identity in the *epistulae* of Pliny', in L. Galli Millic and A. Stoehr-Monjou (eds.), *Au-delà de l'épithalame: le mariage dans la littérature latine/Beyond Wedding Songs: Looking for Marriage in Latin Literature* (Bordeaux).

Gibson, R. K. (f'coming). *Pliny. Epistles Book VI*, Cambridge.

Gibson, R. K., and R. Morello (eds.). 2011. *Pliny the Elder: Themes and Contexts*, Leiden.

Gibson, R. K., and R. Morello. 2012. *Reading the Letters of Pliny the Younger: an Introduction*, Cambridge.

Gibson, R. K., and C. Steel. 2010. 'The indistinct literary careers of Cicero and Pliny the Younger', in P. Hardie and H. Moore (eds.), *Classical Literary Careers and their Reception* (Cambridge), 118–37.

Gibson, R. K., and C. L. Whitton (eds.). 2016. *The Epistles of Pliny: Oxford Readings in Classical Studies*, Oxford.

Gibson, R. K., and C. L. Whitton (eds.). (f'coming). *The Cambridge Critical Guide to Latin Literature*, Cambridge.

Gigante, M. 1989. *Il fungo sul Vesuvio*, Rome = 1979, 'Il racconto Pliniano dell'eruzione del Vesuvio dell'a. 79', *La Parola del Passato* 34: 321–76.

Gill, C. 1996. *Personality in Greek Epic, Tragedy, and Philosophy: the Self in Dialogue*, Oxford.

Gill, C. 1998. 'Personhood and personality: the four-*personae* theory in Cicero, *de Officiis* 1', in J. Annas (ed.), *Oxford Studies in Ancient Philosophy* VI (Oxford), 169–99.

Gill, C. 2006. *The Structured Self in Hellenistic and Roman Thought*, Oxford.

Gill, C. 2013. *Marcus Aurelius: Meditations Books 1–6*, Oxford.

Giovio, B. (B. Iovius Novocomensis). 1629. *Historiae patriae libri duo*, Venice.

Giovio, B. 1982. *Historiae patriae libri duo: storia di Como dalle origini al 1532*, Como.

Gleason, K. L., and M. A. Palmer. 2018. 'Constructing the ancient Roman garden', in Jashemski et al. (eds.), 369–401.

Golden, M. 2009. 'Oedipal complexities', in Hübner and Ratzen (eds.), 41–60.

Goldhill, S. (f'coming). 'Latin literature and Greek', in Gibson and Whitton (eds.).

Gonzalès, A. 2003. *Pline le Jeune: esclaves et affranchis à Rome*, Paris.

Görler, W. 1979. 'Kaltblütiges Schnarchen. Zum literarischen Hintergrund der Vesuvbriefe des jüngeren Plinius', in G. W. Bowersock et al. (eds.), *Arktouros. Hellenic Studies Presented to B. M. W. Knox* (Berlin and New York), 427–33.

Grainger, J. D. 2004. *Nerva and the Roman Succession Crisis of AD 96–99*, London.

Graziosi, B. 2002. *Inventing Homer: the Early Reception of Epic*, Cambridge.

Griffin, M. T. 1999. 'Pliny and Tacitus', *Scripta Classica Israelica* 18: 139–58 = Gibson and Whitton (eds.) 2016: 335–77.

Griffin, M. T. 2000a. 'The Flavians', in Bowman, Garnsey, and Rathbone (eds.), 1–83.

Griffin, M. T. 2000b. 'Nerva to Hadrian', in Bowman, Garnsey, and Rathbone (eds.), 84–131.

Griffin, M. T. 2007. 'The Elder Pliny on philosophers', in E. Bispham, G. Rowe, and E. Matthews (eds.), *Vita Vigilia Est: Essays in Honour of Barbara Levick* (*Bulletin of the Institute of Classical Studies* Supplement 100, (London), 85–101.

Guillemin, A.-M. 1929. *Pline et la vie littéraire de son temps*, Paris.

Günther, S. 2008. *Vectigalia esse nervos rei publicae: Die indirekten Steuern in der Römischen Kaiserzeit von Augustus bis Diokletian*, Wiesbaden.

Güthenke, C. 2016. '"Lives as parameter": the privileging of ancient lives as a category of research, c. 1900', in R. Fletcher and J. Hanink (eds.), *Creative Lives in Classical Antiquity: Poets, Artists and Biographers* (Cambridge), 29–48.

Gwynn, D. M. 2017. 'Augustine in higher society (Rome and Milan)', in Toom (ed.), 44–50.

Habinek, T. 2016. 'The self in Latin literature', *Oxford Classical Dictionary*, 5th edition (online), Oxford.

Habinek, T. 2017. 'Was there a Latin second sophistic?', in Richter and Johnson (eds.), 25–37.

Häger, H.-J. 2015. 'Das Briefcorpus des jüngeren Plinius: neuere Tendenzen in Altertumswissenschaft und Didaktik', *Gymnasium* 122: 559–96.

Hägg, T. 2012. *The Art of Biography in Antiquity*, Cambridge.

Hahn, J. 2011. 'Philosophy as socio-political upbringing', in Peachin (ed.), 119–43.

Hales, S. 2011. 'Cities of the dead', in Hales and Paul (eds.), 153–70.

Hales, S., and J. Paul (eds.) 2011a. *Pompeii in the Public Imagination from Its Rediscovery to Today*, Oxford.

Hales, S., and J. Paul. 2011b. 'Writing Pompeii: an interview with Robert Harris', in Hales and Paul (eds.), 331–9.

Hall, J. M. 2014. *Artifact and Artifice: Classical Archaeology and the Ancient Historian*, Chicago and London.

Hallett, J. P. 2009. 'Absent Roman fathers in the writings of their daughters: Cornelia and Sulpicia', in Hübner and Ratzen (eds.), 175–91.

Hard, R. 2014. *Epictetus: Discourses, Fragments, Handbook*, Oxford.

Harries, J. 2018. 'Saturninus the helmsman, Pliny and friends: legal and literary letter collections', in König and Whitton (eds.), 260–79.

Harrill, J. A. 2006. 'Servile functionaries of priestly leaders? Roman domestic religion, narrative intertextuality, and Pliny's reference to slave Christian *ministrae* (*Ep.* 10.96.8)', *Zeitschrift für die neutestamentliche Wissenschaft* 97: 111–30.

Harris, R. 2003. *Pompeii*, London.

Harris, W. V. 1971. *Rome in Etruria and Umbria*, Oxford.

Harte, R. H. 1935. 'The praetorship of the younger Pliny', *Journal of Roman Studies* 25: 51–4.

Hartswick, K. J. 2018. 'The Roman villa garden', in Jashemski et al. (eds.), 72–86.

Haudebourt, L. P. 1838. *Le Laurentin, maison de campagne de Pline le jeune*, Paris.

Häussler, R. 2007. 'At the margins of Italy: Celts and Ligurians in north-west Italy', in G. Bradley, E. Isayev, and C. Riva (eds.), *Ancient Italy: Regions without Boundaries* (Exeter), 45–78.

Healy, J. F. 1999. *Pliny the Elder on Science and Technology*, Oxford.

Hearne, T. 1703. *C. Plinii Caecilii Secundi epistolae et panegyricus . . . Accedit vita Plinii ordine chronologico digesta*, Oxford.

Henderson, J. G. W. 2002a. *Pliny's Statue. The Letters, Self-portraiture, and Classical Art*, Exeter.

Henderson, J. G. W. 2002b. 'Knowing someone through their books: Pliny on uncle Pliny (*Epistles* 3.5)', *Classical Philology* 97: 256–84 = Gibson and Whitton (eds.) 2016: 378–416.

Henderson, J. G. W. 2002c. 'Funding homegrown talent: Pliny, *Letters* 1.19', *Greece & Rome* 49: 212–26.

Henderson, J. G. W. 2003. 'Portrait of the artist as a figure of style: P.L.I.N.Y's LETTERS', *Arethusa* 36: 115–25.

Hennig, D. 1978. 'Zu Plinius ep. 7, 33', *Historia* 27: 246–9.

Hershkowitz, D. 1995. 'Pliny the poet', *Greece & Rome* 42: 168–81.

Hetland, L. M. 2007. 'Dating the Pantheon', *Journal of Roman Archaeology* 20: 95–112.

Highet, G. 1957. *Poets in a Landscape*, London.

Hindermann, J. 2010. 'Similis excluso a vacuo limine recedo—Plinius' Inszenierung seiner Ehe als elegisches Liebesverhältnis', in M. Formisano and Th. Fuhrer (eds.), *Gender Studies in den Altertumswissenschaften: Gender-Inszenierungen in der antiken Literatur* (Trier), 45–63.

Hindermann, J. 2013. 'Mulier, femina, uxor, coniunx: die begriffliche Kategorisierung von Frauen in den Briefen von Cicero und Plinius dem Jüngeren', *EuGeStA* 3: 142–161.

Hoffer, S. E. 1999. *The Anxieties of Pliny the Younger*, Atlanta, GA ['Models of senators and emperors: Regulus, the bad senator (1.5)', pp. 55–91, reprinted in Gibson and Whitton (eds.) 2016: 225–45].

Hoffer, S. E. 2006. 'Divine comedy? Accession propaganda in Pliny, *Epistles* 10.1–2 and the *Panegyric*', *Journal of Roman Studies* 96: 73–87.

Holleran, C., and A. Claridge (eds.). 2018. *A Companion to the City of Rome*, Chichester and Malden, MA.

Hollis, A. S. 2007. *Fragments of Roman Poetry c. 60 B.C.–A.D. 20*, Oxford.

Hornsby, R. A. 1963. 'The craft of Catullus (*carm.* 4)', *American Journal of Philology* 84: 256–65.

Horster, M. 2011. 'Primary education', in M. Peachin (ed.), 84–100.

Horstkotte, H. 1996. 'Die 1804 Konventseingaben in P. Yale 61', *Zeitschrift für Papyrologie und Epigraphik* 114: 189–93.

Howe, T. N. 2018. 'The social status of the villas of Stabiae', in Marzano and Métraux (eds.), 97–119.

Hübner, S. R., and D. M. Ratzan (eds.). 2009. *Growing up Fatherless in Antiquity*, Cambridge.

Hurley, D. W. 2014. 'Suetonius' rubric sandwich', in Power and Gibson (eds.), 21–37.

Hutchinson, W. M. L. 1915. *Pliny, Letters*, 2 vols., London.

In Stabiano. 2004. = *In Stabiano: Exploring the Ancient Seaside Villas of the Roman Elite*, Castellammare di Stabia.

Jackson, C. R. 2017. 'Dio Chrysostom', in Richter and Johnson (eds.), 217–32.

Jal, P. 1993. 'Pline epistolier, écrivain superficiel? Quelques remarques', *Revue des Études Latines* 71: 212–27.

Janka, M. 2015. 'Plinius und die Poesie', *Gymnasium* 122: 597–618.

Jashemski, W. F., and F. G. Meyer (eds.). 2002. *The Natural History of Pompeii*, Cambridge.

Jashemski, W. F., K. L. Gleason, K. J. Hartswick, and A.-A. Malek (eds.). 2018. *Gardens of the Roman Empire*, Cambridge.

Jenkyns, R. 1998. *Virgil's Experience. Nature and History: Times, Names, and Places*, Oxford.

Jenkyns, R. 2013. *God, Space, and City in the Roman Imagination*, Oxford.

Johnson, G. J. 1988. '*De conspiratione delatorum*. Pliny and the Christians revisited', *Latomus* 47: 417–22.

Johnson, W. A. 2010. *Readers and Reading Culture in the High Roman Empire. A Study of Elite Communities*, Oxford.

Jones, B. W. 1992. *The Emperor Domitian*, London and New York.

Jones, C. P. 1970. 'Sura and Senecio', *Journal of Roman Studies* 60: 98–104.

Jones, C. P. 1971. *Plutarch and Rome*, Oxford.

Jones, C. P. 1978. *The Roman World of Dio Chrysostom*, Cambridge, MA and London.

Jones, C. P. 1986. *Culture and Society in Lucian*, Cambridge, MA.

Jones, C. P. 2015. 'Five letters attributed to Dio of Prusa', *Classical Philology* 110: 124–31.

Jones, N. F. 2001. 'Pliny the younger's Vesuvius letters (6.16 and 6.20)', *Classical World* 95: 31–48.

Jorio, S. 2011. *Le Terme di Como romana: seconda metà I—fine III secolo d.C.*, Milan.

Kaster, R. A. 1995. *C. Suetonius Tranquillus, de Grammaticis et Rhetoribus*, Oxford.

Keeline, T. 2018. 'Model or anti-model? Pliny on uncle Pliny', *Transactions of the American Philological Association* 148: 173–203.

Kehoe, D. P. 1988. 'Allocation of risk and investment on the estates of Pliny the Younger', *Chiron* 18: 15–42.

Kehoe, D. P. 1989. 'Approaches to economic problems in the Letters of Pliny the Younger: the question of risk in agriculture', *Aufstieg und Niedergang der römischen Welt* II.33.1.555–90.

Kehoe, D. P. 1993. 'Investment in estates by upper-class landowners in early imperial Italy: the case of Pliny the Younger', in H. Sancisi-Weerdenburg, R. J. van der Spek, H. C. Teitler, and H. T. Wallinga (eds.), *De Agricultura: In Memoriam Pieter Willem de Neeve* (Amsterdam), 214–37.

Kehoe, D. P. 1997. *Investment, Profit, and Tenancy: the Jurists and the Roman Agrarian Economy*, Ann Arbor.

Kehoe, D. P. 2006. 'Landlords and tenants', in Potter (ed.), 298–311.

Kehoe, D. P. 2007. *Law and the Rural Economy in the Roman Empire*, Ann Arbor.

Kelly, B. 2011. *Petitions, Litigation, and Social Control in Roman Egypt*, Oxford.

Kelly, J. M. 1976. *Studies in the Civil Judicature of the Roman Republic*, Oxford.

Kempf, C. 2012. 'Pliny the Younger (Gaius Caecilius Plinius Secundus minor), *Epistulae*', in C. Walde et al. (eds.), *The Reception of Classical Literature. Brill's New Pauly. Supplements 5* (Leiden), 341–6.

Keppie, L. 2009. *The Romans on the Bay of Naples: an Archaeological Guide*, Stroud.

Ker, J. 2009. 'Seneca on self-examination: rereading *On Anger* 3.36', in Bartsch and Wray (eds.), 16–87.

Klodt. J. 2012. '*Patrem mira similitudine exscripserat*: Plinius' Nachruf auf eine perfekte Tochter (*epist.* 5.16)', *Gymnasium* 119: 23–61.

Kolendo, J. 1969. 'La frontière orientale de l'Étrurie et la localisation de l'un des domaines de Pline le jeune', *ArcheologiaWarsz* 20: 62–8.

König, A. 2013. 'Frontinus' cameo role in Tacitus' *Agricola*', *Classical Quarterly* 63: 361–76.

König, A., and C. L. Whitton (eds.). 2018. *Roman Literature under Nerva, Trajan, and Hadrian: Literary Interactions AD 96–138*, Cambridge.

König, J., K. Oikonomopoulou, and G. Woolf (eds.). 2013. *Ancient Libraries*, Cambridge.

Konstan, D. 2007. 'The contemporary political context', in M. B. Skinner (ed.), *A Companion to Catullus* (Oxford and Malden, MA), 72–91.

Krieckhaus, A. 2004. '*Duae patriae*? C. Plinius Caecilius Secundus zwischen *germana patria* und *urbs*', in L. de Light, E. A. Hemelrijk, and H. W. Singor (eds.), *Roman Rule and Civic Life: Local and Regional Perspectives* (Amsterdam), 299–314.

Krieckhaus, A. 2006. *Senatorische Familien und ihre patriae (1./2. Jahrhundert n. Chr.)*, Hamburg.

Kuijper, D. 1968. 'De honestate Plinii Minoris', *Mnemosyne* 21: 44–70.

Laes, C. 2011. *Children in the Roman Empire: Outsiders Within*, Cambridge.

Laes, C., and J. Strubbe. 2014. *Youth in the Roman Empire: the Young and the Restless Years?*, Cambridge.

Lanciani, R. A. 1909. *Wanderings in the Roman Campagna*, London.

Lane Fox, R. 2015. *Augustine: Conversions and Confessions*, London.

Langlands, R. 2014. 'Pliny's "role models of both sexes": gender and exemplarity in the *Letters*', *EuGeStA* 4: 1–22.

Laurence, R. 1999. *The Roads of Roman Italy: Mobility and Cultural Change*, London and New York.

Laurence, R., S. Esmonde Cleary, and G. Sears 2011. *The City in the Roman West c. 250 BC–AD 250*, Cambridge.

Lauro, M. G. (ed.). 1998. *Castelporziano III: campagne di scavo e restauro 1987–91*, Rome.

Lauro, M. G. (ed.). (f'coming). *Castelporziano IV*.

Lauro, M. G., and A. Claridge. 1998. '*Litus Laurentinum*: carta archaeologia della zona litoranea a Castelporziano', in Lauro (ed.), 39–61.

Lauterbach, I. 1996. 'The gardens of the Milanese "villeggiatura" in the mid-sixteenth century', in J. D. Hunt (ed.), *The Italian Garden: Art, Design, and Culture* (Cambridge), 127–59.

Lavan, M. 2013. *Slaves to Rome: Paradigms of Empire in Roman Culture*, Cambridge.

Lavan, M. 2016. 'The spread of Roman citizenship 14–212 C.E.: quantification in the face of high uncertainty', *Past & Present* 230: 3–46.

Lavan, M. 2018. 'Pliny *Epistles* 10 and imperial correspondence: the empire of letters', in König and Whitton (eds.), 280–301.

Lavan, M. (f'coming). 'Latin and history', in Gibson and Whitton (eds.).

Leach, E. 2003. '*Otium* as *luxuria*: economy of status in the younger Pliny's letters', *Arethusa* 36: 147–66.

Leader, Z. (ed.). 2015. *On Life-Writing*, Oxford.

Lee, G. 1990. *The Poems of Catullus*, Oxford.

Lee, H. 1997. *Virginia Woolf*, London.

Lee, H. 2005. *Body Parts: Essays on Life-Writing*, London.

Lee, H. 2009. *Biography: a Very Short Introduction*, Oxford.

Lee, H. 2013. 'Hermione Lee, the art of biography no. 4', interviewed by L. Thomas in *Paris Review* 205.

Lefèvre, E. 1996. 'Plinius-Studien VI: Der große und der kleine Plinius. Die Vesuv-Briefe (6, 16; 6, 20)', *Gymnasium* 103: 193–215 [= 2009: 123–41].

Lefèvre, E. 2009. *Vom Römertum zum Ästhetizismus: Studien zu den Briefen des jüngeren Plinius*, Berlin.

Lejeune, P. 1989. *On Autobiography*, Minneapolis.

Leonard, A. 2015. 'From *otium* to *imperium*: Propertius and Augustus at Baiae', *Illinois Classical Studies* 40: 139–54.

Levick, B. 1979. 'Pliny in Bithynia—and what followed', *Greece & Rome* 26: 119–31.

Levick, B. 1999. *Vespasian*, London.

Lewis, J. D. 1879. *The Letters of the Younger Pliny*, London.

Lewis, N. 1981. 'The prefect's conventus: proceedings and procedures', *Bulletin of the American Society of Papyrologists* 18:3–4: 119–29.

Liebeschuetz, J. H. W. G. 2001. *Decline and Fall of the Roman City*, Oxford.

Liebeschuetz, J. H. W. G. 2005. *Ambrose of Milan: Political Letters and Speeches*, Liverpool.

Lillge, F. 1918. 'Die literarische Form der Briefe Plinius des Jüngeren über den Ausbruch des Vesuvius', *Sokrates* 6: 209–34 and 273–97.

Lo Cascio, E. 2003. 'L'economia dell'Italia romana nella testimonianza di Plinio il giovane', in Castagna and Lefèvre (eds.), 281–99.

Lomas, K. 2016. 'Roman Naples', in Cooley (ed.), 237–52.

Long, A. A. 2002. *Epictetus: a Stoic and Socratic Guide to Life*, Oxford.

López, J. F. 2007. 'Quintilian as rhetorician and teacher', in Dominik and Hall (eds.), 307–22.

Lucati, V. 1984. 'Plinio il vecchio nella storiografia comasca', in *Plinio, i suoi luoghi, il suo tempo* (Como), 145–68.

Ludolph, M. 1997. *Epistolographie und Selbstdarstellung: Untersuchungen zu den 'Paradebriefen' Plinius des Jüngeren*, Tübingen.

Luongo, G., A. Perrotta, C. Scarpatia, E. De Carolis, G. Patricelli, and A. Ciarallo. 2003. 'Impact of the AD 79 explosive eruption on Pompeii, II. Causes of death of the inhabitants inferred by stratigraphic analysis and areal distribution of the human casualties', *Journal of Volcanology and Geothermal Research* 126: 169–200.

Luraschi, G. 1999a. *Storia di Como antica: saggi di archeologia, diritto e storia*, vol. 1, 2nd edition, Como.

Luraschi, G. 1999b. 'Le due fondazioni di Como', in Luraschi 1999a: 382–98 = 1987, *Quaderni Erbesi* 8: 67–84.

Luraschi, G. 1999c. 'Como romana: le mura', in Luraschi 1999a: 411–22 = 1987, *Como nell' antichità* (Como), 103–113.

Luraschi, G. 1999d. 'Aspetti di vita pubblica nella Como dei Plini', in Luraschi 1999a: 461–504 = 1984, *Plinio, i suoi luoghi, il suo tempo* (Como), 71–105.

Luraschi, G. 1999e. 'Anfiteatro a Como: un problema aperto', in Luraschi 1999a: 505–41 = 1993, *Rivista archeologica dell' antica provincia e diocese di Como* 175: 113–51.

Luraschi, G. 1999f. 'Como romana: la villa di via Zezio', in Luraschi 1999a: 543–60 = 1987 *Como nell' antichità* (Como), 113–31.

Luraschi, G. (ed.). 2013a. *Storia di Como. Volume 1.2 Dalla romanizzazione alla caduta dell' Impero (196 a.C.–476 d.C.)*, Como.

Luraschi, G. 2013b. 'Storia di Como romana: vicende, istituzioni, società', in Luraschi (ed.) 2013a: 7–75.

Madsen, J. M. 2006. 'Intellectual resistance to Roman hegemony and its representativity', in Bekker-Nielsen (ed.), 63–84.

Madsen, J. M. 2009. *Eager to be Roman. Greek Response to Roman Rule in Pontus and Bithynia*, London.

Madsen, J. M., and R. D. Rees (eds.). 2014. *Roman Rule in Greek and Latin Writing: Double Vision*, Leiden and Boston.

Maggi, P. 1993. 'I monumenti di Como romana: le testimonianze scritte', in Sena Chiesa et al. (eds.), 143–50.

Maggi, S. 1993. 'Como romana: la *forma urbis*. Problemi e proposte di studio', in Sena Chiesa et al. (eds.), 163–84.

Maggi, S. 2013. 'L'urbanistica di Como romana', in Luraschi (ed.) 2013a: 131–47.

Magie, D. 1950. *Roman Rule in Asia Minor to the End of the Third Century after Christ*, 2 vols., Princeton.

Malloch, S. J. V. 2013. *The Annals of Tacitus, Book 11*, Cambridge.

Malloch, S. J. V. 2015. 'Frontinus and Domitian: the politics of the *Stratagemata*', *Chiron* 45: 77–100.

Manolaraki, E. 2008. 'Political and rhetorical seascapes in Pliny's *Panegyricus*', *Classical Philology* 103: 374–94.

Manolaraki, E. 2013. *Noscendi Nilum Cupido: Imagining Egypt from Lucan to Philostratus*, Berlin.

Manuwald, G. 2003. 'Eine schule für Novum Comum. Aspekte der *liberalitas* des Plinius', in Castagna and Lefèvre (eds.), 203–17.

Marchesi, I. 2008. *The Art of Pliny's letters. A Poetics of Allusion in the Private Correspondence*, Cambridge.

Marchesi, I. 2013. 'Silenced intertext: Pliny on Martial on Pliny (on Regulus)', *American Journal of Philology* 134: 101–18.

Marchesi, I. (ed.). 2015. *Pliny the Book-Maker: Betting on Posterity in the Epistles*, Oxford.

Marchesi, I. 2018. 'The Regulus connection: displacing Lucan between Martial and Pliny', in König and Whitton (eds.), 349–65.

Marconi, G. 1998. 'Le origini di Centumcellae', *Rivista di Cultura Classica e Medioevale* 40: 195–214.

Marcus, L. 1994. *Auto/biographical Discourses: Theory, Criticism, Practice*, Manchester.

Marcus, L. 2015. 'Autobiography and psychoanalysis', in Leader (ed.), 257–83.

Marek, C. 2003. *Pontus et Bithynia. Die Römischen Provinzen im nordern Kleinasiens*, Mainz am Rhein.

Marsh, D. 2013. 'Cicero in the Renaissance', in C. Steel (ed.), *The Cambridge Companion to Cicero* (Cambridge), 306–17.

Marturano, A., and A. Varone. 2005. 'The A.D. 79 eruption: seismic activity and effects of the eruption on Pompeii', in M. S. Balmuth, D. K. Chester, and P. A. Johnston (eds.), *Cultural Responses to the Volcanic Landscape: The Mediterranean and Beyond* (Boston), 241–60.

Mary, M. 1954. 'Slavery in the writings of St. Augustine', *Classical Journal* 49: 363–9.

Marzano, A. 2007. *Roman Villas in Central Italy: a Social and Economic History*, Leiden.

Marzano, A. 2018. 'Maritime villas and the resource of the sea', in Marzano and Métraux (eds.), 125–39.

Marzano, A., and G. P. R. Métraux (eds.). 2018. *The Roman Villa in the Mediterranean Basin: Late Republic to Late Antiquity*, Cambridge.

Masson, J. 1703. 'C. Plinii Secundi Junioris vita: ordine chronologico breviter digesta', in Hearne 1703: 1–34.

Masson, J. 1709. *C. Plinii Secundi Junioris vita: ordine chronologico sic digesta ut varia dilucidentur Historiae Romanae puncta, quae Flavios Imperatores, uti Nervam Trajanumque spectant*, Amsterdam.

Mastrolorenzo, G., P. Petrone, L. Pappalardo, and F. M. Guarino. 2010. 'Lethal thermal impact at periphery of pyroclastic surges: evidences at Pompeii', *PLoS ONE* 5.6: e11127.

Matthews, J. 1989. *The Roman Empire of Ammianus*, London.

Mayer, R. 1994. *Horace, Epistles Book I*, Cambridge.

Mayer, R. 2003. 'Pliny and *gloria dicendi*', *Arethusa* 36: 227–34.

Mayor, J. E. B. 1880. *Pliny's Letters, Book III*, London.

McDermott, W. C. 1971. 'Pliny the younger and inscriptions', *Classical World* 65: 84–94.

McHam, S. B. 2005. 'Renaissance monuments to favourite sons', *Renaissance Studies* 19: 458–86.

McHam, S. B. 2013. *Pliny and the Artistic Culture of the Italian Renaissance*, New Haven.

McKay, G. 1967. 'Aeneas' landfalls in Hesperia', *Greece & Rome* 14: 3–11.

McLynn, N. 2012. 'Administrator: Augustine in his diocese', in Vessey (ed.), 310–22.

McNeill Poteat, H. 1937. *Selected Letters of Pliny*, London.

Merrill, E. T. 1903. *Selected Letters of the Younger Pliny*, London (2nd edition, 1919).

Merrill, E. T. 1910. 'On the eight-book tradition of Pliny's Letters in Verona', *Classical Philology* 5: 175–88.

Merrill, E. T. 1918. 'Notes on the eruption of Vesuvius in 79 A.D.', *American Journal of Archaeology* 22: 304–9.

Merrill, E. T. 1920. 'Further notes on the eruption of Vesuvius in 79 A.D.', *American Journal of Archaeology* 24: 262–8.

Méthy, N. 2007. *Les lettres de Pline le Jeune. Une représentation de l'homme*, Paris.

Métraux, G. P. R. 2014. 'Some other literary villas of Roman antiquity besides Pliny's', in Reeve (ed.), 27–40.

Meyer, E. 2016. 'Evidence and argument: the truth of prestige and its performance', in du Plessis, Ando, and Tuori (eds.), 270–82.

Migliorati, C. 2008. 'Tifernum Tiberinum: ipotesi per l'identificazione del porto fluviale', in Patterson and Coarelli (eds.), 379–86.

Millar, F. G. B. 1964. 'The *aerarium* and its officials under the empire', *Journal of Roman Studies* 54: 33–44 = 2004c.

Millar, F. G. B. 1965. 'Epictetus and the imperial court', *Journal of Roman Studies* 55: 141–8 = 2004d.

Millar, F. G. B. 1973. 'The imperial cult and the persecutions', in W. den Boer (ed.), *Le Culte des souverains dans l' Empire romain* (Geneva), 145–75 = 2004e.

Millar, F. G. B. 1977. *The Emperor in the Roman World: 31 B.C.–AD 337*, London.

Millar, F. G. B. 2004a. *Rome, the Greek World, and the East. 2: Government, Society & Culture in the Roman Empire* (eds. H. M. Cotton and G. M. Rogers), Chapel Hill, NC.

Millar, F. G. B. 2004b. 'Trajan: government by correspondence', in 2004a: 23–46 = Gibson and Whitton (eds.) 2016: 419–41.

Millar, F. G. B. 2004c. 'The *aerarium* and its officials under the empire', in 2004a: 73–88 = 1964.

Millar, F. G. B. 2004d. 'Epictetus and the imperial court', in 2004a: 105–119 = 1965.

Millar, F. G. B. 2004e. 'The imperial cult and the persecutions', in 2004a: 298–312 = 1973.

Miller, P. A. 1998. 'Catullan consciousness, the "care of the self", and the force of the negative in history', in D. H. J. Larmour, P. A. Miller, and C. Platter (eds.), *Rethinking Sexuality: Foucault and Classical Antiquity* (Princeton), 171–203.

Mirabella Roberti, M. 1993. 'Note su strade e edifice di Como romana', in Sena Chiesa et al. (eds.), 17–22.

Mira Seo, J. 2013. *Exemplary Traits: Reading Characterization in Roman Poetry*, Oxford.

Misch, G. 1907. *Geschichte der Autobiographie*, 2 vols, Leipzig and Berlin.

Mitchell, M. M., and F. M. Young (eds.). 2006. *The Cambridge History of Christianity 1: Origins to Constantine*, Cambridge.

Mitchell, S. 1993. *Anatolia: Land, Men, and Gods in Asia Minor*, 2 vols., Oxford.

Miziotek, J. 2016. *The Villa Laurentina of Pliny the Younger in an Eighteenth Century Vision*, Rome.

Moles, J. L. 1978. 'The career and conversion of Dio Chrysostom', *Journal of Hellenic Studies* 98: 79–100.

Moles, J. L. 1990. 'The kingship orations of Dio Chrysostom', *Papers of Leeds International Latin Seminar* 6: 297–375.

Moles, J. L. 2005. 'The thirteenth oration of Dio Chrysostom: complexity and simplicity, rhetoric and moralism, literature and life', *Journal of Hellenic Studies* 125: 112–38.

Moles, J. L. 2017. '*Romane memento*: Antisthenes, Dio, and Virgil on the education of the strong', in A. J. Woodman and J. Wisse (eds.), *Word and Context in Latin Poetry: Studies in Memory of David West* (Cambridge). 105-30.

Momigliano, A. 1985. 'Marcel Mauss and the quest for the person in Greek biography and autobiography', in Carrithers et al. (eds.), 83–92.

Mommsen, T. 1869. 'Zur Lebensgeschichte des jüngeren Plinius', *Hermes* 3: 31–139 (reprinted in id. 1906; translated as Mommsen 1873).

Mommsen, T. 1873. *Étude sur Pline le Jeune* (trans. C. Morel), Paris.

Mommsen, T. 1906. 'Zur Lebensgeschichte des jüngeren Plinius', in id. (ed. O. Hirschfeld), *Gesammelte Schriften. IV* (Berlin), 366–468.

Morello, R., and R. K. Gibson (eds.). 2003. *Re-imagining Pliny the Younger*, *Arethusa* 36.2.

Morris, C. 1972. *The Discovery of the Individual 1050–1200*, London.

Mortley, R. 2013. *Plotinus, Self and the World*, Cambridge.

Mratschek, S. 2018. 'Images of Domitius Apollinaris in Pliny and Martial: intertextual discourses as aspects of self-definition and differentiation', in König and Whitton (eds.), 208–32.

Mullen, R. L. 2004. *The Expansion of Christianity: a Gazetteer of its First Three Centuries*, Leiden and Boston.

Müller, S. 2009. 'The disadvantages and advantages of being fatherless: the case of Sulla', in Hübner and Ratzen (eds.), 195–206.

Murison, C. L. 2003. 'M. Cocceius Nerva and the Flavians', *Transactions of the American Philological Association* 133: 147–157.

Muth, R. 1982. 'Plinius d. J. und Kaiser Trajan über die Christen. Interpretationen zu Plin. *Ep.* X. 96,97', in P. Neukam (ed.), *Information aus der Vergangenheit* (Munich), 96–128.

Myers, K. S. 2005. '*Docta otia*: garden ownership and configurations of leisure in Statius and Pliny the Younger', *Arethusa* 38: 103–29.

Myers, K. S. 2018. 'Representations of gardens in Roman literature', in Jashemski et al. (eds.), 258–77.

Mynors, R. A. B. 1963. *C. Plini Caecili Secundi Epistularum libri decem*, Oxford (corrected reprint 1968).

Naas, V. 2011. 'Imperialism, *mirabilia*, and knowledge: some paradoxes in the *Naturalis Historia*', in Gibson and Morello (eds.), 57–70.

Nadel, I. B. 1984. *Biography: Fiction, Fact, and Form*, London and Basingstoke.

Naifeh, S., and G. White Smith. 2011. *Van Gogh: the Life*, London.

Nauroy, G. 2017. 'The letter collection of Ambrose of Milan', in C. Sogno, B. K. Storin, and E. K. Watts (eds.), *Late Antique Letter Collections* (Oakland, CA), 146–60.

Nawar, T. 2015. 'Augustine on the dangers of friendship', *Classical Quarterly* 65: 836–51.

Neeve, Pieter W. de. 1990. 'A Roman landowner and his estates: Pliny the Younger', *Athenaeum* 78: 363–402.

Neeve, Pieter W. de. 1992. 'A Roman landowner and his estates: Pliny the Younger', *Studi italiani di Filologia classica* 10: 335–44 (= shortened version of id. 1990).

Newlands, C. 2010. 'The eruption of Vesuvius in the epistles of Statius and Pliny', in A. J. Woodman and J. F. Miller (eds.), *Proxima Poetis: Latin Historiography and Poetry in the Early Empire* (Leiden), 206–21.

Newlands, C. 2012. *Statius, Poet between Rome and Naples*, London.

Nicholls, M. 2013. 'Roman libraries as public buildings in the cities of the empire', in König et al. (eds.), 261–76.

Nicols, J. 2014. *Civic Patronage in the Roman Empire*, Leiden and Boston.

Nikolaidis, A. G. 2014. 'Morality, characterization and individuality', in M. Beck (ed.), *A Companion to Plutarch* (Oxford and Malden, MA), 350–72.

Noreña, C. F. 2007. 'The social economy of Pliny's correspondence with Trajan', *American Journal of Philology* 128: 239–77.

Nutton, V. 1986. 'The perils of patriotism: Pliny and Roman medicine', in R. French and F. Greenaway (eds.), *Science in the Early Roman Empire: Pliny the Elder, His Sources and Influence* (London and Sydney), 30–58.

O'Donnell, J. J. 1992. *Augustine, Confessions*, 3 vols., Oxford.

O'Donnell, J. J. 1999. 'The next life of Augustine', in W. F. Klingshirn and M. Vessey (eds.), *The Limits of Ancient Christianity* (Ann Arbor), 215–31.

O'Donnell, J. J. 2005. *Augustine, Sinner and Saint: a New Biography*, London.

O'Donnell, J. J. 2015. 'Augustine—Cicero "redevivus"', in C. Müller (ed.), *Kampf oder Dialog? Conflict/Dialogue? Begegnung von Kulturen im Horizont von Augustins 'De civitate dei'* (Würzburg), 103–13.

Oertel, F. 1939. 'Zur politischen Haltung des jüngeren Plinius', *Rheinisches Museum* 88: 179–84.

O'Hara, J. J. 2017. *True Names: Vergil and the Alexandrian Tradition of Etymologoical Word Play*, 2nd edition, Ann Arbor.

Otto, W. 1919. *Zur Lebensgeschichte des jüngeren Plinius*, Munich.

Pappalardo, U. 1990. 'L'eruzione pliniana del Vesuvio nel 79 d.C: Ercolano', in C. A. Livadie and F. Widermann (eds.), *Volcanology and Archaeology, Pact* 25: 197–215.

Parker, D. 2010. *Michelangelo and the Art of Letter Writing*, Cambridge.

Parkin, T. 2011. 'The Roman life course and the family', in B. Rawson (ed.), *A Companion to Families in the Greek and Roman Worlds* (Malden, MA and Oxford), 276–90.

Patterson, H., and F. Coarelli (eds.). 2008. *Mercator Placidissimus. New Research in the Upper Tiber Valley*, Rome.

Patterson, J. R. 2006. *Landscapes and Cities: Rural Settlement and Civic Transformation in Early Imperial Italy*, Oxford.

Patterson, J. R. 2008. 'Modelling the urban history of the Tiber valley in the imperial period', in Patterson and Coarelli (eds.), 487–98.

Peachin, M. (ed.). 2011. *The Oxford Handbook of Social Relations in the Roman World*, Oxford and New York.

Peirano Garrison, I. 2017. 'Between biography and commentary: the ancient horizon of expectation of VSD', in A. Powell and P. Hardie (eds.), *The Ancient Lives of Vergil: Literary and Historical Studies* (Swansea), 1–28.

Pelling, C. 1990a. 'Childhood and personality in Greek biography', in id. 1990c: 213–44.

Pelling, C. 1990b. 'Conclusion', in id. 1990c: 245–62.

Pelling, C. (ed.). 1990c. *Characterization and Individuality in Greek Literature*, Oxford.

Pelling, C. 2002. *Plutarch and History: Eighteen Studies*, Swansea.

Pelling, C. 2011. *Plutarch: Caesar*, Oxford.

Peper, B. M., and M. DelCogliano. 2006. 'The Pliny and Trajan correspondence', in A. J. Levine, D. C. Allison Jr., and J. D. Crossan (eds.), *The Historical Jesus in Context* (Princeton), 366–71.

Perry, J. S. 2006. *The Roman collegia: the Modern Evolution of an Ancient Concept*, Leiden.

Pitassi, M. 2009. *The Navies of Rome*, London.

Du Plessis, P. J., C. Ando, and K. Tuori (eds.). 2016. *The Oxford Handbook of Roman Law and Society*, Oxford.

Pölönen, J. 2004. 'Plebeians and repression of crime in the Roman empire: from torture of convicts to torture of suspects', *Revue Internationale des Droits de l' Antiquité* 51: 217–57.

Pomeroy, A. 1991. *The Appropriate Comment: Death Notices in the Ancient Historians*, Frankfurt am Maim.

Potter, D. S. (ed.). 2006a. *A Companion to the Roman Empire*, Oxford and Malden, MA.

Potter, D. S. 2006b. 'The shape of Roman history: the fate of the governing class', in id. 2006a: 1–19.

Powell, J. G. F. 2010. 'Juvenal and the *delatores*', in C. S. Kraus, J. Marincola, and C. Pelling (eds.), *Ancient Historiography and its Contexts: Studies in Honour of A. J. Woodman* (Oxford), 224–44.

Power, T. J. 2010. 'Pliny, *Letters* 5.10 and the literary career of Suetonius', *Journal of Roman Studies* 100: 140–62.

Power, T. J., and R. K. Gibson (eds.). 2014. *Suetonius the Biographer: Studies in Roman Lives*, Oxford.

De Pretis, A. 2003. ' "Insincerity," "facts," and "epistolarity": approaches to Pliny's epistles to Calpurnia', *Arethusa* 36: 127–46.

Pretzler, M. 2007. *Travel Writing in Ancient Greece*, London and New York.

Du Prey, Pierre de la Ruffinière. 1994. *The Villas of Pliny from Antiquity to Posterity*, Chicago.

Du Prey, Pierre de la Ruffinière. 2018. 'Conviviality versus seclusion in Pliny's Tuscan and Laurentine villas', in Marzano and Métraux (eds.), 467–75.

Prichard, C. E., and E. R. Bernard. 1872. *Selected Letters of Pliny*, Oxford.

Procchi, F. 2012. *Plinio il giovane e la difesa di C. Iulius Bassus*, Pisa.

Pucci, J. 2009. 'Catullus among the Christians', in A. Galloway and R. F. Yeager (eds.), *Through A Classical Eye: Transcultural and Transhistorical Visions in Medieval English, Italian, and Latin Literature in Honor of Winthrop Wetherbee* (Toronto), 27–43.

Purcell, N. 1998a. 'Alla scoperta di una costa residenziale romana: il *litus Laurentinum* e l'archaeologia dell'*otium*', in Lauro (ed.), 11–32.

Purcell, N. 1998b. 'Discovering a Roman resort-coast: the *litus Laurentinum* and the archaeology of *otium*', https://intranet.royalholloway.ac.uk/classics/research/laurentine-shore-project/documents/pdf/litus-laurentinum-english-version.pdf.

Purcell, N. 2000. 'Rome and Italy', in Bowman, Garnsey, and Rathbone (eds.), 405–43.

Radice, B. 1962. 'A fresh approach to Pliny's letters', *Greece & Rome* 9: 160–8.

Radice, B. 1969. *Pliny. Letters and Panegyricus*, 2 vols, Cambridge, MA.

Radice, B. 1975. 'The letters of Pliny', in T. A. Dorey (ed.), *Empire and Aftermath* (London), 119–43.

Raepsaet–Charlier, M.-Th. 1987. *Prosopographie des femmes de l'ordre senatorial (Ier – IIe siècles)*, Louvain.

Ramieri, A. M. 1995. 'La villa di Plinio a Castel Fusano', *Archeologia Laziale* 12.2: 407–16.

Rawson, B. 2003. *Children and Childhood in Roman Italy*, Oxford.

Rawson, E. 1983. *Cicero: a Portrait*, 2nd edition, London.

Reeve, M. D. 2011. 'The *vita Plinii*', in Gibson and Morello (eds.), 207–22.

Reeve, M. M. (ed.). 2014. *Tributes to Pierre du Prey: Architecture and the Classical Tradition from Pliny to Posterity*, London and Turnhout.

Reichert, A. 2002. 'Durchdachte Konfusion: Plinius, Trajan und das Christentum', *Zeitschrift für die neutestamentliche Wissenschaft* 93: 227–50.

Reynolds, L. D. 1983. 'The younger Pliny', in id. (ed.) *Texts and Transmission: a Survey of the Latin Classics* (Oxford), 316–22 = Gibson and Whitton (eds.) 2016: 482–88.

Reynolds, L. D., and N. G. Wilson. 2013. *Scribes and Scholars: a Guide to the Transmission of Greek and Latin literature*, 4th edition, Oxford.

Rice, C. M. 2018. 'Rivers, roads and ports', in Holleran and Claridge (eds.), 199–217.

Richardson, J. 2016. 'Provincial administration', in du Plessis, Ando, and Tuori (eds.), 111–23.

Richter, D. S., and W. A. Johnson (eds.). 2017. *The Oxford Handbook of the Second Sophistic*, Oxford and New York.

Ricotti, E. Salza Prina. 1983. 'La villa laurentina di Plinio il Giovane: un'ennesima ricostruzione', in *Lunario romano* (Rome), 229–51.

Ricotti, E. Salza Prina. 1984. 'La c.d. Villa Magna: il Laurentinum di Plinio il Giovane', *Atti Acc. Naz. Dei Lincei Rend.* S. VIII, vol. 39, fasc. 7–12: 339–58.

Ricotti, E. Salza Prina. 1985. 'La Villa Magna a Grotte di Piastra', in *Castelporziano I: campagna di scavo e restauro 1984* (Rome), 53–66.

Ricotti, E. Salza Prina. 1987. 'The importance of water in Roman garden triclinia', in E. B. MacDougall (ed.), *Ancient Roman Villa Gardens* (Washington, DC), 138–83.

Ricotti, E. Salza Prina. 1988. 'Il Laurentino: scavi del 1985', in *Castelporziano II: campagna di scavo e restauro 1985–1986* (Rome), 45–56.

Riggsby, A. M. 1997. ' "Private" and "public" in Roman culture: the case of the cubiculum', *Journal of Roman Archaeology* 10: 36–56.

Riggsby, A. M. 1998. 'Self and community in the younger Pliny', *Arethusa* 31: 75–97 = Gibson and Whitton (eds.) 2016: 225–45.

Riggsby, A. M. 2003. 'Pliny in space (and time)', *Arethusa* 36: 167–86.

Riggsby, A. M. 2004. 'The rhetoric of character in the Roman courts', in J. Powell and J. Paterson (eds.), *Cicero the Advocate* (Oxford), 165–85.

Riikonen, H. 1976. 'The attitude of Roman poets and orators to the countryside as a place for creative work', *Arctos* 10: 75–85.

Rives, J. B. 1999. *Tacitus: Germania*, Oxford.

Rocchi, S. 2015. 'Plinius, Brief 8,17: eine Überschwemmung des Tiber und das Aniene', *Gymnasium* 122: 389–402.

Roche, P. (ed.). 2011a. *Pliny's Praise: the Panegyricus in the Roman World*, Cambridge.

Roche, P. 2011b. 'The *Panegyricus* and the monuments of Rome', in id. 2011a: 45–66.

Rodgers, R. H. 2004. *Frontinus: De Aquaeductu Urbis Romae*, Cambridge.

Rodríguez Almeida, E. 1987, 'Qualche osservazione sulle Esquiliae patrizie e il Lacus Orphei', in *L'Urbs: espace urbain et histoire (Ier siècle av. J. C.–IIIe siècle ap. J. C.)* (Rome), 415–28.

Rolandi, G., and A. Paone, M. Di Lascio, and G. Stefani. 2008. 'The 79 AD eruption of Somma: the relationship between the date of the eruption and the southeast tephra dispersion', *Journal of Volcanology and Geothermal Research* 169: 87–98.

Roller, M. 1998. 'Pliny's Catullus: the politics of literary appropriation', *Transactions of the American Philological Association* 128: 265–304 = Gibson and Whitton (eds.) 2016: 246–88.

Roller, M. 2015. 'The difference an emperor makes: notes on the reception of the republican senate in the imperial age', *Classical Receptions Journal* 7: 11–30.

Roller, M. 2018. 'Amicable and hostile exchange in the culture of recitation', in König and Whitton (eds.), 183–207.

Roman, L. 2010. 'Martial and the city of Rome', *Journal of Roman Studies* 100: 88–117.

Roncaglia, C. E. 2014. ' "Pliny Country" revisited: connectivity and regionalism in Roman Italy', in J. Bodel and N. M. Dimitrova (eds.), *Ancient Documents and Their Contexts: First North American Congress of Greek and Latin Epigraphy (2011)* (Leiden), 199–211.

Roncaglia, C. E. 2018. *Northern Italy and the Roman World: from the Bronze Age to Late Antiquity*, Baltimore.

Rood, T. 2012. 'Black sea variations: Arrian's *Periplus*', *Cambridge Classical Journal* 57: 137–63.

Roskam, G. 2002. 'A *padeia* for the ruler: Plutarch's dream of collaboration between philosopher and ruler', in Stadter and Van der Stockt (eds.), 175–89.

Rossignani, M. P., and F. Sacchi. 1993. 'I documenti architettonici di Como romana', in Sena Chiesa et al. (eds.), 85–142.

Rossiter, J. J. 2003. 'A shady business: building for the seasons at Pliny's villas', *Mouseion* 3: 355–62.

Rowland, I. D. 2014. *From Pompeii: the Afterlife of a Roman Town*, Cambridge, MA and London.

Rüpke, J. (ed.). 2007. *A Companion to Roman Religion*, Oxford and Malden, MA.

Russell, D. A. 1972. *Plutarch*, London and New York.

Rutledge, S. H. 2001. *Imperial Inquisitions: Prosecutors and Informants from Tiberius to Domitian*, London.

Sacchi, F. 2013. 'Como romana. Gli aspetti monumentali della città e del suburbio', in Luraschi (ed.) 2013a: 149–82.

De Ste. Croix, G. E. M. 1963. 'Why were the early Christians persecuted?', *Past & Present* 26: 6–38.

De Ste. Croix, G. E. M. 1964. 'Why were the early Christians persecuted?—a rejoinder', *Past & Present* 27: 28–33.

Saller, R. P. 1994. *Patriarchy, Property, and Death in the Roman Family*, Cambridge.

Salmeri, G. 2000. 'Dio, Rome and the civic life of Asia Minor', in Swain (ed.) 2000a: 53–92.

Salomies, O. 1992. *Adoptive and Polyonymous Nomenclature in the Roman Empire*, Helsinki.

Sarri, A. 2017. *Material Aspects of Letter Writing in the Graeco-Roman World 500 BC–AD 300*, Berlin and Boston.

Sartori, A. 1993. 'Quadro dell' epigrafia comasca', in Sena Chiesa et al. (eds.), 231–58.

Sartori, A. 1994. *Le iscrizioni romane: guida all' esposizione (musei civici Como)*, Como.

Sartori, A. 2013. 'Le pietre e la storia', in Luraschi (ed.) 2013a: 219–44.

Saylor, C. 1972. 'The emperor as *insula*: Pliny *Epist*. 6.31', *Classical Philology* 67: 47–51.

Saylor, C. 1982. 'Overlooking lake Vadimon. Pliny on tourism (*Epist*. VIII, 20)', *Classical Philology* 77: 139–44.

Scandone, R., L. Giacomelli, and P. Gasparini. 1993. 'Mount Vesuvius: 2000 years of volcanological observations', *Journal of Volcanology and Geothermal Research* 58: 5–25.

Scarfi, B. M. 1993. 'Le quattro basi figurate di via 5 Giornate', in Sena Chiesa et al. (eds.), 151–62.

Scarth, A. 2009. *Vesuvius: a Biography*, Princeton and Oxford.

Scheid, J. 1983. 'Note sur les Venuleii Aproniani', *Zeitschrift für Papyrologie und Epigraphik* 52: 225–228.

Scheid, J. 1997. 'Pline le jeune et les sanctuaires d'Italie. Observations sur les lettres IV, 1, VIII, 8 et IX, 39', in A. Chastagnol, S. Demougin, and C. Lepelley (eds.), *Splendidissima Civitas: Études en hommage à Francois Jacques* (Paris), 241–58.

Scheidel, W. 2009. 'The demographic background', in Hübner and Ratzan (eds.), 31–40.

Schönberger, O. 1990. 'Die Vesuv-Briefe des jüngeren Plinius (VI 16 und 20)', *Gymnasium* 97: 526–48.

Schuster, M. 1958. *C. Plini Caecili Secundi Epistularum libri novem. Epistularum ad Traianum liber. Panegyricus*, 3rd edition (revised R. Hanslik), Leipzig.

Scourfield, J. H. D. 2013. 'Towards a genre of consolation', in H. Baltusen (ed.), *Greek and Roman Consolations: Eight Studies of a Tradition and its Afterlife* (Swansea), 1–36.

Sears, G. 2017. 'Augustine in Roman north Africa (Thagaste, Carthage)', in Toom (ed.), 37–43.

Seelentag, G. 2004. *Taten und Tugenden Traians: Herrschaftsdarstellung im Principat*, Stuttgart.

Seelentag, G. 2011. 'Imperial representation and reciprocation: the case of Trajan', *Classical Journal* 107: 73–97.

Seigel, J. 2005. *The Idea of the Self: Thought and Experience in Western Europe since the Seventeenth Century*, Cambridge.

Sena Chiesa, G., P. Angelo Donati, and A. Sartori (eds.). 1993. *Novum Comum 2050. Atti del convegno celebrativo della fondazione di Como romana, 1992*, Como.

Seydl, J. L. 2012. 'Decadence, apocalypse, resurrection', in Gardner Coates, Lapatin, and Seydl (eds.), 14–31.

Shanks, H. 2010. 'The destruction of Pompeii—God's revenge?', *Biblical Archaeology Review* 36.4: 60–67.

Shanzer, D. 1992. 'Latent narrative patterns, allegorical choices, and literary unity in Augustine's *Confessions*', *Vigiliae Christianae* 46: 40–56.

Shanzer, D. 2012. 'Augustine and the Latin classics', in M. Vessey (ed.), 161–74.

Shapiro, J. 2015. 'Unravelling Shakespeare's life', in Leader (ed.), 7–24.

Shaw, B. D. 1987. 'The family in late antiquity: the experience of Augustine', *Past & Present* 115: 3–51.

Shaw, B. D. 2000. 'Rebels and outsiders', in Bowman, Garnsey, and Rathbone (eds.), 361–404.

Shelton, J.-A. 1987. 'Pliny's Letter 3.11: rhetoric and autobiography', *Classica et Mediaevalia* 38: 121–39.

Shelton, J.-A. 1990. 'Pliny the younger, and the ideal wife', *Classica et Mediaevalia* 41: 163–86 = Gibson and Whitton (eds.) 2016: 159–84.

Shelton, J.-A. 2013. *The Women of Pliny's Letters*, Abingdon and New York.

Sherwin-White, A. N. 1952. 'The early persecutions and Roman law again', *Journal of Theological Studies* 3: 199–213.

Sherwin-White, A. N. 1964. 'Why were the early Christians persecuted?—an amendment', *Past & Present* 27: 23–7.

Sherwin-White, A. N. 1966. *The Letters of Pliny: a Historical and Social commentary*, Oxford (reissued 1985).

Sherwin-White, A. N. 1969. 'Pliny, the man and his letters', *Greece & Rome* 16: 76–90.

Shotter, D. C. A. 1967. 'Tacitus and Verginius Rufus', *Classical Quarterly* 17: 370–81.

Shotter, D. C. A. 2001. 'A considered epitaph', *Historia* 50: 253–55.

Sider, D. 2005. *The Library of the Villa dei Papiri*, Los Angeles.

Sigurdsson, H., and S. Carey. 2002. 'The eruption of Vesuvius in A.D. 79', in Jashemski and Meyer (eds.), 37–64.

Sigurdsson, H., S. Carey, W. Cornell, and T. Pescatore. 1985. 'The eruption of Vesuvius in A.D. 79', *National Geographic Research* 1.3: 332–87.

Sigurdsson, H., S. Cashdollar, and R. S. J. Sparks. 1982. 'The eruption of Vesuvius in A.D. 79: reconstruction from historical and vulcanological evidence', *American Journal of Archaeology* 86: 39–51, with addendum at *American Journal of Archaeology* 86: 315–16.

Sisani, S. 2008. '*Dirimens Tiberis*? I confini tra Etruria e Umbria', in Patterson and Coarelli (eds.), 45–86.

Small, J. P. 2007. 'Memory and the Roman orator', in Dominik and Hall (eds.), 195–206.

Snyder, H. G. 2013. 'Early Christianity', in B. Spaeth (ed.), *The Cambridge Companion to Ancient Mediterranean Religion* (Cambridge), 177–98.

Sorabji, R. 2006. *Self. Ancient and Modern Insights about Individuality, Life, and Death*, Oxford.

Spawforth, A. J. S., and S. Walker. 1985. 'The world of the Panhellenion: I. Athens and Eleusis', *Journal of Roman Studies* 75: 78–104.

Spencer, D. 2010. *Roman Landscape: Culture and Identity*, Cambridge.

Stadter, P. 2006. 'Pliny and the ideology of empire: the correspondence with Trajan', *Prometheus* 32: 61–76.

Stadter, P. 2015. *Plutarch and his Roman Readers*, Oxford.

Stadter, P., and L. Van der Stockt (eds.). 2000. *Sage and Emperor: Plutarch, Greek Intellectuals, and Roman Power in the Time of Trajan*, Leuven.

Stähli, A. 2012. 'Screening Pompeii: the last days of Pompeii in cinema', in Gardner Coates, Lapatin, and Seydl (eds.), 78–87.

Stanfield, J. F. 1813. *Essays on the Study and Composition of Biography*, Sunderland.

Stark, R. 1996. *The Rise of Christianity*, Princeton.

Starr, C. G. 1983. *The Roman Imperial Navy, 31 B.C.—A.D. 324*, 3rd edition, Chicago.

Stefani, G., and M. Borgongino. 2007. 'Ancora sulla data dell'eruzione', *Rivista di Studi Pompeiani* 18: 204–6.

Sterk, A. 2017. 'Augustine as a bishop (Hippo)', in Toom (ed.), 51–8.

Stock, B. 2017. *The Integrated Self: Augustine, the Bible, and Ancient Thought*, Philadelphia.

Storr, A. 1995. 'Psychiatry and literary biography', in J. Batchelor (ed.), *The Art of Literary Biography* (Oxford), 73–86.

Stout, S. E. 1962. *Plinius, Epistulae: a Critical Edition*, Bloomington, IA.

Strawson, G. 2004. 'Against narrativity', *Ratio* 17: 428–52.

Strawson, G. 2015. 'The unstoried life', in Leader (ed.), 284–301.

Strobel, K. 1983. 'Laufbahn und Vermächtnis des jüngeren Plinius. Zu CIL V 5262', in W. Huß and K. Strobel (eds.), *Beiträge zur Geschichte* (Bamberg), 37–56.

Strobel, K. 2003. 'Plinius und Domitian: Der willige Helfer eines Unrechtssystems? Zur Problematik historischer Aussagen in den Werken des jüngeren Plinius', in Castagna and Lefèvre (eds.), 303–14.

Strunk, T. E. 2012. 'Pliny the pessimist', *Greece & Rome* 59: 178–92.

Strunk, T. E. 2013. 'Domitian's lightning bolts and close shaves in Pliny', *Classical Journal* 109: 88–113.

Strunk, T. E. 2015. 'Collaborators amongst the opposition? Deconstructing the imperial *cursus honorum*', *Arethusa* 48: 47–58.

Sturrock, J. 1977. 'The new model autobiographer', *New Literary History* 9: 51–63.

Sturrock, J. 1993. *The Language of Autobiography: Studies in the First Person Singular*, Cambridge.

Sullivan, J. P. 1991. *Martial: the Unexpected Classic*, Cambridge.

Swain, S. (ed.). 2000a. *Dio Chrysostom: Politics, Letters, and Philosophy*, Oxford.

Swain, S. 2000b. 'Reception and interpretation', in id. 2000a: 13–52.

Syme, R. 1958. *Tacitus*, Oxford.

Syme, R. 1960. 'Pliny's less successful friends', *Historia* 9: 362–79 = *RP* 2.477–95 = Gibson and Whitton (eds.) 2016: 67–88.

Syme, R. 1964. 'Pliny and the Dacian wars', *Latomus* 23: 750–9 = *RP* 6.142–49.

Syme, R. 1968a. 'People in Pliny', *Journal of Roman Studies* 58: 135–51 = *RP* 2.694–723.

Syme, R. 1968b. 'The Ummidii', *Historia* 17: 72–105 = *RP* 2.659–93.

Syme, R.1969. 'Pliny the procurator', *Harvard Studies in Classical Philology* 73: 201–36 = *RP* 2.742–73.

Syme, R. 1979 'Ummidius Quadratus, *capax imperii*', *Harvard Studies in Classical Philology* 82: 287–310 = *RP* 3.1158–78.

Syme, R. 1980. *Some Arval Brethren*, Oxford.

Syme, R. 1982. 'Hadrianic governors of Syria', in G. Wirth (ed.), *Romanitas-Christianitas: Untersuchungen zur Geschichte und Literatur der römischen Kaiserzeit Johannes Straub zum 70 Geburtstag am 18. Oktober 1982 gewidmet* (Berlin and New York), 230–43 = *RP* 4.50–61.

Syme, R. 1984a. 'Clues to testamentary adoption', *Epigrafia e ordine senatorio i*: 397–410 = *RP* 4.159–73

Syme, R. 1984b. 'Hadrian and the senate', *Athenaeum* 62: 31–60 = *RP* 4.295–324.

Syme, R. 1985a. 'Correspondents of Pliny', *Història* 34: 324–59 = *RP* 5.440–77.

Syme, R. 1985b. 'The dating of Pliny's latest letters', *Classical Quarterly* 35: 176–85 = *RP* 5.478–89.

Syme, R. 1985c. 'The paternity of polyonomous consuls', *Zeitschrift für Papyrologie und Epigraphik* 61: 191–8 = *RP* 5.639–47.

Syme, R. 1985d. 'Hadrian as philhellene: neglected aspects', *Bonner Historia-Augusta-Colloquium 1982/83*, 341–62 = *RP* 5.546–62.

Syme, R. 1985e. 'Superior suffect consuls', *Zeitschrift für Papyrologie und Epigraphik* 68: 235–43 = *RP* 5.490–8.

Syme, R. 1991. *Roman Papers* VII (ed. A. R. Birley), Oxford.

Syme, R. 1999. *The Provincial at Rome/Rome and the Balkans 80 BC–AD 14* (ed. A. R. Birley), Exeter.

Syme, R. 2016. *Approaching the Roman Revolution: Papers on Republican History* (ed. F. Santangelo), Oxford.

Tacoma, L. E. 2015. 'Roman elite mobility under the principate', in N. Fisher and H. van Wees (eds.), *'Aristocracy' in Antiquity: Redefining Greek and Roman Elites* (Swansea), 125–45.

Talbert, R. J. A. 1980. 'Pliny the Younger as governor of Bithynia-Pontus', in C. Deroux (ed.), *Studies in Latin Literature and Roman History II* (Brussels), 412–35.

Talbert, R. J. A. 1984. *The Senate of Imperial Rome*, Princeton.

Tanzer, H. 1924. *The Villas of Pliny the Younger*, New York.

Tatum, W. J. 1997. 'Friendship, politics, and literature in Catullus: poems 1, 65, and 66, 116', *Classical Quarterly* 47: 482–500.

Taylor, C. 1989. *Sources of the Self: the Making of Modern Identity*, Cambridge MA.

Taylor, T. S. 2016. 'Social status, legal status, and legal privilege', in du Plessis, Ando, and Tuori (eds.), 349–61.

Tempest, K. 2014. *Cicero: Politics and Persuasion in Ancient Rome*, London and New York.

Tempest, K. 2017. 'Oratorical performance in Pliny's *Letters*', in S. Papaiannou, A. Serafim, and B. de Vela (eds.), *The Theatre of Justice: Aspects of Performance in Greco-Roman Oratory and Rhetoric* (Leiden and Boston), 175–97.

Thomas, R. F. 1982. *Lands and Peoples in Roman Poetry: the Ethnographical Tradition*, Cambridge.

Thompson, G. H. 1942. 'Pliny's want of humour', *Classical Journal* 37: 201–9.

Thorsteinsson, R. M. 2010. *Roman Christianity and Roman Stoicism: a Comparative Study of Ancient Morality*, Oxford.

Thraede, K. 2004. 'Noch einmal: Plinius d.j. und die Christen', *Zeitschrift für die neutestamentliche Wissenschaft* 93: 105–28.

Toom, T. (ed.). 2017. *Augustine in Context*, Cambridge.

Della Torre, S. 1984. 'Note per l'iconografia di Plinio il vecchio', in *Plinio, i suoi luoghi, il suo tempo* (Como), 169–86.

Trapp, M. B. 2007. 'Biography in letters; biography and letters', in B. M. McGing and J. Mossman (eds.), *The Limits of Ancient Biography* (London), 335–50.

Traub, H. W. 1955. 'Pliny's treatment of history in epistolary form', *Transactions of the American Philological Association* 86: 213–32 = Gibson and Whitton (eds.) 2016: 67–88.

Treggiari, S. 2007. *Terentia, Tullia, and Publilia: the Women of Cicero's Family*, Abingdon and New York.

Trevett, C. 2006. 'Asian Minor and Achaea', in Mitchell and Young (eds.), 314–29.

Trombley, F. 2006. 'Overview: the geographical spread of Christianity', in Mitchell and Young (eds.), 302–13.

Tucci, P. L. 2013. 'Flavian libraries in the city of Rome', in König et al. (eds.), 277–311.

Tzounakas, S. 2012. 'Pliny and his elegies in Icaria', *Classical Quarterly* 62: 301–6.

Uden, J. 2018. 'Childhood education and the boundaries of interaction: [Plutarch], Quintilian, Juvenal', in König and Whitton (eds.), 385–401.

Uroz Sáez, J. 1999a. 'I bolli laterizi', in Braconi and Uroz Sáez (eds.), 43–50.

Uroz Sáez, J. 1999b. 'Domini e proprietà agrararia', in Braconi and Uroz Sáez (eds.), 191–208.

Uroz Sáez, J. 2008. 'Fundiary property and brick production in the high Tiber valley', in Patterson and Coarelli (eds.), 123–42.

Van Hoof, L. 2010. Plutarch's Practical Ethics: the Social Dynamics of Philosophy, Oxford.

Várhelyi, Z. 2010. The Religion of Roman Senators in the Roman Empire, Cambridge

De Verger, A. R. 1997–98. 'Erotic language in Pliny, Ep. 7.5', Glotta 74: 114–16.

Vervaet, F. 2007. 'The principle of the summum imperium auspiciumque under the Roman republic', Studia et Documenta Historiae et Iuris 73: 1–148.

Vessey, M. (ed.). 2012. A Companion to Augustine, Malden, MA and Oxford.

Vidal, J. M. 2008. 'Mercantile trade in the upper Tiber valley: the villa of Pliny the Younger in Tuscis', in Patterson and Coarelli (eds.), 215–50.

Vidman, L. 1980. Fasti Ostienses, 2nd edition, Prague.

Wallace-Hadrill, A. 2011. Herculaneum: Past and Future, London.

Walsh, P. G. 2006. Pliny the Younger: Complete Letters, Oxford.

Ward-Perkins, B. 1997. 'Continuitists, catastrophists, and the towns of post-Roman northern Italy', Papers of the British School at Rome 65: 157–76.

Ward-Perkins, J. B. 1970. 'From republic to empire: reflections on the early provincial architecture of the Roman west', Journal of Roman Studies 60: 1–19.

Watson, N. 2006. The Literary Tourist: Readers and Places in Romantic and Victorian Britain, Basingstoke and New York.

Watts, E. 2014. 'The historical context: the rhetoric of suffering in Libanius' Monodies, Letters and Autobiography', in L. Van Hoof (ed.), Libanius: a Critical Introduction (Cambridge), 39–58.

Watts, W. J. 1971. 'The birthplaces of Latin writers', Greece & Rome 18: 91–101.

Wear, A. 2008. 'Place, health, and disease: the Airs, Waters, Places tradition in early modern England and North America', Journal of Medieval and Early Modern Studies 38: 443–465.

White, J. A. 2005. Biondo Flavio: Italy Illuminated. Volume 1, Books 1–4, Cambridge, MA and London.

White, J. L. 1986. Light from Ancient Letters, Philadelphia.

White, P. 2010. Cicero in Letters. Epistolary Relations of the Late Republic, Oxford.

Whitmarsh, T. 2001. Greek Literature and the Roman Empire, Oxford.

Whitmarsh, T. 2005. The Second Sophistic, Cambridge.

Whitton, C. L. 2010. 'Pliny, Epistles 8.14: slavery, senate and the Agricola', Journal of Roman Studies 100: 118–39.

Whitton, C. L. 2011. 'Trapdoors: the falsity of closure in Pliny's Epistles', in F. Grewing and B. Acosta-Hughes (eds.), The Door Ajar: False Closure in Greek and Roman Literature and Art (Heidelberg), 43–61.

Whitton, C. L. 2012. '"Let us tread our path together": Tacitus and the younger Pliny', in V. E. Pagán (ed.), A Companion to Tacitus (Oxford and Malden, MA), 345–68.

Whitton, C. L.2013. Pliny the Younger: Epistles Book II, Cambridge.

Whitton, C. L. 2014. 'Minerva on the Surrey Downs: reading Pliny (and Horace) with John Toland', Cambridge Classical Journal 60: 127–57.

Whitton, C.L. 2015a. 'Grand designs/unrolling Epistles 2', in Marchesi (ed.), 109–43.

Whitton, C. L. 2015b. 'Pliny's progress: on a troublesome Domitianic career', *Chiron* 45: 1–22.

Whitton, C. L. 2018. 'Quintilian, Pliny, Tacitus', in König and Whitton (eds.), 37–62.

Whitton, C. L. 2019. *The Arts of Imitation in Latin Prose: Pliny Epistles/Quintilian in Brief*, Cambridge.

Whitton, C. L., and R. K. Gibson. 2016. 'Introduction: readers and readings of Pliny's *Epistles*', in Gibson and Whitton (eds.), 1–48.

Wilamowitz-Möllendorff, U. von. 1907. 'Die Autobiographie im Altertum', *Internationale Wochenschrift fur Wissenschaft, Kunst und Technik* 1: 1105–14 = 1972, *Kleine Schriften* (Berlin and Amsterdam), 120–27.

Wilder, T. 1948. *The Ides of March*, London.

Williams, K. F. 2006. 'Pliny and the murder of Larcius Macedo', *Classical Journal* 101: 409–24.

Williams, W. 1990. *Pliny: Correspondence with Trajan from Bithynia (Epistles X)*, Warminster.

Wills, G. 2010. 'Vergil and St. Augustine', in J. Farrell and M. C. J. Putnam (eds.), *A Companion to Vergil's Aeneid and its Tradition* (Malden, MA and Oxford), 123–32.

Wilson, E. 2014. *The Greatest Empire: a Life of Seneca*, Oxford and New York.

Winsbury, R. 2014. *Pliny the Younger: a Life in Roman Letters*, London.

Wiseman, T. P. 1986. *Catullus and His World: a Reappraisal*, Cambridge.

Witcher, R. 2016. 'Agricultural production in Roman Italy', in Cooley (ed.), 459–82.

Wolff, E. 2003. *Pline le jeune, ou le refus de pessimisme*, Rennes.

Woodman, A. J. 2009. 'Tacitus and the contemporary scene', in id. (ed.), *The Cambridge Companion to Tacitus* (Cambridge), 31–43.

Woodman, A. J. 2012. 'The preface to Tacitus' *Agricola*', in id., *From Poetry to History: Selected Papers* (Oxford), 257–90.

Woodman, A. J. 2017. *The Annals of Tacitus, Books 5 and 6*, Cambridge.

Woodman, A. J., with C. S. Kraus. 2014. *Tacitus: Agricola*, Cambridge.

Woodman, A. J., and R. H. Martin. 1996. *The Annals of Tacitus Book 3*, Cambridge.

Woolf, G. 1990. 'Food, poverty, and patronage: the significance of the epigraphy of the Roman alimentary scheme in early imperial Italy', *Papers of the British School at Rome* 58: 197–228.

Woolf, G. 1998. *Becoming Roman: the Origins of Provincial Civilization in Gaul*, Cambridge.

Woolf, G. 2006a. 'Pliny's province', in Bekker-Nielsen (ed.), 93–108 = Gibson and Whitton (eds.) 2016: 442–60.

Woolf, G. 2006b. 'Playing games with Greeks: one Roman on Greekness', in D. Konstan and S. Saïd (eds.), *Greeks on Greekness: Viewing the Past under the Roman Empire* (Cambridge), 162–78.

Woolf, G. 2015. 'Pliny/Trajan and the poetics of empire', *Classical Philology* 110: 132–51.

Woolf, V. 1927. 'The new biography', *New York Herald Tribune*, 30 October 1927, reprinted in D. Bradshaw (ed.), *Virginia Woolf: Selected Essays* (Oxford), 95–100.

Woolf, V. 1939. 'The art of biography', *Atlantic Monthly* 163/4 (April 1939), 506–10, reprinted in D. Bradshaw (ed.), *Virginia Woolf: Selected Essays* (Oxford), 116–22.

Woolf, V. 1940. *Roger Fry: a Biography*, London.

Woolf, V. 2004. *Orlando: a Biography*, London (originally published 1928).

Young, E. 2011. 'Catullus' *phaselus* (C. 4): mastering a new wave of poetic speech', *Arethusa* 44: 69–88.

Yuge, T. 1986. 'Die einstellung Plinius des Jüngeren zur Sklaverei', in H. Kalyck, B. B. Gullath, and A. Graeber (eds.), *Studien zur Alten Geschichte: Festschrift S. Lauffer* (Rome), III.1089–1102.

Zanker, P. 2000. 'The city as symbol: Rome and the creation of an urban image', in E. Fentress (ed.), *Romanization and the City: Creation, Transformations, and Failures* (*Journal of Roman Archaeology* Supplements 38: Portsmouth, RI), 25–41.

Zarmakoupi, M. 2014. *Designing for Luxury on the Bay of Naples: Villas and Landscapes (c. 100 B.C.E.–79 C.E.)*, Oxford.

Zarmakoupi, M. 2018. 'Landscape at the "villa of Poppaea" (Villa A) at Torre Annunziata', in Marzano and Métraux (eds.), 85–96.

Zecchini, G. 2002. 'Plutarch as political theorist and Trajan: some reflections', in Stadter and Van der Stockt (eds.), 191–200.

Zehnacker, H. 2009–12. *Pline le Jeune. Lettres I–IX*, 3 vols (French translation by N. Méthy from vol. 2), Paris.

Zelzer, K. 1989. '*Plinius Christianus*: Ambrosius als Epistograph', *Studia Patristica* 23: 203–8.

Zeitlin, F. I. 2012. 'Gendered ambiguities, hybrid formations, and the imaginary of the body in Achilles Tatius', in M. Pinheiro, M. Skinner, and F. I. Zeitlin (eds.), *Narrating Desire: Eros, Sex, and Gender in the Ancient World* (Berlin), 105–26.

Zimmermann, T. C. P. 1995. *Paolo Giovio: the Historian and the Crisis of Sixteenth-Century Italy*, Princeton.

Zwerdling, A. 2017. *The Rise of the Memoir*, Oxford.

Index of Passages

For the benefit of digital users, indexed terms that span two pages (e.g., 52–53) may, on occasion, appear on only one of those pages.

General Index

For the benefit of digital users, indexed terms that span two pages (e.g., 52–53) may, on occasion, appear on only one of those pages.

Unless otherwise specified, all references to Pliny are to the Younger Pliny.

Figures are indicated by *f* following the page number